FROM SAVAGE WIT
TO STUBBORN DEFIANCE

THE FEMININE MIND—H. L. Mencken's caustic comments on women, "the possessors of a rare and subtle super-logic."

ON THE PLEASURE OF HATING—William Hazlitt lashes out at a world that denies external violence, but refuses to part with the principle of hostility.

OF FRIENDSHIP—Francis Bacon's warning about the pit-falls of companionship.

THE POWER OF LAUGHTER: WEAPON AGAINST EVIL—Sean O'Casey expresses his belief that one cannot live without laughter, the wine for the soul.

ON WITCHES AND WITCHCRAFT—Joseph Addison views the myth of the old woman who "fills the whole Country with extravagant Fancies, imaginary Distempers, and ter-rifying Dreams."

LIFE WITHOUT PRINCIPLE—Henry David Thoreau's im-mortal defense of the rights of those who refuse to com-promise with conscience.

FIFTY GREAT ESSAYS

Fifty brilliant works by the greatest essayists of all time

BANTAM LITERATURE

FIFTY
GREAT ESSAYS

EDITED BY ELIZABETH
AND EDWARD HUBERMAN

A NATIONAL GENERAL COMPANY

FIFTY GREAT ESSAYS

A Bantam Classic / published October 1964

2nd printing .... *April 1966*	*4th printing* ...... *March 1968*
3rd printing ... *November 1966*	*5th printing* ... *September 1968*

6th printing ...... *April 1970*
Bantam edition published May 1971

ACKNOWLEDGMENTS

Beerbohm, Max: "Hosts and Guests" from *And Even Now*. Copyright, 1921, by E. P. Dutton & Company, Inc. Renewal Copyright, 1949, by Max Beerbohm. Reprinted by permission of E. P. Dutton & Company, Inc., and William Heinemann Ltd. Publishers.

Borges, Jorge Luis: "Parables" from *Labyrinths: Selected Stories and Other Writings by Jorge Luis Borges*. Edited by Donald A. Yates and James E. Irby. Copyright © 1962 by New Directions. Reprinted by permission of New Directions.

Broun, Heywood: "Holding a Baby" from *The Collected Edition of Heywood Broun*. Copyright © 1921, 1941 by Heywood Broun. Reprinted by permission of Heywood Hale Broun and Constance Broun.

Edman, Irwin: "How to Be Sweet Though Sophisticated." Reprinted by permission of the Irwin Edman Estate.

Eiseley, Loren: "Endure the Night." Copyright © 1963 by The Atlantic Monthly Company. Reprinted by permission of the Publisher and the Author.

Huxley, Aldous: "Wordsworth in the Tropics" from *Do What You Will*. Copyright © 1929 by Aldous Huxley. Reprinted by permission of Harper & Row, Publishers, Inc. and Chatto & Windus Ltd. Publishers.

Lawrence, D. H.: "Mercury" from *Phoenix*. Copyright © 1936 by Frieda Lawrence. Reprinted by permission of The Viking Press, Inc., Laurence Pollinger Limited and the Estate of the late Mrs. Frieda Lawrence.

Lynd, Robert: "Un-English" from *Essays on Life and Literature*. Everyman's Library. Reprinted by permission of E. P. Dutton & Company, Inc. and J. M. Dent & Sons Ltd. Publishers.

Mencken, H. L.: "The Feminine Mind" from *A Mencken Chrestomathy*. Copyright © 1922 by Alfred A. Knopf, Inc. Reprinted by permission of the Publisher.

O'Casey, Sean: "The Power of Laughter: Weapon Against Evil" from *The Green Crow*; George Braziller, Inc., 1956. Originally printed in *Saturday Night*, October 1953. Reprinted by permission of George Braziller, Inc., Saturday Night, and the Author.

Oppenheimer, Robert: "Prospects in the Arts and Sciences" from the CBS Lecture Series, December 1954, and printed as a part of Columbia University's Bicentennial Volume, *A Man's Right to Knowledge*. Reprinted by permission of the Board of Trustees of Columbia University in the City of New York, and the Author.

Piel, Gerard: "The Acceleration of History." Delivered at the dedication of Thomas M. Evans Hall, Phillips Academy, Andover, Massachusetts, April 27, 1963. Reprinted by permission of Gerard Piel.

Priestley, J. B.: "The Hesperides Conference" from *Thoughts in the Wilderness*. William Heinemann Ltd. Publishers, 1957. Reprinted by permission of A. D. Peters, Literary Agent on behalf of the Author.

Rilke, Rainer Maria: "Some Reflections on Dolls" from *Selected Works of Rainer Maria Rilke*, Volume I: *Prose*, translated by G. Craig Houston. All rights reserved. Reprinted by permission of New Directions, Publishers, and The Hogarth Press Ltd.

Russell, Bertrand: "The Harm That Good Men Do" from *Sceptical Essays*. Reprinted by permission of George Allen & Unwin Ltd.

Santayana, George: "Hermes the Interpreter" from *Soliloquies in England*. Reprinted by permission of Constable & Company Limited.

Thurber, James: "How to Name a Dog" from *Thurber's Dogs*, Simon and Schuster, 1955. Reprinted by permission of Mrs. James Thurber.

White, E. B.: "Getting Ready for a Cow" from *One Man's Meat*. Copyright © 1942 by E. B. White. Reprinted by permission of Harper & Row, Publishers, Inc.

Woolf, Virginia: "The Death of the Moth" from *The Death of the Moth and Other Essays*. Copyright © 1942 by Harcourt, Brace & World, Inc. Reprinted by permission of Harcourt, Brace & World Inc., and Leonard Woolf.

Bantam Books are published by Bantam Books, Inc., a National General company. Its trade-mark, consisting of the words "Bantam Books" and the portrayal of a bantam, is registered in the United States Patent Office and in other countries. Marca Registrada. Bantam Books, Inc., 666 Fifth Avenue, New York, N.Y. 10019.

PRINTED IN THE UNITED STATES OF AMERICA

Contents

Introduction

According to William Wordsworth, the key with which Shakespeare unlocked his heart was the sonnet; and the sonnet, the ode, the lyric of every variety, have traditionally been keys to poets' hearts. Yet the very form of a poem often sets a screen between writer and reader. The demands of rhyme and meter shape and disguise the writer's original impulse. For opening the door directly into an author's mind, there is no better key than the essay.

Here certainly the writer reveals his heart, and Wordsworth must have known it. All his friends—Coleridge, Lamb, De Quincey, Hazlitt—were publishing essays that disclosed their most intimate thoughts. They were, moreover, following a literary line that stretched back to the originator of the essay as we know it today, Michel Eyquem de Montaigne. "Reader, I am myself the subject of my book," Montaigne announced, and he kept to his subject. Whatever he discussed—and his mind ranged from details of his digestion to lost Atlantis—he discussed in relation to himself. He was not self-centered; he was interested in humanity; but Michel Eyquem de Montaigne happened to be a fascinating example of humanity, and conveniently at hand for observation and analysis.

Since the time of Wordsworth and his circle, too, the essayist's subject has continued to be himself. The term "essay" is of course infinitely elastic. Some genealogists of the form prefer to extend its lineage far back of Montaigne to the meditations of Seneca and Cicero. Others emphasize the moral strain, descending again from Seneca through Bacon's aphoristic wisdom and the "characters" of the seventeenth century, such as Thomas Fuller's "Good Schoolmaster," to Addison and Steele's lessons in manners and morals for the rising middle class of the eighteenth century. Even in that century, the term had a multitude of applications. Pope's "Essay on Man" was a poem, and Locke's "Essay Concerning Human Understanding," a lengthy philosophical treatise. Dr. Johnson, himself a master of the essay, provided in his dictionary a definition of the word that was the quintessence of the amorphous: "A loose sally of the mind; an irregular indigested piece; not a regular and orderly composition." But then Dr. Johnson had a sense of humor. In the succeeding century, essayists were frequently sterner. It was the self-appointed task of Arnold, Emerson, Huxley, to educate the public in new concepts of literature, science, and philosophy, and they did not regard their compositions as loose, irregular, or indigested. They did, however, extend the limits of the form to include informative popular lectures, and they thus prepared the way for the type of essay which has dominated the periodicals of the twentieth century: the methodical exposition of impersonal fact. Yet this dominance of the impersonal has been merely quantitative. Literally tons of newsprint covered with such essays are produced each day, and each day forgotten. The essays that are not forgotten are still the articles, the columns, the profiles, where the subject is the writer; where he unlocks his heart.

In this book there are fifty essays, gathered from different writers of different times and countries, but in them all the personal element prevails. All of them convey the sense of immediate contact with a thinking mind. Whether the writer is John Donne contemplating the prospect of death, Samuel Johnson meditating sagely on old age, or J. Robert Oppenheimer pleading for a community of creative thinkers in the midst of an open, windy world, the effect is the same: here is the man himself. The form of discourse may vary. Lamb chats informally; Milton builds elaborate sentences; Sir Thomas Browne and De Quincey embroider their prose with gilt and purple; Abraham Lincoln speaks with the simple strength of the Bible; D. H. Lawrence tells a story; and Landor writes a dramatic dialogue. Through dialogue and story, however, through formal address and cosy chat, it is the writer who speaks his own thoughts. No mask, no fictitious personality intervenes.

It is impossible to meet another mind so directly without reacting personally in return. There is, in consequence, as the reader will observe, a consistent note of admiration running through all the introductory statements to these fifty essays. For only those essays to which we reacted with admiration are included here. Our problem was not to find essays we admired, but to limit them to fifty; the fifty printed in this book are therefore those for which we had the highest praise, the warmest sympathy. Others, equally fine, had to be discarded for technical reasons: some were too long, some too short. Some offered insurmountable problems of permission and copyright, and some had been too often anthologized already. Whatever the reason, they had to be left out, and we herewith apologize to them all, and to the readers whose favorites they were. The nature of an anthology, unfortunately, is to exclude. But presumably the excellence of what is included is thereby guaranteed.

Among "what is included" here are many examples from the seventeenth and early eighteenth centuries, when spelling and punctuation often differed considerably from modern usage. Where these differences seemed likely to interfere with ease of reading, we have used modern English versions. Where no loss of clarity was involved, we have retained the original texts, for their power to suggest the flavor of the time and place where they were written and the personalities of the men who wrote them. Addison's frequent capital letters seem to add emphasis to Sir Roger de Coverley's comments on witches, and Donne's "Meditations" gain intensity from their seventeenth-century syntax and spelling. In one other way we have varied from the original texts, and this is of course in our use of a small number of translations. We have made no attempt to provide a representative selection of essays from other languages, but have rather hoped to indicate to the reader the existence of a vast new area for exploration.

In every other way, the essays in this book remain exactly as they were written. Their greatness lies in the greatness of the minds that speak directly through them, and on human magnanimity no editor should dare to cast a shadow.

JOSEPH ADDISON
1672–1719

Because of their collaboration in writing *The Tatler* and *The Spectator,* during the years from 1709 to 1714, the names of Richard Steele and Joseph Addison are indissolubly linked. They seem at times like one person. Yet they were actually very different in character: Steele was rash, generous, gay, endlessly interested in people; Addison, cautious, cold, withdrawn, and above all, discreet. In their writing they were equally different, for Addison dealt more with ideas and morals than with manners and people. He wished to have it said of him that he "brought Philosophy out of Closets and Libraries, Schools and Colleges, to dwell in Clubs and Assemblies, at Tea-Tables, and in Coffee-Houses." To bring Philosophy to such popular resorts, however, he had often to give her a human form, as he does here in the July 14, 1711 issue of *The Spectator,* where he and Sir Roger engage in a humane discussion of witchcraft, personified in old Moll White.

On Witches and Witchcraft
. . . Ipsi sibi somnia fingunt.—Virg.

There are some Opinions in which a Man should stand Neuter, without engaging his Assent to one side or the other. Such a hovering Faith as this, which refuses to settle upon any Determination, is absolutely necessary in a Mind that is careful to avoid Errors and Prepossessions. When the Arguments press equally on both sides in Matters that are indifferent to us, the safest Method is to give up our selves to neither.

It is with this Temper of Mind that I consider the Subject of Witchcraft. When I hear the Relations that are made from all Parts of the World, not only from *Norway* and *Lapland,* from the *East* and *West Indies,* but from every particular Nation in *Europe,* I cannot forbear thinking that there is such an Intercourse and Commerce with Evil Spirits, as that which

1

we express by the Name of Witchcraft. But when I consider
that the ignorant and credulous Parts of the World abound
most in these Relations, and that the Persons among us who
are supposed to engage in such an Infernal Commerce are
People of a weak Understanding and crazed Imagination, and
at the same time reflect upon the many Impostures and De-
lusions of this Nature that have been detected in all Ages, I
endeavour to suspend my Belief till I hear more certain
Accounts than any which have yet come to my Knowledge.
In short, when I consider the Question, Whether there are
such Persons in the World as those we call Witches? my Mind
is divided between the two opposite Opinions; or rather (to
speak my Thoughts freely) I believe in general that there is,
and has been such a thing as Witchcraft; but at the same time
can give no Credit to any Particular Instance of it.

I am engaged in this Speculation, by some Occurrences
that I met with Yesterday, which I shall give my Reader an
Account of at large. As I was walking with my Friend Sir
ROGER by the side of one of his Woods, an old Woman applied her self to me for my Charity. Her Dress and Figure put
me in mind of the following Description in *Otway*.

> In a close Lane as I pursu'd my Journey,
> I spy'd a wrinkled *Hag*, with Age grown double,
> Picking dry Sticks, and mumbling to her self.
> Her Eyes with scalding Rheum were gall'd and red;
> Cold Palsy shook her Head; her Hands seem'd wither'd;
> And on her Crooked Shoulders had she wrapp'd
> The tatter'd Remnants of an old striped Hanging,
> Which serv'd to keep her Carcass from the Cold:
> So there was nothing of a-piece about her.
> Her lower Weeds were all o'er coarsely patch'd
> With diff'rent-colour'd Rags, black, red, white, yellow,
> And seem'd to speak Variety of Wretchedness.

As I was musing on this Description, and comparing it
with the object before me, the Knight told me, that this very
old Woman had the Reputation of a Witch all over the Country, that her Lips were observed to be always in Motion, and
that there was not a Switch about her House which her Neighbours did not believe had carried her several hundreds of
Miles. If she chanced to stumble, they always found Sticks
or Straws that lay in the Figure of a Cross before her. If she
made any Mistake at Church, and cryed *Amen* in a wrong
Place, they never failed to conclude that she was saying her

Prayers backwards. There was not a Maid in the Parish that would take a Pin of her, though she should offer a Bag of Money with it. She goes by the Name of *Moll White,* and has made the Country ring with several imaginary Exploits which are palmed upon her. If the Dairy Maid does not make her Butter come so soon as she would have it, *Moll White* is at the bottom of the Churn. If a Horse sweats in the Stable, *Moll White* has been upon his Back. If a Hare makes an unexpected Escape from the Hounds, the Huntsman curses *Moll White.* Nay, (says Sir ROGER) I have known the Master of the Pack, upon such an Occasion, send one of his Servants to see if *Moll White* had been out that Morning.

This Account raised my Curiosity so far, that I begged my Friend Sir ROGER to go with me into her Hovel, which stood in a solitary Corner under the side of the Wood. Upon our first entring Sir ROGER winked to me, and pointed at something that stood behind the Door, which upon looking that way I found to be an old Broomstaff. At the same time he whispered me in the Ear to take notice of a Tabby Cat that sat in the Chimney-Corner, which, as the old Knight told me, lay under as bad a Report as *Moll White* her self; for besides that *Moll* is said often to accompany her in the same Shape, the Cat is reported to have spoken twice or thrice in her Life, and to have played several Pranks above the Capacity of an ordinary Cat.

I was secretly concerned to see Human Nature in so much Wretchedness and Disgrace, but at the same time could not forbear smiling to hear Sir ROGER, who is a little puzzled about the old Woman, advising her as a Justice of Peace to avoid all Communication with the Devil, and never to hurt any of her Neighbours' Cattle. We concluded our Visit with a Bounty, which was very acceptable.

In our Return home Sir ROGER told me, that old *Moll* had been often brought before him for making Children spit Pins, and giving Maids the Night-Mare; and that the Country People would be tossing her into a Pond and trying Experiments with her every Day, if it was not for him and his Chaplain.

I have since found, upon Enquiry, that Sir ROGER was several times staggered with the Reports that had been brought him concerning this old Woman, and would frequently have bound her over to the County Sessions, had not his Chaplain with much ado perswaded him to the contrary.

I have been the more particular in this Account, because

I hear there is scarce a Village in *England* that has not a *Moll White* in it. When an old Woman begins to doat, and grow chargeable to a Parish, she is generally turned into a Witch, and fills the whole Country with extravagant Fancies, imaginary Distempers, and terrifying Dreams. In the mean time, the poor Wretch that is the innocent Occasion of so many Evils begins to be frighted at her self, and sometimes confesses secret Commerce and Familiarities that her Imagination forms in a delirious old Age. This frequently cuts off Charity from the greatest Objects of Compassion, and inspires People with a Malevolence towards those poor decrepid Parts of our Species, in whom Human Nature is defaced by Infirmity and Dotage.

MATTHEW ARNOLD
1822–1888

"The trouble with England," said H. G. Wells in *Mr. Britling Sees It Through,* "is that she did not listen to Arnold." Whether Wells was right, or even in earnest in saying this, is not the point. The point is that Matthew Arnold was a man who wanted the English public to listen to him. "Such a public as it is," he wrote in one of his letters, "and such a work one wants to do with it." That work was nothing less than to shatter the material comfort, the moral complacency of his fellow Victorians; to open their minds to the great literatures, the great ideas, of the rest of the world; and to challenge them with a vision of human excellence. He directed their attention in the following essay, which was his inaugural lecture as Professor of Poetry at Oxford in 1857, to the literature of ancient Greece, because it was, "even for modern times, a mighty agent of intellectual deliverance." The Greeks of the great age of Pericles, in other words, understood their age; their literature was "adequate" to their epoch, and gave to them and to succeeding generations—even to the Victorians and to us— a "point of view from which to contemplate," with serenity and dignity, the error and confusion of ordinary life.

On the Modern Element in Literature

It is related in one of those legends which illustrate the history of Buddhism, that a certain disciple once presented himself before his master, Buddha, with the desire to be permitted to undertake a mission of peculiar difficulty. The compassionate teacher represented to him the obstacles to be surmounted and the risks to be run. Pourna—so the disciple was called—insisted, and replied, with equal humility and adroitness, to the successive objections of his adviser. Satisfied at last by his answers of the fitness of his disciple, Buddha accorded to him the desired permission; and dismissed him to his task with these remarkable words, nearly identical with those in which he himself is said to have been admonished by a divinity at the outset of his own career:—"Go then, O Pourna," are his words; "having been delivered, deliver; having been consoled, console; being arrived thyself at the farther bank, enable others to arrive there also."

It was a moral deliverance, eminently, of which the great Oriental reformer spoke; it was a deliverance from the pride, the sloth, the anger, the selfishness, which impair the moral activity of man—a deliverance which is demanded of all individuals and in all ages. But there is another deliverance for the human race, hardly less important, indeed, than the first —for in the enjoyment of both united consists man's true freedom—but demanded far less universally, and even more rarely and imperfectly obtained; a deliverance neglected, apparently hardly conceived, in some ages, while it has been pursued with earnestness in others, which derive from that very pursuit their peculiar character. This deliverance is an intellectual deliverance.

An intellectual deliverance is the peculiar demand of those ages which are called modern; and those nations are said to be imbued with the modern spirit most eminently in which the demand for such a deliverance has been made with most zeal, and satisfied with most completeness. Such a deliverance is emphatically, whether we will or no, the demand of the age in which we ourselves live. All intellectual pursuits our age judges according to their power of helping to satisfy this demand; of all studies it asks, above all, the question, how far they can contribute to this deliverance.

I propose, on this my first occasion of speaking here, to attempt such a general survey of ancient classical literature and history as may afford us the conviction—in presence of the doubts so often expressed of the profitableness, in the present day, of our study of this literature—that, even admitting to their fullest extent the legitimate demands of our age, the literature of ancient Greece is, even for modern times, a mighty agent of intellectual deliverance; even for modern times, therefore, an object of indestructible interest.

But first let us ask ourselves why the demand for an intellectual deliverance arises in such an age as the present, and in what the deliverance itself consists? The demand arises, because our present age has around it a copious and complex present, and behind it a copious and complex past; it arises, because the present age exhibits to the individual man who contemplates it the spectacle of a vast multitude of facts awaiting and inviting his comprehension. The deliverance consists in man's comprehension of this present and past. It begins when our mind begins to enter into possession of the general ideas which are the law of this vast multitude of facts. It is perfect when we have acquired that harmonious acquiescence of mind which we feel in contemplating a grand spectacle that is intelligible to us; when we have lost that impatient irritation of mind which we feel in presence of an immense, moving, confused spectacle which, while it perpetually excites our curiosity, perpetually baffles our comprehension.

This, then, is what distinguishes certain épochs in the history of the human race, and our own amongst the number; —on the one hand, the presence of a significant spectacle to contemplate; on the other hand, the desire to find the true point of view from which to contemplate this spectacle. He who has found that point of view, he who adequately comprehends this spectacle, has risen to the comprehension of his age: he who communicates that point of view to his age, he who interprets to it that spectacle, is one of his age's intellectual deliverers.

The spectacle, the facts, presented for the comprehension of the present age, are indeed immense. The facts consist of the events, the institutions, the sciences, the arts, the literatures, in which human life has manifested itself up to the present time: the spectacle is the collective life of humanity. And everywhere there is connexion, everywhere there is illustration: no single event, no single literature, is adequately comprehended except in its relation to other events, to other literatures. The literature of ancient Greece, the literature of the Christian Middle Age, so long as they are regarded as two isolated literatures, two isolated growths of the human spirit, are not adequately comprehended; and it is adequate comprehension which is the demand of the present age. "We must compare,"—the illustrious Chancellor of Cambridge said the other day to his hearers at Manchester,—"we must compare the works of other ages with those of our own age and country; that, while we feel proud of the immense development of knowledge and power of production which we possess, we may learn humility in contemplating the refinement of feeling and intensity of thought manifested in the works of the older schools." To know how others stand, that we may know how we ourselves stand; and to know how we ourselves stand, that we may correct our mistakes and achieve our deliverance—that is our problem.

But all facts, all the elements of the spectacle before us, have not an equal value—do not merit a like attention: and it is well that they do not, for no man would be adequate to the task of thoroughly mastering them all. Some have more significance for us, others have less; some merit our utmost attention in all their details, others it is sufficient to comprehend in their general character, and then they may be dismissed.

What facts, then, let us ask ourselves, what elements of the spectacle before us, will naturally be most interesting to a highly developed age like our own, to an age making the demand which we have described for an intellectual deliverance by means of the complete intelligence of its own situation? Evidently, the other ages similarly developed, and making the same demand. And what past literature will naturally be most interesting to such an age as our own? Evidently, the literatures which have most successfully solved for *their* ages the problem which occupies ours: the literatures which in their day and for their own nation have adequately comprehended, have adequately represented, the spectacle before them. A significant, a highly-developed, a culminating epoch, on the one hand,—a comprehensive, a commensurate, an adequate literature, on the other,—these will naturally be the objects of deepest interest to our modern age. Such an epoch and such a literature are, in fact, *modern,* in the same sense in which our own age and literature are modern; they are founded upon a rich past and upon an instructive fulness of experience.

It may, however, happen that a great epoch is without a perfectly adequate literature; it may happen that a great age, a great nation, has attained a remarkable fulness of political and social development, without intellectually taking the complete measure of itself, without adequately representing that development in its literature. In this case, the *epoch,* the *nation* itself, will still be an object of the greatest interest to us; but the *literature* will be an object of less interest to us: the facts, the material spectacle are there; but the contemporary view of the facts, the intellectual interpretation, are inferior and inadequate.

It may happen, on the other hand, that great authors, that a powerful literature, are found in an age and nation less great and powerful than themselves; it may happen that a literature, that a man of genius, may arise adequate to the representation of a greater, a more highly developed age than that in which they appear; it may happen that a literature completely interprets its epoch, and yet has something over; that it has a force, a richness, a geniality, a power of view which the materials at its disposition are insufficient adequately to employ. In such a case, the literature will be more interesting to us than the epoch. The interpreting power, the illuminating and revealing intellect, are there; but the spectacle on which they throw their light is not fully worthy of them.

And I shall not, I hope, be thought to magnify too much my office if I add, that it is to the poetical literature of an age that we must, in general, look for the most perfect, the most adequate interpretation of that age,—for the performance of a work which demands the most energetic and harmonious activity of all the powers of the human mind. Because that activity of the whole mind, that genius, as Johnson nobly describes it, "without which judgment is cold and knowledge is inert; that energy which collects, combines, amplifies, and animates," is in poetry at its highest stretch and in its most energetic exertion.

What we seek, therefore, what will most enlighten us, most contribute to our intellectual deliverance, is the union of two things; it is the coexistence, the simultaneous appearance, of a great epoch and a great literature.

Now the culminating age in the life of ancient Greece I call, beyond question, a great epoch; the life of Athens in the fifth century before our era I call one of the highly developed, one of the marking, one of the modern periods in the life of the whole human race. It has been said that the "Athens of Pericles was a vigorous man, at the summit of his bodily strength and mental energy." There was the utmost energy of life there, public and private; the most entire freedom, the most unprejudiced and intelligent observation of human affairs. Let us rapidly examine some of the characteristics which distinguish modern epochs; let us see how far the culminating century of ancient Greece exhibits them; let us compare it, in respect of them, with a much later, a celebrated century; let us compare it with the age of Elizabeth in our own country.

To begin with what is exterior. One of the most characteristic outward features of a *modern* age, of an age of advanced civilization, is the banishment of the ensigns of war and bloodshed from the intercourse of civil life. Crime still

exists, and wars are still carried on; but within the limits of
civil life a circle has been formed within which man can move
securely, and develop the arts of peace uninterruptedly. The
private man does not go forth to his daily occupation prepared to assail the life of his neighbour or to have to defend
his own. With the disappearance of the constant means of
offence the occasions of offence diminish; society at last
acquires repose, confidence, and free activity. An important
inward characteristic, again, is the growth of a tolerant spirit;
that spirit which is the offspring of an enlarged knowledge;
a spirit patient of the diversities of habits and opinions. Other
characteristics are the multiplication of the conveniences of
life, the formation of taste, the capacity for refined pursuits.
And this leads us to the supreme characteristic of all: the
intellectual maturity of man himself; the tendency to observe
facts with a critical spirit; to search for their law, not to wander among them at random; to judge by the rule of reason,
not by the impulse of prejudice or caprice.

Well, now, with respect to the presence of all these characteristics in the age of Pericles, we possess the explicit
testimony of an immortal work,—of the history of Thucydides. "The Athenians first," he says—speaking of the gradual
development of Grecian society up to the period when the
Peloponnesian war commenced—"the Athenians first left off
the habit of wearing arms": that is, this mark of superior
civilization had, in the age of Pericles, become general in
Greece, had long been visible at Athens. In the time of
Elizabeth, on the other hand, the wearing of arms was universal in England and throughout Europe. Again, the conveniences, the ornaments, the luxuries of life, had become
common at Athens at the time of which we are speaking. But
there had been an advance even beyond this; there had been
an advance to that perfection, that propriety of taste which
prescribes the excess of ornament, the extravagance of
luxury. The Athenians had given up, Thucydides says, had
given up, although not very long before, an extravagance
of dress and an excess of personal ornament which, in the
first flush of newly-discovered luxury, had been adopted by
some of the richer classes. The height of civilization in this
respect seems to have been attained; there was general elegance and refinement of life, and there was simplicity. What
was the case in this respect in the Elizabethan age? The
scholar Casaubon, who settled in England in the reign of
James I, bears evidence to the want here, even at that time, of

conveniences of life which were already to be met with on the continent of Europe. On the other hand, the taste for fantastic, for excessive personal adornment, to which the portraits of the time bear testimony, is admirably set forth in the work of a great novelist, who was also a very truthful antiquarian—in the *Kenilworth* of Sir Walter Scott. We all remember the description, in the thirteenth and fourteenth chapters of the second volume of *Kenilworth*, of the barbarous magnificence, the "fierce vanities," of the dress of the period.

Pericles praises the Athenians that they had discovered sources of recreation for the spirit to counterbalance the labours of the body: compare these, compare the pleasures which charmed the whole body of the Athenian people through the yearly round of their festivals with the popular shows and pastimes in *Kenilworth*. "We have freedom," says Pericles, "for individual diversities of opinion and character; we do not take offence at the tastes and habits of our neighbour if they differ from our own." Yes, in Greece, in the Athens of Pericles, there is toleration; but in England, in the England of the sixteenth century?—the Puritans are then in full growth. So that with regard to these characteristics of civilization of a modern spirit which we have hitherto enumerated, the superiority, it will be admitted, rests with the age of Pericles.

Let us pass to what we said was the supreme characteristic of a highly developed, a modern age—the manifestation of a critical spirit, the endeavour after a rational arrangement and appreciation of facts. Let us consider one or two of the passages in the masterly introduction which Thucydides, the contemporary of Pericles, has prefixed to his history. What was his motive in choosing the Peloponnesian War for his subject? Because it was, in his opinion, the most important, the most instructive event which had, up to that time, happened in the history of mankind. What is his effect in the first twenty-three chapters of his history? To place in their correct point of view all the facts which had brought Grecian society to the point at which that dominant event found it; to strip these facts of their exaggeration, to examine them critically. The enterprises undertaken in the early times of Greece were on a much smaller scale than had been commonly supposed. The Greek chiefs were induced to combine in the expedition against Troy, not by their respect for an oath taken by them all when suitors to Helen, but by their respect for the

preponderating influence of Agamemnon; the siege of Troy
had been protracted not so much by the valour of the be-
sieged as by the inadequate mode of warfare necessitated by
the want of funds of the besiegers. No doubt Thucydides'
criticism of the Trojan War is not perfect; but observe how
in these and many other points he labours to correct popular
errors, to assign their true character to facts, complaining,
as he does so, of men's habit of *uncritical* reception of current stories. "So little a matter of care to most men," he says,
"is the search after truth, and so inclined are they to take
up any story which is ready to their hand." "He himself," he
continues, "has endeavoured to give a true picture, and be-
lieves that in the main he has done so. For some readers his
history may want the charm of the uncritical, half-fabulous
narratives of earlier writers; but for such as desire to gain a
clear knowledge of the past, and thereby of the future also,
which will surely, after the course of human things, represent
again hereafter, if not the very image, yet the near resemblance
of the past—if such shall judge my work to be profitable, I
shall be well content."

What language shall we properly call this? It is *modern*
language; it is the language of a thoughtful philosophic man
of our own days; it is the language of Burke or Niebuhr as-
signing the true aim of history. And yet Thucydides is no
mere literary man; no isolated thinker, speaking far over the
heads of his hearers to a future age—no: he was a man of
action, a man of the world, a man of his time. He represents,
at its best indeed, but he represents, the general intelligence of
his age and nation; of a nation the meanest citizens of which
could follow with comprehension the profoundly thoughtful
speeches of Pericles.

Let us now turn for a contrast to a historian of the Elizabethan age, also a man of great mark and ability, also a man
of action, also a man of the world, Sir Walter Ralegh. Sir
Walter Ralegh writes the *History of the World,* as Thucydides has written the "History of the Peloponnesian War"; let
us hear his language; let us mark his point of view; let us see
what problems occur to him for solution. "Seeing," he says,
"that we digress in all the ways of our lives—yea, seeing the
life of man is nothing else but digression—I may be the better
excused in writing their lives and actions." What are the preliminary facts which he discusses, as Thucydides discusses
the Trojan War and the early naval power of Crete, and
which are to lead up to his main inquiry? Open the table of

contents of his first volume. You will find:—"Of the firmament, and of the waters above the firmament, and whether
there be any crystalline Heaven, or any primum mobile." You
will then find:—"Of Fate, and that the stars have great influence, and that their operations may diversely be prevented
or furthered." Then you come to two entire chapters on the
place of Paradise, and on the two chief trees in the garden of
Paradise. And in what style, with what power of criticism,
does Ralegh treat the subjects so selected? I turn to the 7th
section of the third chapter of his first book, which treats "Of
their opinion which make Paradise as high as the moon, and
of others which make it higher than the middle region of the
air." Thus he begins the discussion of this opinion:—"Whereas Beda saith, and as the schoolmen affirm Paradise to be a
place altogether removed from the knowledge of men (*'locus
a cognitione hominum remotissimus'*) and Barcephas conceived that Paradise was far in the east, but mounted above
the ocean and all the earth, and near the orb of the moon
(which opinion, though the schoolmen charge Beda withal,
yet Pererius lays it off from Beda and his master Rabanus);
and whereas Rupertus in his geography of Paradise doth not
much differ from the rest, but finds it seated next or nearest
Heaven—" So he states the error, and now for his own criticism of it. "First, such a place cannot be commodious to live
in, for being so near the moon it had been too near the
sun and other heavenly bodies. Secondly, it must have been
too joint a neighbour to the element of fire. Thirdly, the air
in that region is so violently moved and carried about with
such swiftness as nothing in that place can consist or have
abiding. Fourthly,"—but what has been quoted is surely
enough, and there is no use in continuing.

Which is the ancient here, and which is the modern? Which
uses the language of an intelligent man of our own days?
which a language wholly obsolete and unfamiliar to us? Which
has the rational appreciation and control of his facts? which
wanders among them helplessly and without a clue? Is it
our own countryman, or is it the Greek? And the language
of Ralegh affords a fair sample of the critical power, of the
point of view, possessed by the majority of intelligent men
of his day; as the language of Thucydides affords us a fair
sample of the critical power of the majority of intelligent men
in the age of Pericles.

Well, then, in the age of Pericles, we have, in spite of its
antiquity, a highly-developed, a modern, a deeply interesting

epoch. Next comes the question: Is this epoch adequately interpreted by its highest literature? Now, the peculiar characteristic of the highest literature—the poetry—of the fifth century in Greece before the Christian era, is its *adequacy;* the peculiar characteristic of the poetry of Sophocles is its consummate, its unrivalled *adequacy;* that it represents the highly developed human nature of that age—human nature developed in a number of directions, politically, socially, religiously, morally developed—in its completest and most harmonious development in all these directions; while there is shed over this poetry the charm of that noble serenity which always accompanies true insight. If in the body of Athenians of that time there was, as we have said, the utmost energy of mature manhood, public and private; the most entire freedom, the most unprejudiced and intelligent observation of human affairs—in Sophocles there is the same energy, the same maturity, the same freedom, the same intelligent observation; but all these idealized and glorified by the grace and light shed over them from the noblest poetical feeling. And therefore I have ventured to say of Sophocles, that he "saw life steadily, and saw it whole." Well may we understand how Pericles—how the great statesman whose aim was, it has been said, "to realize in Athens the idea which he had conceived of human greatness," and who partly succeeded in his aim—should have been drawn to the great poet whose works are the noblest reflection of his success.

I assert, therefore, though the detailed proof of the assertion must be reserved for other opportunities, that, if the fifth century in Greece before our era is a significant and modern epoch, the poetry of that epoch—the poetry of Pindar, Aeschylus, and Sophocles—is an adequate representation and interpretation of it.

The poetry of Aristophanes is an adequate representation of it also. True, this poetry regards humanity from the comic side; but there is a comic side from which to regard humanity as well as a tragic one; and the distinction of Aristophanes is to have regarded it from the true point of view on the comic side. He too, like Sophocles, regards the human nature of his time in its fullest development; the boldest creations of a riotous imagination are in Aristophanes, as has been justly said, based always upon the foundation of a serious thought: politics, education, social life, literature—all the great modes in which the human life of his day manifested itself—are the subjects of his thoughts, and of his penetrating comment.

There is shed, therefore, over his poetry the charm, the vital freshness, which is felt when man and his relations are from any side adequately and therefore genially, regarded. Here is the true difference between Aristophanes and Menander. There has been preserved an epitome of a comparison by Plutarch between Aristophanes and Menander, in which the grossness of the former, the exquisite truth to life and felicity of observation of the latter, are strongly insisted upon; and the preference of the refined, the learned, the intelligent men of a later period for Menander loudly proclaimed. "What should take a man of refinement to the theatre," asks Plutarch, "except to see one of Menander's plays? When do you see the theatre filled with cultivated persons, except when Menander is acted? and he is the favourite refreshment" he continues, "to the overstrained mind of the laborious philosopher." And every one knows the famous line of tribute to this poet by an enthusiastic admirer in antiquity:—"O Life and Menander, which of you painted the other?" We remember, too, how a great English statesman is said to have declared that there was no lost work of antiquity which he so ardently desired to recover as a play of Menander. Yet Menander has perished, and Aristophanes has survived. And to what is this to be attributed? To the instinct of self-preservation in humanity. The human race has the strongest, the most invincible tendency to *live*, to *develop* itself. It retains, it clings to what fosters its life, what favours its development, to the literature which exhibits it in its vigour; it rejects, it abandons what does not foster its development, the literature which exhibits it arrested and decayed. Now, between the times of Sophocles and Menander a great check had befallen the development of Greece;—the failure of the Athenian expedition to Syracuse, and the consequent termination of the Peloponnesian War in a result unfavourable to Athens. The free expansion of her growth was checked; one of the noblest channels of Athenian life, that of political activity, had begun to narrow and to dry up. That was the true catastrophe of the ancient world; it was then that the oracles of the ancient world should have become silent, and that its gods should have forsaken their temples; for from that date the intellectual and spiritual life of Greece was left without an adequate material basis of political and practical life; and both began inevitably to decay. The opportunity of the ancient world was then lost, never to return; for neither the Macedonian nor the Roman world, which possessed an adequate material basis, possessed, like the Athens of earlier times, an adequate intellect and soul to inform and inspire them; and there was left of the ancient world, when Christianity arrived, of Greece only a head without a body, and of Rome only a body without a soul.

It is Athens after this check, after this diminution of vitality, —it is man with part of his life shorn away, refined and intelligent indeed, but sceptical, frivolous, and dissolute,—which the poetry of Menander represented. The cultivated, the accomplished might applaud the dexterity, the perfection of the representation—might prefer it to the free genial delineation of a more living time with which they were no longer in sympathy. But the instinct of humanity taught it, that in the one poetry there was the seed of life, in the other poetry the seed of death; and it has rescued Aristophanes, while it has left Menander to his fate.

In the flowering period of the life of Greece, therefore, we have a culminating age, one of the flowering periods of the life of the human race: in the poetry of that age we have a literature commensurate with its epoch. It is most perfectly commensurate in the poetry of Pindar, Aeschylus, Sophocles, Aristophanes; these, therefore, will be the supremely interesting objects in this literature; but the stages in literature which led up to this point of perfection, the stages in literature which led downward from it, will be deeply interesting also. A distinguished person, who has lately been occupying himself with Homer, has remarked that an undue preference is given, in the studies of Oxford, to these poets over Homer. The justification of such a preference, even if we put aside all philological considerations, lies, perhaps, in what I have said. Homer himself is eternally interesting; he is a greater poetical power than even Sophocles or Aeschylus; but his age is less interesting than himself. Aeschylus and Sophocles represent an age as interesting as themselves; the names, indeed, in their dramas are the names of the old heroic world, from which they were far separated; but these names are taken, because the use of them permits to the poet that free and ideal treatment of his characters which the highest tragedy demands; and into these figures of the old world is poured all the fulness of life and of thought which the new world had accumulated. This new world in its maturity of reason resembles our own; and the advantage over Homer in their greater significance for *us,* which Aeschylus and Sophocles gain by belonging to this new world, more than compensates for their poetical inferiority to him.

Let us now pass to the Roman world. There is no necessity to accumulate proofs that the culminating period of Roman history is to be classed among the leading, the significant, the modern periods of the world. There is universally current, I think, a pretty correct appreciation of the high development of the Rome of Cicero and Augustus; no one doubts that material civilization and the refinements of life were largely diffused in it; no one doubts that cultivation of mind and intelligence were widely diffused in it. Therefore, I will not occupy time by showing that Cicero corresponded with his friends in the style of the most accomplished, the most easy letter-writers of modern times; that Cicero did not write history like Sir Walter Ralegh. The great period of Rome is, perhaps, on the whole, the greatest, the fullest, the most significant period on record; it is certainly a greater, a fuller period than the age of Pericles. It is an infinitely larger school for the men reared in it; the relations of life are immeasurably multiplied, the events which happen are on an immeasurably grander scale. The facts, the spectacle of this Roman world, then, are immense: let us see how far the literature, the interpretation of the facts, has been adequate.

Let us begin with a great poet, a great philosopher, Lucretius. In the case of Thucydides I called attention to the fact that his habit of mind, his mode of dealing with questions, were modern; that they were those of an enlightened, reflecting man among ourselves. Let me call attention to the exhibition in Lucretius of a modern *feeling* not less remarkable than the modern *thought* in Thucydides. The predominance of thought, of reflection, in modern epochs is not without its penalties; in the unsound, in the over-tasked, in the over-sensitive, it has produced the most painful, the most lamentable results; it has produced a state of feeling unknown to less enlightened but perhaps healthier epochs—the feeling of depression, the feeling of *ennui*. Depression and *ennui;* these are the characteristics stamped on how many of the representative works of modern times! they are also the characteristics stamped on the poem of Lucretius. One of the most powerful, the most solemn passages of the work of Lucretius, one of the most powerful, the most solemn passages in the literature of the whole world, is the well-known conclusion of the third book. With masterly touches he exhibits the lassitude, the incurable tedium which pursue men in their amusements; with indignant irony he upbraids them for the cowardice with which they cling to a life which for most is miserable; to a life which contains, for the most fortunate, nothing but the old dull round of the same unsatisfying objects for ever presented. "A man rushes abroad," he says, "because he is sick of being at home; and suddenly comes home again because he finds himself no whit easier abroad. He posts as fast as his horses can take him to his country-seat: when he has got there he hesitates what to do; or he throws himself down moodily to sleep, and seeks forgetfulness in that; or he makes the best of his way back to town again with the same speed as he fled from it. Thus every one flies from himself." What a picture of *ennui!* of the disease of the most modern societies, the most advanced civilizations! "O man," he exclaims again, "the lights of the world, Scipio, Homer, Epicurus, are dead; wilt thou hesitate and fret at dying, whose life is well-nigh dead whilst thou art yet alive; who consumest in sleep the greater part of thy span, and when awake dronest and ceasest not to dream; and carriest about a mind troubled with baseless fear, and canst not find what it is that aileth thee when thou staggerest like a drunken wretch in the press of thy cares, and welterest hither and thither in the unsteady wandering of thy spirit!" And again: "I have nothing more than you have already seen," he makes Nature say to man, "to invent for your amusement; *eadem sunt omnia semper*—all things continue the same for ever."

Yes, Lucretius is modern; but is he adequate? And how can a man adequately interpret the activity of his age when he is not in sympathy with it? Think of the varied, the abundant, the wide spectacle of the Roman life of his day; think of its fulness of occupation, its energy of effort. From these Lucretius withdraws himself, and bids his disciples to withdraw themselves; he bids them to leave the business of the world, and to apply themselves *"naturam cognoscere rerum*—to learn the nature of things"; but there is no peace, no cheerfulness for him either in the world from which he comes, or in the solitude to which he goes. With stern effort, with gloomy despair, he seems to rivet his eyes on the elementary reality, the naked framework of the world, because the world in its fulness and movement is too exciting a spectacle for his discomposed brain. He seems to feel the spectacle of it at once terrifying and alluring; and to deliver himself from it he has to keep perpetually repeating his formula of disenchantment and annihilation. In reading him, you understand the tradition which represents him as having been driven mad by a poison administered as a love-charm by his mistress, and as having composed his great work in the intervals of his madness. Lucretius is, therefore, overstrained, gloom-weighted, morbid; and he who is morbid is no adequate interpreter of his age.

I pass to Virgil; to the poetical name which of all poetical names has perhaps had the most prodigious fortune; the name which for Dante, for the Middle Ages, represented the perfection of classical antiquity. The perfection of classical antiquity Virgil does not represent; but far be it from me to add my voice to those which have decried his genius; nothing that I shall say is, or can ever be, inconsistent with a profound, an almost affectionate veneration for him. But with respect to him, as with respect to Lucretius, I shall freely ask the question, *Is he adequate?* Does he represent the epoch in which he lived, the mighty Roman world of his time, as the great poets of the great epoch of Greek life represented theirs in all its fulness, in all its significance?

From the very form itself of his great poem, the Aeneid, one would be led to augur that this was impossible. The epic form, as a form for representing contemporary or nearly contemporary events, has attained, in the poems of Homer, an unmatched, an immortal success; the epic form as employed by learned poets for the reproduction of the events of a past age has attained a very considerable success. But for *this* purpose, for the poetic treatment of the events of a *past* age, the epic form is a less vital form than the dramatic form. The great poets of the modern period of Greece are accordingly, as we have seen, the *dramatic* poets. The chief of these— Aeschylus, Sophocles, Euripides, Aristophanes—have survived: the distinguished epic poets of the same period— Panyasis, Choerilus, Antimachus—though praised by the Alexandrian critics, have perished in a common destruction with the undistinguished. And what is the reason of this? It is, that the dramatic form exhibits, above all, *the actions of man as strictly determined by his thoughts and feelings;* it exhibits, therefore, what may be always accessible, always intelligible, always interesting. But the epic form takes a wider range; it represents not only the thought and passion of man, that which is universal and eternal, but also the forms of outward life, the fashion of manners, the aspects of nature, that which is local or transient. To exhibit adequately what is local and transient, only a witness, a contemporary, can suffice. In the *reconstruction*, by learning and antiquarian ingenuity, of the local and transient features of a past age, in their representation by one who is not a witness or contemporary, it is impossible to feel the liveliest kind of interest. What, for instance, is the most interesting portion of the Aeneid,—the portion where Virgil seems to be moving most freely, and therefore to be most animated, most forcible? Precisely that portion which has most a *dramatic* character; the episode of Dido; that portion where locality and manners are nothing— where persons and characters are everything. We might pre- sume beforehand, therefore, that if Virgil, at a time when contemporary epic poetry was no longer possible, had been in- spired to represent human life in its fullest significance, he would not have selected the epic form. Accordingly, what is, in fact, the character of the poem, the frame of mind of the poet? Has the poem the depth, the completeness of the poems of Aeschylus or Sophocles, of those adequate and consum- mate representations of human life? Has the poet the serious cheerfulness of Sophocles, of a man who has mastered the problem of human life, who knows its gravity, and is therefore serious, but who knows that he comprehends it, and is there- fore cheerful? Over the whole of the great poem of Virgil, over the whole Aeneid, there rests an ineffable melancholy: not a rigid, a moody gloom, like the melancholy of Lucretius; no, a sweet, a touching sadness, but still a sadness; a melan- choly which is at once a source of charm in the poem, and a testimony to its incompleteness. Virgil, as Niebuhr has well said, expressed no affected self-disparagement, but the haunt- ing, the irresistible self-dissatisfaction of his heart, when he desired on his death-bed that his poem might be destroyed. A man of the most delicate genius, the most rich learning, but of weak health, of the most sensitive nature, in a great and overwhelming world; conscious, at heart, of his inade- quacy for the thorough spiritual mastery of that world and its interpretation in a work of art; conscious of this inadequacy— the one inadequacy, the one weak place in the mighty Roman nature! This suffering, this graceful-minded, this finely-gifted man is the most beautiful, the most attractive figure in literary history; but he is not the adequate interpreter of the great period of Rome.

We come to Horace: and if Lucretius, if Virgil want cheer- fulness, Horace wants seriousness. I go back to what I said of Menander: as with Menander so it is with Horace: the men of taste, the men of cultivation, the men of the world are enchanted with him; he has not a prejudice, not an illusion, not a blunder. True! yet the best men in the best ages have never been thoroughly satisfied with Horace. If human life were complete without faith, without enthusiasm, without energy, Horace, like Menander, would be the perfect interpreter of human life: but it is not; to the best, to the most living sense of humanity, it is not; and because it is not, Horace is inadequate. Pedants are tiresome, men of reflection and enthusiasm are unhappy and morbid; therefore Horace is a sceptical man of the world. Men of action are without ideas, men of the world are frivolous and sceptical; therefore Lucretius is plunged in gloom and in stern sorrow. So hard, nay, so impossible for most men is it to develop themselves in their entireness; to rejoice in the variety, the movement of human life with the children of the world; to be serious over the depth, the significance of human life with the wise! Horace warms himself before the transient fire of human animation and human pleasure while he can, and is only serious when he reflects that the fire must soon go out:—

Damna tamen celeres reparant coelestia lunae:
Nos, ubi decidimus—

"For nature there is renovation, but for man there is none!" —it is exquisite, but it is not interpretative and fortifying.

In the Roman world, then, we have found a highly modern, a deeply significant, an interesting period—a period more significant and more interesting, because fuller, than the great period of Greece; but we have not a commensurate literature. In Greece we have seen a highly modern, a most significant and interesting period, although on a scale of less magnitude and importance than the great period of Rome; but then, coexisting with the great epoch of Greece there is what is wanting to that of Rome, a commensurate, an interesting literature.

The intellectual history of our race cannot be clearly understood without applying to other ages, nations, and literatures the same method of inquiry which we have been here imperfectly applying to what is called classical antiquity. But enough has at least been said, perhaps, to establish the absolute, the enduring interest of Greek literature, and, above all, of Greek poetry.

FRANCIS BACON
1561–1626

Sir Francis Bacon embodied the ideal figure of the Renaissance:
the Universal Man. He was lawyer, statesman, philosopher,
scientist, writer, all on a grand scale; even when he falls from
greatness he retains a certain grandeur. Yet he has always been
more admired than revered. Blake characterized his essays as "good
advice for Satan's kingdom" because Bacon's voice seemed the
voice of reason, not of love. Bacon offers wise counsel on how
to succeed in the world, how to derive most profit from every
occasion. Even the essay on the following pages describes rather
the advantages of having friends than the emotion of friendship.
Within these limits, however, Bacon is superb. By the lapidary
precision, the extreme conciseness, the brilliant wit of his "dispersed Meditacions," which he called by Montaigne's new word,
essays, he engendered in the English language a form of writing
which has flourished mightily ever since.

Of Friendship

It had been hard for him that spake it to have put more
truth and untruth together in a few words, than in that speech,
*Whosoever is delighted in solitude is either a wild beast or a
god.* For it is most true that a natural and secret hatred and
aversation towards society, in any man, hath somewhat of the
savage beast; but it is most untrue that it should have any
character at all of the divine nature; except it proceed, not
out of a pleasure in solitude, but out of a love and desire to
sequester a man's self for a higher conversation: such as is
found to have been falsely and feignedly in some of the
heathen; as Epimenides the Candian, Numa the Roman, Em-
pedocles the Sicilian, and Apollonius of Tyana; and truly and
really in divers of the ancient hermits and holy fathers of the
church. But little do men perceive what solitude is, and how
far it extendeth. For a crowd is not company, and faces are
but a gallery of pictures, and talk but a tinkling cymbal,
where there is no love. The Latin adage meeteth with it a

22

little, *Magna civitas, magna solitudo;* because in a great town friends are scattered; so that there is not that fellowship, for the most part, which is in less neighbourhoods. But we may go further and affirm most truly, that it is a mere and miserable solitude to want true friends, without which the world is but a wilderness; and even in this sense also of solitude, whosoever in the frame of his nature and affections is unfit for friendship, he taketh it of the beast, and not from humanity.

A principal fruit of friendship is the ease and discharge of the fulness and swellings of the heart, which passions of all kinds do cause and induce. We know diseases of stoppings and suffocations are the most dangerous in the body; and it is not much otherwise in the mind: you may take sarza to open the liver, steel to open the spleen, flowers of sulphur for the lungs, castoreum for the brain; but no receipt openeth the heart, but a true friend, to whom you may impart griefs, joys, fears, hopes, suspicions, counsels, and whatsoever lieth upon the heart to oppress it, in a kind of civil shrift or confession.

It is a strange thing to observe how high a rate great kings and monarchs do set upon this fruit of friendship whereof we speak: so great, as they purchase it many times at the hazard of their own safety and greatness. For princes, in regard of the distance of their fortune from that of their subjects and servants, cannot gather this fruit, except (to make themselves capable thereof) they raise some persons to be as it were companions and almost equals to themselves, which many times sorteth to inconvenience. The modern languages give unto such persons the name of *favourites,* or *privadoes;* as if it were matter of grace, or conversation. But the Roman name attaineth the true use and cause thereof, naming them *participes curarum;* for it is that which tieth the knot. And we see plainly that this hath been done, not by weak and passionate princes only, but by the wisest and most politic that ever reigned; who have oftentimes joined to themselves some of their servants, whom both themselves have called *friends,* and allowed others likewise to call them in the same manner, using the word which is received between private men.

L. Sylla, when he commanded Rome, raised Pompey (after surnamed the Great) to that height, that Pompey vaunted himself for Sylla's overmatch. For when he had carried the consulship for a friend of his, against the pursuit of Sylla, and that Sylla did a little resent thereat, and began to speak great, Pompey turned upon him again, and in effect bade him be

quiet; *for that more men adored the sun rising than the sun
setting.* With Julius Cæsar, Decimus Brutus had obtained that
interest, as he set him down in his testament for heir in remainder after his nephew. And this was the man that had
power with him to draw him forth to his death. For when
Cæsar would have discharged the senate, in regard of some
ill presages, and specially a dream of Calpurnia, this man
lifted him gently by the arm out of his chair, telling him he
hoped he would not dismiss the senate till his wife had
dreamt a better dream. And it seemeth his favour was so
great, as Antonius, in a letter which is recited *verbatim* in one
of Cicero's *Philippics,* calleth him *venefica,* "witch"; as if he
had enchanted Cæsar. Augustus raised Agrippa (though of
mean birth) to that height, as, when he consulted with
Mæcenas about the marriage of his daughter Julia, Mæcenas
took the liberty to tell him, *that he must either marry his
daughter to Agrippa, or take away his life; there was no third
way, he had made him so great.* With Tiberius Cæsar, Sejanus
had ascended to that height, as they two were termed and
reckoned as a pair of friends. Tiberius in a letter to him
saith, *Hæc pro amicitiâ nostrâ non occultavi;* and the whole
senate dedicated an altar to Friendship, as to a goddess, in
respect of the great dearness of friendship between them two.
The like or more was between Septimius Severus and Plautianus. For he forced his eldest son to marry the daughter of
Plautianus; and would often maintain Plautianus in doing
affronts to his son; and did write also in a letter to the senate
by these words: *I love the man so well, as I wish he may
over-live me.* Now if these princes had been as a Trajan,
or a Marcus Aurelius, a man might have thought that this
had proceeded of an abundant goodness of nature; but being
men so wise, for such strength and severity of mind, and so
extreme lovers of themselves, as all these were, it proveth
most plainly that they found their own felicity (though as
great as ever happened to mortal men) but as an half piece,
except they mought have a friend to make it entire: and yet,
which is more, they were princes that had wives, sons, neph-
ews; and yet all these could not supply the comfort of
friendship.

It is not to be forgotten, what Commineus observeth of his
first master, Duke Charles the Hardy; namely, that he would
communicate his secrets with none; and least of all, those
secrets which troubled him most. Whereupon he goeth on and
saith, that towards his latter time *that closeness did impair and*

a little perish his understanding. Surely Commineus mought
have made the same judgement also, if it had pleased him, of
his second master, Lewis the Eleventh, whose closeness was
indeed his tormentor. The parable of Pythagoras is dark, but
true; *Cor ne edito,* "Eat not the heart." Certainly, if a man
would give it a hard phrase, those that want friends to open
themselves unto are cannibals of their own hearts. But one
thing is most admirable (wherewith I will conclude this first
fruit of friendship), which is, that this communicating of a
man's self to his friend works two contrary effects; for it
redoubleth joys, and cutteth griefs in halfs. For there is no man
that imparteth his joys to his friend, but he joyeth the more;
and no man that imparteth his griefs to his friend, but he
grieveth the less. So that it is in truth of operation upon a
man's mind, of like virtue as the alchymists use to attribute to
their stone for man's body; that it worketh all contrary effects,
but still to the good and benefit of nature. But yet, without
praying in aid of alchymists, there is a manifest image of this
in the ordinary course of nature. For in bodies, union strength-
eneth and cherisheth any natural action; and, on the other
side, weakeneth and dulleth any violent impression: and
even so is it of minds.

The second fruit of friendship is healthful and sovereign
for the understanding, as the first is for the affections. For
friendship maketh indeed a fair day in the affections, from
storm and tempests; but it maketh daylight in the understanding, out of darkness and confusion of thoughts. Neither
is this to be understood only of faithful counsel, which a man
receiveth from his friend; but before you come to that, certain it is that whosoever hath his mind fraught with many
thoughts, his wits and understanding do clarify and break up,
in the communicating and discoursing with another: he tosseth
his thoughts more easily; he marshalleth them more orderly;
he seeth how they look when they are turned into words;
finally, he waxeth wiser than himself; and that more by an
hour's discourse than by a day's meditation. It was well
said by Themistocles to the king of Persia, *that speech was
like cloth of Arras, opened and put abroad; whereby the imagery doth appear in figure; whereas in thoughts they lie but
as in packs.* Neither is this second fruit of friendship, in opening the understanding, restrained only to such friends as are
able to give a man counsel: (they indeed are best); but even
without that, a man learneth of himself, and bringeth his own
thoughts to light, and whetteth his wits as against a stone,

which itself cuts not. In a word, a man were better relate himself to a statua or picture, than to suffer his thoughts to pass in smother.

Add now, to make this second fruit of friendship complete, that other point, which lieth more open, and falleth within vulgar observation; which is faithful counsel from a friend. Heraclitus saith well in one of his enigmas, *Dry light is ever the best*. And certain it is that the light that a man receiveth by counsel from another is drier and purer than that which cometh from his own understanding and judgment; which is ever infused and drenched in his affections and customs. So as there is as much difference between the counsel that a friend giveth, and that a man giveth himself, as there is between the counsel of a friend and of a flatterer. For there is no such flatterer as is a man's self; and there is no such remedy against flattery of a man's self as the liberty of a friend. Counsel is of two sorts; the one concerning manners, the other concerning business. For the first; the best preservative to keep the mind in health is the faithful admonition of a friend. The calling of a man's self to a strict account is a medicine, sometime, too piercing and corrosive. Reading good books of morality is a little flat and dead. Observing our faults in others is sometimes unproper for our case. But the best receipt (best, I say, to work, and best to take) is the admonition of a friend. It is a strange thing to behold what gross errors and extreme absurdities many (especially of the greater sort) do commit, for want of a friend to tell them of them, to the great damage both of their fame and fortune. For, as S. James saith, they are as men, *that look sometimes into a glass, and presently forget their own shape and favour*. As for business, a man may think, if he will, that two eyes see no more than one; or that a gamester seeth always more than a looker-on; or that a man in anger is as wise as he that hath said over the four and twenty letters; or that a musket may be shot off as well upon the arm as upon a rest; and such other fond and high imaginations, to think himself all in all. But when all is done, the help of good counsel is that which setteth business straight. And if any man think that he will take counsel, but it shall be by pieces; asking counsel in one business of one man, and in another business of another man; it is well (that is to say, better perhaps than if he asked none at all); but he runneth two dangers. One, that he shall not be faithfully counselled; for it is a rare thing, except it be from a perfect and entire friend, to have counsel given, but such as shall be bowed and crooked to some ends which he hath that giveth it. The other, that he shall have counsel given, hurtful and unsafe (though with good meaning), and mixed partly of mischief and partly of remedy: even as if you would call a physician, that is thought good for the cure of the disease you complain of, but is unacquainted with your body; and therefore may put you in way for a present cure, but overthroweth your health in some other kind; and so cure the disease and kill the patient. But a friend that is wholly acquainted with a man's estate will beware, by furthering any present business, how he dasheth upon other inconvenience. And therefore rest not upon scattered counsels; they will rather distract and mislead than settle and direct.

After these two noble fruits of friendship (peace in the affections, and support of the judgment) followeth the last fruit, which is like the pomegranate, full of many kernels; I mean aid and bearing a part in all actions and occasions. Here the best way to represent to life the manifold use of friendship is to cast and see how many things there are which a man cannot do himself; and then it will appear that it was a sparing speech of the ancients, to say, *that a friend is another himself:* for that a friend is far more than himself. Men have their time, and die many times in desire of some things which they principally take to heart; the bestowing of a child, the finishing of a work, or the like. If a man have a true friend, he may rest almost secure that the care of those things will continue after him. So that a man hath as it were two lives in his desires. A man hath a body, and that body is confined to a place; but where friendship is, all offices of life are as it were granted to him and his deputy. For he may exercise them by his friend. How many things are there which a man cannot, with any face or comeliness, say or do himself! A man can scarce allege his own merits with modesty, much less extol them; a man cannot sometimes brook to supplicate or beg; and a number of the like. But all these things are graceful in a friend's mouth, which are blushing in a man's own. So again, a man's person hath many proper relations which he cannot put off. A man cannot speak to his son but as a father; to his wife but as a husband; to his enemy but upon terms: whereas a friend may speak as the case requires, and not as it sorteth with the person. But to enumerate these things were endless: I have given the rule, where a man cannot fitly play his own part: if he have not a friend, he may quit the stage.

MAX BEERBOHM
1872–1956

Max Beerbohm, in the essay printed below, divides mankind into two great classes: hosts and guests. He himself, he confesses, was one of the guests, and no host could have wished for more charming company. Merely to hear his voice was a pleasure; "he made one aware of how beautiful spoken English can sound," noted S. N. Behrman. And the things he talked of: literature, art, ideas, people, all captured in words with the same diabolical wit he used in his drawings! Yet his wit was not unkind. He had a sympathy, indeed, for the lowly, the failure, such as the nameless clergyman who "solicited his imagination" because Dr. Johnson once crushed him so mercilessly at the Thrales'. After Oscar Wilde's disgrace, Beerbohm regretted one of his caricatures of Wilde; he hadn't realized "how wicked it was," how it could be used as evidence against the man. A satirist Beerbohm always was, from his days as drama critic for the London *Saturday Review* in the nineties, through his more leisurely years as the novelist (*Zuleika Dobson*) and essayist supreme—"the prince of his profession," according to Virginia Woolf. But underlying and enriching the satire was a modesty and a warm humanity that canceled all offense. Small wonder that George Bernard Shaw, not lightly given to praise, called him "the incomparable Max."

Hosts and Guests

Beautifully vague though the English language is, with its meanings merging into one another as softly as the facts of landscape in the moist English climate, and much addicted though we always have been to ways of compromise, and averse from sharp hard logical outlines, we do not call a host a guest, nor a guest a host. The ancient Romans did so. They, with a language that was as lucid as their climate and was a perfect expression of the sharp hard logical outlook fostered by that climate, had but one word for those two things. Nor have their equally acute descendants done what might have been expected of them in this matter. *Hôte* and *ospite* and *héspide* are as mysteriously equivocal as *hospes*. By weight of all this authority I find myself being dragged to the conclusion that a host and a guest must be the same thing, after all. Yet in a dim and muzzy way, deep down in my breast, I feel sure that they are different. Compromise, you see, as usual. I take it that strictly the two things *are* one, but that our division of them is yet another instance of that sterling common-sense by which, etc., etc.

I would go even so far as to say that the difference is more than merely circumstantial and particular. I seem to discern also a temperamental and general difference. You ask me to dine with you in a restaurant, I say I shall be delighted, you order the meal, I praise it, you pay for it, I have the pleasant sensation of not paying for it; and it is well that each of us should have a label according to the part he plays in this transaction. But the two labels are applicable in a larger and more philosophic way. In every human being one or the other of these two instincts is predominant: the active or positive instinct to offer hospitality, the negative or passive instinct to accept it. And either of these instincts is so significant of character that one might well say that mankind is divisible into two great classes: hosts and guests.

I have already (see third sentence of foregoing paragraph) somewhat prepared you for the shock of a confession which candour now forces from me. I am one of the guests. You are, however, so shocked that you will read no more of me? Bravo! Your refusal indicates that you have not a guestish soul. Here am I trying to entertain you, and you will not be entertained. You stand shouting that it is more blessed to give than to receive. Very well. For my part, I would rather read than write, any day. You shall write this essay for me. Be it never so humble, I shall give it my best attention and manage to say something nice about it. I am sorry to see you calming suddenly down. Nothing but a sense of duty to myself, and to guests in general, makes me resume my pen. I believe guests to be as numerous, really, as hosts. It may be that even you, if you examine yourself dispassionately, will find that you are one of them. In which case, you may yet thank me for some comfort. I think there are good qualities to be found in guests, and some bad ones in even the best hosts.

Our deepest instincts, bad or good, are those which we

share with the rest of the animal creation. To offer hospitality, or to accept it, is but an instinct which man has acquired in the long course of his self-development. Lions do not ask one another to their lairs, nor do birds keep open nest. Certain wolves and tigers, it is true, have been so seduced by man from their natural state that they will deign to accept man's hospitality. But when you give a bone to your dog, does he run out and invite another dog to share it with him?—and does your cat insist on having a circle of other cats around her saucer of milk? Quite the contrary. A deep sense of personal property is common to all these creatures. Thousands of years hence they may have acquired some willingness to share things with their friends. Or rather, dogs may; cats, I think, not. Meanwhile, let us not be censorious. Though certain monkeys assuredly were of finer and more malleable stuff than any wolves or tigers, it was a very long time indeed before even we began to be hospitable. The cavemen did not entertain. It may be that now and again—say, towards the end of the Stone Age—one or another among the more enlightened of them said to his wife, while she plucked an eagle that he had snared the day before, 'That red-haired man who lives in the next valley seems to be a decent, harmless sort of person. And sometimes I fancy he is rather lonely. I think I will ask him to dine with us to-night,' and, presently going out, met the red-haired man and said to him, 'Are you doing anything to-night? If not, won't you dine with us? It would be a great pleasure to my wife. Only ourselves. Come just as you are.' 'That is most good of you, but,' stammered the red-haired man, 'as ill-luck will have it, I *am* engaged to-night. A long-standing, formal invitation. I wish I could get out of it, but I simply can't. I have a morbid conscientiousness about such things.' Thus we see that the will to offer hospitality was an earlier growth than the will to accept it. But we must beware of thinking these two things identical with the mere will to give and the mere will to receive. It is unlikely that the red-haired man would have refused a slice of eagle if it had been offered to him where he stood. And it is still more unlikely that his friend would have handed it to him. Such is not the way of hosts. The hospitable instinct is not wholly altruistic. There is pride and egoism mixed up with it, as I shall show.

Meanwhile, why did the red-haired man babble those excuses? It was because he scented danger. He was not by nature suspicious, but—what possible motive, except murder, could this man have for enticing him to that cave? Acquaintance in the open valley was all very well and pleasant, but a strange den after dark—no, no! You despise him for his fears? Yet these were not really so absurd as they may seem. As man progressed in civilisation, and grew to be definitely gregarious, hospitality became more a matter of course. But even then it was not above suspicion. It was not hedged around with those unwritten laws which make it the safe and eligible thing we know to-day. In the annals of hospitality there are many pages that make painful reading; many a great dark blot is there which the Recording Angel may wish, but will not be able to wipe out with a tear.

If I were a host, I should ignore those tomes. Being a guest, I sometimes glance into them, but with more of horror, I assure you, than of malicious amusement. I carefully avoid those which treat of hospitality among barbarous races. Things done in the best periods of the most enlightened peoples are quite bad enough. The Israelites were the salt of the earth. But can you imagine a deed of colder-blooded treachery than Jael's? You would think it must have been held accursed by even the basest minds. Yet thus sang Deborah and Barak, 'Blessed above women shall Jael the wife of Heber the Kenite be, blessed shall she be among women in the tent.' And Barak, remember, was a gallant soldier, and Deborah was a prophetess who 'judged Israel at that time.' So much for the ideals of hospitality among the children of Israel.

Of the Homeric Greeks it may be said that they too were the salt of the earth; and it may be added that in their pungent and antiseptic quality there was mingled a measure of sweetness, not to be found in the children of Israel. I do not say outright that Odysseus ought not to have slain the suitors. That is a debatable point. It is true that they were guests under his roof. But he had not invited them. Let us give him the benefit of the doubt. I am thinking of another episode in his life. By what Circe did, and by his disregard of what she had done, a searching light is cast on the laxity of Homeric Greek notions as to what was due to guests. Odysseus was a clever, but not a bad man, and his standard of general conduct was high enough. Yet, having foiled Circe in her purpose to turn him into a swine, and having forced her to restore his comrades to human shape, he did not let pass the barrier of his teeth any such winged words as 'Now will I bide no more under thy roof, Circe, but fare across the sea with my dear comrades, even unto mine own

home, for that which thou didst was an evil thing, and one
not meet to be done unto strangers by the daughter of a god.'
He seems to have said nothing in particular, to have accepted
with alacrity the invitation that he and his dear comrades
should prolong their visit, and to have prolonged it with them
for a whole year, in the course of which Circe bore him a
son, named Telegonus. As Matthew Arnold would have said,
'What a set!'

My eye roves, for relief, to those shelves where the later
annals are. I take down a tome at random. Rome in the fifteenth century: civilisation never was more brilliant than there
and then, I imagine; and yet—no, I replace that tome. I
saw enough in it to remind me that the Borgias selected and
laid down rare poisons in their cellars with as much thought
as they gave to their vintage wines. Extraordinary!—but the
Romans do not seem to have thought so. An invitation to
dine at the Palazzo Borghese was accounted the highest social
honour. I am aware that in recent books of Italian history
there has been a tendency to whiten the Borgias' characters.
But I myself hold to the old romantic black way of looking
at the Borgias. I maintain that though you would often in the
fifteenth century have heard the snobbish Roman say, in a
would-be off-hand tone, 'I am dining with the Borgias to-night,'
no Roman ever was able to say 'I dined last night with the
Borgias.'

To mankind in general Macbeth and Lady Macbeth stand
out as the supreme type of all that a host and hostess should
not be. Hence the marked coolness of Scotsmen towards
Shakespeare, hence the untiring efforts of that proud and sensitive race to set up Burns in his stead. It is a risky thing to
offer sympathy to the proud and sensitive, yet I must say that
I think the Scots have a real grievance. The two actual, historic Macbeths were no worse than innumerable other
couples in other lands that had not yet fully struggled out of
barbarism. It is hard that Shakespeare happened on the story
of that particular pair, and so made it immortal. But he meant
no harm, and, let Scotsmen believe me, did positive good.
Scotch hospitality is proverbial. As much in Scotland as in
America does the English visitor blush when he thinks how
perfunctory and niggard, in comparison, English hospitality
is. It was Scotland that first formalised hospitality, made of
it an exacting code of honour, with the basic principle that
the guest must in all circumstances be respected and at all
costs protected. Jacobite history bristles with examples of the

heroic sacrifices made by hosts for their guests, sacrifices of their own safety and even of their own political convictions, for fear of infringing, however slightly, that sacred code of theirs. And what was the origin of all this noble pedantry? Shakespeare's 'Macbeth.'

Perhaps if England were a bleak and rugged country, like Scotland, or a new country, like America, the foreign visitor would be more overwhelmed with kindness here than he is. The landscapes of our country-side are so charming, London abounds in public monuments so redolent of history, so romantic and engrossing, that we are perhaps too apt to think the foreign visitor would have neither time nor inclination to sit dawdling in private dining-rooms. Assuredly there is no lack of hospitable impulse among the English. In what may be called mutual hospitality they touch a high level. The French, also the Italians, entertain one another far less frequently. In England the native guest has a very good time indeed—though of course he pays for it, in some measure, by acting as host too, from time to time.

In practice, no, there cannot be any absolute division of mankind into my two categories, hosts and guests. But psychologically a guest does not cease to be a guest when he gives a dinner, nor is a host not a host when he accepts one. The amount of entertaining that a guest need do is a matter wholly for his own conscience. He will soon find that he does not receive less hospitality for offering little; and he would not receive less if he offered none. The amount received by him depends wholly on the degree of his agreeableness. Pride makes an occasional host of him; but he does not shine in that capacity. Nor do hosts want him to assay it. If they accept an invitation from him, they do so only because they wish not to hurt his feelings. As guests they are fish out of water.

Circumstances do, of course, react on character. It is conventional for the rich to give, and for the poor to receive. Riches do tend to foster in you the instincts of a host, and poverty does create an atmosphere favorable to the growth of guestish instincts. But strong bents make their own way. Not all guests are to be found among the needy, nor all hosts among the affluent. For sixteen years after my education was, by courtesy, finished—from the age, that is, of twenty-two to the age of thirty-eight—I lived in London, seeing all sorts of people all the while; and I came across many a rich man who, like the master of the shepherd Corin,

was 'of churlish disposition' and little recked 'to find the way
to heaven by doing deeds of hospitality.' On the other hand, I
knew quite poor men who were incorrigibly hospitable.

To such men, all honour. The most I dare claim for myself
is that if I had been rich I should have been better than
Corin's master. Even as it was, I did my best. But I had no
authentic joy in doing it. Without the spur of pride I might
conceivably have not done it at all. There recurs to me from
among memories of my boyhood an episode that is rather
significant. In my school, as in most others, we received now
and again 'hampers' from home. At the mid-day dinner, in
every house, we all ate together; but at breakfast and supper
we ate in four or five separate 'messes.' It was customary for
the receiver of a hamper to share the contents with his mess-
mates. On one occasion I received, instead of the usual varie-
gated hamper, a box containing twelve sausage-rolls. It happened that when this box arrived and was opened by me
there was no one around. Of sausage-rolls I was particularly
fond. I am sorry to say that I carried the box up to my
cubicle, and, having eaten two of the sausage-rolls, said nothing to my friends, that day, about the other ten, nor anything
about them when, three days later, I had eaten them all—
all, up there, alone.

Thirty years have elapsed, my school-fellows are scattered
far and wide, the chance that this page may meet the eyes of
some of them does not much dismay me; but I am glad there
was no collective and contemporary judgment by them on my
strange exploit. What defence could I have offered? Suppose I
had said 'You see, I am so essentially a guest,' the plea would
have carried little weight. And yet it would not have been
a worthless plea. On receipt of a hamper, a boy did rise,
always, in the esteem of his mess-mates. His sardines, his
marmalade, his potted meat, at any rate while they lasted,
did make us think that his parents 'must be awfully decent'
and that he was a not unworthy son. He had become our
central figure, we expected him to lead the conversation, we
liked listening to him, his jokes were good. With those twelve
sausage-rolls I could have dominated my fellows for a while.
But I had not a dominant nature. I never trusted myself as
a leader. Leading abashed me. I was happiest in the comity of
the crowd. Having received a hamper, I was always glad
when it was finished, glad to fall back into the ranks. Humility is a virtue, and it is a virtue innate in guests.

Boys (as will have been surmised from my record of the

effect of hampers) are all of them potential guests. It is only as they grow up that some of them harden into hosts. It is likely enough that if I, when I grew up, had been rich, my natural bent to guestship would have been diverted, and I too have become a (sort of) host. And perhaps I should have passed muster. I suppose I did pass muster whenever, in the course of my long residence in London, I did entertain friends. But the memory of those occasions is not dear to me —especially not the memory of those that were in the more distinguished restaurants. Somewhere in the back of my brain, while I tried to lead the conversation brightly, was always the haunting fear that I had not brought enough money in my pocket. I never let this fear master me. I never said to any one 'Will you have a liqueur?'—always 'What liqueur will you have?' But I postponed as far as possible the evil moment of asking for the bill. When I had, in the proper casual tone (I hope and believe), at length asked for it, I wished always it were not brought to me *folded* on a plate, as though the amount were so hideously high that I alone must be privy to it. So soon as it was laid beside me, I wanted to know the worst at once. But I pretended to be so occupied in talk that I was unaware of the bill's presence; and I was careful to be always in the middle of a sentence when I raised the upper fold and took my not (I hope) frozen glance. In point of fact, the amount was always much less than I had feared. Pessimism does win us great happy moments.

Meals in the restaurants of Soho tested less severely the pauper guest masquerading as host. But to them one could not ask rich persons—nor even poor persons unless one knew them very well. Soho is so uncertain that the fare is often not good enough to be palmed off on even one's poorest and oldest friends. A very magnetic host, with a great gift for bluffing, might, no doubt, even in Soho's worst moments, diffuse among his guests a conviction that all was of the best. But I never was good at bluffing. I had always to let food speak for itself. 'It's cheap' was the only pæan that in Soho's bad moments ever occurred to me, and this of course I did not utter. And *was* it so cheap, after all? Soho induces a certain optimism. A bill there was always larger than I had thought it would be.

Every one, even the richest and most munificent of men, pays much by cheque more light-heartedly than he pays little in specie. In restaurants I should have liked always to give cheques. But in any restaurant I was so much more often seen as guest than as host that I never felt sure the proprietor would trust me. Only in my club did I know the luxury, or rather the painlessness, of entertaining by cheque. A cheque— especially if it is a club cheque, as supplied for the use of members, not a leaf torn out of his own book—makes so little mark on any man's imagination. He dashes off some words and figures, he signs his name (with that vague momentary pleasure which the sight of his own signature anywhere gives him), he walks away and forgets. Offering hospitality in my club, I was inwardly calm. But even there I did not glow (though my face and manner, I hoped, glowed). If my guest was by nature a guest, I managed to forget somewhat that I myself was a guest by nature. But if, as now and then happened, my guest was a true and habitual host, I did feel that we were in an absurdly false relation; and it was not without difficulty that I could restrain myself from saying to him 'This is all very well, you know, but—frankly: your place is at the head of your own table.'

The host as guest is far, far worse than the guest as host. He never even passes muster. The guest, in virtue of a certain hability that is part of his natural equipment, can more or less ape the ways of a host. But the host, with his more positive temperament, does not even attempt the graces of a guest. By 'graces' I do not mean to imply anything artificial. The guest's manners are, rather, as wild flowers springing from good rich soil—the soil of genuine modesty and gratitude. He honourably wishes to please in return for the pleasure he is receiving. He wonders that people should be so kind to him, and, without knowing it, is very kind to *them*. But the host, as I said earlier in this essay, is a guest against his own will. That is the root of the mischief. He feels that it is more blessed, etc., and that he is conferring rather than accepting a favour. He does not adjust himself. He forgets his place. He leads the conversation. He tries genially to draw you out. He never comments on the goodness of the food or wine. He looks at his watch abruptly and says he must be off. He doesn't say he has had a delightful time. In fact, his place is at the head of his own table.

His own table, over his own cellar, under his own roof— it is only there that you see him at his best. To a club or restaurant he may sometimes invite you, but not there, not there, my child, do you get the full savour of his quality. In life or literature there has been no better host than Old Wardle. Appalling though he would have been as a guest in club or restaurant, it is hardly less painful to think of him as a host there. At Dingley Dell, with an ample gesture, he made you free of all that was his. He could not have given you a club or a restaurant. Nor, when you come to think of it, did he give you Dingley Dell. The place remained his. None knew better than Old Wardle that this was so. Hospitality, as we have agreed, is not one of the most deep-rooted instincts in man, whereas the sense of possession certainly is. Not even Old Wardle was a communist. 'This,' you may be sure he said to himself, 'is *my* roof, these are *my* horses, that's a picture of *my* dear old grandfather.' And 'This,' he would say to us, 'is *my* roof: sleep soundly under it. These are *my* horses: ride them. That's a portrait of *my* dear old grandfather: have a good look at it.' But he did not ask us to walk off with any of these things. Not even what he actually did give us would he regard as having passed out of his possession. 'That,' he would muse if we were torpid after dinner, 'is *my* roast beef,' and 'That,' if we staggered on the way to bed, 'is *my* cold milk punch.' 'But surely,' you interrupt me, 'to give and then not feel that one has given is the very best of all ways of giving.' I agree. I hope you didn't think I was trying to disparage Old Wardle. I was merely keeping my promise to point out that from among the motives of even the best hosts pride and egoism are not absent.

Every virtue, as we were taught in youth, is a mean between two extremes; and I think any virtue is the better understood by us if we glance at the vice on either side of it. I take it that the virtue of hospitality stands midway between churlishness and mere ostentation. Far to the left of the good host stands he who doesn't want to see anything of any one; far to the right, he who wants a horde of people to be always seeing something of *him*. I conjecture that the figure on the left, just discernible through my field-glasses, is that of old Corin's master. His name was never revealed to us, but Corin's brief account of his character suffices. 'Deeds of hospitality' is a dismal phrase that could have occurred only to the servant of a very dismal master. Not less tell-tale is Corin's idea that men who do these 'deeds' do them only to save their souls in the next world. It is a pity Shakespeare did not actually bring Corin's master on to the stage. One would have liked to see the old man genuinely touched by the charming eloquence of Rosalind's appeal for a crust of bread, and conscious that he would probably go to heaven if he granted it, and yet not quite able to grant it. Far away though he stands to the left of the good host, he has yet something in common with that third person discernible on the right—that speck yonder, which I believe to be Lucullus. Nothing that we know of Lucullus suggests that he was less inhuman than the churl of Arden. It does not appear that he had a single friend, nor that he wished for one. His lavishness was indiscriminate except in that he entertained only the rich. One would have liked to dine with him, but not even in the act of digestion could one have felt that he had a heart. One would have acknowledged that in all the material resources of his art he was a master, and also that he practiced his art for sheer love of it, wishing to be admired for nothing but his mastery, and cocking no eye on any of those ulterior objects but for which some of the most prominent hosts would not entertain at all. But the very fact that he was an artist is repulsive. When hospitality becomes an art it loses its very soul. With this reflection I look away from Lucullus and, fixing my gaze on the middle ground, am the better able to appreciate the excellence of the figure that stands before me—the figure of Old Wardle. Some pride and egoism in that capacious breast, yes, but a great heart full of kindness, and ever a warm spontaneous welcome to the stranger in need, and to all old friends and young. Hark! He is shouting something. He is asking us both down to Dingley Dell. And you have shouted back that you will be delighted. Ah, did I not suspect from the first you too were perhaps a guest?

But—I constrain you in the act of rushing off to pack your things—one moment: this essay has yet to be finished. We have yet to glance at those two extremes between which the mean is good guestship. Far to the right of the good guest, we descry the parasite; far to the left, the churl again. Not the same churl, perhaps. We do not know that Corin's master was ever sampled as a guest. I am inclined to call yonder speck Dante—Dante Alighieri, of whom we do know that he received during his exile much hospitality from many hosts and repaid them by writing how bitter was the bread in their houses, and how steep the stairs were. To think of dour Dante as a guest is less dispiriting only than to think what he would have been as a host had it ever occurred to him to entertain any one or anything except a deep regard for Beatrice; and one turns with positive relief to have a glimpse of the parasite—Mr. Smurge, I presume, 'whose gratitude was as boundless as his appetite, and his presence as unsought as it appeared to be inevitable.' But now, how gracious and admirable is the central figure—radiating gratitude, but not too much of it; never intrusive, ever within call; full of dignity, yet all amenable; quiet, yet lively; never echoing, ever amplifying; never contradicting, but often lighting the way to truth; an ornament, an inspiration, anywhere.

Such is he. But *who* is he? It is easier to confess a defect than to claim a quality. I have told you that when I lived in London I was nothing as a host; but I will not claim to have been a perfect guest. Nor indeed was I. I was a good one, but, looking back, I see myself not quite in the centre—slightly to the left, slightly to the churlish side. I was rather *too* quiet, and I did sometimes contradict. And, though I always liked to be invited anywhere, I very often preferred to stay at home. If any one hereafter shall form a collection of the notes written by me in reply to invitations, I am afraid he will gradually suppose me to have been more in request than ever I really was, and to have been also a great invalid, and a great traveller.

JORGE LUIS BORGES
1899——

Argentine Jorge Luis Borges is a writer of poetry, stories, and essays that are very little known in this country, because in this country very little is known of any Latin American writer. In Europe, on the other hand, his reputation is great and growing. André Maurois wrote the admiring preface for a collection of Borges' stories and essays published in English in 1962; and in 1961 Borges shared with Samuel Beckett the International For- mentor Prize. Among his literary ancestors critics list Poe, Baude- laire, Valéry, Kafka, but ultimately Borges resembles no one so much as himself. Like Sir Thomas Browne, he delights in mystery and paradox; and indeed in the rapid progression of his mind from one association to another, he shows a kinship with the metaphysical writers of the seventeenth century. He rejects, how- ever, their theological certainty. All metaphysics, from Zeno to Kierkegaard, provide him material for intellectual games; he puts his faith in none. Yet he is not uncommitted. The problems of time, of identity, of reality and illusion, of dreamer and dreamed, with which he plays, are the inescapable problems of the human spirit, and Borges plays with them in earnest. The translation is by James E. Irby.

Parables

I. Ragnarök

In our dreams (writes Coleridge) images represent the sen- sations we think they cause; we do not feel horror because we are threatened by a sphinx; we dream of a sphinx in order to explain the horror we feel. If this is so, how could a mere chronicle of its forms transmit the stupor, the exaltation, the alarm, the menace and the jubilance which made up the fabric of that dream that night? I shall attempt such a chronicle, however; perhaps the fact that the dream was composed of one single scene may remove or mitigate this essential difficulty.

The place was the School of Philosophy and Letters; the time, toward sundown. Everything (as usually happens in dreams) was somewhat different; a slight magnification altered things. We were electing officials: I was talking with Pedro Henríquez Ureña, who in the world of waking reality died many years ago. Suddenly we were stunned by the clamor of a demonstration or disturbance. Human and animal cries came from the Bajo. A voice shouted "Here they come!" and then "The Gods! The Gods!" Four or five individuals emerged from the mob and occupied the platform of the main lecture hall. We all applauded, tearfully; these were the Gods returning after a centuries-long exile. Made larger by the platform, their heads thrown back and their chests thrust forward, they arrogantly received our homage. One held a branch which no doubt conformed to the simple botany of dreams; another, in a broad gesture, extended his hand which was a claw; one of the faces of Janus looked with distrust at the curved beak of Thoth. Perhaps aroused by our applause, one of them—I no longer know which—erupted in a victorious clatter, unbelievably harsh, with something of a gargle and of a whistle. From that moment, things changed.

It all began with the suspicion (perhaps exaggerated) that the Gods did not know how to talk. Centuries of fell and fugitive life had atrophied the human element in them; the moon of Islam and the cross of Rome had been implacable with these outlaws. Very low foreheads, yellow teeth, stringy mulatto or Chinese mustaches and thick bestial lips showed the degeneracy of the Olympian lineage. Their clothing corresponded not to a decorous poverty but rather to the sinister luxury of the gambling houses and brothels of the Bajo. A carnation bled crimson in a lapel and the bulge of a knife was outlined beneath a close-fitting jacket. Suddenly we sensed that they were playing their last card, that they were cunning, ignorant and cruel like old beasts of prey and that, if we let ourselves be overcome by fear or pity, they would finally destroy us.

We took out our heavy revolvers (all of a sudden there were revolvers in the dream) and joyfully killed the Gods.

II. The Witness

In a stable which is almost in the shadow of the new stone church, a man with gray eyes and gray beard, lying amidst the odor of the animals, humbly seeks death as one would seek sleep. The day, faithful to vast and secret laws, is shifting and confusing the shadows inside the poor shelter; outside are the plowed fields and a ditch clogged with dead leaves and the tracks of a wolf in the black mud where the forests begin. The man sleeps and dreams, forgotten. He is awakened by the bells tolling the Angelus. In the kingdoms of England the ringing of bells is now one of the customs of the evening, but this man, as a child, has seen the face of Woden, the divine horror and exultation, the crude wooden idol hung with Roman coins and heavy clothing, the sacrificing of horses, dogs and prisoners. Before dawn he will die and with him will die, and never return, the last immediate images of these pagan rites; the world will be a little poorer when this Saxon has died.

Deeds which populate the dimensions of space and which reach their end when someone dies may cause us wonderment, but one thing, or an infinite number of things, dies in every final agony, unless there is a universal memory as the theosophists have conjectured. In time there was a day that extinguished the last eyes to see Christ; the battle of Junín and the love of Helen died with the death of a man. What will die with me when I die, what pathetic or fragile form will the world lose? The voice of Macedonio Fernández, the image of a red horse in the vacant lot at Serrano and Charcas, a bar of sulphur in the drawer of a mahogany desk?

III. Borges and I

The other one, the one called Borges, is the one things happen to. I walk through the streets of Buenos Aires and stop for a moment, perhaps mechanically now, to look at the arch of an entrance hall and the grillwork on the gate; I know of Borges from the mail and see his name on a list of professors or in a biographical dictionary. I like hourglasses, maps, eighteenth-century typography, the taste of coffee and the prose of Stevenson; he shares these preferences, but in a vain way that turns them into the attributes of an actor. It would be an exaggeration to say that ours is a hostile relationship; I live, let myself go on living, so that Borges may contrive his literature, and this literature justifies me. It is no effort for me to confess that he has achieved some valid pages, but those pages cannot save me, perhaps because what is good belongs to no one, not even to him, but rather to the language and to tradition. Besides, I am destined to perish, definitively, and only some instant of myself can survive in him. Little by little, I am giving over everything to him, though I am quite aware of his perverse custom of falsifying and magnifying things. Spinoza knew that all things long to persist in their being; the stone eternally wants to be a stone and the tiger a tiger. I shall remain in Borges, not in myself (if it is true that I am someone), but I recognize myself less in his books than in many others or in the laborious strumming of a guitar. Years ago I tried to free myself from him and went from the mythologies of the suburbs to the games with time and infinity, but those games belong to Borges now and I shall have to imagine other things. Thus my life is a flight and I lose everything and everything belongs to oblivion, or to him.

I do not know which of us has written this page.

IV. Everything and Nothing

There was no one in him; behind his face (which even through the bad paintings of those times resembles no other) and his words, which were copious, fantastic and stormy, there was only a bit of coldness, a dream dreamt by no one. At first he thought that all people were like him, but the astonishment of a friend to whom he had begun to speak of this emptiness showed him his error and made him feel always that an individual should not differ in outward appearance. Once he thought that in books he would find a cure for his ill and thus he learned the small Latin and less Greek a contemporary would speak of; later he considered that what he sought might well be found in an elemental rite of humanity, and let himself be initiated by Anne Hathaway one long June afternoon. At the age of twenty-odd years he went to London. Instinctively he had already become proficient in the habit of simulating that he was someone, so that others would not discover his condition as no one; in London he found the profession to which he was predestined, that of the actor, who on a stage plays at being another before a gathering of people who play at taking him for that other person. His histrionic tasks brought him a singular satisfaction, perhaps the first he had ever known; but once the last verse had been acclaimed and the last dead man withdrawn from the stage, the hated flavor of unreality returned to him. He ceased to be Ferrex or Tamerlane and became no one again. Thus hounded, he took to imagining other heroes and other tragic fables. And so, while his flesh fulfilled its destiny as flesh in the taverns and brothels of London, the soul that inhabited him was Caesar, who disregards the augur's admonition, and Juliet, who abhors the lark, and Macbeth, who converses on the plain with the witches who are also Fates. No one has ever been so many men as this man, who like the Egyptian Proteus could exhaust all the guises of reality. At times he would leave a confession hidden away in some corner of his work, certain that it would not be deciphered; Richard affirms that in his person he plays the part of many and Iago claims with curious words "I am not what I am." The fundamental identity of existing, dreaming and acting inspired famous passages of his.

For twenty years he persisted in that controlled hallucination, but one morning he was suddenly gripped by the tedium and the terror of being so many kings who die by the sword and so many suffering lovers who converge, diverge and melodiously expire. That very day he arranged to sell his theater. Within a week he had returned to his native village, where he recovered the trees and rivers of his childhood and did not relate them to the others his muse had celebrated, illustrious with mythological allusions and Latin terms. He had to be someone; he was a retired impresario who had made his fortune and concerned himself with loans, lawsuits and petty usury. It was in this character that he dictated the arid will and testament known to us, from which he deliberately excluded all traces of pathos or literature. His friends from London would visit his retreat and for them he would take up again his role as poet.

History adds that before or after dying he found himself in the presence of God and told Him: "I who have been so many men in vain want to be one and myself." The voice of the Lord answered from a whirlwind: "Neither am I anyone; I have dreamt the world as you dreamt your work, my Shakespeare, and among the forms in my dream are you, who like myself are many and no one."

HEYWOOD BROUN
1888–1939

Heywood Broun on the lecture platform looked "like a mammoth elf." That was his image to countless devoted readers, too, who followed his famous column, "It Seems to Me," for almost twenty years in the old New York *World* and other newspapers: a great, lovable, laughable bear of a man with a shrewd wit and a disarming innocence. This is the side of Broun that shows in the following essay, "Holding a Baby." But there was another side, hard, courageous, passionate, that many of his readers first learned about when he insisted on using his column to defend Sacco and Vanzetti, in defiance of editorial objection. Out of this issue came his break with the *World,* but Broun went on with undiminished fervor to the *Telegram,* to fight injustice, intolerance, and all the miseries of the Depression. He jolted the complacency of Manhattan's Seventeenth District by campaigning for Congress there on the Socialist ticket. He helped to organize the American Newspaper Guild and became its militant president. He marched on picket lines, talked back to the police, and even got himself arrested. Not from any wish for violence or notoriety, but in order to prove by act as well as by word, he wrote as his belief on his fiftieth birthday: "The underdog can and will lick his weight in the wildcats of the world."

Holding a Baby

When Adam delved and Eve span, the fiction that man is incapable of housework was first established. It would be interesting to figure out just how many foot-pounds of energy men have saved themselves, since the creation of the world, by keeping up the pretense that a special knack is required for washing dishes and for dusting, and that the knack is wholly feminine. The pretense of incapacity is impudent in its audacity, and yet it works.

45

Men build bridges and throw railroads across deserts, and yet they contend successfully that the job of sewing on a button is beyond them. Accordingly, they don't have to sew buttons.

It might be said, of course, that the safety of suspension bridges is so much more important than that of suspenders that the division of labor is only fair, but there are many of us who have never thrown a railroad in our lives, and yet swagger in all the glory of masculine achievement without undertaking any of the drudgery of odd jobs.

Probably men alone could never have maintained the fallacy of masculine incapacity without the aid of women. As soon as that rather limited sphere, once known as woman's place, was established, women began to glorify and exaggerate its importance, by the pretense that it was all so special and difficult that no other sex could possibly begin to accomplish the tasks entailed. To this declaration men gave immediate and eager assent and they have kept it up. The most casual examination will reveal the fact that all the jokes about the horrible results of masculine cooking and sewing are written by men. It is all part of a great scheme of sex propaganda.

Naturally there are other factors. Biology has been unscrupulous enough to discriminate markedly against women, and men have seized upon this advantage to press the belief that, since the bearing of children is exclusively the province of women, it must be that all the caring for them belongs properly to the same sex. Yet how ridiculous this is.

Most things which have to be done for children are of the simplest sort. They should tax the intelligence of no one. Men profess a total lack of ability to wash baby's face simply because they believe there's no great fun in the business, at either end of the sponge. Protectively, man must go the whole distance and pretend that there is not one single thing which he can do for baby. He must even maintain that he doesn't know how to hold one. From this pretense has grown the shockingly transparent fallacy that holding a baby correctly is one of the fine arts; or, perhaps even more fearsome than that, a wonderful intuition, which has come down after centuries of effort to women only.

"The thing that surprised Richard most," says a recent woman novelist, "was the ease and the efficiency with which Eleanor handled Annabel. . . . She seemed to know by instinct, things that Richard could not understand and that he could not understand how she came by. If she reached out her hands to take Annabel, her fingers seemed, of themselves, to curve into the places where they would fit the spineless bundle and give it support."

At this point, interruption is inevitable. Places indeed! There are one hundred and fifty-two distinctly different ways of holding a baby—and all are right! At least all will do. There is no need of seeking out special places for the hands. A baby is so soft that anybody with a firm grip can make places for an effective hold wherever he chooses. But to return to our quotation: "If Richard tried to take up the bundle, his fingers fell away like the legs of the brittle crab and the bundle collapsed, incalculable and helpless. 'How do you do it?' he would say. And he would right Annabel and try to still her protests. And Eleanor would only smile gently and send him on some masculine errand, while she soothed Annabel's feelings in the proper way."

You may depend upon it that Richard also smiled as soon as he was safely out of the house and embarked upon some masculine errand, such as playing eighteen holes of golf. Probably, by the time he reached the tenth green, he was too intent upon his game to remember how guile had won him freedom. Otherwise, he would have laughed again, when he holed a twenty-foot putt over a rolling green and recollected that he had escaped an afternoon of carrying Annabel because he was too awkward. I once knew the wife of the greatest billiard player in the world, and she informed me with much pride that her husband was incapable of carrying the baby. "He doesn't seem to have the proper touch," she explained.

As a matter of fact, even if men in general were as awkward as they pretend to be at home, there would still be small reason for their shirking the task of carrying a baby. Except that right side up is best, there is not much to learn. As I ventured to suggest before, almost any firm grip will do. Of course the child may cry, but that is simply because he has become over-particular through too much coddling. Nature herself is cavalier. Young rabbits don't even whimper when picked up by the ears, and kittens are quite contented to be lifted by the scruff of the neck.

This same Nature has been used as the principal argument for woman's exclusive ability to take care of the young. It is pretty generally held that all a woman needs to do to know all about children is to have some. This wisdom is attributed to instinct. Again and again we have been told by rapturous grandmothers that: "It isn't something which can be read in a book or taught in a school. Nature is the great teacher." This simply isn't true. There are many mothers in America who have learned far more from the manuals of Dr. Holt than instinct ever taught them—and Dr. Holt is a man. I have seen mothers give beer and spaghetti and Neapolitan ice-cream to children in arms, and, if they got that from instinct, the only conclusion possible is that instinct did not know what it was talking about. Instinct is not what it used to be.

I have no feeling of being a traitor to my sex, when I say that I believe in at least a rough equality of parenthood. In shirking all the business of caring for children we have escaped much hard labor. It has been convenient. Perhaps it has been too convenient. If we have avoided arduous tasks, we have also missed much fun of a very special kind. Like children in a toy shop, we have chosen to live with the most amusing of talking-and-walking dolls, without ever attempting to tear down the sign which says, "Do not touch." In fact we have helped to set it in place. That is a pity.

Children mean nothing at long range. For our own sake we ought to throw off the pretense of incapacity and ask that we be given a half share in them. I hope that this can be done without its being necessary for us to share the responsibility of dishes also. I don't think there are any concealed joys in washing dishes. Washing children is quite a different matter. After you have washed somebody else's face you feel that you know him better. This may be the reason why so many trained nurses marry their patients—but that is another story. A dish is an unresponsive thing. It gives back nothing. A child's face offers competitive possibilities. It is interesting to see just how high a polish can be achieved without making it cry.

There is also a distinct sense of elation in doing trifling practical things for children. They are so small and so helpless that they contribute vastly to a comforting glow in the ego of the grown-up. When you have completed the rather difficult task of preparing a child for bed and actually getting him there, you have a sense of importance almost divine in its extent. This is to feel at one with Fate, to be the master of another's destiny, of his waking and his sleeping and his going out into the world. It is a brand-new world for the child. He is a veritable Adam and you loom up in his life as more than mortal. Golf is well enough for a Sunday sport, but it is a trifling thing beside the privilege of taking a small son to the zoo and letting him see his first lion, his first tiger and, best of all, his first elephant. Probably he will think that they are part of your own handiwork turned out for his pleasure.

To a child, at least, even the meanest of us may seem glamourous with magic and wisdom. It seems a pity not to take the fullest advantage of this chance before the opportunity is lost. There must come a day when even the most nimble-witted father has to reply, "I don't know." On that day the child comes out of Eden and you are only a man again. Cortes on his lonely peak in Darien was a pigmy discoverer beside the child eating his first spoonful of ice-cream. There is the immediate frightened and angry rebellion against the coldness of it, and then the amazing sensation as the strange substance melts into magic of pleasant sweetness. The child will go on to high adventure, but I doubt whether the world holds for any one more soul-stirring surprise than the first adventure with ice-cream. No, there is nothing dull in feeding a child.

There is less to be said for dressing a child, from the point of view of recreation. This seems to us laborious and rather tiresome, both for father and child. Still I knew one man who managed to make an adventure of it. He boasted that he had broken all the records of the world for changing all or any part of a child's clothing. He was a skilled automobile mechanic, much in demand in races, where tires are whisked on and off. He brought his technic into the home. I saw several of his demonstrations. He was a silent man who habitually carried a mouthful of safety pins. Once the required youngster had been pointed out, he wasted no time in preliminary wheedlings but tossed her on the floor without more ado. Even before her head had bumped, he would be hard at work. With him the thrill lay in the inspiration of the competitive spirit. He endeavored always to have his task completed before the child could begin to cry. He never lost. Often the child cried afterward, but by that time my friend felt that his part of the job was completed—and would turn the youngster over to her mother.

SIR THOMAS BROWNE
1605–1682

In a period when, according to Dr. Johnson, every writer was experimenting with the English language, "moulding it according to his own fancy," Sir Thomas Browne fashioned for himself a style of unsurpassed sonority and splendor. More, he "poured" into the language a "multitude of exotic words," some of which have remained exotic, while others, such as *electricity* and *medical,* have passed into common use. Yet Browne was more than stylist and innovator; he was an eminent physician, a scientific experimenter, and an explorer of the heights and depths of religious experience. Perhaps most important in our eyes, he remained sane and charitable in an age of bitter religious controversy. *Religio Medici,* from which the following passage is taken, was a statement of Browne's own faith, not a prescription for a single other soul.

Of Charity

SECT. I.—Now, for that other virtue of charity, without which faith is a mere notion and of no existence, I have ever endeavoured to nourish the merciful disposition and humane inclination I borrowed from my parents, and regulate it to the written and prescribed laws of charity. And, if I hold the true anatomy of myself, I am delineated and naturally framed to such a piece of virtue—for I am of a constitution so general that it consorts and sympathizeth with all things; I have no antipathy, or rather idiosyncrasy, in diet, humour, air, anything. I wonder not at the French for their dishes of frogs, snails, and toadstools, nor at the Jews for locusts and grasshoppers; but, being amongst them, make them my common viands; and I find they agree with my stomach as well as theirs. I could digest a salad gathered in a churchyard as well as in a garden. I cannot start at the presence of a serpent, scorpion, lizard, or salamander; at the sight of a toad or viper, I find in me no desire to take up a stone to destroy them. I feel not in myself those common antipathies that I can discover in others: those national repugnances do not touch me, nor do I behold with prejudice the French, Italian, Spaniard, or Dutch; but, where I find their actions in balance with my countrymen's, I honour, love, and embrace them, in the same degree. I was born in the eighth climate, but seem to be framed and constellated unto all. I am no plant that will not prosper out of a garden. All places, all airs, make unto me one country; I am in England everywhere, and under any meridian. I have been shipwrecked, yet am not enemy with the sea or winds; I can study, play, or sleep in a tempest. In brief, I am averse from nothing: my conscience would give me the lie if I should say I absolutely detest or hate any essence, but the devil; or so at least abhor anything, but that we might come to composition. If there be any among those common objects of hatred I do contemn and laugh at, it is that great enemy of reason, virtue, and religion, the multitude; that numerous piece of monstrosity, which, taken asunder, seem men, and the reasonable creatures of God, but, confused together, make but one great beast, and a monstrosity more prodigious than Hydra. It is no breach of charity to call these fools; it is the style all holy writers have afforded them, set down by Solomon in canonical scripture, and a point of our faith to believe so. Neither in the name of multitude do I only include the base and minor sort of people: there is a rabble even amongst the gentry; a sort of plebeian heads, whose fancy moves with the same wheel as those; men in the same level with mechanicks, though their fortunes do somewhat gild their infirmities, and their purses compound for their follies. But, as in casting account three or four men together come short in account of one man placed by himself below them, so neither are a troop of these ignorant Doradoes of that true esteem and value as many a forlorn person, whose condition doth place him below their feet. Let us speak like politicians; there is a nobility without heraldry, a natural dignity, whereby one man is ranked with another, another filed before him, according to the quality of his desert, and pre-eminence of his good parts. Though the corruption of these times, and the bias of present practice, wheel another way, thus it was in the first and primitive commonwealths, and is yet in the integrity and cradle of well ordered politics: till corruption getteth ground;—ruder desires labouring after that which wiser considerations contemn;—every one having a liberty to amass and heap up riches, and they a licence or faculty to do or purchase anything.

SECT. II.—This general and indifferent temper of mine doth more nearly dispose me to this noble virtue. It is a happiness to be born and framed unto virtue, and to grow up from the seeds of nature, rather than the inoculations and forced grafts of education: yet, if we are directed only by our particular natures, and regulate our inclinations by no higher rule than that of our reasons, we are but moralists; divinity will still call us heathens. Therefore this great work of charity must have other motives, ends, and impulsions. I give no alms to satisfy the hunger of my brother, but to fulfil and accomplish the will and command of my God; I draw not my purse for his sake that demands it, but his that enjoined it; I relieve no man upon the rhetorick of his miseries, nor to content mine own commiserating disposition; for this is still but moral charity, and an act that oweth more to passion than reason. He that relieves another upon the bare suggestion and bowels of pity doth not this so much for his sake as for his own: for by compassion we make another's misery our own; and so, by relieving them, we relieve ourselves also. It is as erroneous a conceit to redress other men's misfortunes upon the common considerations of merciful natures, that it may be one day our own case; for this is a sinister and politick kind of charity, whereby we seem to bespeak the pities of men in the like occasions. And truly I have observed that those professed eleemosynaries, though in a crowd or multitude, do yet direct and place their petitions on a few and selected persons; there is surely a physiognomy, which those experienced and master mendicants observe, whereby they instantly discover a merciful aspect, and will single out a face, wherein they spy the signatures and marks of mercy. For there are mystically in our faces certain characters which carry in them the motto of our souls, wherein he that cannot read A B C may read our natures. I hold, moreover, that there is a phytognomy, or physiognomy, not only of men, but of plants and vegetables; and in every one of them some outward figures which hang as signs or bushes of their inward forms. The finger of God hath left an inscription upon all his works, not graphical, or composed of letters, but of their several forms, constitutions, parts, and operations, which, aptly joined together, do make one word that doth express their natures. By these letters God calls the stars by their names; and by this alphabet Adam assigned to every creature a name peculiar to its nature. Now, there are, besides these characters in our faces, certain mystical figures in our hands, which I dare not call mere dashes, strokes *à la volée* or at random, because delineated by a pencil that never works in vain; and hereof I take more particular notice, because I carry that in mine own hand which I could never read of nor discover in another. Aristotle, I confess, in his acute and singular book of physiognomy, hath made no mention of chiromancy: yet I believe the Egyptians, who were nearer addicted to those abstruse and mystical sciences, had a knowledge therein: to which those vagabond and counterfeit Egyptians did after pretend, and perhaps retained a few corrupted principles, which sometimes might verify their prognosticks.

It is the common wonder of all men, how, among so many millions of faces, there should be none alike: now, contrary, I wonder as much how there should be any. He that shall consider how many thousand several words have been carelessly and without study composed out of twenty-four letters; withal, how many hundred lines there are to be drawn in the fabrick of one man; shall easily find that this variety is necessary: and it will be very hard that they shall so concur as to make one portrait like another. Let a painter carelessly limn out a million of faces, and you shall find them all different; yea, let him have his copy before him, yet, after all his art, there will remain a sensible distinction: for the pattern or example of everything is the perfectest in that kind, whereof we still come short, though we transcend or go beyond it; because herein it is wide, and agrees not in all points unto its copy. Nor doth the similitude of creatures disparage the variety of nature, nor any way confound the works of God. For even in things alike there is diversity; and those that do seem to accord do manifestly disagree. And thus is man like God; for, in the same things that we resemble him we are utterly different from him. There was never anything so like another as in all points to concur; there will ever some reserved difference slip in, to prevent the identity; without which two several things would not be alike, but the same, which is impossible.

SECT. III.—But, to return from philosophy to charity, I hold not so narrow a conceit of this virtue as to conceive, that to give alms is only to be charitable, or think a piece of liberality can comprehend the total of charity. Divinity hath wisely divided the act thereof into many branches, and hath taught us, in this narrow way, many paths unto goodness; as many ways as we may do good, so many ways we may be charitable. There are infirmities not only of body, but of soul and fortunes, which do require the merciful hand of our abilities. I cannot contemn a man for ignorance, but behold him with as much pity as I do Lazarus. It is no greater charity to clothe his body than to apparel the nakedness of his soul. It is an honourable object to see the reasons of other men wear our liveries, and their borrowed understandings do homage to the bounty of ours. It is the cheapest way of beneficence, and, like the natural charity of the sun, illuminates another without obscuring itself. To be reserved and caitiff in this part of goodness is the sordidest piece of covetousness, and more contemptible than the pecuniary avarice. To this (as calling myself a scholar) I am obliged by the duty of my condition. I make not therefore my head a grave, but a treasury of knowledge. I intend no monoply, but a community in learning. I study not for my own sake only, but for theirs that study not for themselves. I envy no man that knows more than myself, but pity them that know less. I instruct no man as an exercise of my knowledge, or with an intent rather to nourish and keep it alive in mine own head than beget and propagate it in his. And, in the midst of all my endeavours, there is but one thought that dejects me, that my required parts must perish with myself, nor can be legacied among my honoured friends. I cannot fall out or contemn a man for an error, or conceive why a difference in opinion should divide an affection; for controversies, disputes, and argumentations, both in philosophy and in divinity, if they meet with discreet and peaceable natures, do not infringe the laws of charity. In all disputes, so much as there is of passion, so much there is of nothing to the purpose; for then reason, like a bad hound, spends upon a false scent, and forsakes the question first started. And this is one reason why controversies are never determined; for, though they be amply proposed, they are scarce at all handled; they do so swell with unnecessary digressions; and the parenthesis on the party is often as large as the main discourse upon the subject. The foundations of religion are already established, and the principles of salvation subscribed unto by all. There remain not many controversies worthy a passion, and yet never any dispute it without, not only in divinity but inferior arts. What a βατραχομυομαχία and hot skirmish is betwixt S. and T. in Lucian! How do grammarians hack and slash for the genitive case[1] in Jupiter! How do they break their own pates, to salve that of Priscian! *Si foret in terris, rideret Democritus.* Yea, even amongst wiser militants, how many wounds have been given and credits slain, for the poor victory of an opinion, or beggarly conquest of a distinction! Scholars are men of peace, they bear no arms, but their tongues are sharper than Actius's razor; their pens carry further, and give a louder report than thunder. I had rather stand in the shock of a basilisk than in the fury of a merciless pen. It is not mere zeal to learning, or devotion to the muses, that wiser princes patron the arts, and carry an indulgent aspect unto scholars; but a desire to have their names eternized by the memory of their writings, and a fear of the revengeful pen of succeeding ages: for these are the men that, when they have played their parts, and had their *exits,* must step out and give the moral of their scenes, and deliver unto posterity an inventory of their virtues and vices. And surely there goes a great deal of conscience to the compiling of an history: there is no reproach to the scandal of a story; it is such an authentick kind of falsehood, that with authority belies our good names to all nations and posterity.

[1] Whether Jovis or Jupitris.

THOMAS CARLYLE
1795–1881

Essayist, historian and philosopher, Thomas Carlyle called himself a radical. A bitter enemy of conformity, he loathed popular political institutions, damned the French Revolution and scorned mass production as the bane of fine craftsmanship. At times he lapsed into a pessimistic tone, mourning the world's materialistic and low moral principles which, he felt, were grasping too firm a hold on society. The mannerisms and exaggerations in his writings annoyed many of his contemporaries. Matthew Arnold advised a flight from "Carlylese," which he considered analagous to fleeing the devil. In the essay, "Happy," Carlyle expressed many of his ideas in a characteristically intense and somewhat raucous style.

Happy

All work, even cotton-spinning, is noble; work is alone noble: be that here said and asserted once more. And in like manner too, all dignity is painful; a life of ease is not for any man, nor for any god. The life of all gods figures itself to us as a Sublime Sadness,—earnestness of Infinite Battle against Infinite Labour. Our highest religion is named the 'Worship of Sorrow.' For the son of man there is no noble crown, well worn or even ill worn, but is a crown of thorns!—These things, in spoken words, or still better, in felt instincts alive in every heart, were once well known.

Does not the whole wretchedness, the whole *Atheism* as I call it, of man's ways, in these generations, shadow itself for us in that unspeakable Life-philosophy of his: The pretension to be what he calls 'happy'? Every pitifulest whipster that walks within a skin has his head filled with the notion that he is, shall be, or by all human and divine laws ought to be 'happy.' His wishes, the pitifulest whipster's, are to be fulfilled for him; his days, the pitifulest whipster's, are to flow on in ever-gentle current of enjoyment, impossible even for the gods. The prophets preach to us, Thou shalt be happy; thou shalt love pleasant things, and find them. The people clamour, Why have we not found pleasant things?

We construct our theory of Human Duties, not on any Greatest-Nobleness Principle, never so mistaken; no, but on a Greatest-Happiness Principle. 'The word *Soul* with us, as in some Slavonic dialects, seems to be synonymous with *Stomach*.' We plead and speak, in our Parliaments and elsewhere, not as from the Soul, but from the Stomach;—wherefore indeed our pleadings are so slow to profit. We plead not for God's Justice; we are not ashamed to stand clamouring and pleading for our own 'interests,' our own rents and trade-profits; we say, They are the 'interests' of so many; there is such an intense desire in us for them! We demand Free-Trade, with much just vociferation and benevolence, That the poorer classes, who are terribly ill-off at present, may have cheaper New-Orleans bacon. Men ask on Free-trade platforms, How can the indomitable spirit of Englishmen be kept up without plenty of bacon? We shall become a ruined Nation!—Surely, my friends, plenty of bacon is good and indispensable: but, I doubt, you will never get even bacon by aiming only at that. You are men, not animals of prey, well-used or ill-used! Your Greatest-Happiness Principle seems to me fast becoming a rather unhappy one.—What if we should cease babbling about 'happiness,' and leave *it* resting on its own basis, as it used to do!

A gifted Byron rises in his wrath; and feeling too surely that he for his part is not 'happy,' declares the same in very violent language, as a piece of news that may be interesting. It evidently has surprised him much. One dislikes to see a man and poet reduced to proclaim on the streets such tidings but on the whole, as matters go, that is not the most dislikable. Byron speaks the *truth* in this matter. Byron's large audience indicates how true it is felt to be.

'Happy,' my brother? First of all, what difference is it whether thou art happy or not! Today becomes Yesterday so fast, all Tomorrows become Yesterdays; and then there is no question whatever of the 'happiness,' but quite another question. Nay, thou hast such a sacred pity left at least for thyself, thy very pains, once gone over into Yesterday, become joys to thee. Besides, thou knowest not what heavenly blessedness and indispensable sanative virtue was in them; thou shalt only know it after many days, when thou art wiser!

—A benevolent old Surgeon sat once in our company, with a
Patient fallen sick by gourmandising, whom he had just, too
briefly in the Patient's judgment, been examining. The foolish
Patient still at intervals continued to break in on our discourse,
which rather promised to take a philosophic turn: 'But I
have lost my appetite,' said he, objurgatively, with a tone of
irritated pathos; 'I have no appetite; I can't eat!'—'My
dear fellow,' answered the Doctor in mildest tone, 'it isn't of
the slightest consequence';—and continued his philosophical
discoursings with us!

Or does the reader not know the history of that Scottish
iron Misanthrope? The inmates of some town-mansion, in
those Northern parts, were thrown into the fearfulest alarm by
indubitable symptoms of a ghost inhabiting the next house,
or perhaps even the partition-wall! Ever at a certain hour,
with preternatural gnarring, growling, and screeching, which
attended as running bass, there began, in a horrid, semi-artic-
ulate, unearthy voice, this song: 'Once I was hap-hap-happy,
but now I am *mees*erable! Clack-clack-clack, gnarr-r-r,
whuz-z: Once I was hap-hap-happy, but now I'm *mees*erable!'—Rest, rest, perturbed spirit;—or indeed, as the good
old Doctor said: My dear fellow, it isn't of the slightest consequence! But no; the perturbed spirit could not rest; and
to the neighbours, fretted, affrighted, or at least insufferably
bored by him, it *was* of such consequence that they had to go
and examine in his haunted chamber. In his haunted chamber, they find that the perturbed spirit is an unfortunate—
Imitator of Byron? No, is an unfortunate rusty Meat-jack,
gnarring and creaking with rust and work; and this, in
Scottish dialect, is *its* Byronian musical Life-philosophy, sung
according to ability!

Truly, I think the man who goes about pothering and up-
roaring for his 'happiness,'—pothering, and were it ballot-
boxing, poem-making, or in what way soever fussing and
exerting himself,—he is not the man that will help us to 'get
our knaves and dastards arrested'! No; he rather is on the
way to increase the number,—by at least one unit and his
tail! Observe, too, that this is all a modern affair; belongs
not to the old heroic times, but to these dastard new times.
'Happiness our being's end and aim,' all that very paltry
speculation is at bottom, if we will count well, not yet two
centuries old in the world.

The only happiness a brave man ever troubled himself with

asking much about was, happiness enough to get his work done. Not 'I can't eat!' but 'I can't work!' that was the burden of all wise complaining among men. It is, after all, the one unhappiness of a man, That he cannot work; that he cannot get his destiny as a man fulfilled. Behold, the day is passing swiftly over, our life is passing swiftly over; and the night cometh, wherein no man can work. The night once come, our happiness, our unhappiness,—it is all abolished, vanished, clean gone; a thing that has been: 'not of the slightest consequence' whether we were happy as eupeptic Curtis, as the fattest pig of Epicurus, or unhappy as Job with potsherds, as musical Byron with Giaours and sensibilities of the heart; as the unmusical Meat-jack with hard labour and rust! But our work,—behold that is not abolished, that has not vanished; our work, behold, it remains, or the want of it remains;—for endless Times and Eternities, remains; and that is now the sole question with us for evermore! Brief brawling Day, with its noisy phantasms, its poor paper-crowns tinsel-gilt, is gone; and divine everlasting Night, with her star-diadems, with her silences and her veracities, is come! What hast thou done, and how? Happiness, unhappiness: all that was but the *wages* thou hadst; thou hast spent all that, in sustaining thyself hitherward; not a coin of it remains with thee, it is all spent, eaten: and now thy work, where is thy work? Swift, out with it; let us see thy work!

Of a truth, if man were not a poor hungry dastard, and even much of a blockhead withal, he would cease criticising his victuals to such extent; and criticise himself rather, what he does with his victuals!

SAMUEL LANGHORNE CLEMENS
1835–1910

"The trouble with Mr. Clemens," said the *Springfield Republican* when *Huckleberry Finn* was published in this country in 1885, "is that he has no reliable sense of propriety." Mr. Clemens, as everyone knows, was that roving printer, prospector, reporter, and Mississippi River pilot who took his pen name from the boatman's cry: "Mark Twain!," and the *Springfield Republican* was quite right about him. He had no sense of propriety, reliable or otherwise, and he wanted none. He wrote about the life he knew on the River and on the Western frontier, where freedom was large, speech colorful and racy, and humor uninhibited. Although proper Massachusetts critics might disapprove, readers were happy; they bought 50,000 copies of *Huckleberry Finn* within only a few weeks after publication. And although it is now the critical fashion to dwell on Twain's sterner aspect as a critic of society, or to delve into the depths of his subconscious, readers still prefer simply to be happy. The popular Twain is the Twain who keeps his public laughing, as he does in the following sketch on "Political Economy," with its burlesque of philosophical mumbo-jumbo and its frontier-style fabulous tall tale.

Political Economy

Political Economy is the basis of all good government. The wisest men of all ages have brought to bear upon this subject the——

[Here I was interrupted and informed that a stranger wished to see me down at the door. I went and confronted him, and asked to know his business, struggling all the time to keep a tight rein on my seething political economy ideas, and not let them break away from me or get tangled in their harness. And privately I wished the stranger was in the bottom of the canal with a cargo of wheat on top of him. I was all in a fever, but he was cool. He said he was sorry to disturb me, but as he was passing he noticed that I needed some lightning-rods. I said, "Yes, yes—go on—what about it?" He said there was nothing about it, in particular—nothing except that he would like to put them up for me. I am new to housekeeping; have been used to hotels and boarding-houses all my life. Like anybody else of similar experience, I try to appear (to strangers) to be an old housekeeper; consequently I said in an off-hand way that I had been intending for some time to have six or eight lightning-rods put up, but— The stranger started, and looked inquiringly at me, but I was serene. I thought that if I chanced to make any mistakes, he would not catch me by my countenance. He said he would rather have my custom than any man's in town. I said, "All right," and started off to wrestle with my great subject again, when he called me back and said it would be necessary to know exactly how many "points" I wanted put up, what parts of the house I wanted them on, and what quality of rod I preferred. It was close quarters for a man not used to the exigencies of housekeeping; but I went through creditably, and he probably never suspected that I was a novice. I told him to put up eight "points," and put them all on the roof, and use the best quality of rod. He said he could furnish the "plain" article at 20 cents a foot; "coppered," 25 cents; "zinc-plated spiral-twist," at 30 cents, that would stop a streak of lightning any time, no matter where it was bound, and "render its errand harmless and its further progress apocryphal." I said apocryphal was no slouch of a word, emanating from the source it did, but, philology aside, I liked the spiral-twist and would take that brand. Then he said he *could* make two hundred and fifty feet answer; but to do it right, and make the best job in town of it, and attract the admiration of the just and the unjust alike, and compel all parties to say they never saw a more symmetrical and hypothetical display of lightning-rods since they were born, he supposed he really couldn't get along without four hundred, though he was not vindictive, and trusted he was willing to try. I said, go ahead and use four hundred, and make any kind of a job he pleased out of it, but let me get back to my work. So I got rid of him at last; and now, after half an hour spent in getting my train of political economy thoughts coupled together again, I am ready to go on once more.]

richest treasures of their genius, their experience of life, and their learning. The great lights of commercial jurisprudence, international confraternity, and biological deviation, of all ages, all civilizations, and all nationalities, from Zoroaster down to Horace Greeley, have——

[Here I was interrupted again, and required to go down and confer further with that lightning-rod man. I hurried off, boiling and surging with prodigious thoughts wombed in words of such majesty that each one of them was in itself a straggling procession of syllables that might be fifteen minutes passing a given point, and once more I confronted him—he so calm and sweet, I so hot and frenzied. He was standing in the contemplative attitude of the Colossus of Rhodes, with one foot on my infant tuberose, and the other among my pansies, his hands on his hips, his hat-brim tilted forward, one eye shut and the other gazing critically and admiringly in the direction of my principal chimney. He said now *there* was a state of things to make a man glad to be alive; and added, "I leave it to *you* if you ever saw anything more deliriously picturesque than eight lightning-rods on one chimney?" I said I had no present recollection of anything that transcended it. He said that in his opinion nothing on earth but Niagara Falls was superior to it in the way of natural scenery. All that was needed now, he verily believed, to make my house a perfect balm to the eye, was to kind of touch up the other chimneys a little, and thus "add to the generous *coup d'œil* a soothing uniformity of achievement which would allay the excitement naturally consequent upon the first *coup d'état*." I asked him if he learned to talk out of a book, and if I could borrow it anywhere? He smiled pleasantly, and said that his manner of speaking was not taught in books, and that nothing but familiarity with lightning could enable a man to handle his conversational style with impunity. He then figured up an estimate, and said that about eight more rods scattered about my roof would about fix me right, and he guessed five hundred feet of stuff would do it; and added that the first eight had got a little the start of him, so to speak, and used up a mere trifle of material more than he had calculated on—a hundred feet or along there. I said I was in a dreadful hurry, and I wished we could get this business permanently mapped out, so that I could go on with my work. He said, "I *could* have put up those eight rods, and marched off about my business—some men *would* have done it. But no; I said to myself, this man is a stranger to me, and I will die before I'll wrong him; there ain't lightning-rods enough on that house, and for one

I'll never stir out of my tracks till I've done as I would be done by, and told him so. Stranger, my duty is accomplished; if the recalcitrant and dephlogistic messenger of heaven strikes your—" "There, now, there," I said, "put on the other eight—add five hundred feet of spiral-twist—do anything and everything you want to do; but calm your sufferings, and try to keep your feelings where you can reach them with the dictionary. Meanwhile, if we understand each other now, I will go to work again."

I think I have been sitting here a full hour this time, trying to get back to where I was when my train of thought was broken up by the last interruption; but I believe I have accomplished it at last, and may venture to proceed again.]

wrestled with this great subject, and the greatest among them have found it a worthy adversary, and one that always comes up fresh and smiling after every throw. The great Confucius said that he would rather be a profound political economist than chief of police. Cicero frequently said that political economy was the grandest consummation that the human mind was capable of consuming; and even our own Greeley has said vaguely but forcibly that *"Political——*

[Here the lightning-rod man sent up another call for me. I went down in a state of mind bordering on impatience. He said he would rather have died than interrupt me, but when he was employed to do a job, and that job was expected to be done in a clean, workmanlike manner, and when it was finished and fatigue urged him to seek the rest and recreation he stood so much in need of, and he was about to do it, but looked up and saw at a glance that all the calculations had been a little out, and if a thunder storm were to come up, and that house, which he felt a personal interest in, stood there with nothing on earth to protect it but sixteen lightning-rods—"Let us have peace!" I shrieked. "Put up a hundred and fifty! Put some on the kitchen! Put a dozen on the barn! Put a couple on the cow!—Put one on the cook!—scatter them all over the persecuted place till it looks like a zinc-plated, spiral-twisted, silver-mounted cane-brake! Move! Use up all the material you can get your hands on, and when you run out of lightning-rods put up ram-rods, cam-rods, stair-rods, piston-rods—*anything* that will pander to your dismal appetite for artificial scenery, and bring respite to my raging brain and healing to my lacerated soul!" Wholly unmoved— further than to smile sweetly—this iron being simply turned back his wristbands daintily, and said he would now proceed to hump himself. Well, all that was nearly three hours ago.

It is questionable whether I am calm enough yet to write on the noble theme of political economy, but I cannot resist the desire to try, for it is the one subject that is nearest to my heart and dearest to my brain of all this world's philosophy.]

"——*economy is heaven's best boon to man*." When the loose but gifted Byron lay in his Venetian exile he observed that, if it could be granted him to go back and live his misspent life over again, he would give his lucid and unintoxicated intervals to the composition, not of frivolous rhymes, but of essays upon political economy. Washington loved this exquisite science; such names as Baker, Beckwith, Judson, Smith, are imperishably linked with it; and even imperial Homer, in the ninth book of the Iliad, has said:—

> Fiat justitia, ruat coelum,
> Post mortem unum, ante bellum,
> Hic jacet hoc, ex-parte res,
> Politicum e-conomico est.

The grandeur of these conceptions of the old poet, together with the felicity of the wording which clothes them, and the sublimity of the imagery whereby they are illustrated, have singled out that stanza, and made it more celebrated than any that ever—

["Now, not a word out of you—not a single word. Just state your bill and relapse into impenetrable silence for ever and ever on these premises. Nine hundred dollars? Is that all? This check for the amount will be honored at any respectable bank in America. What is that multitude of people gathered in the street for? How?—'looking at the lightning-rods!' Bless my life, did they never see any lightning-rods before? Never saw 'such a stack of them on one establishment,' did I understand you to say? I will step down and critically observe this popular ebullition of ignorance."]

THREE DAYS LATER.—We are all about worn out. For four-and-twenty hours our bristling premises were the talk and wonder of the town. The theaters languished, for their happiest scenic inventions were tame and commonplace compared with my lightning-rods. Our street was blocked night and day with spectators, and among them were many who came from the country to see. It was a blessed relief on the second day when a thunder storm came up and the lightning began to "go for" my house, as the historian Josephus quaintly phrases it. It cleared the galleries, so to speak. In five minutes there was not a spectator within half a mile of my place; but all the high houses about that distance away were full, windows, roof, and all. And well they might be, for all the falling stars and Fourth of July fireworks of a generation, put together and rained down simultaneously out of heaven in one brilliant shower upon one helpless roof, would not have any advantage of the pyrotechnic display that was making my house so magnificently conspicuous in the general gloom of the storm. By actual count, the lightning struck at my establishment seven hundred and sixty-four times in forty minutes, but tripped on one of those faithful rods every time, and slid down the spiral-twist and shot into the earth before it probably had time to be surprised at the way the thing was done. And through all that bombardment only one patch of slates was ripped up, and that was because, for a single instant, the rods in the vicinity were transporting all the lightning they could possibly accommodate. Well, nothing was ever seen like it since the world began. For one whole day and night not a member of my family stuck his head out of the window but he got the hair snatched off it as smooth as a billiard-ball; and, if the reader will believe me, not one of us ever dreamt of stirring abroad. But at last the awful siege came to an end— because there was absolutely no more electricity left in the clouds above us within grappling distance of my insatiable rods. Then I sallied forth, and gathered daring workmen together, and not a bite or a nap did we take till the premises were utterly stripped of all their terrific armament except just three rods on the house, one on the kitchen, and one on the barn—and, behold, these remain there even unto this day. And then, and not till then, the people ventured to use our street again. I will remark here, in passing, that during that fearful time I did not continue my essay upon political economy. I am not even yet settled enough in nerve and brain to resume it.

To Whom It May Concern.—Parties having need of three thousand two hundred and eleven feet of best quality zinc-plated spiral-twist lightning-rod stuff, and sixteen hundred and thirty-one silver-tipped points, all in tolerable repair (and, although much worn by use, still equal to any ordinary emergency), can hear of a bargain by addressing the publisher.

SAMUEL TAYLOR COLERIDGE
1772–1834

To introduce Samuel Taylor Coleridge, there are no fitter words than his own lines from "Kubla Khan":

> And all should cry, Beware! Beware!
> His flashing eyes, his floating hair!
> Weave a circle round him thrice,
> And close your eyes with holy dread,
> For he on honey-dew hath fed,
> And drunk the milk of Paradise.

For this was the effect Coleridge himself had on other people. All who encountered him testified to the magic of his presence, the enchantment of his conversation. "The light of his genius shone in my soul, like the sun's rays glittering in the puddles of the road," wrote Hazlitt of his first acquaintance with Coleridge. Dorothy Wordsworth spoke of his eye, large, full and grey, which "speaks every motion of his animated mind; it has more of 'the poet's eye in a fine frenzy rolling' than I ever witnessed." And Dorothy's brother, William, called Coleridge "the most wonderful man I have ever known." His talk, according to De Quincey, was "a continuous strain of eloquent dissertation . . . traversing the most spacious fields of thought." In this vast terrain, his listeners sometimes lost their way; and in his prose writings, too, it is easy for the casual reader to mistake the part for the whole, to flounder among the fragments of mighty thought without seeing the unifying pattern. Yet Coleridge always had a pattern in view; there is always a unity in him for the reader to find; but it is the unity of a very "deep well," of the ocean whose only bound is the horizon.

On the "Lyrical Ballads"

During the first year that Mr. Wordsworth and I were neighbours our conversations turned frequently on the two cardinal points of poetry, the power of exciting the sympathy of the reader by a faithful adherence to the truth of nature, and the power of giving the interest of novelty by the modifying colors of imagination. The sudden charm, which accidents of light and shade, which moon-light or sun-set diffused over a known and familiar landscape, appeared to represent the practicability of combining both. These are the poetry of nature. The thought suggested itself (to which of us I do not recollect) that a series of poems might be composed of two sorts. In the one, the incidents and agents were to be, in part at least, supernatural; and the excellence aimed at was to consist in the interesting of the affections by the dramatic truth of such emotions, as would naturally accompany such situations, supposing them real. And real in *this* sense they have been to every human being who, from whatever source of delusion, has at any time believed himself under supernatural agency. For the second class, subjects were to be chosen from ordinary life; the characters and incidents were to be such, as will be found in every village and its vicinity, where there is a meditative and feeling mind to seek after them, or to notice them, when they present themselves.

In this idea originated the plan of the "Lyrical Ballads"; in which it was agreed, that my endeavours should be directed to persons and characters supernatural, or at least romantic; yet so as to transfer from our inward nature a human interest and a semblance of truth sufficient to procure for these shadows of imagination that willing suspension of disbelief for the moment, which constitutes poetic faith. Mr. Wordsworth, on the other hand, was to propose to himself as his object, to give the charm of novelty to things of every day, and to excite a feeling analogous to the supernatural, by awakening the mind's attention from the lethargy of custom, and directing it to the loveliness and the wonders of the world before us; an inexhaustible treasure, but for which, in consequence of the film of familiarity and selfish solicitude we have eyes, yet see not, ears that hear not, and hearts that neither feel nor understand.

With this view I wrote "The Ancient Mariner," and was preparing among other poems, "The Dark Ladie," and the "Christabel," in which I should have more nearly realized my ideal, than I had done in my first attempt. But Mr. Wordsworth's industry had proved so much more successful, and the number of his poems so much greater, that my compositions, instead of forming a balance, appeared rather an interpolation of heterogeneous matter: Mr. Wordsworth added two or three poems written in his own character, in the impassioned, lofty, and sustained diction, which is characteristic of his genius. In this form the "Lyrical Ballads" were published; and were presented by him, as an *experiment,* whether subjects, which from their nature rejected the usual ornaments and extra-colloquial style of poems in general, might not be so managed in the language of ordinary life as to produce the pleasurable interest, which it is the peculiar business of poetry to impart. To the second edition he added a preface of considerable length; in which, notwithstanding some passages of apparently a contrary import, he was understood to contend for the extension of this style to poetry of all kinds, and to reject as vicious and indefensible all phrases and forms of style that were not included in what he (unfortunately, I think, adopting an equivocal expression) called the language of *real* life. From this preface, prefixed to poems in which it was impossible to deny the presence of original genius, however mistaken its direction might be deemed, arose the whole long-continued controversy. For from the conjunction of perceived power with supposed heresy I explain the inveteracy and in some instances, I grieve to say, the acrimonious passions, with which the controversy has been conducted by the assailants.

Had Mr. Wordsworth's poems been the silly, the childish things, which they were for a long time described as being; had they been really distinguished from the compositions of other poets merely by meanness of language and inanity of thought; had they indeed contained nothing more than what is found in the parodies and pretended imitations of them; they must have sunk at once, a dead weight, into the slough of oblivion, and have dragged the preface along with them. But year after year increased the number of Mr. Wordsworth's admirers. They were found too not in the lower classes of the reading public, but chiefly among young men of strong sensibility and meditative minds; and their admiration (inflamed perhaps in some degree by opposition) was distinguished by its intensity, I might almost say, by its *religious* fervor. These facts, and the intellectual energy of the author, which was more or less consciously felt, where it was outwardly and even boisterously denied, meeting with sentiments of aversion to his opinions, and of alarm at their consequences, produced an eddy of criticism, which would of itself have borne up the poems by the violence, with which it whirled them round and round. With many parts of this preface, in the sense attributed to them, and which the words undoubtedly seem to authorize, I never concurred; but on the contrary objected to them as erroneous in principle, and as contradictory (in appearance at least) both to other parts of the same preface, and to the author's own practice in the greater number of the poems themselves. Mr. Wordsworth in his recent collection has, I find, degraded this prefatory disquisition to the end of his second volume, to be read or not at the reader's choice. But he has not, as far as I can discover, announced any change in his poetic creed. At all events, considering it as the source of a controversy, in which I have been honored more than I deserve by the frequent conjunction of my name with his, I think it expedient to declare once for all, in what points I coincide with his opinions, and in what points I altogether differ. But in order to render myself intelligible I must previously, in as few words as possible, explain my ideas, first, of a POEM; and secondly, of POETRY itself, in *kind,* and in *essence.*

The office of philosophical *disquisition* consists in just *distinction;* while it is the privilege of the philosopher to preserve himself constantly aware, that distinction is not division. In order to obtain adequate notions of any truth, we must intellectually separate its distinguishable parts; and this is the technical *process* of philosophy. But having so done, we must then restore them in our conceptions to the unity, in which they actually co-exist; and this is the *result* of philosophy. A poem contains the same elements as a prose composition; the difference therefore must consist in a different combination of them, in consequence of a different object being proposed. According to the difference of the object will be the difference of the combination. It is possible, that the object may be merely to facilitate the recollection of any given facts or observations by artificial arrangement; and the composition will be a poem, merely because it is distinguished from prose by metre, or by rhyme, or by both conjointly. In this, the lowest sense, a man might attribute the name of a poem to the well-known enumeration of the days in the several months;

> "Thirty days hath September,
> April, June, and November," &c.

and others of the same class and purpose. And as a particular pleasure is found in anticipating the recurrence of sounds and quantities, all compositions that have this charm super-added, whatever be their contents, *may* be entitled poems.

So much for the superficial *form*. A difference of object and contents supplies an additional ground of distinction. The immediate purpose may be the communication of truths; either of truth absolute and demonstrable, as in works of science; or of facts experienced and recorded, as in history. Pleasure, and that of the highest and most permanent kind, may *result* from the *attainment* of the end; but it is not itself the immediate end. In other works the communication of pleasure may be the immediate purpose; and though truth, either moral or intellectual, ought to be the *ultimate* end, yet this will distinguish the character of the author, not the class to which the work belongs. Blest indeed is that state of society, in which the immediate purpose would be baffled by the perversion of the proper ultimate end; in which no charm of diction or imagery could exempt the Bathyllus even of an Anacreon, or the Alexis of Virgil, from disgust and aversion!

But the communication of pleasure may be the immediate object of a work not metrically composed; and that object may have been in a high degree attained, as in novels and romances. Would then the mere superaddition of metre, with or without rhyme, entitle *these* to the name of poems? The answer is, that nothing can permanently please, which does not contain in itself the reason why it is so, and not otherwise. If metre be superadded, all other parts must be made consonant with it. They must be such, as to justify the perpetual and distinct attention to each part, which an exact correspondent recurrence of accent and sound are calculated to excite. The final definition then, so deduced, may be thus worded. A poem is that species of composition, which is opposed to works of science, by proposing for its *immediate* object pleasure, not truth; and from all other species (having *this* object in common with it) it is discriminated by proposing to itself such delight from the *whole*, as is compatible with a distinct gratification from each component *part*.

Controversy is not seldom excited in consequence of the disputants attaching each a different meaning to the same word; and in few instances has this been more striking, than in disputes concerning the present subject. If a man chooses to call every composition a poem, which is rhyme, or measure, or both, I must leave his opinion uncontroverted. The distinction is at least competent to characterize the writer's intention. If it were subjoined, that the whole is likewise entertaining or affecting, as a tale, or as a series of interesting reflections, I of course admit this as another fit ingredient of a poem, and an additional merit. But if the definition sought for be that of a *legitimate* poem, I answer, it must be one, the parts of which mutually support and explain each other; all in their proportion harmonizing with, and supporting the purpose and known influences of metrical arrangement. The philosophic critics of all ages coincide with the ultimate judgement of all countries, in equally denying the praises of a just poem, on the one hand, to a series of striking lines or distiches, each of which, absorbing the whole attention of the reader to itself, disjoins it from its context, and makes it a separate whole, instead of an harmonizing part; and on the other hand, to an unsustained composition, from which the reader collects rapidly the general result, unattracted by the component parts. The reader should be carried forward, not merely or chiefly by the mechanical impulse of curiosity, or by a restless desire to arrive at the final solution; but by the pleasureable activity of mind excited by the attractions of the journey itself. Like the motion of a serpent, which the Egyptians made the emblem of intellectual power; or like the path of sound through the air; at every step he pauses and half recedes, and from the retrogressive movement collects the force which again carries him onward. "Præcipitandus est *liber* spiritus," says Petronius Arbiter most happily. The epithet, *liber*, here balances the preceding verb; and it is not easy to conceive more meaning condensed in fewer words.

But if this should be admitted as a satisfactory character of a poem, we have still to seek for a definition of poetry. The writings of PLATO, and Bishop TAYLOR, and the "Theoria Sacra" of BURNET, furnish undeniable proofs that poetry of the highest kind may exist without metre, and even without the contra-distinguishing objects of a poem. The first chapter of Isaiah (indeed a very large portion of the whole book) is poetry in the most emphatic sense; yet it would be not less irrational than strange to assert, that pleasure, and not truth, was the immediate object of the prophet. In short, whatever *specific* import we attach to the word, poetry, there will be found involved in it, as a necessary consequence, that a poem of any length neither can be, or ought to be, all poetry. Yet if an harmonious whole is to be produced, the remaining parts must be preserved *in keeping* with the poetry; and this can be no otherwise effected than by such a studied selection and artificial arrangement, as will partake of *one,* though not a *peculiar* property of poetry. And this again can be no other than the property of exciting a more continuous and equal attention than the language of prose aims at, whether colloquial or written.

My own conclusions on the nature of poetry, in the strictest use of the word, have been in part anticipated in the preceding disquisition on the fancy and imagination. What is poetry? is so nearly the same question with, what is a poet? that the answer to the one is involved in the solution of the other. For it is a distinction resulting from the poetic genius itself, which sustains and modifies the images, thoughts, and emotions of the poet's own mind.

The poet, described in *ideal* perfection, brings the whole soul of man into activity, with the subordination of its faculties to each other, according to their relative worth and dignity. He diffuses a tone and spirit of unity, that blends, and (as it were) *fuses,* each into each, by that synthetic and magical power, to which we have exclusively appropriated the name of imagination. This power, first put in action by the will and understanding, and retained under their irremissive, though gentle and unnoticed, controul (*laxis effertur habenis*) reveals itself in the balance or reconciliation of opposite or discordant qualities: of sameness, with difference; of the general, with the concrete; the idea, with the image; the individual, with the representative; the sense of novelty and freshness, with old and familiar objects; a more than usual state of emotion, with more than usual order; judgement ever awake and steady self-possession, with enthusiasm and feeling profound or vehement; and while it blends and harmonizes the natural and the artificial, still subordinates art to nature; the manner to the matter; and our admiration of the poet to our sympathy with the poetry. "Doubtless," as Sir John Davies observes of the soul (and his words may with slight alteration be applied, and even more appropriately, to the poetic IMAGINATION)

> "Doubtless this could not be, but that she turns
>   Bodies to spirit by sublimation strange,
> As fire converts to fire the things it burns,
>   As we our food into our nature change.
>
> From their gross matter she abstracts their forms,
>   And draws a kind of quintessence from things;
> Which to her proper nature she transforms,
>   To bear them light on her celestial wings.

> Thus does she, when from individual states
> She doth abstract the universal kinds;
> Which then re-clothed in divers names and fates
> Steal access through our senses to our minds."

Finally, GOOD SENSE is the BODY of poetic genius, FANCY its DRAPERY, MOTION its LIFE, and IMAGINATION the SOUL that is everywhere, and in each; and forms all into one graceful and intelligent whole.

—*Biographia Literaria,* Chapter XIV.

ABRAHAM COWLEY
1618–1667

"Who now reads Cowley?" asked Alexander Pope of a man who a century before had been regarded as the greatest poet of his time. The answer was, of course, that very few read Cowley, for his seventeenth-century "metaphysical" verse, as Dr. Johnson termed it, had gone out of fashion. "But still," continued Pope, "I love the language of his heart." And it is the simple, affecting language of the heart that Cowley used in his eleven "essays in verse and prose" that we read and love today. He charms us here with the little, the intimate; for he confessed, "I love littleness almost in all things"; and when, like Montaigne, he wrote "Of Myself," it was the small details of his life he chose to dwell on: the volume of Spenser lying on his mother's table, or the grammar rules he never learned. Dr. Johnson abhorred Cowley's poetry, but of the prose he wrote, with his usual acumen: "His thoughts are natural, and his style has a smooth and placid equability, which has never yet obtained its due commendation." Now, after the passage of two more centuries, Cowley's prose has everywhere its due commendation.

Of Myself

It is a hard and nice subject for a man to write of himself; it grates his own heart to say any thing of disparagement, and the reader's ears to hear any thing of praise from him. There is no danger from me of offending him in this kind; neither my mind, nor my body, nor my fortune, allow me any materials for that vanity. It is sufficient for my own contentment, that they have preserved me from being scandalous, or remarkable on the defective side. But, besides that, I shall here speak of myself, only in relation to the subject of these precedent discourses, and shall be likelier thereby to fall into the contempt, than rise up to the estimation, of most people.

As far as my memory can return back into my past life,
before I knew, or was capable of guessing, what the world,
or the glories or business of it, were, the natural affections of
my soul gave me a secret bent of aversion from them, as some
plants are said to turn away from others, by an antipathy im-
perceptible to themselves, and inscrutable to man's understanding. Even when I was a very young boy at school, instead of running about on holy-days and playing with my
fellows, I was wont to steal from them, and walk into the
fields, either alone with a book, or with some one companion,
if I could find any of the same temper. I was then, too, so
much an enemy to all constraint, that my masters could never
prevail on me, by any persuasions or encouragements, to
learn without book the common rules of grammar; in which
they dispensed with me alone, because they found I made a
shift to do the usual exercise out of my own reading and
observation. That I was then of the same mind as I am now
(which, I confess, I wonder at, myself) may appear by the
latter end of an ode, which I made when I was but thirteen
years old, and which was then printed with many other verses.
The beginning of it is boyish; but of this part, which I here
set down (if a very little were corrected), I should hardly
now be much ashamed.

9.

This only grant me, that my means may lie
Too low for envy, for contempt too high.
    Some honour I would have,
Not from great deeds, but good alone;
The unknown are better, than ill known:
    Rumour can ope the grave.
Acquaintance I would have, but when 't depends
Not on the number, but the choice of friends.

10.

Books should, not business, entertain the light,
And sleep, as undisturb'd as death, the night.
    My house a cottage more
Than palace; and should fitting be
For all my use, no luxury.
    My garden painted o'er
With nature's hand, not art's; and pleasures yield,
Horace might envy in his Sabin field.

11.

Thus would I double my life's fading space;
For he, that runs it well, twice runs his race.

And in this true delight,
These unbought sports, this happy state,
I would not fear, nor wish, my fate;
    But boldly say each night,
To-morrow let my sun his beams display,
Or, in clouds hide them; I have liv'd, to-day.

You may see by it, I was even then acquainted with the
poets (for the conclusion is taken out of Horace); and perhaps it was the immature and immoderate love of them,
which stampt first, or rather engraved, these characters in
me: they were like letters cut into the bark of a young tree,
which with the tree still grow proportionably. But, how this
love came to be produced in me so early, is a hard question:
I believe, I can tell the particular little chance that filled my
head first with such chimes of verse, as have never since left
ringing there: for I remember, when I began to read, and to
take some pleasure in it, there was wont to lie in my mother's
parlour (I know not by what accident, for she herself never
in her life read any book but of devotion) but there was
wont to lie Spenser's works: this I happened to fall upon,
and was infinitely delighted with the stories of the knights, and
giants, and monsters, and brave houses, which I found every
where there (though my understanding had little to do with
all this); and, by degrees, with the tinkling of the rhyme and
dance of the numbers; so that, I think, I had read him all over
before I was twelve years old, and was thus made a poet as
immediately as a child is made an eunuch.

With these affections of mind, and my heart wholly set
upon letters, I went to the university; but was soon torn from
thence by that violent public storm, which would suffer nothing to stand where it did, but rooted up every plant, even
from the princely cedars to me the hyssop. Yet, I had as good
fortune as could have befallen me in such a tempest; for I was
cast by it into the family of one of the best persons, and into
the court of one of the best princesses, of the world. Now,
though I was here engaged in ways most contrary to the
original design of my life, that is, into much company, and
no small business, and into a daily sight of greatness, both
militant and triumphant (for that was the state then of the
English and French courts); yet all this was so far from
altering my opinion, that it only added the confirmation of
reason to that which was before but natural inclination. I saw
plainly all the paint of that kind of life, the nearer I came
to it; and that beauty, which I did not fall in love with, when,

for aught I knew, it was real, was not like to bewitch or entice me, when I saw that it was adulterate. I met with several great persons, whom I liked very well; but could not perceive that any part of their greatness was to be liked or desired, no more than I would be glad or content to be in a storm, though I saw many ships which rid safely and bravely in it: a storm would not agree with my stomach, if it did with my courage. Though I was in a crowd of as good company as could be found any where, though I was in business of great and honourable trust, though I ate at the best table, and enjoyed the best conveniences for present subsistence that ought to be desired by a man of my condition in banishment and public distresses; yet I could not abstain from renewing my old schoolboy's wish, in a copy of verses to the same effect:

> Well then; I now do plainly see
> This busy world and I shall ne'er agree, &c.

And I never then proposed to myself any other advantage from his majesty's happy Restoration, but the getting into some moderately convenient retreat in the country; which I thought, in that case, I might easily have compassed, as well as some others, who with no greater probabilities or pretenses, have arrived to extraordinary fortune: but I had before written a shrewd prophecy against myself; and I think Apollo inspired me in the truth, though not in the elegance, of it:

> Thou neither great at court, nor in the war,
> Nor at th' exchange shall be, nor at the wrang-
>   ling bar.
> Content thyself with the small barren praise,
>   Which neglected verse does raise.
>   She spake; and all my years to come
>   Took their unlucky doom.
> Their several ways of life let others chuse,
>   Their several pleasures let them use;
> But I was born for Love, and for a Muse.

> 4.

> With Fate what boots it to contend?
> Such I began, such am, and so must end.
>   The star, that did my being frame,
>   Was but a lambent flame,
>   And some small light it did dispense,
>   But neither heat nor influence.
> No matter, Cowley; let proud Fortune see,

> That thou canst her despise no less than she does thee.
>> Let all her gifts the portion be
>> Of folly, lust, and flattery,
>> Fraud, extortion, calumny,
>> Murder, infidelity,
>> Rebellion and hypocrisy.
> Do thou nor grieve nor blush to be,
> As all th' inspired tuneful men,
> And all thy great forefathers were, from Homer down
>> to Ben.

However, by the failing of the forces which I had expected, I did not quit the design which I had resolved on; I cast myself into it a *corps perdu*, without making capitulations, or taking counsel of fortune. But God laughs at a man, who says to his soul, *Take thy ease:* I met presently not only with many little incumbrances and impediments, but with so much sickness (a new misfortune to me) as would have spoiled the happiness of an emperor as well as mine: yet I do neither repent, nor alter my course. "Non ego perfidum dixi sacramentum;" nothing shall separate me from a mistress, which I have loved so long, and have now at last married; though she neither has brought me a rich portion, nor lived yet so quietly with me as I hoped from her:

> ——"Nec vos, dulcissima mundi
> Nomina, vos Musæ, Libertas, Otia, Libri,
> Hortique Sylvæque, animâ remanente, relinquam."

>> Nor by me e'er shall you,
> You, of all names the sweetest, and the best,
> You, Muses, books, and liberty, and rest;
> You, gardens, fields, and woods, forsaken be,
> As long as life itself forsakes not me.

But this is a very pretty ejaculation; because I have concluded all the other chapters with a copy of verses, I will maintain the humour to the last.

MARTIAL, LIB. X. EPIGR. XLV.

> "Vitam quæ faciunt beatiorem,
> Jucundissime Martialis, hæc sunt:
> Res non parta labore, sed relicta;
> Non ingratus ager, focus perennis,
> Lis nunquam; toga rara; mens quieta;
> Vires ingenuæ; salubre corpus;
> Prudens simplicitas; pares amici;
> Convictus facilis; sinè arte mensa;
> Nox non ebria, sed soluta curis;
> Non tristis torus, et tamen pudicus;

Somnus, qui faciat breves tenebras;
Quod sis, esse velis, nihílque malis:
Summum nec metuas diem, nec optes."

Since, dearest friend, 'tis your desire to see
A true receipt of happiness from me;
These are the chief ingredients, if not all:
Take an estate neither too great nor small,
Which *quantum sufficit* the doctors call.
Let this estate from parents' care descend;
The getting it too much of life does spend.
Take such a ground, whose gratitude may be
A fair encouragement for industry.
Let constant fires the winter's fury tame;
And let thy kitchen's be a vestal flame.
Thee to the town let never suit at law,
And rarely, very rarely, business draw.
Thy active mind in equal temper keep,
In undisturbed peace, yet not in sleep.
Let exercise a vigorous health maintain,
Without which all the composition's vain.
In the same weight prudence and innocence take,
Ana of each does the just mixture make.
But a few friendships wear, and let them be
By nature and by fortune fit for thee.
Instead of art and luxury in food,
Let mirth and freedom make thy table good.
If any cares into thy day-time creep,
At night, without wine's opium, let them sleep.
Let rest, which nature does to darkness wed,
And not lust, recommend to thee thy bed.
Be satisfied, and pleas'd with what thou art,
Act chearfully and well th' allotted part;
Enjoy the present hour, be thankful for the past,
And neither fear, nor wish, th' approaches of the last.

MARTIAL, LIB. X. EPIGR. LXXXVII.

Sæpe loquar nimiùm gentes quòd, avite, remotas,
  Miraris, Latiâ factus in urbe senex;
Auriferùmque Tagum sitiam, patriùmque Salo-
    nem,
  Et repetam saturæ sordida rura casæ.
Illa placet tellus, in quâ res parva beatum
  Me facit, et tenues luxuriantur opes.
Pascitur hìc; ibi pascit ager: tepet igne maligno
  Hìc focus, ingenti lumine lucet ibi.
Hìc pretiosa fames, conturbatórque macellus,
  Mensa ibi divitiis ruris operta sui.
Quatuor hìc æstate togæ, plurésve teruntur;
  Autumnis ibi me quatuor una tegit.
I, cole nunc reges: quicquid non præstat amicus,
  Cùm præstare tibi possit, avite, locus."

Me, who have liv'd so long among the great,

You wonder to hear talk of a retreat:
And a retreat so distant, as may show
No thoughts of a return, when once I go.
Give me a country, how remote so e'er;
Where happiness a mod'rate rate does bear,
Where poverty itself in plenty flows,
And all the solid use of riches knows.
The ground about the house maintains it there,
The house maintains the ground about it here.
Here even hunger's dear; and a full board
Devours the vital substance of the lord.
The land itself does there the feast bestow,
The land itself must here to market go.
Three or four suits one winter here does waste,
One suit does there three or four winters last.
Here every frugal man must oft be cold,
And little luke-warm fires are to you sold.
There fire's an element, as cheap and free,
Almost as any of the other three.
Stay you then here, and live among the great,
Attend their sports, and at their tables eat.
When all the bounties here of men you score,
The place's bounty there shall give me more.

EPITAPHIUM VIVI AUCTORIS.

Hic, o viator, sub lare parvulo
Couleius hîc est conditus, hic jacet;
    Defunctus humani laboris
        Sorte, supervacuâque vitâ.

Non indecorâ pauperie nitens,
Et non inerti nobilis otio,
    Vanoque dilectis popello
        Divitiis animosus hostis.

Possis ut illum dicere mortuum;
En terra jam nunc quantula sufficit!
    Exempta sit curis, viator,
        Terra sit illa levis, precare.

Hîc sparge flores, sparge breves rosas,
Nam vita gaudet mortua floribus,
    Herbisque odoratis corona
        Vatis adhuc cinerem calentem."

EPITAPH ON THE LIVING AUTHOR.

1.

Here, stranger, in this humble nest,
    Here, Cowley sleeps; here lies,
Scap'd all the toils, the life molest,
    And its superfluous joys.

2.

Here, in no sordid poverty,
  And no inglorious ease,
He braves the world, and can defy
  Its frowns and flatteries.

3.

The little earth, he asks, survey:
  Is he not dead, indeed?
"Light lye that earth," good stranger, pray,
  "Nor thorn upon it breed!"

4.

With flow'rs, fit emblem of his fame,
  Compass your poet round;
With flow'rs of ev'ry fragrant name
  Be his warm ashes crown'd!

THOMAS DE QUINCEY
1785–1859

"What wouldn't one give to have him in a box and take him out to talk!" said Jane Carlyle of Thomas De Quincey. For De Quincey, blue-eyed, bright-faced, and scarcely five feet in height, appeared to her like a marvelous talking doll. Jane's husband, Thomas Carlyle, admitted De Quincey's "gentle-winding courtesies and ingenuities in conversation," but all this in the end he found "inconclusive and long-winded." And in that beautiful doll's or child's face, there was something that said to Carlyle, "*Eccovi*—this child has been in hell." That he had been in a dream of hell, and heaven too, De Quincey himself revealed in his *Confessions of an English Opium-Eater*. His *Autobiographic Sketches*, beginning with "The Afflictions of Childhood," indicate a real life not much this side of hell. He endured a succession of miseries, only moderately relieved by the love of children, the enduring loyalty of a patient wife, some friendships, and some literary success. The bulk of his writing turned out like his conversation to be "inconclusive and long-winded"; it barely earned him a living in his lifetime, and it is now forgotten. In that discursive mass, however, are a few unforgettable chapters: penetrating analyses of human nature; explorations of the world of drugs and dreams; or passages like the following "Levana and Our Ladies of Sorrow," which recall, for pure gorgeousness, the prose of the seventeenth century and of Sir Thomas Browne.

Levana and Our Ladies of Sorrow

Oftentimes at Oxford I saw Levana in my dreams. I knew her by her Roman symbols. Who is Levana? Reader, that do not pretend to have leisure for very much scholarship, you will not be angry with me for telling you. Levana was the Roman goddess that performed for the new-born infant the earliest office of ennobling kindness—typical, by its mode, of that grandeur which belongs to man everywhere, and of that benignity in powers invisible which even in Pagan worlds sometimes descends to sustain it. At the very moment of birth, just as the infant tasted for the first time the atmosphere of our troubled planet, it was laid on the ground. *That* might bear different interpretations. But immediately, lest so grand a creature should grovel there for more than one instant, either the paternal hand, as proxy for the goddess Levana, or some near kinsman, as proxy for the father, raised it upright, bade it look erect as the king of all this world, and presented its forehead to the stars, saying, perhaps, in his heart, "Behold what is greater than yourselves!" This symbolic act represented the function of Levana. And that mysterious lady, who never revealed her face (except to me in dreams), but always acted by delegation, had her name from the Latin verb (as still it is the Italian verb) *levare*, to raise aloft.

This is the explanation of Levana. And hence it has arisen that some people have understood by Levana the tutelary power that controls the education of the nursery. She, that would not suffer at his birth even a prefigurative or mimic degradation for her awful ward, far less could be supposed to suffer the real degradation attaching to the non-development of his power. She therefore watches over human education. Now, the word *educo*, with the penultimate short, was derived (by a process often exemplified in the crystallisation of languages) from the word *educo*, with the penultimate long. Whatsoever *educes*, or develops, *educates*. By the education of Levana, therefore, is meant,—not the poor machinery that moves by spelling-books and grammars, but by that mighty system of central forces hidden in the deep bosom of human life, which by passion, by strife, by temptation, by the energies of resistance, works forever upon children,—resting not day or night, any more than the mighty wheel of day and night themselves, whose moments, like restless spokes, are glimmering forever as they revolve.

If, then, *these* are the ministries by which Levana works, how profoundly must she reverence the agencies of grief! But you, reader, think that children generally are not liable to grief such as mine. There are two senses in the word *generally*,—the sense of Euclid, where it means *universally* (or in the whole extent of the *genus*), and a foolish sense of this word, where it means *usually*. Now, I am far from saying that children universally are capable of grief like mine. But there are more than you ever heard of who die of grief in this

island of ours. I will tell you a common case. The rules of
Eton require that a boy on the *foundation* should be there
twelve years: he is superannuated at eighteen; consequently
he must come at six. Children torn away from mothers and
sisters at that age not unfrequently die. I speak of what I
know. The complaint is not entered by the registrar as grief;
but *that* it is. Grief of that sort, and at that age, has killed
more than ever have been counted amongst its martyrs.

Therefore it is that Levana often communes with the powers
that shake man's heart; therefore it is that she dotes upon
grief. "These ladies," said I softly to myself, on seeing the
ministers with whom Levana was conversing, "these are the
Sorrows; and they are three in number: as the *Graces* are
three, who dress man's life with beauty; the *Parcae* are three,
who weave the dark arras of man's life in their mysterious
loom always with colours sad in part, sometimes angry with
tragic crimson and black; the *Furies* are three, who visit with
retributions, called from the other side of the grave, offences
that walk upon this; and once even the *Muses* were but three,
who fit the harp, the trumpet, or the lute, to the great burdens
of man's impassioned creations. These are the Sorrows; all
three of whom I know." The last words I say *now;* but in
Oxford I said "one of whom I know, and the others too surely I *shall* know." For already, in my fervent youth, I saw
(dimly relieved upon the dark background of my dreams)
the imperfect lineaments of the awful Sisters.

These Sisters—by what name shall we call them? If I
say simply "The Sorrows," there will be a chance of mistaking
the term; it might be understood of individual sorrow,—
separate cases of sorrow,—whereas I want a term expressing
the mighty abstractions that incarnate themselves in all
individual sufferings of man's heart, and I wish to have these
abstractions presented as impersonations,—that is, as clothed
with human attributes of life, and with functions pointing to
flesh. Let us call them, therefore, *Our Ladies of Sorrow*.

I know them thoroughly, and have walked in all their
kingdoms. Three sisters they are, of some mysterious household; and their paths are wide apart; but of their dominion
there is no end. Them I saw often conversing with Levana,
and sometimes about myself. Do they talk, then? O no!
Mighty phantoms like these disdain the infirmities of language.
They may utter voices through the organs of man when they
dwell in human hearts, but amongst themselves is no voice nor
sound; eternal silence reigns in *their* kingdoms. They spoke

not as they talked with Levana; they whispered not; they sang not; though oftentimes methought they *might* have sung; for I upon earth had heard their mysteries oftentimes deciphered by harp and timbrel, by dulcimer and organ. Like God, whose servants they are, they utter their pleasure not by sounds that perish, or by words that go astray, but by signs in heaven, by changes on earth, by pulses in secret rivers, heraldries painted on darkness, and hieroglyphics written on the tablets of the brain. *They* wheeled in mazes; *I* spelled the steps. *They* telegraphed from afar; *I* read the signals. *They* conspired together; and on the mirrors of darkness *my* eye traced the plots. *Theirs* were the symbols; *mine* are the words.

What is it the Sisters are? What is it that they do? Let me describe their form and their presence, if form it were that still *fluctuated* in its outline, or presence it were that forever advanced to the front or forever receded amongst shades.

The eldest of the three is named *Mater Lachrymarum,* Our Lady of Tears. She it is that night and day raves and moans, calling for vanished faces. She stood in Rama, where a voice was heard of lamentation,—Rachel weeping for her children, and refusing to be comforted. She it was that stood in Bethlehem on the night when Herod's sword swept its nurseries of Innocents, and the little feet were stiffened forever which, heard at times as they trotted along floors overhead, woke pulses of love in household hearts that were not unmarked in heaven. Her eyes are sweet and subtle, wild and sleepy, by turns; oftentimes rising to the clouds, oftentimes challenging the heavens. She wears a diadem round her head. And I knew by my childish memories that she could go abroad upon the winds, when she heard the sobbing of litanies, or the thundering of organs, and when she beheld the mustering of summer clouds. This Sister, the elder, it is that carries keys more than papal at her girdle, which open every cottage and every palace. She, to my knowledge, sat all last summer by the bedside of the blind beggar, him that so often and so gladly I talked with, whose pious daughter, eight years old, with the sunny countenance, resisted the temptations of play and village mirth, to travel all day long on dusty roads with her afflicted father. For this did God send her a great reward. In the spring time of the year, and whilst yet her own spring was budding, He recalled her to himself. But her blind father mourns forever over *her;* still he dreams at midnight that the little guiding hand is locked within his own; and still he wakens to a darkness that is *now* within a second and a deeper darkness.

This *Mater Lachrymarum* also has been sitting all this winter of 1844–5 within the bedchamber of the Czar, bringing before his eyes a daughter (not less pious) that vanished to God not less suddenly, and left behind her a darkness not less profound. By the power of the keys it is that Our Lady of Tears glides, a ghostly intruder, into the chambers of sleepless men, sleepless women, sleepless children, from Ganges to the Nile, from Nile to Mississippi. And her, because she is the first-born of her house, and has the widest empire, let us honour with the title of "Madonna."

The second Sister is called *Mater Suspiriorum,* Our Lady of Sighs. She never scales the clouds, nor walks abroad upon the winds. She wears no diadem. And her eyes, if they were ever seen, would be neither sweet nor subtle; no man could read their story; they would be found filled with perishing dreams, and with wrecks of forgotten delirium. But she raises not her eyes; her head, on which sits a dilapidated turban, droops forever, forever fastens on the dust. She weeps not. She groans not. But she sighs inaudibly at intervals. Her sister, Madonna, is oftentimes stormy and frantic, raging in the highest against heaven, and demanding back her darlings. But Our Lady of Sighs never clamours, never defies, dreams not of rebellious aspirations. She is humble to abjectness. Hers is the meekness that belongs to the hopeless. Murmur she may, but it is in her sleep. Whisper she may, but it is to herself in the twilight. Mutter she does at times, but it is in solitary places that are desolate as she is desolate, in ruined cities, and when the sun has gone down to his rest. This Sister is the visitor of the Pariah, of the Jew, of the bondsman to the oar in the Mediterranean galleys; of the English criminal in Norfolk Island, blotted out from the books of remembrance in sweet far-off England; of the baffled penitent reverting his eyes forever upon a solitary grave, which to him seems the altar overthrown of some past and bloody sacrifice, on which altar no oblations can now be availing, whether towards pardon that he might implore, or towards reparation that he might attempt. Every slave that at noonday looks up to the tropical sun with timid reproach, as he points with one hand to the earth, our general mother, but for *him* a stepmother, as he points with the other hand to the Bible, our general teacher, but against *him* sealed and sequestered; every woman sitting in darkness, without love to shelter her head, or hope to illumine her solitude, because the heaven-born instincts kindling in her nature germs of holy affections, which God implanted in her womanly bosom, having been stifled by social necessities, now burn sullenly to waste, like sepulchral lamps amongst the ancients; every nun defrauded of her unreturning Maytime by wicked kinsman, whom God will judge; every captive in every dungeon; all that are betrayed, and all that are rejected; outcasts by traditionary law, and children of *hereditary* disgrace: all these walk with Our Lady of Sighs. She also carries a key; but she needs it little. For her kingdom is chiefly amongst the tents of Shem, and the houseless vagrant of every clime. Yet in the very highest ranks of man she finds chapels of her own; and even in glorious England there are some that, to the world, carry their heads as proudly as the reindeer, who yet secretly have received her mark upon their foreheads.

But the third Sister, who is also the youngest——! Hush! whisper whilst we talk of *her!* Her kingdom is not large, or else no flesh should live; but within that kingdom all power is hers. Her head, turreted like that of Cybele, rises almost beyond the reach of sight. She droops not; and her eyes, rising so high, *might* be hidden by distance. But, being what they are, they cannot be hidden: through the treble veil of crape which she wears the fierce light of a blazing misery, that rests not for matins or for vespers, for noon of day or noon of night, for ebbing or for flowing tide, may be read from the very ground. She is the defier of God. She also is the mother of lunatics, and the suggestress of suicides. Deep lie the roots of her power; but narrow is the nation that she rules. For she can approach only those in whom a profound nature has been upheaved by central convulsions; in whom the heart trembles and the brain rocks under conspiracies of tempest from without and tempest from within. Madonna moves with uncertain steps, fast or slow, but still with tragic grace. Our Lady of Sighs creeps timidly and stealthily. But this youngest Sister moves with incalculable motions, bounding, and with tiger's leaps. She carries no key; for, though coming rarely amongst men, she storms all doors at which she is permitted to enter at all. And *her* name is *Mater Tenebrarum*,—our Lady of Darkness.

These were the *Semnai Theai* or Sublime Goddesses, these were the *Eumenides* or Gracious Ladies (so called by antiquity in shuddering propitiation), of my Oxford dreams. Madonna spoke. She spoke by her mysterious hand. Touching my head, she beckoned to Our Lady of Sighs; and *what* she spoke, translated out of the signs which (except in dreams) no man reads, was this:—

"Lo! here is he whom in childhood I dedicated to my altars. This is he that once I made my darling. Him I led astray, him I beguiled; and from heaven I stole away his young heart to mine. Through me did he become idolatrous; and through me it was, by languishing desires, that he worshipped the worm, and prayed to the wormy grave. Holy was the grave to him; lovely was its darkness; saintly its corruption. Him, this young idolater, I have seasoned for thee, dear gentle Sister of Sighs! Do thou take him now to *thy* heart, and season him for our dreadful sister. And thou,"—turning to the *Mater Tenebrarum,* she said,—"wicked sister, that temptest and hatest, do thou take him from *her.* See that thy sceptre lie heavy on his head. Suffer not woman and her tenderness to sit near him in his darkness. Banish the frailties of hope; wither the relenting of love; scorch the fountains of tears; curse him as only *thou* canst curse. So shall he be accomplished in the furnace; so shall he see the things that ought *not* to be seen, sights that are abominable, and secrets that are unutterable. So shall he read elder truths, sad truths, grand truths, fearful truths. So shall he rise again *before* he dies. And so shall our commission be accomplished which before God we had,—to plague his heart until we had unfolded the capacities of his spirit."

JOHN DONNE
1571–1631

John Donne was one who "knew the anguish of the marrow/
The ague of the skeleton." He knew too, and very well, the delights of the flesh, and a love, beyond flesh, that was "inter-assured
of the mind." But the substantial presence of death and final corruption was constantly in the mind of this man who became Dean
of St. Paul's; and never more so than in the year 1623, when he
suffered the severe illness which motivated his "Meditations." A
single phrase from these "Meditations," "for whom the bell tolls,"
has become familiar since Ernest Hemingway chose it for the title
of his novel; but here is the phrase in its elaborately developed
setting, where the bell that tolls the death of one man tolls for all,
and at the same time tolls the dead into eternal life.

Meditations

> Intereà insomnes noctes Ego duco, Diesque.
> *I sleepe not day nor night.*

XV

Naturall men have conceived a twofold use of *sleepe;* That
it is a *refreshing* of the body in this life; That it is a *preparing*
of the *soule* for the next; That it is a *feast,* and it is the *grace*
at that *feast;* That it is our *recreation,* and cheeres us, and it
is our *Catechisme* and instructs us; wee lie downe in a hope,
that wee shall rise the stronger; and we lie downe in a knowledge, that wee may rise no more. *Sleepe* is an *Opiate* which
gives us *rest,* but such an *Opiate,* as perchance, being under
it, we shall wake no more. But though naturall men, who
have induced secondary and figurative considerations, have
found out this second, this *emblematicall* use of *sleepe,* that
it should be a *representation of death, God,* who wrought and
perfected his worke, before *Nature* began, (for *Nature* was

but his *Apprentice,* to learne in the first *seven daies,* and now is his *foreman,* and works next under him) *God,* I say, intended *sleepe* onely for the *refreshing* of man by bodily rest, and not for a *figure of death,* for he intended not *death* it selfe then. But *Man* having induced *death* upon himselfe, *God* hath taken *Mans Creature, death,* into his hand, and mended it; and whereas it hath in itselfe a fearefull forme and aspect, so that Man is afraid of his own *Creature, God* presents it to him, in a *familiar,* in an *assiduous,* in an *agreeable* and *acceptable* forme, in *sleepe,* that so when hee awakes from *sleepe,* and saies to himselfe, shall I bee no otherwise when I am dead, than I was even now, when I was asleep, hee may bee ashamed of his waking *dreames,* and of his *Melancholique* fancying out a horrid and an affrightfull figure of that *death* which is so like sleepe. As then wee need *sleepe* to live out our *threescore and ten yeeres,* so we need *death,* to live that *life* which we cannot *out-live.* And as *death* being our *enemie, God* allowes us to defend ourselves against it (for wee *victuall* ourselves against *death, twice* every day, as often as we *eat)* so *God* having so sweetned *death* unto us as hee hath in *sleepe,* wee put ourselves into our *enemies* hands *once* every day; so farre, as *sleepe* is *death,* and *sleepe* is as much *death,* as *meat* is *life.* This then is the *misery* of my *sicknesse,* That death as it is produced from mee, and is mine owne *Creature,* is now before mine *Eyes,* but in that forme, in which *God* hath mollified it to us, and made it acceptable, in *sleepe,* I cannot see it: how many *prisoners,* who have even hollowed themselves their *graves* upon that *Earth,* on which they have lien long under heavie fetters, yet at this *houre* are *asleepe,* though they bee yet working upon their owne *graves* by their owne *waight!* Hee that hath seene his *friend* die to *day,* or knowes hee shall see it to *morrow,* yet will sinke into a sleepe betweene. I cannot; and oh, if I be entring now into *Eternitie,* where there shall bee no more distinction of *houres,* why is it al my businesse now *to tell Clocks?* Why is none of the heavinesse of my *heart,* dispensed into mine *Eye-lids,* that they might fall as my heart doth? And why, since I have lost my delight in all objects, cannot I discontinue the facultie of seeing them, by closing mine *eyes* in *sleepe?* But why rather being entring into that presence, where I shall wake continually and never sleepe more, doe I not interpret my continuall waking here, to bee a *parasceve,* and a *preparation* to that?

Et properare meum clamant, è Turre propinqua,
Obstreperæ Campanæ aliorum in funere, funus.

*From the Bells of the Church adjoyning, I am
daily remembred of my buriall in the funeralls
of others.*

XVI

We have a *Convenient Author*, who writ a *Discourse of Bells*,
when hee was prisoner in *Turky*. How would hee have enlarged himselfe if he had beene my *fellow-prisoner* in this
sicke bed, so neere to that *Steeple*, which never ceases, no
more than the *harmony of the spheres*, but is more heard.
When the *Turkes* took *Constantinople*, they melted the *Bells*
into *Ordnance;* I have heard both *Bells* and *Ordnance*, but
never been so much affected with those, as with these *Bells*.
I have *lien* near a *Steeple*, in which there are said to be more
than *thirty Bels;* And neere another, where there is one so
bigge, as that the *Clapper* is said to weigh more than *six
hundred pound*, yet never so affected as here. Here the *Bells*
can scarse solemnise the funerall of any person, but that I
knew him, or knew that he was my *Neighbour:* we dwelt in
houses neere to one another before, but now hee is gone into
that house, into which I must follow him. There is a way of
correcting the *Children* of great persons, that other *Children*
are corrected in their *behalfe*, and in their *names*, and this
workes upon them, who indeed had more deserved it. And
when these *Bells* tell me, that now one, and now another is
buried, must not I acknowledge, that they have the *correction*
due to me, and paid the *debt* that I owe? There is a story of
a *Bell* in a *Monastery* which, when any of the house was
sicke to death, rung alwaies *voluntarily*, and they knew the
inevitablenesse of the danger by that. It rung once, when no
man was sick; but the next day one of the house, fell from
the *steeple*, and died, and the *Bell* held the reputation of a
Prophet still. If these *Bells* that warne to a *Funerall* now,
were appropriated to none, may not I, by the houre of the
Funerall, supply? How many men that stand at an *execution*,
if they would aske, for what dies that man, should heare
their owne faults condemned, and see themselves executed, by

Atturney? We scarce heare of any man *preferred,* but wee thinke of our selves, that wee might very well have beene that *Man;* Why might not I have beene that *Man,* that is carried to his *grave* now? Could I fit my selfe, to *stand,* or *sit* in any mans *place,* and not to lie in any mans *grave?* I may lacke much of the *good parts* of the meanest, but I lacke nothing of the *mortality* of the weakest; They may have acquired better *abilities* than I, but I was borne to as many *infirmities* as they. To be an *Incumbent* by lying down in a *grave,* to be a *Doctor* by teaching *Mortification* by *Example,* by *dying,* though I may have *seniors,* others may be *elder* than I, yet I have proceeded apace in a good *University,* and gone a great way in a little time, by the furtherance of a vehement *Fever;* and whomsoever these *Bells* bring to the ground to day, if hee and I had beene compared yesterday, perchance I should have been thought likelier to come to this preferment, then, than he. *God* hath kept the power of *death* in his owne hands, lest any man should *bribe death.* If man knew the *gaine of death,* the *ease of death,* he would solicite, he would provoke *death* to assist him, by any hand, which he might use. But as when men see many of their owne professions preferd, it ministers a hope that that may light upon them; so when these hourely *Bells* tell me of so many *funerals* of men like me, it presents, if not a *desire* that it may, yet a *comfort* whensoever mine shall come.

Nunc lento sonitu dicunt, Morieris.

*Now, this Bell tolling softly for an-
other, saies to me, Thou must die.*

XVII

Perchance hee for whom this *Bell* tolls, may be so ill, as that he knowes not it tolls for him; And perchance I may thinke my selfe so much better than I am, as that they who are about mee, and see my state, may have caused it to toll for mee, and I know not that. The *Church* is *Catholike, universall,* so are all her *Actions; All* that she does, belongs to *all.* When she *baptizes a child,* that action concernes mee; for that child is thereby connected to that *Head* which is my *Head* too, and engraffed into that *body,* whereof I am a *member.* And when she *buries a Man,* that action concernes me: All *mankinde* is of one *Author,* and is one *volume;* when one Man dies, one *Chapter* is not *torne* out of the *booke,* but *translated* into a better *language;* and every *Chapter* must be so *translated; God* emploies several *translators;* some peeces are translated by *age,* some by *sicknesse,* some by *warre,* some by *justice;* but *Gods* hand is in every *translation;* and his hand shall binde up all our scattered leaves againe, for that *Librarie* where every *booke* shall lie open to one another: As therefore the *Bell* that rings to a *Sermon,* calls not upon the *Preacher* onely, but upon the *Congregation* to come; so this *Bell* calls us all: but how much more mee, who am brought so neere the *doore* by this *sicknesse.* There was a *contention* as farre as a *suite,* (in which both *pietie* and *dignitie, religion,* and *estimation,* were mingled) which of the religious *Orders* should ring to *praiers* first in the *Morning;* and it was *determined,* that *they should ring first that rose earliest.* If we understand aright the *dignitie* of this *Bell* that tolls for our *evening prayer,* wee would bee glad to make it ours, by rising early, in that *application,* that it might bee ours, as wel as his, whose indeed it is. The *Bell* doth toll for him that *thinkes* it doth; and though it *intermit* againe, yet from that *minute,* that that occasion wrought upon him, hee is united to *God.* Who casts not up his *Eye* to the *Sunne* when it rises? but who takes off his *Eye* from a *Comet* when that breaks out? Who bends not his *eare* to any *bell,* which upon any occasion rings? but who can remove it from that *bell,* which is passing a *peece of himselfe* out of this *world?* No man is an *Iland,* intire of it selfe; every man is a peece of the *Continent,* a part of the *maine;* if a *Clod* bee washed away by the *Sea, Europe* is the lesse, as well as if a *Promontorie* were, as well as if a *Mannor* of thy *friends* or of *thine owne* were; any mans *death* diminishes *me,* because I am involved in *Mankinde;* And therefore never send to know for whom the *bell* tolls; It tolls for *thee.* Neither can we call this a *begging* of *Miserie* or a *borrowing* of *Miserie,* as though wee were not miserable enough of our selves, but must fetch in more from the next house, in taking upon us the *Miserie* of our *Neighbours.* Truly it were an excusable covetousnesse if wee did; for *affliction* is a *treasure,* and scarce any man hath *enough* of it. No man hath *affliction* enough that is not matured, and ripened by it, and made fit for *God* by that *affliction.* If a man carry *treasure* in *bullion,* or in a *wedge* of *gold,* and have none coined into *currant Monies,* his *treasure* will not defray him as he travells. *Tribulation* is *Treasure* in the *nature* of it, but it is not *currant money* in the *use* of it, except wee get nearer and nearer our *home*, *Heaven*, by it. Another man may be sicke too, and sick to *death*, and this *affliction* may lie in his *bowels*, as *gold* in a *Mine*, and be of no use to him; but this *bell*, that tells me of his *affliction*, digs out, and applies that *gold* to *mee*: if by this consideration of anothers danger, I take mine owne into contemplation, and so secure my selfe, by making my recourse to my *God*, who is our onely securitie.

IRWIN EDMAN
1896–1954

In the preface to *Adam, the Baby, and the Man from Mars,*
the volume from which the following essay is taken, Irwin Edman
writes that he "happens to be engaged in the profession of what
is commonly called philosophy. He happens likewise to be living
in the twentieth century, in America, and in New York. He has
been educated in, or exposed to, a point of view that might
roughly be called naturalism, the world that science reveals."
Yet, he confesses, he has also "a nostalgic passion for what may
be called Platonism, the world that poetry remembers." To this
self-portrait, little except routine biographical details need be
added. New York, for example, was even more specifically Columbia University, where Edman studied and then taught from
1918 until his death. The philosophy he professed, that mixture
of naturalism and Platonism, charmed and fortified generations
of students, just as the same philosophy, expressed with wit,
warmth, and urbanity, in his many books and magazine articles,
attracted hosts of readers not ordinarily addicted to the "love of
wisdom."

How to Be Sweet Though Sophisticated

One can learn as much about the prevailing temper of a
generation by studying its contempts as by remembering its
loves. It is indeed very difficult in our time to tell what we
love, the old objects of our adoration having been riddled
with suspicion, and love itself, in the skeptical hands of our
contemporary wise men, having come into disrepute. To the
Spartan, the ideal of life was represented by the warrior, dis-
ciplined and taut. To the medieval, the ideal of the good life
was typified by the martyr, the ascetic or the saint. In the
Renaissance one wished to be something like Castiglione's
courtier, a polished fusion of the gentleman, the scholar, the

soldier and the man of the world. The contemporary hero, the mythical pattern in the imitation of whom we would live, remains as yet undefined. We have no hero; what is more to the point, we suspect hero worship.

But it is only necessary to read the books of our more circumspect novelists or to move for an evening in the society of our more intelligent friends, to detect what we do not wish to be, or at least what we do not wish to be thought to be. To the modern spirit, disillusioned or at least unillusioned, the great evil to be avoided is sentimentality. We will forgive almost all sins save those of slushiness. We will condone all defects save those of the soft mind. There is going to be no nonsense about us, and though we may wince a little in private, or cause others to wince in public, we are not going to be children. We are not going to cry for the moon, swear by the stars, or go roller-skating on the rainbow. Not for us the sorrows of Werther, the melancholy of Byron, the purified ecstasies of Coventry Patmore's version, so angelic and so silly, of love. We have both learned and unlearned too much, we think, for that sort of thing. First as to what we have learned.

Science has ceased to be the esoteric possession of experts in a laboratory; it has become the popular jargon of the men in the street or at least of the women in the salon. We know enough about glands to be incredulous of our own or of anybody else's melancholy. When we are depressed we know that it is probably not the cosmos in general but the thyroid in particular that is wrong with us. We are more and more conversant with the chemistry of that clod of clay on a speck of star-dust, that we call human life. We are, therefore, increasingly impatient with the romantic expectation that the universe should conform exactly with the human heart's desire.

Love, again, may among adolescents parade its ancient recognizable rhetoric. But we know better. We see through the disguise, ornate and thin, by which lust conceals itself— even from itself. Every schoolboy, almost, has read Freud. Every adult can quote Havelock Ellis. Our devotion may seem deep, but its depths are in the seamier profundities of our psyches. And as for that eternity with which we credit every passing affection—well, we smile ourselves at that outmoded sentimentalism. Eternal love! Eternal nonsense! A generation that has busied itself with the meaning of time and the flux of consciousness knows enough to discount the permanence of its passions. Another year, another place, and this so vivid absorption will be a memory regarded at best with ironic regret.

Besides all of which, we have lived through a war and its aftermath. We have learned the hollowness of high-sounding words masking low deeds. We have observed the terrible consequences of acting in a world of brutal fact with soft evasions, with the respectable rubbish of a sentimental moral tradition. We have acquired a wisdom cool and aseptic; we have unlearned the moralities, outwardly benign, actually perilous, on which we were brought up.

So having discarded the old myths, we have gradually been forming a hero-myth of our own. He—or she—we thank the stars (or we would, if we were in a mood to thank anything) is no hero. Every one has met an example of the blueprint Modern acceptable to the contemporary intelligence. It is to be met with at any current social gathering. Enter the Modern. It makes no difference whether it be a man or a woman. In either case, the ideas, like the figure and headdress, will be much the same. He will not talk of love or admit it. He will not believe in the Good Life or be publicly seen leading it. He will have no nonsense about religion or believe that relic of primitive mentality still exists. He will be 'anæsthetized to all that Jesus or that Plato prized.' He will have little patience with politeness or allow himself to practice it. He will try to be a tough mind gayly indifferent in a tough world. The last obscenity he will permit himself will be nobility. The last weakness he will indulge in will be to be sweet or soft. He will talk like a character out of Ernest Hemingway, act like one of Aldous Huxley's bizarre London intelligentsia—or pretend he does—and try to think in such terms as James Joyce's heroines use in their more untrammeled moments.

Now obviously if human nature changes—and it has changed only very little since paleolithic days—it certainly has not gone a complete metamorphosis in the last quarter of a century. Sophisticated people, whatever they may say, have feelings like their more naïve brothers. They love and hate, are stirred to wonder and beauty, hunger and thirst much like the Victorians whom they mock and the living boobies whom they despise. But the new lingo has become a cult and, thanks to the surgical psychologies, the new self-consciousness has become a fashion. It is now in the best circles indecent to be decent, shameful to be shy, offensive to be courteous, suspicious to be simple. Many of our newly smart would rather be found murdering their children than being kind to their parents. They would prefer to be damned for rudeness than to be snickered at for courtesy. They suspect even themselves for any outworn noble sentiment they may happen to experience, any unpremeditated act of kindness they may do, any spontaneous impulse of affection to which they may give way. How many gentle souls does one know who go about being gentle *sub rosa!* How many little amenities of life are people, for fear of being thought ridiculous, beginning to practice behind closed doors. As for love, what roundabout ways a lover will take to express it, for fear that his beloved may set him down as old-fashioned and suburban.

It is not merely fear of what people will say, but fear of what one will think of one's self that makes it difficult in our time to be at once a 'tough mind' and a gentle heart. All the new realism of thinking and writing and conversation have made us self-skeptical. Any one acquainted with the new psychiatry knows why. That gesture we intended to be generous we know to be timid or vain. The kindness we tried to utter we are told is a defense against our own weakness, a fear of not being kind. Enthusiasm is a symptom of prolonged adolescence. Rapture is a psychological debauch that is a vulgar truancy from reason.

Now it would seem to be high time to find out whether this sort of thing has not gone too far. The sophisticates themselves, I suspect, feel that it has. How else is one to account for the joy with which in our most advanced circles intelligentlemen, intelligentlewomen hail any naïveté in literature or art. Exhibitions of primitive Negro sculpture are visited by the best minds. For a season cultivated New York crowded to see a simple little Spanish play entitled 'Cradle Song,' which was compacted of old-fashioned tenderness and peace, a story of simple nuns, their demure ward, and her love-affair, all lavender and lace.

As for the respectable bourgeois rabble whom our sophisticated despise, these comfortable bumpkins cannot get enough of the traditional simple virtues and simple souls. Write them a story, as an Englishman did recently, of a brave father come down in the world, fighting the good fight against slimy obstacles for the love of his pure and devoted son, and you will have hundreds of thousands at your feet and at your publisher's. And what of the whole English-speaking world that quotes with glee the childlike whimsicalities of 'Christopher Robin' and 'Winnie-the-Pooh.'

The question indeed comes down to this: Is it possible to be at once sweet and sophisticated? In our generation can one be at once honest and kindly, intelligent and courteous, informed and gay? Is the price of modern knowledge ill humor and ill temper? Must we pay for having eaten of the tree of good and evil by losing our heritage of urbanity and our saving faith in people and things? Is this the folly that one calls being wise?

These are rhetorical questions and they are intended to be such. This observer at least wishes to bear humble testimony to the conviction that contemporary wisdom has overreached itself. It is submitted that it is the easiest thing in the world, even the contemporary world, to find life agreeable, and to live it agreeably. It is easy to do these things without being a sentimentalist, or what is perhaps the equivalent, without being a fool. I submit that we are the only half-willing followers of fashion when we identify sophistication with the discourteous in manners, the brutal in action and the cynical in thought. It is diffidently proposed that insight into truth, and charm of life need not necessarily be contradictions in terms.

First as to thought! There is a presumption, at once common and fallacious, that to be cynical is by definition to be honest and profound. The young man who has first had his eyes opened to the shallowness and mockery of conventional morals has a fine brusque sense of wisdom at no longer being taken in. He hears the preacher intone, 'Our Father which art in Heaven,' and he thinks of all the human peccadilloes of all the preachers he has ever known. He hears the political orator bellow of justice and the people's rights and his alert memory ruminates upon all the patent injustices of our social order, the travesties of criminal procedure, the mockeries of representative government, the robberies and swinish deceits practiced upon a gullible public. His professors use high words about the Good and he knows and sees what happens daily in the market-place. He hears of the goodness of God and he hears also of wars and rumors of wars and acts of God, floods and earthquakes, that cannot remotely be construed as beneficent.

The honest mind insists, in our generation, to an unprecedented degree, on being realistic. To be realistic is tantamount to acknowledging that there is a deal of tinsel in our lives and our pretensions. God may still be in His Heaven, but there is more than sufficient evidence that all is not right with the world. But to be realistic is also to admit that an indictment of evils is not the whole story nor the whole universe.

Sophistication demands honesty; it does not require ill temper. There is a kind of wisdom called mellowness and the history of literature is amiably strewn with its exemplars. Montaigne is the prince of these; his essays are the perfectly urbane expression of a man who kept his mind clear and his blood sweet. He knew as well as the latest contemporary futilitarian knows how much there is to bewail in the world. At its best life is short; half of its felicities are illusions and the other half are fatal in their consequences. There is little of which we can be certain, and much of which we must be regretful or ashamed.

But it is not clear now as it was to Montaigne that ill temper is hardly the mood with which to live pleasantly, nor the spirit which reason will commend to adopt toward the world. The light may have gone out of Heaven and meaning out of the earth. We may be fated animals crawling anxiously through the palpitation brief and confused, that we call life. But that chaotic interval is at moments clear with wonder or beauty, and even the disorder of our current societies permits moments of delight. These are clearly on the debit side of the ledger, and a realism that denies the doughnut in affirming the hole is both jaundiced and dishonest.

Nor is it any more honest or reasonable to be continually suspicious of our pleasures, our kindnesses or our raptures because the laboratory has been revealing the machinery by which these operate. Love, we are told, is merely a matter of glandular secretions. But to admit the truth of this physiological fact is far from denying that love exists. There may be a thousand subconscious reasons why we aid a friend in distress or sacrifice our life and energies for some lost or forlorn ideal. The causes of the late war may be demonstrated to have been sordid and mean, but even the most cynical will not deny that thousands of men gave their lives in the generous belief that they were not. It matters not what produces our raptures or our loves or loyalties. Even the most hardened can hardly contest their existence.

To know the material origins of our flights is not to deny their being or their value. To recognize the horrors and evils in the texture of existence is not to blind us to all the loveliness and liveliness there is to enjoy and to commemorate under the sun. It may be said indeed that the essence of being adult rather than childish is to cease to be sulky and irritable at finding life and existence to be what they are. It means among other things to be able to face life steadily and without illusion—but also without disillusion.

And once one has surrendered the cult of disillusion it will not seem necessary any longer to parade a hard-boiled manner, a tough language, and a sour mind. Many of our contemporaries are disappointed sentimentalists who try to conceal from their public their disappointment by the language of the prize-ring or the gutter. Those who have really learned to look candidly upon existence will not need to apologize for their candor with fighting words. If life is really tragic, we are all in the same boat, and the least we can do is to greet each other *pro tem* with a decent courtesy, if only to mitigate by friendliness the dark interval in which we live. It will not seem necessary to those truly gifted with a tragic sense of life to use the language of the street to prove they are not sentimental. No one was more profoundly candid about the universe than Thomas Hardy. No one had a gentler tongue. Nor is it necessary, finally, to be rough-neck in one's thinking. There is after all, little use in defying a universe that is *a priori* defined as indifferent.

Sentimentalism is usually attributed to a prolonged adolescence, a perpetual refusal to emerge from the mirage of cherished illusions to the candid prospect of realities. But the convention has risen in our own day that cynicism or perpetual disillusion is the symptom of maturity. The fallacy of sentimentalism is that it paints to itself a picture that conforms comfortably with its own roseate desires. The fallacy of cynicism is that it paints the universe as in league against human ideals. A persistent satire upon life is hardly more adult than a persistent prettifying of it. One of the worst sins Dante could think of was to sulk in the sunlight: To those who did he assigned the eternal punishment of wallowing in the mud. To be understanding is to be equable, and to be equable is to escape the need for being smart or sulky or hard. 'Heartbreak,' says a character in Shaw's 'Heartbreak House,' 'is the end of happiness and the beginning of peace.' If our hearts were at peace, we should not need to put up so elaborate a smoke-screen of pert defense. We should not need to insist on singing our satirical praises to a God from whom all evils flow. We should not need to think of existence as a psychiatric clinic, nor to be its perpetual *enfants terribles*.

One might set up as a conceivable ideal for our generation the combination of the tough mind and the gentle heart. The tough mind will be undismayed by any fact or any horror; it will not be misled by any pleasure or mirage. It will know that man is neither an ape nor an angel, but a precarious and harassed animal living in an uncertain, sometimes abominable, sometimes exquisite world. The gentle heart will know how far even lust and hypocrisy have their understandable causes. It will know enough to discern good and forgive evil. Some one once called John Stuart Mill 'the saint of rationalism.' The ideal of character for our generation, for any generation, is, perhaps, a union of the reasoner and the saint. Reason has led men into inhumanity; religion has led them into illusion. A fusion of the two spirits may be possible in an age that has learned to think candidly and has, since we are still human, not forgotten how to feel.

One has an image of what that modern type of the 'high-minded man' will be like. He is to be met with at least in potentiality in some of the educated youth of our own day. I have known a dozen myself, young men and women who were not fooled by ancient illusions, were not hardened by a modern cult. Their minds were steel-like in their precision and taut in their honesty. Their hearts were, like those that Dante valued, gentle. They could relish the goods of life without blinding themselves to its nightmares. They could discern the tragedy of existence and laugh at its diversions. Of such, as it was said of old, may be the Kingdom of Heaven. From such may be forming the modern temper.

LOREN EISELEY
1907——

In the tradition of Francis Bacon, Sir Thomas Browne, and T. H. Huxley, the author of "Endure the Night" is a man of letters as well as a man of science. A Fellow of the American Association for the Advancement of Science as well as a past President of the American Institute for Human Paleontology, Loren Eiseley is a distinguished anthropologist who has combined his scientific and literary lives with an active career in the academic world. After teaching at the University of Kansas and Oberlin College, he was for several years Chairman of the Department of Anthropology, then Provost, then Professor of the History of Science at the University of Pennsylvania. His books include *The Immense Journey, Darwin's Century,* and *The Firmament of Time;* his essays have appeared in *Harper's* and *The American Scholar,* as well as in *Science* and *Scientific American.* Dr. Eiseley has lectured at many American universities, and has won numerous honors and awards. When asked by one of the editors of this anthology, in a television broadcast, how he managed to find time for literary activity in addition to his demanding work in science and education, Dr. Eiseley replied, "Well, you see, I have insomnia. . . ." Readers of the essay reprinted here from the *Atlantic Monthly* of June, 1963 will understand.

Endure the Night

There is always a soft radiance beyond the bedroom door from a night-light behind my chair. I have lived this way for many years now. I sleep or I do not sleep, and the light makes no difference except if I wake. Then, as I awaken, the dim forms of objects sustain my grip on reality. The familiar chair, the walls of the book-lined study reassert my own existence.

I do not lie and toss with doubt any longer, as I did in

earlier years. I get up and write, as I am writing now, or I read in the old chair that is as worn as I am. I read philosophy, metaphysics, difficult works that sometime, soon or late, draw a veil over my eyes so that I drowse in my chair.

It is not that I fail to learn from these midnight examinations of the world. It is merely that I choose that examination to remain as remote and abstruse as possible. Even so, I cannot always prophesy the result. An obscure line may whirl me into a wide-awake, ferocious concentration in which ideas like animals leap at me out of the dark, in which sudden odd trains of thought drive me inexorably to my desk and paper. I am, in short, a victim of insomnia—sporadic, wearing, violent, and melancholic. In the words of Shakespeare, for me the world "does murder sleep." It has been so since my twentieth year.

In that year my father died—a man well loved, the mainstay of a small afflicted family. He died slowly in severe bodily torture. My mother was stone-deaf. I, his son, saw and heard him die. We lived in a place and time not free with the pain-alleviating drugs of later decades. When this episode of many weeks' duration was over, a curious thing happened: I could no longer bear the ticking of the alarm clock in my own bedroom.

At first I smothered it with an extra blanket in a box beside my cot, but the ticking persisted as though it came from my own head. I used to lie for hours staring into the dark of the sleeping house, feeling the loneliness that only the sleepless know when the queer feeling comes that it is the sleeping who are alive and that those awake are disembodied ghosts. Finally, in desperation, I gave up the attempt to sleep and turned to reading, though it was difficult to concentrate.

It was then that human help appeared. My grandmother saw the light burning through the curtains of my door and came to sit with me. A few years later, when I touched her hair in farewell at the beginning of a journey from which I would not return to see her alive, I knew she had saved my sanity. Into that lonely room at midnight she had come, abandoning her own sleep, in order to sit with one in trouble. We had not talked much, but we had sat together by the lamp, reasserting our common humanity before the great empty dark that is the universe.

It did not matter that she knew nothing of psychiatry. She had not re-established my sleep patterns, but she had done something more important. She had brought me out of a dark room and retied my thread of life to the living world. Henceforward, by night or day, though I have been subject to the moods of depression or gaiety which are a part of the lives of all of us, I have been able not merely to endure but to make the best of what many regard as an unbearable affliction.

It is true that as an educational administrator I can occasionally be caught nodding in lengthy committee meetings, but so, I have observed, can men who come from sound nights on their pillows. Strangely, I, who frequently grow round-eyed and alert as an owl at the stroke of midnight, find it pleasant to nap in daylight among friends. I can roll up on a couch and sleep peacefully while my wife and chatting friends who know my peculiarities keep the daytime universe safely under control. Or so it seems. For, deep-seated in my subconscious is perhaps the idea that the black bedroom door is the gateway to the tomb.

I try in that bedroom to sleep high on two pillows, to have ears and eyes alert. Something shadowy has to be held in place and controlled. At night one has to sustain reality without help. One has to hear lest hearing be lost, see lest sight not return to follow moonbeams across the floor, touch lest the sense of objects vanish. Oh, sleeping, soundlessly sleeping ones, do you ever think who knits your universe together safely from one day's memory to the next? It is the insomniac, not the night policeman on his beat.

Many will challenge this point of view. They will say that electric power does the trick, that many a roisterer stumbles down the long street at dawn, after having served his purpose of holding the links of the gay world together. There are parts of the nighttime world, men say to me, that it is just as well I do not know. Go home and sleep, man. Others will keep your giddy world together. Let the thief pass quickly in the shadow, he is awake. Let the juvenile gangs which sidle like bands of evil crabs up from the dark waters of poverty into prosperous streets pass without finding you at midnight.

The advice is good, but in the city or the country, small things important to our lives have no reporter except as he who does not sleep may observe them. And that man must be disencumbered of reality. He must have no commitments to the dark, as do the murderer and thief. Only he must see, though what he sees may come from the night side of the planet that no man knows well. For even in the early dawn, while men lie unstirring in their sleep or stumble sleepy-eyed to work, some single episode may turn the whole world for a moment into the place of marvel that it is, but that we grow too day-worn to accept.

For example, I call the place where I am writing now the bay of broken things. In the February storms, spume wraiths climb the hundred-foot cliff to fight and fall like bitter rain in the moonlight upon the cabin roof. The earth shakes from the drum roll of the surf. I lie awake and watch through the window beyond my bed. This is no ticking in my brain; this is the elemental night of chaos. This is the sea chewing its million-year way into the heart of the continent.

The caves beneath the cliff resound with thunder. Again those warring wraiths shoot high over the house. Impelled as though I were a part of all those leaping ghosts, I dress in the dark and come forth. With my back against the door, like an ancient necromancer, I hurl my mind into the white spray and try to summon back, among those leaping forms, the faces and features of the dead I know. The shapes rise endlessly, but pass inland before the wind, indifferent to my mortal voice.

I walk a half mile to a pathway that descends upon a little beach. Below me is a stretch of white sand. No shell is ever found unbroken, even on quiet days upon that shore. Everything comes over the rocks to seaward. Wood is riven into splinters; the bones of seamen and of sea lions are pounded equally into white and shining sand. Throughout the night the long black rollers, like lines of frothing cavalry, form ranks, drum towering forward, and fall, fall till the mind is dizzy with the spume that fills it. I wait in the shelter of a rock for daybreak. At last the sea eases a trifle. The tide is going out.

I stroll shivering along the shore, and there, exposed in inescapable nakedness, I see the elemental cruelty of the natural world. A broken-winged gull, hurled by the wind against the cliff, runs before me wearily along the beach. It will starve or, mercifully, the dogs will find it. I try not to hurry it, and walk on. A little later in a quieter bend of the shore, I see ahead of me a bleeding, bedraggled blot on the edge of the white surf. As I approach, it starts warily to its feet. We look at each other. It is a wild duck, also with a shattered wing. It does not run ahead of me like the longer-limbed gull. Before I can cut off its retreat it waddles painfully from its brief refuge into the water.

The sea continues to fall heavily. The duck dives awkwardly, but with long knowledge and instinctive skill, under the fall of the first two inshore waves. I see its head working seaward. A long green roller, far taller than my head, rises and crashes forward. The black head of the water-logged duck disappears. This is the way wild things die, without question, without knowledge of mercy in the universe, knowing only themselves and their own pathway to the end. I wonder, walking further up the beach, if the man who shot that bird will die as well.

We say that this is the old chaos before man came, before sages imbued with pity walked the earth. Indeed it is true, and in my faraway study my hands have often touched with affection the backs of the volumes which line my shelves. Nevertheless, I have endured the nights and mornings of the city. I have seen old homeless men who have slept for hours sitting upright on ledges along the outer hallway of one of the great Eastern stations straighten stiffly in the dawn and limp away with feigned businesslike aloofness before the approach of the policeman on his rounds. I know that on these cold winter mornings sometimes a man, like the pigeons I have seen roosting as closely as possible over warm hotel air vents, will fall stiffly and not awaken. It is true that there are shelters for the homeless, but some men, like their Ice Age forebears, prefer their independence to the end.

But the loneliness of the city was brought home to me one early sleepless morning, not by men like me tossing in lonely rooms, not by poverty and degradation, not by old men trying with desperate futility to be out among others in the great roaring hive, but by a single one of those same pigeons which I had seen from my hotel window, looking down at midnight upon the smoking air vents and chimneys.

The pigeon, *Columba livia*, is the city bird par excellence. He is a descendant of the rock pigeon that in the Old World lived among the cliffs and crevices above the caves that early man inhabited. He has been with us since our beginning and has adapted as readily as ourselves to the artificial cliffs of man's first cities. He has known the Roman palaces and the cities of Byzantium. His little flat feet, suited to high and precarious walking, have sauntered in the temples of vanished gods as readily as in New York's Pennsylvania Station. In my dim morning strolls, waiting for the restaurants to open, I have seen him march quickly into the back end of a delivery truck while the driver was inside a store engaged in his orders with the proprietor. Yet for all its apparent tolerance of these highly adapted and often comic birds, New York also has a beach of broken things more merciless than the reefs and rollers of the ocean shore.

One morning, strolling sleepless as usual toward early breakfast time in Manhattan, I saw a sick pigeon huddled at an uncomfortable slant against a building wall on a street corner. I felt worry for the bird but I had no box, no instrument of help, and had learned long ago that pursuing wounded birds on city streets is a hopeless, dangerous activity. Pigeons, like men, die in scores every day in New York. As I hesitantly walked on, however, I wondered why the doomed bird was assuming such a desperately contorted position under the cornice that projected slightly over it.

At this moment I grew aware of something I had heard more loudly in European streets as the factory whistles blew, but never in such intensity as here, even though American shoes are built of softer materials. All around me the march of people was intensifying. It was New York on the way to work. Space was shrinking before my eyes. The tread of innumerable feet from an echo passed to the steady murmuring of a stream, then to a drumming. A dreadful robot rhythm began to rack my head, a sound like the boots of Nazis in their heyday of power. I was carried along in an irresistible surge of bodies.

A block away, jamming myself between a waste-disposal basket and a lightpost, I managed to look back. No one hesitated at that corner. The human tide pressed on, jostling and pushing. My bird had vanished under that crunching, multifooted current as remorselessly as the wounded duck under the indifferent combers of the sea. I watched this human ocean, of which I was an unwilling droplet, rolling past, its individual faces like whitecaps passing on a night of storm, fixed, merciless, indifferent; man in the mass marching like the machinery of which he is already a replaceable part, toward desks, computers, missiles, and machines, marching like the waves toward his own death with a conscious ruthlessness no watery shore could ever duplicate. I have never returned to search in that particular street for the face of humanity. I prefer the endlessly rolling pebbles of the tide, the moonstones polished by the pulling moon.

And yet, plunged as I am in dire memories and midnight reading, I have said that it is the sufferer from insomnia who knits the torn edges of men's dreams together in the hour before dawn. It is he from his hidden, winter vantage point who sees the desperate high-hearted bird fly through the doorway of the grand hotel while the sleepy doorman nods, a deed equivalent in human terms to that of some starving wretch evading Peter at heaven's gate, and an act, I think, very likely to be forgiven.

It is a night more mystical, however, that haunts my memory. Around me I see again the parchment of old books and remember how, on one rare evening, I sat in the shadows while a firefly flew from volume to volume lighting its small flame, as if in literate curiosity. Choosing the last volume whose title it had illuminated, I came immediately upon these words from St. Paul: "Beareth all things, believeth all things, hopeth all things, endureth all things." In this final episode I shall ask you to bear with me and also to believe.

I sat, once more in the late hours of darkness, in the airport of a foreign city. I was tired as only both the sufferer from insomnia and the traveler can be tired. I had missed a plane and had almost a whole night's wait before me. I could not sleep. The long corridor was deserted. Even the cleaning women had passed by.

In that white efficient glare I grew ever more depressed and weary. I was tired of the endless comings and goings of my profession; I was tired of customs officers and police. I was lonely for home. My eyes hurt. I was, unconsciously perhaps, looking for that warm stone, that hawthorn leaf where, in the words of the poet, man trades in at last his wife and friend. I had an ocean to cross; the effort seemed unbearable. I rested my aching head upon my hand.

Later, beginning at the far end of that desolate corridor, I saw a man moving slowly toward me. In a small corner of my eye I merely noted him. He limped, painfully and grotesquely, upon a heavy cane. He was far away, and it was no matter to me. I shifted the unpleasant mote out of my eye.

But, after a time, I could still feel him approaching, and in one of those white moments of penetration which are so dreadful, my eyes were drawn back to him as he came on. With an anatomist's eye I saw this amazing conglomeration of sticks and broken, misshapen pulleys which make up the body of man. Here was an apt subject, and I flew to a raging mental dissection. How could anyone, I contended, trapped in this mechanical thing of joints and sliding wires expect the acts it performed to go other than awry?

The man limped on, relentlessly.

How, oh God, I entreated, did we become trapped within this substance out of which we stare so hopelessly upon our own eventual dissolution? How for a single minute could we dream or imagine that thought would save us, children deliver us from the body of this death? Not in time, my mind rang with my despair; not in mortal time, not in this place, not anywhere in the world would blood be stanched, or the dark wrong be forever righted, or the parted be rejoined. Not in this time, not mortal time. The substance was too gross, our utopias bought with too much pain.

The man was almost upon me, breathing heavily, lunging and shuffling upon his cane. Though an odor emanated from him, I did not draw backward. I had lived with death too many years. And then this strange thing happened, which I do not mean physically, and cannot explain. The man entered me. From that moment I saw him no more. For a moment I was contorted within his shape, and then out of this body—those bodies, rather—there arose some inexplicable sweetness of union, some understanding between spirit and body which I had never before experienced. Was it I, the joints and pulleys only, who desired this peace so much?

I limped with growing age as I gathered up my luggage. Something of that terrible passer lingered in my bones, yet I was released, the very room had dilated. As I went toward my plane the words the firefly had found for me came automatically to my lips. "Beareth all things," believe, believe. It is thus that one day and the next are welded together, that one night's dying becomes tomorrow's birth. I, who do not sleep, can tell you this.

RALPH WALDO EMERSON
1803–1882

The popular image of Emerson today is one he would be the first to disown: the lofty Sage of Concord, the misty transcendentalist, far removed from earthly flesh and blood. Certain traits in Emerson did encourage such fantasies. His thinking could be muddled, his sentiments rarefied, his optimism, especially for the twentieth-century reader, unbearable. But in the long run, he kept close to reality; it was always there, like the wood to be gathered from his woodlot or the blueberries along the cowpath. When many of his Concord literary friends were planning a new Utopia, Brook Farm, Emerson "sat aloof," for his sense of the practical was stronger than theirs. Stronger than theirs, too, was his taste for robust talk. He liked the "language of the street," words that would "bleed" if cut; and although he phrased his essays and lectures with due decorum, it is an undercurrent of these "vascular," concrete terms that gives his writing much of its force. Force comes as well from his down-to-earth wit, often as biting as Mark Twain's, whose piece of foolery called "Political Economy" (pages 60-65), echoes the title of Emerson's "Politics," printed below. And the final source of Emerson's power, as a reading of "Politics" will show, is his unassailable moral strength, as granite as his New England hills. Mystic Emerson may sometimes seem, but a common-sense Yankee he certainly was—and if the two images do not coincide, why, then, as Emerson wrote in his *Journal:* "Damn Consistency!"

Politics

Gold and iron are good
To buy iron and gold;
All earth's fleece and food
For their like are sold.
Boded Merlin wise,

Proved Napoleon great,—
Nor kind nor coinage buys
Aught above its rate.
Fear, Craft and Avarice
Cannot rear a State.
Out of dust to build
What is more than dust,—
Walls Amphion piled
Phœbus stablish must.
When the Muses nine
With the Virtues meet,
Find to their design
An Atlantic seat,
By green orchard boughs
Fended from the heat,
Where the statesman ploughs
Furrow for the wheat;
When the Church is social worth,
When the state-house is the hearth,
Then the perfect State is come,
The republican at home.

In dealing with the State we ought to remember that its institutions are not aboriginal, though they existed before we were born; that they are not superior to the citizen; that every one of them was once the act of a single man; every law and usage was a man's expedient to meet a particular case; that they all are imitable, all alterable; we may make as good, we may make better. Society is an illusion to the young citizen. It lies before him in rigid repose, with certain names, men and institutions rooted like oak-trees to the centre, round which all arrange themselves the best they can. But the old statesman knows that society is fluid; there are no such roots and centres, but any particle may suddenly become the centre of the movement and compel the system to gyrate round it; as every man of strong will, like Pisistratus or Cromwell, does for a time, and every man of truth, like Plato or Paul, does forever. But politics rest on necessary foundations, and cannot be treated with levity. Republics abound in young civilians who believe that the laws make the city, that grave modifications of the policy and modes of living and employments of the population, that commerce, education and religion may be voted in or out; and that any measure, though it were absurd, may be imposed on a people if only you can get sufficient voices to make it a law. But the wise know that foolish legislation is a rope of sand which perishes in the twisting; that the State must follow and not lead the character and progress of the citizen; the strongest usurper is quickly got rid of; and they only who build on Ideas, build for eternity; and that the form of government which prevails is the expression of what cultivation exists in the population which permits it. The law is only a memorandum. We are superstitious, and esteem the statute somewhat: so much life as it has in the character of living men is its force. The statute stands there to say, Yesterday we agreed so and so, but how feel ye this article to-day? Our statute is a currency which we stamp with our own portrait: it soon becomes unrecognizable, and in process of time will return to the mint. Nature is not democratic, nor limited-monarchical, but despotic, and will not be fooled or abated of any jot of her authority by the pertest of her sons; and as fast as the public mind is opened to more intelligence, the code is seen to be brute and stammering. It speaks not articulately, and must be made to. Meantime the education of the general mind never stops. The reveries of the true and simple are prophetic. What the tender poetic youth dreams, and prays, and paints to-day, but shuns the ridicule of saying aloud, shall presently be the resolutions of public bodies; then shall be carried as grievance and bill of rights through conflict and war, and then shall be triumphant law and establishment for a hundred years, until it gives place in turn to new prayers and pictures. The history of the State sketches in coarse outline the progress of thought, and follows at a distance the delicacy of culture and of aspiration.

The theory of politics which has possessed the mind of men, and which they have expressed the best they could in their laws and in their revolutions, considers persons and property as the two objects for whose protection government exists. Of persons, all have equal rights in virtue of being identical in nature. This interest of course with its whole power demands a democracy. While the rights of all as persons are equal, in virtue of their access to reason, their rights in property are very unequal. One man owns his clothes, and another owns a county. This accident, depending primarily on the skill and virtue of the parties, of which there is every degree, and secondarily on patrimony, falls unequally, and its rights of course are unequal. Personal rights, universally the same, demand a government framed on the ratio of the census; property demands a government framed on the ratio of owners and of owning. Laban, who has flocks and herds, wishes them looked after by an officer on the frontiers, lest the Midianites shall drive them off; and pays a tax to that end. Jacob has no flocks or herds and no fear of the Midianites, and pays no tax to the officer. It seemed fit that Laban and Jacob should have equal rights to elect the officer who is to defend their persons, but that Laban and not Jacob should elect the officer who is to guard the sheep and cattle. And if question arise whether additional officers or watch-towers should be provided, must not Laban and Isaac, and those who must sell part of their herds to buy protection for the rest, judge better of this, and with more right, than Jacob, who, because he is a youth and a traveller, eats their bread and not his own?

In the earliest society the proprietors made their own wealth, and so long as it comes to the owners in the direct way, no other opinion would arise in any equitable community than that property should make the law for property, and persons the law for persons.

But property passes through donation or inheritance to those who do not create it. Gift, in one case, makes it as really the new owner's, as labor made it the first owner's: in the other case, of patrimony, the law makes an ownership which will be valid in each man's view according to the estimate which he sets on the public tranquillity.

It was not, however, found easy to embody the readily admitted principle that property should make law for property, and persons for persons; since persons and property mixed themselves in every transaction. At last it seemed settled that the rightful distinction was that the proprietors should have more elective franchise than non-proprietors, on the Spartan principle of "calling that which is just, equal; not that which is equal, just."

That principle no longer looks so self-evident as it appeared in former times, partly because doubts have arisen whether too much weight had not been allowed in the laws to property, and such a structure given to our usages as allowed the rich to encroach on the poor, and to keep them poor; but mainly because there is an instinctive sense, however obscure and yet inarticulate, that the whole constitution of property, on its present tenures, is injurious, and its influence on persons deteriorating and degrading; that truly the only interest for the consideration of the State is persons; that property will always follow persons; that the highest end of government is the culture of men; and that if men can be educated, the institutions will share their improvement and the moral sentiment will write the law of the land.

If it be not easy to settle the equity of this question, the peril is less when we take note of our natural defences. We are kept by better guards than the vigilance of such magistrates as we commonly elect. Society always consists in greatest part of young and foolish persons. The old, who have seen through the hypocrisy of courts and statesmen, die and leave no wisdom to their sons. They believe their own newspaper, as their fathers did at their age. With such an ignorant and deceivable majority, States would soon run to ruin, but that there are limitations beyond which the folly and ambition of governors cannot go. Things have their laws, as well as men; and things refuse to be trifled with. Property will be protected. Corn will not grow unless it is planted and manured; but the farmer will not plant or hoe it unless the chances are a hundred to one that he will cut and harvest it. Under any forms, persons and property must and will have their just sway. They exert their power, as steadily as matter its attraction. Cover up a pound of earth never so cunningly, divide and subdivide it; melt it to liquid, convert it to gas; it will always weigh a pound; it will always attract and resist other matter by the full virtue of one pound weight:—and the attributes of a person, his wit and his moral energy, will exercise, under any law or extinguishing tyranny, their proper force,—if not overtly, then covertly; if not for the law, then against it; if not wholesomely, then poisonously; with right, or by might.

The boundaries of personal influence it is impossible to fix, as persons are organs of moral or supernatural force. Under the dominion of an idea which possesses the minds of multitudes, as civil freedom, or the religious sentiment, the powers of persons are no longer subjects of calculation. A nation of men unanimously bent on freedom or conquest can easily confound the arithmetic of statists, and achieve extravagant actions out of all proportion to their means; as the Greeks, the Saracens, the Swiss, the Americans, and the French have done.

In like manner to every particle of property belongs its own attraction. A cent is the representative of a certain quantity of corn or other commodity. Its value is in the necessities of the animal man. It is so much warmth, so much bread, so much water, so much land. The law may do what it will with the owner of property; its just power will still attach to the cent. The law may in a mad freak say that all shall have power except the owners of property; they shall have no vote. Nevertheless, by a higher law, the property will, year after year, write every statute that respects property. The non-proprietor will be the scribe of the proprietor. What the owners wish to do, the whole power of property will do, either through the law or else in defiance of it. Of course I speak of all the property, not merely of the great estates. When the rich are outvoted, as frequently happens, it is the joint treasury of the poor which exceeds their accumulations. Every man owns something, if it is only a cow, or a wheelbarrow, or his arms, and so has that property to dispose of.

The same necessity which secures the rights of person and property against the malignity or folly of the magistrate, determines the form and methods of governing, which are proper to each nation and to its habit of thought, and nowise transferable to other states of society. In this country we are very vain of our political institutions, which are singular in this, that they sprung, within the memory of living men, from the character and condition of the people, which they still express with sufficient fidelity,—and we ostentatiously prefer them to any other in history. They are not better, but only fitter for us. We may be wise in asserting the advantage in modern times of the democratic form, but to other states of society, in which religion consecrated the monarchical, that and not this was expedient. Democracy is better for us, because the religious sentiment of the present time accords better with it. Born democrats, we are nowise qualified to judge of monarchy, which, to our fathers living in the monarchical idea, was also relatively right. But our institutions, though in coincidence with the spirit of the age, have not any exemption from the practical defects which have discredited other forms. Every actual State is corrupt. Good men must not obey the laws too well. What satire on government can equal the severity of censure conveyed in the word *politic,* which now for ages has signified *cunning,* intimating that the State is a trick?

The same benign necessity and the same practical abuse appear in the parties, into which each State divides itself, of opponents and defenders of the administration of the government. Parties are also founded on instincts, and have better guides to their own humble aims than the sagacity of their leaders. They have nothing perverse in their origin, but rudely mark some real and lasting relation. We might as wisely reprove the east wind or the frost, as a political party, whose members, for the most part, could give no account of their position, but stand for the defence of those interests in which they find themselves. Our quarrel with them begins when they quit this deep natural ground at the bidding of some leader, and obeying personal considerations, throw themselves into the maintenance and defence of points nowise belonging to their system. A party is perpetually corrupted by personality. Whilst we absolve the association from dishonesty, we cannot extend the same charity to their leaders. They reap the rewards of the docility and zeal of the masses which they direct. Ordinarily our parties are parties of circumstance, and not of principle; as the planting interest in conflict with the commercial; the party of capitalists and that of operatives: parties which are identical in their moral character, and which can easily change ground with each other in the support of many of their measures. Parties of principle, as, religious sects, or the party of free-trade, of universal suffrage, of abolition of slavery, of abolition of capital punishment, degenerate into personalities, or would inspire enthusiasm. The vice of our leading parties in this country (which may be cited as a fair specimen of these societies of opinion) is that they do not plant themselves on the deep and necessary grounds to which they are respectively entitled, but lash themselves to fury in the carrying of some local and momentary measure, nowise useful to the commonwealth. Of the two great parties which at this hour almost share the nation between them, I should say that one has the best cause, and the other contains the best men. The philosopher, the poet, or the religious man, will of course wish to cast his vote with the democrat, for free-trade, for wide suffrage, for the abolition of legal cruelties in the penal code, and for facilitating in every manner the access of the young and the poor to the sources of wealth and power. But he can rarely accept the persons whom the so-called popular party propose to him as representatives of these liberalities. They have not at heart the ends which give to the name of democracy what hope and virtue are in it. The spirit of our American radicalism is destructive and aimless: it is not loving; it has no ulterior and divine ends, but is destructive only out of hatred and selfishness. On the other side, the conservative party, composed of the most moderate, able and cultivated part of the population, is timid, and merely defensive of property. It vindicates no right, it aspires to no real good, it brands no crime, it proposes no generous policy; it does not build, nor write, nor cherish the arts, nor foster religion, nor establish schools, nor encourage science, nor emancipate the slave, nor befriend the poor, or the Indian, or the immigrant. From neither party, when in power, has the world any benefit to expect in science, art, or humanity, at all commensurate with the resources of the nation.

I do not for these defects despair of our republic. We are not at the mercy of any waves of chance. In the strife of ferocious parties, human nature always finds itself cherished; as the children of the convicts at Botany Bay are found to have as healthy a moral sentiment as other children. Citizens of feudal states are alarmed at our democratic institutions lapsing into anarchy, and the older and more cautious among ourselves are learning from Europeans to look with some terror at our turbulent freedom. It is said that in our license of construing the Constitution, and in the despotism of public opinion, we have no anchor; and one foreign observer thinks he has found the safeguard in the sanctity of Marriage among us; and another thinks he has found it in our Calvinism. Fisher Ames expressed the popular security more wisely, when he compared a monarchy and a republic, saying that a monarchy is a merchantman, which sails well, but will sometimes strike on a rock and go to the bottom; whilst a republic is a raft, which would never sink, but then your feet are always in water. No forms can have any dangerous importance whilst we are befriended by the laws of things. It makes no difference how many tons' weight of atmosphere presses on our heads, so long as the same pressure resists it within the lungs. Augment the mass a thousand fold, it cannot begin to crush us, as long as reaction is equal to action. The fact of two poles, of two forces, centripetal and centrifugal, is universal, and each force by its own activity develops the other. Wild liberty develops iron conscience. Want of liberty, by strengthening law and decorum, stupefies conscience. "Lynch-law" prevails only where there is greater hardihood and self-subsistency in the leaders. A mob cannot be a permanency; everybody's interest requires that it should not exist, and only justice satisfies all.

We must trust infinitely to the beneficent necessity which shines through all laws. Human nature expresses itself in them as characteristically as in statues, or songs, or railroads; and an abstract of the codes of nations would be a transcript of the common conscience. Governments have their origin in the moral identity of men. Reason for one is seen to be reason for another, and for every other. There is a middle measure which satisfies all parties, be they never so many or so resolute for their own. Every man finds a sanction for his simplest claims and deeds, in decisions of his own mind, which he calls Truth and Holiness. In these decisions all the citizens find a perfect agreement, and only in these; not in what is good to eat, good to wear, good use of time, or what amount of land or of public aid each is entitled to claim. This truth and justice men presently endeavor to make application of to the measuring of land, the apportionment of service, the protection of life and property. Their first endeavors, no doubt, are very awkward. Yet absolute right is the first governor; or, every government is an impure theocracy. The idea after which each community is aiming to make and mend its law, is the will of the wise man. The wise man it cannot find in nature, and it makes awkward but earnest efforts to secure his government by contrivance; as by causing the entire people to give their voices on every measure; or by a double choice to get the representation of the whole; or by a selection of the best citizens; or to secure the advantages of efficiency and internal peace by confiding the government to one, who may himself select his agents. All forms of government symbolize an immortal government, common to all dynasties and independent of numbers, perfect where two men exist, perfect where there is only one man.

Every man's nature is a sufficient advertisement to him of the character of his fellows. My right and my wrong is their right and their wrong. Whilst I do what is fit for me, and abstain from what is unfit, my neighbor and I shall often agree in our means, and work together for a time to one end. But whenever I find my dominion over myself not sufficient for me, and undertake the direction of him also, I overstep the truth, and come into false relations to him. I may have so much more skill or strength than he that he cannot express adequately his sense of wrong, but it is a lie, and hurts like a lie both him and me. Love and nature cannot maintain the assumption; it must be executed by a practical lie, namely by force. This undertaking for another is the blunder which stands in colossal ugliness in the governments of the world. It is the same thing in numbers, as in a pair, only not quite so intelligible. I can see well enough a great difference between my setting myself down to a self-control, and my going to make somebody else act after my views; but when a quarter of the human race assume to tell me what I must do, I may be too much disturbed by the circumstances to see so clearly the absurdity of their command. Therefore all public ends look vague and quixotic beside private ones. For any laws but those which men make for themselves are laughable. If I put myself in the place of my child, and we stand in one thought and see that things are thus or thus, that perception is law for him and me. We are both there, both act. But if, without carrying him into the thought, I look over into his plot, and, guessing how it is with him, ordain this or that, he will never obey me. This is the history of governments,—one man does something which is to bind another. A man who cannot be acquainted with me, taxes me; looking from afar at me ordains that a part of my labor shall go to this or that whimsical end,—not as I, but as he happens to fancy. Behold the consequence. Of all debts men are least willing to pay the taxes. What a satire is this on government! Everywhere they think they get their money's worth, except for these.

Hence the less government we have the better,—the fewer laws, and the less confided power. The antidote to this abuse of formal government is the influence of private character, the growth of the Individual; the appearance of the principal to supersede the proxy; the appearance of the wise man; of whom the existing government is, it must be owned, but a shabby imitation. That which all things tend to educe; which freedom, cultivation, intercourse, revolutions, go to form and deliver, is character; that is the end of Nature, to reach unto this coronation of her king. To educate the wise man the State exists, and with the appearance of the wise man the State expires. The appearance of character makes the State unnecessary. The wise man is the State. He needs no army, fort, or navy,—he loves men too well; no bribe, or feast, or palace, to draw friends to him; no vantage ground, no favorable circumstance. He needs no library, for he has not done thinking; no church, for he is a prophet; no statute-book, for he has the lawgiver; no money, for he is value; no road, for he is at home where he is; no experience, for the life of the creator shoots through him, and looks from his eyes. He has no personal friends, for he who has the spell to draw the prayer and the piety of all men unto him needs not husband and educate a few to share with him a select and poetic life. His relation to men is angelic; his memory is myrrh to them; his presence, frankincense and flowers.

We think our civilization near its meridian, but we are yet only at the cock-crowing and the morning star. In our barbarous society the influence of character is in its infancy. As a political power, as the rightful lord who is to tumble all rulers from their chairs, its presence is hardly yet suspected. Malthus and Ricardo quite omit it; the Annual Register is silent; in the Conversations' Lexicon it is not set down; the President's Message, the Queen's Speech, have not mentioned it; and yet it is never nothing. Every thought which genius and piety throw into the world, alters the world. The gladiators in the lists of power feel, through all their frocks of force and simulation, the presence of worth. I think the very strife of trade and ambition is confession of this divinity; and successes in those fields are the poor amends, the fig-leaf with which the shamed soul attempts to hide its nakedness. I find the like unwilling homage in all quarters. It is because we know how much is due from us that we are impatient to show some petty talent as a substitute for worth. We are haunted by a conscience of this right to grandeur of character, and are false to it. But each of us has some talent, can do somewhat useful, or graceful, or formidable, or amusing, or lucrative. That we do, as an apology to others and to ourselves for not reaching the mark of a good and equal life. But it does not satisfy *us,* whilst we thrust it on the notice of our companions. It may throw dust in their eyes, but does not smooth our own brow, or give us the tranquillity of the strong when we walk abroad. We do penance as we go. Our talent is a sort of expiation, and we are constrained to reflect on our splendid moment with a certain humiliation, as somewhat too fine, and not as one act of many acts, a fair expression of our permanent energy. Most persons of ability meet in society with a kind of tacit appeal. Each seems to say, "I am not all here." Senators and presidents have climbed so high with pain enough, not because they think the place specially agreeable, but as an apology for real worth, and to vindicate their manhood in our eyes. This conspicuous chair is their compensation to themselves for being of a poor, cold, hard nature. They must do what they can. Like one class of forest animals, they have nothing but a prehensile tail; climb they must, or crawl. If a man found himself so rich-natured that he could enter into strict relations with the best persons and make life serene around him by the dignity and sweetness of his behavior, could he afford to circumvent the favor of the caucus and the press, and covet relations so hollow and pompous as those of a politician? Surely nobody would be a charlatan who could afford to be sincere.

The tendencies of the times favor the idea of self-government, and leave the individual, for all code, to the rewards and penalties of his own constitution; which work with more energy than we believe whilst we depend on artificial restraints. The movement in this direction has been very marked in modern history. Much has been blind and discreditable, but the nature of the revolution is not affected by the vices of the revolters; for this is a purely moral force. It was never adopted by any party in history, neither can be. It separates the individual from all party, and unites him at the same time to the race. It promises a recognition of higher rights than those of personal freedom, or the security of property. A man has a right to be employed, to be trusted, to be loved, to be revered. The power of love, as the basis of a State, has never been tried. We must not imagine that all things are lapsing into confusion if every tender protestant be not compelled to bear his part in certain social conventions; nor doubt that roads can be built, letters carried, and the fruit of labor secured, when the government of force is at an end. Are our methods now so excellent that all competition is hopeless? could not a nation of friends even devise better ways? On the other hand, let not the most conservative and timid fear anything from a premature surrender of the bayonet and the system of force. For, according to the order of nature, which is quite superior to our will, it stands thus; there will always be a government of force where men are selfish; and when they are pure enough to abjure the code of force they will be wise enough to see how these public ends of the post-office, of the highway, of commerce and the exchange of property, of museums and libraries, of institutions of art and science can be answered.

We live in a very low state of the world, and pay unwilling tribute to governments founded on force. There is not, among the most religious and instructed men of the most religious and civil nations, a reliance on the moral sentiment and a sufficient belief in the unity of things, to persuade them that society can be maintained without artificial restraints, as well as the solar system; or that the private citizen might be reasonable and a good neighbor, without the hint of a jail or a confiscation. What is strange too, there never was in any man sufficient faith in the power of rectitude to inspire him with the broad design of renovating the State on the principle of right and love. All those who have pretended this design have been partial reformers, and have admitted in some manner the supremacy of the bad State. I do not call to mind a single human being who has steadily denied the authority of the laws, on the simple ground of his own moral nature. Such designs, full of genius and full of faith as they are, are not entertained except avowedly as air-pictures. If the individual who exhibits them dare to think them practicable, he disgusts scholars and churchmen; and men of talent and women of superior sentiments cannot hide their contempt. Not the less does nature continue to fill the heart of youth with suggestions of this enthusiasm, and there are now men,—if indeed I can speak in the plural number,—more exactly, I will say, I have just been conversing with one man, to whom no weight of adverse experience will make it for a moment appear impossible that thousands of human beings might exercise towards each other the grandest and simplest sentiments, as well as a knot of friends, or a pair of lovers.

THOMAS FULLER
1608–1661

In the years 1645 to 1660, Thomas Fuller published three books: *Good Thoughts in Bad Times, Good Thoughts in Worse Times,* and *Mixt Contemplations in Better Times.* The bad and worse times were England's Civil War, when Fuller, an Anglican divine who remained loyal to church and king, naturally found life difficult. Yet no difficulties could keep him from having "Good Thoughts." On the other hand, when the Restoration brought "Better Times," Fuller was moved only to "Mixt Contemplations," not to unseemly glee. This happy moderation, this just and reasonable balance, is typical of Thomas Fuller in all his works. In *The Holy State,* for example, from which the sketch of "The Good Schoolmaster" is taken, there is all the wit and the verbal juggling commonly found in the popular seventeenth-century "character" books. But there is also charity, understanding, and the warmth of Fuller's own personality. He remains still what he was to Charles Lamb: a "dear, fine, silly old angel."

The Good Schoolmaster

There is scarce any profession in the commonwealth more necessary which is so slightly performed. The reasons whereof I conceive to be these: first, young scholars make this calling their refuge, yea, perchance, before they have taken any degree in the university, commence schoolmasters in the country, as if nothing else were required to set up this profession but only a rod and a ferula. Secondly, others who are able use it only as a passage to better preferment, to patch the rents in their present fortune till they can provide a new one, and betake themselves to some more gainful calling. Thirdly, they are disheartened from doing their best with the miserable reward which in some places they receive, being masters to the children and slaves to their parents. Fourthly, being grown rich, they grow negligent, and scorn to touch the school but by the proxy of an usher. But see how well our schoolmaster behaves himself.

His genius inclines him with delight to his profession. Some men had as lief be schoolboys as schoolmasters, to be tied to the school, as Cooper's "Dictionary" and Scapula's "Lexicon" are chained to the desks therein; and though great scholars, and skillful in other arts, are bunglers in this: but God of His goodness hath fitted several men for several callings, that the necessity of Church and State in all conditions may be provided for. So that he who beholds the fabric thereof may say, "God hewed out this stone, and appointed it to lie in this very place, for it would fit none other so well, and here it doth most excellent." And thus God mouldeth some for a schoolmaster's life, undertaking it with desire and delight, and discharging it with dexterity and happy success.

He studieth his scholars' natures as carefully as they their books, and ranks their dispositions into several forms. And though it may seem difficult for him in a great school to descend to all particulars, yet experienced schoolmasters may quickly make a grammar of boys' natures, and reduce them all, saving some few exceptions, to these general rules:

1. Those that are ingenious and industrious. The conjunction of two such planets in a youth presages much good unto him. To such a lad a frown may be a whipping, and a whipping a death; yea, where their master whips them once, shame whips them all the week after. Such natures he useth with all gentleness.

2. Those that are ingenious and idle. These think, with the hare in the fable, that running with snails (so they count the rest of their schoolfellows) they shall come soon enough to the post, though sleeping a good while before their starting. Oh, a good rod would finely take them napping.

3. Those that are dull and diligent. Wines, the stronger they be, the more lees they have when they are new. Many boys are muddy-headed till they be clarified with age, and such afterwards prove the best. Bristol diamonds are both bright and squared and pointed by nature, and yet are soft and worthless; whereas orient ones in India are rough and rugged naturally. Hard, rugged, and dull natures of youth acquit themselves afterwards the jewels of the country, and therefore their dullness at first is to be borne with, if they be diligent. That schoolmaster deserves to be beaten himself who beats nature in a boy for a fault. And I question whether all the whipping in

the world can make their parts, which are naturally sluggish, rise one minute before the hour nature hath appointed.

4. Those that are invincibly dull and negligent also. Correction may reform the latter, not amend the former. All the whetting in the world can never set a razor's edge on that which hath no steel in it. Such boys he consigneth over to other professions. Shipwrights and boatmakers will choose those crooked pieces of timber which other carpenters refuse. Those may make excellent merchants and mechanics who will not serve for scholars.

He is able, diligent, and methodical in his teaching; not leading them rather in a circle than forwards. He minces his precepts for children to swallow, hanging clogs on the nimbleness of his own soul, that his scholars may go along with him.

He is and will be known to be an absolute monarch in his school. If cockering mothers proffer him money to purchase their sons an exemption from his rod (to live as it were in a peculiar, out of their master's jurisdiction), with disdain he refuseth it, and scorns the late custom, in some places, of commuting whipping into money, and ransoming boys from the rod at a set price. If he hath a stubborn youth, correction-proof, he debaseth not his authority by contesting with him, but fairly, if he can, puts him away before his obstinacy hath affected others.

He is moderate in inflicting deserved correction. Many a school master better answereth the name παιδοτρίβης than παιδαγωγός, rather tearing his scholars' flesh with whipping than giving them good education. No wonder if his scholars hate the muses, being presented unto them in the shapes of fiends and furies. Junius complains *de insolenti carnificina* of his school master, by whom *conscindebatur flagris septies aut octies in dies singulos.* Yea, hear the lamentable verses of poor Tusser in his own life:

> "From Paul's I went, to Eton sent,
> To learn straightways the Latin phrase,
> Where fifty-three stripes, given to me
>   At once I had.

> "For fault but small, or none at all,
> It came to pass thus beat I was;
> See Udall, see, the mercy of thee,
>   To me, poor lad."

Such an Orbilius mars more scholars than he makes: their tyranny hath caused many tongues to stammer, which spake plain by nature, and whose stuttering at first was nothing else but fears quavering on their speech at their master's presence; and whose mauling them about their heads hath dulled those who, in quickness, exceeded their master.

He makes his school free to him who sues to him in forma pauperis. And surely learning is the greatest alms that can be given. But he is a beast who, because the poor scholar cannot pay him his wages, pays the scholar in his whipping. Rather are diligent lads to be encouraged with all excitements to learning. This minds me of what I have heard concerning Mr. Bust, that worthy late schoolmaster of Eton, who would never suffer any wandering begging scholar (such as justly the statute hath ranked in the forefront of rogues) to come into his school, but would thrust him out with earnestness (however privately charitable unto him), lest his schoolboys should be disheartened from their books by seeing some scholars, after their studying in the university, preferred to beggary.

He spoils not a good school to make thereof a bad college, therein to teach his scholars logic. For, besides that logic may have an action to trespass against grammar for encroaching on her liberties, syllogisms are solecisms taught in the school, and oftentimes they are forced afterwards in the university to unlearn the fumbling skill they had before.

Out of his school he is no whit pedantical in carriage or discourse; contenting himself to be rich in Latin, though he doth not jingle with it in every company wherein he comes.

To conclude, let this amongst other motives make schoolmasters careful in their place, that the eminencies of their scholars have commended the memories of their schoolmasters to posterity, who otherwise in obscurity had altogether been forgotten. Who had ever heard of R. Bond, in Lancashire, but for the breeding of learned Ascham, his scholar? or of Hartgrave, in Brundly school, in the same county, but because he was the first did teach worthy Dr. Whitaker? Nor do I honour the memory of Mulcaster for anything so much as for his scholar, that gulf of learning, Bishop Andrews. This made the Athenians, the day before the great feasts of Theseus, their founder, to sacrifice a ram to the memory of Conidas, his schoolmaster that first instructed him.

OLIVER GOLDSMITH
1730–1774

In a friendly contest of mock epitaphs among the members of a literary club gathered at the St. James's Coffee-house, David Garrick declaimed:

> "Here lies Nolly Goldsmith, for shortness called Noll,
> Who wrote like an angel, but talked like poor Poll."

How Goldsmith talked, no one now can tell; but about his writing we know that Garrick was right. Goldsmith wrote with the instinctive wisdom, the unassuming ease, the natural charm we would expect from an angel turned essayist, poet, and playwright. And with infinitely more humor. These are the qualities he displays in this essay, "On the Education of Youth," plus an angelic clairvoyance about certain problems in education we still face today.

On the Education of Youth

N.B. This treatise was published before Rousseau's *Emilius*: if there be a similitude in any one instance, it is hoped the author of the present essay will not be deemed a plagiarist.

As few subjects are more interesting to society, so few have been more frequently written upon, than the education of youth. Yet it is a little surprising, that it has been treated almost by all in a declamatory manner. They have insisted largely on the advantages that result from it, both to individuals and to society; and have expatiated in the praise of what none have ever been so hardy as to call in question.

Instead of giving us fine but empty harangues upon this subject, instead of indulging each his particular and whimsical systems, it had been much better if the writers on this subject had treated it in a more scientific manner, repressed all the sallies of imagination, and given us the result of their observations with didactic simplicity. Upon this subject, the smallest errors are of the most dangerous consequence; and the author should venture the imputation of stupidity upon a topic, where his slightest deviations may tend to injure posterity. However, such are the whimsical and erroneous productions written upon this subject. Their authors have studied to be uncommon, not to be just; and, at present, we want a treatise upon education, not to tell us anything new, but to explode the errors which have been introduced by the admirers of novelty. It is in this manner books become numerous; a desire of novelty produces a book, and other books are required to destroy this production.

The manner in which our youth of London are at present educated, is, some in free-schools in the city, but the far greater number in boarding-schools about town. The parent justly consults the health of his child, and finds an education in the country tends to promote this, much more than a continuance in town. Thus far he is right: if there were a possibility of having even our free-schools kept a little out of town, it would certainly conduce to the health and vigour of, perhaps, the mind as well as the body. It may be thought whimsical, but it is truth; I have found, by experience, that they who have spent all their lives in cities, contract not only an effeminacy of habit, but even of thinking.

But when I have said that the boarding-schools are preferable to free-schools, as being in the country, this is certainly the only advantage I can allow them, otherwise it is impossible to conceive the ignorance of those who take upon them the important trust of education. Is any man unfit for any of the professions, he finds his last resource in setting up a school. Do any become bankrupts in trade, they still set up a boarding-school, and drive a trade this way, when all others fail: nay, I have been told of butchers and barbers who have turned schoolmasters; and, more surprising still, made fortunes in their new profession.

Could we think ourselves in a country of civilized people —could it be conceived that we have a regard for posterity, when such persons are permitted to take the charge of the morals, genius, and health of those dear little pledges, who may one day be the guardians of the liberties of Europe, and who may serve as the honour and bulwark of their aged parents? The care of our children, is it below the state? Is it fit to indulge the caprice of the ignorant with the disposal of their children in this particular? For the state to take the charge of all its children, as in Persia or Sparta, might at present be inconvenient; but surely, with great ease, it might cast an eye to their instructors. Of all professions in society, I do not know a more useful or a more honourable one than a schoolmaster; at the same time that I do not see any more generally despised, or men whose talents are so ill rewarded.

Were the salaries of schoolmasters to be augmented from a diminution of useless sinecures, how might it turn to the advantage of this people; a people whom, without flattery, I may, in other respects, term the wisest and greatest upon earth. But while I would reward the deserving, I would dismiss those utterly unqualified for their employment: in short, I would make the business of a schoolmaster every way more respectable, by increasing their salaries, and admitting only men of proper abilities.

It is true, we have already schoolmasters appointed, and they have small salaries; but where at present there is only one schoolmaster appointed, there should at least be two; and wherever the salary is at present twenty pounds, it should be augmented to an hundred. Do we give immoderate benefices to our own instructors, and shall we deny even subsistence to those who instruct our children? Every member of society should be paid in proportion as he is necessary; and I will be bold enough to say, that schoolmasters in a state are more necessary than clergymen, as children stand in more need of instruction than their parents.

But instead of this, as I have already observed, we send them to board in the country to the most ignorant set of men that can be imagined; and, lest the ignorance of the master be not sufficient, the child is generally consigned to the usher. This is commonly some poor needy animal, little superior to a footman either in learning or spirit, invited to his place by an advertisement, and kept there merely from his being of a complying disposition, and making the children fond of him. 'You give your child to be educated to a slave,' says a philosopher to a rich man; 'instead of one slave, you will then have two.'

It were well, however, if parents, upon fixing their children in one of these houses, would examine the abilities of the usher, as well as the master; for, whatever they are told to the contrary, the usher is generally the person most employed in their education. If, then, a gentleman, upon putting out his son to one of these houses, sees the usher disregarded by the master, he may depend upon it, that he is equally disregarded by the boys: the truth is, in spite of all their endeavours to please, they are generally the laughing-stock of the school. Every trick is played upon the usher; the oddity of his manners, his dress, or his language, are a fund of eternal ridicule; the master himself, now and then, cannot avoid joining in the laugh; and the poor wretch, eternally resenting this ill usage, seems to live in a state of war with all the family. This is a very proper person, is it not, to give children a relish for learning? They must esteem learning very much, when they see its professors used with such ceremony. If the usher be despised, the father may be assured his child will never be properly instructed.

But let me suppose, that there are some schools without these inconveniences, where the masters and ushers are men of learning, reputation, and assiduity. If there are to be found such, they cannot be prized in a state sufficiently. A boy will learn more true wisdom in a public school in a year, than by a private education in five. It is not from masters, but from their equals, youth learn a knowledge of the world; the little tricks they play each other, the punishment that frequently attends the commission, is a just picture of the great world, and all the ways of men are practised in a public school in miniature. It is true, a child is early made acquainted with some vices in a school; but it is better to know these when a boy, than be first taught them when a man; for their novelty then may have irresistible charms.

In a public education boys early learn temperance; and if the parents and friends would give them less money upon their usual visits, it would be much to their advantage; since it may justly be said, that a great part of their disorders arise from surfeit,—*plus occidit gula quam gladius*. And now I am come to the article of health, it may not be amiss to observe, that Mr. Locke and some others have advised that children should be inured to cold, to fatigue, and hardship, from their youth; but Mr. Locke was but an indifferent physician. Habit, I grant, has great influence over our constitutions, but we have not precise ideas upon this subject.

We know, that among savages, and even among our peasants, there are found children born with such constitutions, that they cross rivers by swimming, endure cold, thirst, hunger, and want of sleep, to a surprising degree; that when they happen to fall sick, they are cured without the help of medicine, by nature alone. Such examples are adduced to persuade us to imitate their manner of education, and accustom ourselves betimes to support the same fatigues. But had these gentlemen considered first, how many lives are lost in this ascetic discipline; had they considered, that these savages and peasants are generally not so long-lived as those who have led a more indolent life; that the more laborious the life is, the less populous is the country: had they considered that what physicians call the *stamina vitae* by fatigue and labour become rigid, and thus anticipate old age: that the numbers who survive those rude trials, bear no proportion to those who die in the experiment; had these things been properly considered, they would not have thus extolled an education begun in fatigue and hardships. Peter the Great, willing to inure the children of his seamen to a life of hardship, ordered that they should only drink sea-water, but they unfortunately all died under the trial.

But while I would exclude all unnecessary labours, yet still I would recommend temperance in the highest degree. No luxurious dishes with high seasoning, nothing given children to force an appetite, as little sugared or salted provisions as possible, though ever so pleasing; but milk, morning and night, should be their constant food. This diet would make them more healthy than any of those slops that are usually cooked by the mistress of a boarding-school; besides, it corrects any consumptive habits, not infrequently found amongst the children of city parents.

As boys should be educated with temperance, so the first greatest lesson that should be taught them is, to admire frugality. It is by the exercise of this virtue alone, they can ever expect to be useful members of society. It is true, lectures continually repeated upon this subject, may make some boys, when they grow up, run into an extreme, and become misers; but it were well, had we more misers than we have among us. I know few characters more useful in society; for a man's having a larger or smaller share of money lying useless by him, no way injures the commonwealth; since, should every miser now exhaust his stores, this might make gold more plenty, but it would not increase the commodities or pleasures of life; they would still remain as they are at present: it matters not, therefore, whether men are misers or not, if they be only frugal, laborious, and fill the station they have chosen. If they deny themselves the necessaries of life, society is no way injured by their folly.

Instead, therefore, of romances, which praise young men of spirit, who go through a variety of adventures, and at last conclude a life of dissipation, folly, and extravagance, in riches and matrimony, there should be some men of wit employed to compose books that might equally interest the passions of our youth; where such an one might be praised for having resisted allurements when young and how he, at last, became Lord Mayor; how he was married to a lady of great sense, fortune, and beauty: to be as explicit as possible, the old story of Whittington, were his cat left out, might be more serviceable to the tender mind, than either *Tom Jones*, *Joseph Andrews*, or an hundred others, where frugality is the only good quality the hero is not possessed of. Were our schoolmasters, if any of them have sense enough to draw up such a work, thus employed, it would be much more serviceable to their pupils than all the grammars and dictionaries they may publish these ten years.

Children should early be instructed in the arts from which they may afterwards draw the greatest advantages. When the wonders of nature are never exposed to our view, we have no great desire to become acquainted with those parts of learning which pretend to account for the phenomena. One of the ancients complains, that as soon as young men have left school, and are obliged to converse in the world, they fancy themselves transported into a new region. 'Ut cum in forum venerint existiment se in alium terrarum orbem delatos.' We should early, therefore, instruct them in the experiments, if I may so express it, of knowledge, and leave to maturer age the accounting for the causes. But, instead of that, when boys begin natural philosophy in colleges, they have not the least curiosity for those parts of the science which are proposed for their instruction; they have never before seen the phenomena, and consequently have no curiosity to learn the reasons. Might natural philosophy, therefore, be made their pastime at school, by this means it would in college become their amusement.

In several of the machines now in use, there would be ample field both for instruction and amusement; the different sorts of the phosphorus, the artificial pyrites, magnetism, electricity, the experiments upon the rarefaction and weight of the air, and those upon elastic bodies, might employ their idle hours, and none should be called from play to see such experiments, but such as thought proper. At first then it would be sufficient if the instruments, and the effects of their combination, were only shown; the causes should be deferred to a maturer age, or to those times when natural curiosity prompts us to discover the wonders of nature. Man is placed in this world as a spectator; when he is tired of wondering at all the novelties about him, and not till then, does he desire to be made acquainted with the causes that create those wonders.

What I have observed with regard to natural philosophy, I would extend to every other science whatsoever. We should teach them as many of the facts as possible, and defer the causes until they seemed of themselves desirous of knowing them. A mind thus leaving school, stored with all the simple experiences of science, would be the fittest in the world for the college course; and though such a youth might not appear so bright, or so talkative, as those who had learned the real principles and causes of some of the sciences, yet he would make a wiser man, and would retain a more lasting passion for letters, than he who was early burdened with the disagreeable institution of cause and effect.

In history, such stories alone should be laid before them as might catch the imagination: instead of this, at present, they are too frequently obliged to toil through the four empires, as they are called, where their memories are burdened by a number of disgusting names, that destroy all their future relish for our best historians, who may be termed the truest teachers of wisdom.

Every species of flattery should be carefully avoided; a boy who happens to say a sprightly thing is generally applauded so much, that he sometimes continues a coxcomb all his life after. He is reputed a wit at fourteen, and becomes a blockhead at twenty. Nurses, footmen, and such, should therefore be driven away as much as possible. I was even going to add, that the mother herself should stifle her pleasure, or her vanity, when little master happens to say a good or a smart thing. Those modest lubberly boys who seem to want spirit, become at length more shining men; and at school generally go through their business with more ease to themselves, and more satisfaction to their instructors.

There has of late a gentleman appeared, who thinks the study of rhetoric essential to a perfect education. That bold male eloquence, which often, without pleasing, convinces, is generally destroyed by such an institution. Convincing eloquence is infinitely more serviceable to its possessor than the most florid harangue, or the most pathetic tones that can be imagined; and the man who is thoroughly convinced himself, who understands his subject, and the language he speaks in, will be more apt to silence opposition than he who studies the force of his periods, and fills our ears with sounds, while our minds are destitute of conviction.

It was reckoned the fault of the orators at the decline of the Roman empire, when they had been long instructed by rhetoricians, that their periods were so harmonious, that they could be sung as well as spoken. What a ridiculous figure must one of these gentlemen cut, thus measuring syllables, and weighing words, when he should plead the cause of his client! Two architects were once candidates for the building a certain temple at Athens: the first harangued the crowd very learnedly upon the different orders of architecture, and showed them in what manner the temple should be built; the other, who got up after him, only observed, that what his brother had spoken, he could do; and thus he at once gained his cause.

To teach men to be orators, is little less than to teach them to be poets; and, for my part, I should have too great a regard for my child, to wish him a manor only in a bookseller's shop.

Another passion which the present age is apt to run into, is to make children learn all things; the languages, the sciences, music, the exercises, and painting. Thus the child soon becomes a Talker in all, but a Master in none. He thus acquires a superficial fondness for everything, and only shows his ignorance when he attempts to exhibit his skill.

As I deliver my thoughts without method or connexion, so the reader must not be surprised to find me once more addressing schoolmasters on the present method of teaching the learned languages, which is commonly by literal translations. I would ask such, if they were to travel a journey, whether those parts of the road in which they found the greatest difficulties, would not be the most strongly remembered? Boys who, if I may continue the allusion, gallop through one of the ancients with the assistance of a translation, can have but a very slight acquaintance either with the author or his language. It is by the exercise of the mind alone, that a language is learned; but a literal translation, on the opposite page, leaves no exercise for the memory at all. The boy will not be at the fatigue of remembering, when his doubts are at once satisfied by a glance of the eye; whereas, were every word to be sought from a dictionary, the learner would attempt to remember them, to save himself the trouble of looking out for the future.

To continue in the same pedantic strain, of all the various grammars now taught in the schools about town, I would recommend only the old common one; I have forgot whether Lilly's, or an emendation of him. The others may be improvements; but such improvements seem, to me, only mere grammatical niceties, no way influencing the learner, but perhaps loading him with trifling subtleties, which, at a proper age, he must be at some pains to forget.

Whatever pains a master may take to make the learning of the languages agreeable to his pupil, he may depend upon it, it will be at first extremely unpleasant. The rudiments of every language, therefore, must be given as a task, not as an amusement. Attempting to deceive children into instruction of this kind, is only deceiving ourselves; and I know no passion capable of conquering a child's natural laziness, but fear. Solomon has said it before me; nor is there any more certain, though perhaps more disagreeable truth, than the proverb in verse, too well known to repeat on the present occasion. It is very probable that parents are told of some masters who never use the rod, and consequently are thought the properest instructors for their children; but, though tenderness is a requisite quality in an instructor, yet there is too often the truest tenderness in well-timed correction.

Some have justly observed, that all passion should be banished on this terrible occasion; but, I know not how, there is a frailty attending human nature, that few masters are able to keep their temper whilst they correct. I knew a good-natured man, who was sensible of his own weakness in this respect, and consequently had recourse to the following expedient to prevent his passions from being engaged, yet at the same time administer justice with impartiality. Whenever any of his pupils committed a fault, he summoned a jury of his peers, I mean of the boys of his own or the next classes to him: his accusers stood forth; he had liberty of pleading in his own defence; and one or two more had the liberty of pleading against him: when found guilty by the panel, he was consigned to the footman, who attended in the house, and had previous orders to punish, but with lenity. By this means the master took off the odium of punishment from himself; and the footman, between whom and the boys there could not be even the slightest intimacy, was placed in such a light as to be shunned by every boy in the school.

WILLIAM HAZLITT
1778–1830

That William Hazlitt should be represented in this collection by "The Pleasure of Hating" is peculiarly appropriate, for he was much hated in his time, and he hated in return. His was a healthy, righteous hate, however; he could not abide "meanness, spite, cowardice, want of feeling"; he lashed out at hypocrisy and despotism. He was still loyal to the principles of the French Revolution in an age of reaction against that Revolution, and his opinions accordingly were not popular. But popularity was not important to Hazlitt. "The love of life" for him was "the effect not of our enjoyments but of our passions." Whether he was hating or loving, attacking or resisting attack, did not matter; he was then living, and enjoying it. This turbulence and torment, reflected in his writing, led Virginia Woolf to deny Hazlitt a place in the first rank of essayists. Yet to other critics the same qualities seemed the source of his excellence. "He is himself in fact the very best," writes J. B. Priestley, a devoted admirer of Hazlitt; while Robert Louis Stevenson's saying is well known: "We are all of us fine fellows, but no one can write like William Hazlitt." Nor was Hazlitt dissatisfied with himself. On his deathbed, after a life of discomfort, abuse, and thwarted desires, he could still say, and say in earnest, "Well, I have had a happy life."

On the Pleasure of Hating

There is a spider crawling along the matted floor of the room where I sit (not the one which has been so well allegorised in the admirable *Lines to a Spider,* but another of the same edifying breed); he runs with heedless, hurried haste, he hobbles awkwardly towards me, he stops: he sees the giant shadow before him, and, at a loss whether to retreat or proceed, meditates his huge foe. But as I do not start up and seize upon the straggling caitiff, as he would upon a hapless fly within his toils, he takes heart, and ventures on, with mingled cunning, impudence, and fear. As he passes me, I lift up the matting to assist his escape, am glad to get rid of the unwelcome intruder, and shudder at the recollection after he is gone. A child, a woman, a clown, or a moralist a century ago, would have crushed the little reptile to death: my philosophy has got beyond that. I bear the creature no ill-will, but still I hate the very sight of it. The spirit of malevolence survives the practical exertion of it. We learn to curb our will and keep our overt actions within the bounds of humanity, long before we can subdue our sentiments and imaginations to the same mild tone. We give up the external demonstration, the *brute* violence, but cannot part with the essence or principle of hostility. We do not tread upon the poor little animal in question (that seems barbarous and pitiful!) but we regard it with a sort of mystic horror and superstitious loathing. It will ask another hundred years of fine writing and hard thinking to cure us of the prejudice, and make us feel towards this ill-omened tribe with something of "the milk of human kindness," instead of their own shyness and venom.

Nature seems (the more we look into it) made up of antipathies: without something to hate, we should lose the very spring of thought and action. Life would turn to a stagnant pool, were it not ruffled by the jarring interests, the unruly passions, of men. The white streak in our own fortunes is brightened (or just rendered visible) by making all around it as dark as possible; so the rainbow paints its form upon the cloud. Is it pride? Is it envy? Is it the force of contrast? Is it weakness or malice? But so it is, that there is a secret affinity, *a hankering* after evil in the human mind, and that it takes a perverse, but a fortunate delight in mischief, since it is a never-failing source of satisfaction. Pure good soon grows insipid, wants variety and spirit. Pain is a bitter-sweet, which never surfeits. Love turns, with a little indulgence, to indifference or disgust: hatred alone is immortal. Do we not see this principle at work everywhere? Animals torment and worry one another without mercy: children kill flies for sport: every one reads the accidents and offences in a newspaper, as the cream of the jest: a whole town runs to be present at a fire, and the spectator by no means exults to see it extinguished. It is better to have it so, but it diminishes the interest; and our feelings take part with our passions rather than with our understandings. Men assemble in crowds, with eager enthusiasm, to witness a tragedy: but if there were an execution going forward in the next street, as Mr. Burke observes, the theater would be left empty. A strange cur in a village, an idiot, a crazy woman, are set upon and baited by the whole community. Public nuisances are in the nature of public benefits. How long did the Pope, the Bourbons, and the Inquisition keep the people of England in breath, and supply them with nick-names to vent their spleen upon! Had they done us any harm of late? No: but we have always a quantity of superfluous bile upon the stomach, and we wanted an object to let it out upon. How loth were we to give up our pious belief in ghosts and witches, because we liked to persecute the one, and frighten ourselves to death with the other! It is not the quality so much as the quantity of excitement that we are anxious about: we cannot bear a state of indifference and *ennui:* the mind seems to abhor a *vacuum* as much as ever matter was supposed to do. Even when the spirit of the age (that is, the progress of intellectual refinement, warring with our natural infirmities) no longer allows us to carry our vindictive and headstrong humours into effect, we try to revive them in description, and keep up the old bugbears, the phantoms of our terror and our hate, in imagination. We burn Guy Fawkes in effigy, and the hooting and buffeting and maltreating that poor tattered figure of rags and straw makes a festival in every village in England once a year. Protestants and Papists do not now burn one another at the stake: but we subscribe to new editions of *Fox's Book of Martyrs;* and the secret of the success of the *Scotch Novels* is much the same: they carry us back to the feuds, the heartburnings, the havoc, the dismay, the wrongs and the revenge of a barbarous age and people—to the rooted prejudices and deadly animosities of sects and parties in politics and religion, and contending chiefs and clans in war and intrigue. We feel the full force of the spirit of hatred with all of them in turn. As we read, we throw aside the trammels of civilisation, the flimsy veil of humanity. "Off, you lendings!" The wild beast resumes its sway within us, we feel like hunting-animals, and as the hound starts in his sleep and rushes on the chase in fancy, the heart rouses itself in its native lair, and utters a wild cry of joy, at being restored once more to freedom and lawless, unrestrained impulses. Every one has his full swing, or goes to the Devil his own way. Here are no Jeremy Bentham Panopticons, none of Mr. Owen's impassable Parallelograms, (Rob Roy would have spurned and poured a thousand curses on them), no long calculations of self-interest:

the will takes its instant way to its object, as the mountain-torrent flings itself over the precipice: the greatest possible good of each individual consists in doing all the Mischief he can to his neighbour: that is charming, and finds a sure and sympathetic chord in every breast! So Mr. Irving, the celebrated preacher, has rekindled the old, original, almost exploded hell-fire in the aisles of the Caledonian Chapel, as they introduce the real water of the New River at Sadler's Wells, to the delight and astonishment of his fair audience. *'Tis pretty, though a plague,* to sit and peep into the pit of Tophet, to play at *snap-dragon* with flames and brimstone (it gives a smart electrical shock, a lively fillip to delicate constitutions), and to see Mr. Irving, like a huge Titan, looking as grim and swarthy as if he had to forge tortures for all the damned! What a strange being man is! Not content with doing all he can to vex and hurt his fellows here, "upon this bank and shoal of time," where one would think there were heart-aches, pain, disappointment, anguish, tears, sighs, and groans enough, the bigoted maniac takes him to the top of the high peak of school divinity to hurl him down the yawning gulf of penal fire; his speculative malice asks eternity to wreak its infinite spite in, and calls on the Almighty to execute its relentless doom! The cannibals burn their enemies and eat them in good-fellowship with one another: meek Christian divines cast those who differ from them but a hair's breadth, body and soul, into hell-fire, for the glory of God and the good of his creatures! It is well that the power of such persons is not coördinate with their wills: indeed, it is from the sense of their weakness and inability to control the opinions of others, that they thus "outdo termagant," and endeavour to frighten them into conformity by big words and monstrous denunciations.

The pleasure of hating, like a poisonous mineral, eats into the heart of religion, and turns it to rankling spleen and bigotry; it makes patriotism an excuse for carrying fire, pestilence, and famine into other lands: it leaves to virtue nothing but the spirit of censoriousness, and a narrow, jealous, inquisitorial watchfulness over the actions and motives of others. What have the different sects, creeds, doctrines in religion been but so many pretexts set up for men to wrangle, to quarrel, to tear one another in pieces about, like a target as a mark to shoot at? Does any one suppose that the love of country in an Englishman implies any friendly feeling or disposition to serve another bearing the same name? No, it means only hatred to the French or the inhabitants of any other country that we happen to be at war with for the time. Does the love of virtue denote any wish to discover or amend our own faults? No, but it atones for an obstinate adherence to our own vices by the most virulent intolerance to human frailties. This principle is of a most universal application. It extends to good as well as evil: if it makes us hate folly, it makes us no less dissatisfied with distinguished merit. If it inclines us to resent the wrongs of others, it impels us to be as impatient of their prosperity. We revenge injuries: we repay benefits with ingratitude. Even our strongest partialities and likings soon take this turn. "That which was luscious as locusts, anon becomes bitter as coloquintida;" and love and friendship melt in their own fires. We hate old friends: we hate old books: we hate old opinions; and at last we come to hate ourselves.

I have observed that few of those, whom I have formerly known most intimate, continue on the same friendly footing, or combine the steadiness with the warmth of attachment. I have been acquainted with two or three knots of inseparable companions, who saw each other "six days in the week," that have broken up and dispersed. I have quarrelled with almost all my old friends, (they might say this is owing to my bad temper, but) they have also quarrelled with one another. What is become of "that set of whist-players," celebrated by ELIA in his notable *Epistle to Robert Southey, Esq.* (and now I think of it—that I myself have celebrated in this very volume) "that for so many years called Admiral Burney friend?" They are scattered, like last year's snow. Some of them are dead, or gone to live at a distance, or pass one another in the street like strangers; or if they stop to speak, do it as coolly and try to *cut* one another as soon as possible. Some of us have grown rich, others poor. Some have got places under Government, others a *niche* in the Quarterly Review. Some of us have dearly earned a name in the world; whilst others remain in their original privacy. We despise the one, and envy and are glad to mortify the other. Times are changed; we cannot revive our old feelings; and we avoid the sight and are uneasy in the presence of those who remind us of our infirmity, and put us upon an effort at seeming cordiality, which embarrasses ourselves and does not impose upon our *quondam* associates. Old friendships are like meats served up repeatedly, cold, comfortless, and distasteful. The stomach turns against them. Either constant intercourse and familiarity breed weariness and contempt; or if we meet again after an interval of absence, we appear no longer the same. One is too wise, another too foolish, for us; and we wonder we did not find this out before. We are disconcerted and kept in a state of continual alarm by the wit of one, or tired to death of the dullness of another. The *good things* of the first (besides leaving stings behind them) by repetition grow stale, and lose their startling effect; and the insipidity of the last becomes intolerable. The most amusing or instructive companion is at best like a favourite volume, that we wish after a time to *lay upon the shelf;* but as our friends are not willing to be laid there, this produces a misunderstanding and ill-blood between us. Or if the zeal and integrity of friendship is not abated, or its career interrupted by any obstacle arising out of its own nature, we look out for other subjects of complaint and sources of dissatisfaction. We begin to criticise each other's dress, looks, and general character. "Such a one is a pleasant fellow, but it is a pity he sits so late!" Another fails to keep his appointments, and that is a sore that never heals. We get acquainted with some fashionable young men or with a mistress, and wish to introduce our friend; but he is awkward and a sloven, the interview does not answer, and this throws cold water on our intercourse. Or he makes himself obnoxious to opinion—and we shrink from our own convictions on the subject as an excuse for not defending him. All or any of these causes mount up in time to a ground of coolness or irritation—and at last they break out into open violence as the only amends we can make ourselves for suppressing them so long, or the readiest means of banishing recollections of former kindness so little compatible with our present feelings. We may try to tamper with the wounds or patch up the carcass of departed friendship; but the one will hardly bear the handling, and the other is not worth the trouble of embalming! The only way to be reconciled to old friends is to part with them for good: at a distance we may chance to be thrown back (in a waking dream) upon old times and old feelings: or at any rate we should not think of renewing our intimacy, till we have fairly *spit our spite,* or said, thought, and felt all the ill we can of each other. Or if we can pick a quarrel with some one else, and make him the scapegoat, this is an excellent contrivance to heal a broken bone. I think I must be friends with Lamb again, since he has written that magnanimous Letter to Southey, and told him a piece of his mind! I don't know what it is that attaches me to H—— so much, except that he and I, whenever we meet, sit in judgment on another set of old friends, and "carve them as a dish fit for the gods." There was L—— H——, John Scott, Mrs. M——, whose dark raven locks made a picturesque background to our discourse, B——, who is grown fat and is, they say, married, R——; these had all separated long ago, and their foibles are the common link that holds us together. We do not affect to condole or whine over their follies; we enjoy, we laugh at them till we are ready to burst our sides, *"sans* intermission, for hours by the dial." We serve up a course of anecdotes, *traits,* master-strokes of character, and cut and hack at them till we are weary. Perhaps some of them are even with us. For my own part, as I once said, I like a friend the better for having faults that one can talk about. "Then," said Mrs. M——, "you will never cease to be a philanthropist!" Those in question were some of the choice-spirits of the age, not "fellows of no mark or likelihood;" and we so far did them justice: but it is well they did not hear what we sometimes said of them. I care little what any one says of me, particularly behind my back, and in the way of critical and analytical discussion: it is looks of dislike and scorn that I answer with the worst venom of my pen. The expression of the face wounds me more than the expressions of the tongue. If I have in one instance mistaken this expression, or resorted to this remedy where I ought not, I am sorry for it. But the face was too fine over which it mantled, and I am too old to have misunderstood it! . . . I sometimes go up to ——'s; and as often as I do, resolve never to go again. I do not find the old homely welcome. The ghost of friendship meets me at the door, and sits with me all dinner-time. They have got a set of fine notions and new acquaintance. Allusions to past occurrences are thought trivial, nor is it always safe to touch upon more general subjects. M. does not begin as he formerly did every five minutes, "Fawcett used to say," &c. That topic is something worn. The girls are grown up, and have a thousand accomplishments. I perceive there is a jealousy on both sides. They think I give myself airs, and I fancy the same of them. Every time I am asked, "If I do not think Mr. Washington Irving a very fine writer?" I shall not go again till I receive an invitation for Christmas Day in company with Mr. Liston. The only intimacy I never found to flinch or fade was a purely intellectual one. There was none of the cant of candour in it, none of the whine of mawkish sensibility. Our mutual acquaintance were considered merely as subjects of conversation and knowledge, not at all of affection. We regarded them no more in our experiments than "mice in an air pump:" or like malefactors, they were regularly cut down and given over to the dissecting-knife. We spared neither friend nor foe. We sacrificed human infirmities at the shrine of truth. The skeletons of character might be seen, after the juice was extracted, dangling in the air like flies in cobwebs: or they were kept for future inspection in some refined acid. The demonstration was as beautiful as it was new. There is no surfeiting on gall: nothing keeps so well as a decoction of spleen. We grow tired of every thing but turning others into ridicule, and congratulating ourselves on their defects.

We take a dislike to our favourite books, after a time, for the same reason. We cannot read the same works for ever. Our honeymoon, even though we wed the Muse, must come to an end; and is followed by indifference, if not by disgust. There are some works, those indeed that produce the most striking effect at first by novelty and boldness of outline, that will not bear reading twice: others of a less extravagant character, and that excite and repay attention by a greater nicety of details, have hardly interest enough to keep alive our continued enthusiasm. The popularity of the most successful writers operates to wean us from them, by the cant and fuss that is made about them, by hearing their names everlastingly repeated, and by the number of ignorant and indiscriminate admirers they draw after them:—we as little like to have to drag others from their unmerited obscurity, lest we should be exposed to the charge of affectation and singularity of taste. There is nothing to be said respecting an author that all the world have made up their minds about: it is a thankless as well as hopeless task to recommend one that nobody has ever heard of. To cry up Shakespear as the god of our idolatry, seems like a vulgar national prejudice: to take down a volume of Chaucer, or Spenser, or Beaumont and Fletcher, or Ford, or Marlowe, has very much the look of pedantry and egotism. I confess it makes me hate the very name of Fame and Genius when works like these are "gone into the wastes of time," while each successive generation of fools is busily employed in reading the trash of the day, and women of fashion gravely join with their waiting-maids in discussing the preference between the Paradise Lost and Mr. Moore's Loves of the Angels. I was pleased the other day on going into a shop to ask, "If they had any of the *Scotch*

Novels?" to be told—"That they had just sent out the last, Sir Andrew Wylie!"—Mr. Galt will also be pleased with this answer! The reputation of some books is raw and *unaired:* that of others is worm-eaten and mouldy. Why fix our affections on that which we cannot bring ourselves to have faith in, or which others have long ceased to trouble themselves about? I am half afraid to look into Tom Jones, lest it should not answer my expectations at this time of day; and if it did not, I should certainly be disposed to fling it into the fire, and never look into another novel while I lived. But surely, it may be said, there are some works that, like nature, can never grow old; and that must always touch the imagination and passions alike! Or there are passages that seem as if we might brood over them all our lives, and not exhaust the sentiments of love and admiration they excite: they become favourites, and we are fond of them to a sort of dotage. Here is one:

> ——"Sitting in my window
> Printing my thoughts in lawn, I saw a god,
> I thought (but it was you), enter our gates;
> My blood flew out and back again, as fast
> As I had puffed it forth and sucked it in
> Like breath; then was I called away in haste
> To entertain you: never was a man
> Thrust from a sheepcote to a sceptre, raised
> So high in thoughts as I; you left a kiss
> Upon these lips then, which I mean to keep
> From you for ever. I did hear you talk
> Far above singing!"

A passage like this indeed leaves a taste on the palate like nectar, and we seem in reading it to sit with the gods at their golden tables: but if we repeat it often in ordinary moods, it loses its flavour, becomes vapid, "the wine of *poetry* is drank, and but the lees remain." Or, on the other hand, if we call in the aid of extraordinary circumstances to set it off to advantage, as the reciting it to a friend, or after having our feelings excited by a long walk in some romantic situation, or while we

> ——"play with Amaryllis in the shade,
> Or with the tangles of Neæra's hair"—

we afterwards miss the accompanying circumstances, and instead of transferring the recollection of them to the favourable side, regret what we have lost, and strive in vain to bring back "the irrevocable hour"—wondering in some instances how we survive it, and at the melancholy blank that is left behind! The pleasure rises to its height in some moment of calm solitude or intoxicating sympathy, declines ever after, and from the comparison and a conscious falling-off, leaves rather a sense of satiety and irksomeness behind it. . . . "Is it the same in pictures?" I confess it is, with all but those from Titian's hand. I don't know why, but an air breathes from his landscapes, pure, refreshing, as if it came from other years; there is a look in his faces that never passes away. I saw one the other day. Amidst the heartless desolation and glittering finery of Fonthill, there is a portfolio of the Dresden Gallery. It opens, and a young female head looks from it; a child, yet woman grown; with an air of rustic innocence and the graces of a princess, her eyes like those of doves, the lips about to open, a smile of pleasure dimpling the whole face, the jewels sparkling in her crisped hair, her youthful shape compressed in a rich antique dress, as the bursting leaves contain the April buds! Why do I not call up this image of gentle sweetness, and place it as a perpetual barrier between mischance and me?—It is because pleasure asks a greater effort of the mind to support it than pain; and we turn, after a little idle dalliance, from what we love to what we hate!

As to my old opinions, I am heartily sick of them. I have reason, for they have deceived me sadly. I was taught to think, and I was willing to believe, that genius was not a bawd, that virtue was not a mask, that liberty was not a name, that love had its seat in the human heart. Now I would care little if these words were struck out of the dictionary, or if I had never heard them. They are become to my ears a mockery and a dream. Instead of patriots and friends of freedom, I see nothing but the tyrant and the slave, the people linked with kings to rivet on the chains of despotism and superstition. I see folly join with knavery, and together make up public spirit and public opinions. I see the insolent Tory, the blind Reformer, the coward Whig! If mankind had wished for what is right, they might have had it long ago. The theory is plain enough; but they are prone to mischief, "to every good work reprobate." I have seen all that had been done by the mighty yearnings of the spirit and intellect of men, "of whom the world was not worthy," and that promised a proud opening to truth and good through the vista of future years, undone by one man, with just glimmering of understanding enough to feel that he was a king, but not to comprehend how he could be king of a free people! I have seen this triumph celebrated by poets, the friends of my youth and the friends of man, but who were carried away by the infuriate tide that, setting in from a throne, bore down every distinction of right reason before it; and I have seen all those who did not join in applauding this insult and outrage on humanity proscribed, hunted down (they and their friends made a byword of), so that it has become an understood thing that no one can live by his talents or knowledge who is not ready to prostitute those talents and that knowledge to betray his species, and prey upon his fellow-man. "This was some time a mystery: but the time gives evidence of it." The echoes of liberty had awakened once more in Spain, and the morning of human hope dawned again: but that dawn has been overcast by the foul breath of bigotry, and those reviving sounds stifled by fresh cries from the time-rent towers of the Inquisition: man yielding (as it is fit he should) first to brute force, but more to the innate perversity and dastard spirit of his own nature, which leaves no room for farther hope or disappointment. And England, that arch-reformer, that heroic deliverer, that mouther about liberty and tool of power, stands gaping by, not feeling the blight and mildew coming over it, nor its very bones crack and turn to a paste under the grasp and circling folds of this new monster—Legitimacy! In private life do we not see hypocrisy, servility, selfishness, folly, and impudence succeed, while modesty shrinks from the encounter, and merit is trodden under foot? How often is "the rose plucked from the forehead of a virtuous love to plant a blister there!" What chance is there of the success of real passion? What certainty of its continuance? Seeing all this as I do, and unravelling the web of human life into its various threads of meanness, spite, cowardice, want of feeling, and want of understanding, of indifference towards others and ignorance of ourselves—seeing custom prevail over all excellence, itself giving way to infamy—mistaken as I have been in my public and private hopes, calculating others from myself, and calculating wrong; always disappointed where I placed most reliance; the dupe of friendship, and the fool of love;—have I not reason to hate and to despise myself? Indeed I do; and chiefly for not having hated and despised the world enough.

DAVID HUME
1711–1776

The Scotsman David Hume, "le bon David" to his friends, "the atheist Hume" to those who disagreed with him, was in his own eyes "a man of mild dispositions," who simply insisted on pursuing an idea to its limits. Thus, in his *Treatise on Human Nature* and his *Enquiry into Human Understanding,* Hume used reason to destroy reason. By reason, he held, we are led to doubt both mind and matter. Yet like a sensible Scot, he did not let this conclusion disturb him. He was content to rely on "the instinct by which we live," and to leave to the great Immanuel Kant the task of rehabilitating reason. Hume himself, with the same combination of pertinacity and common sense, went on to inquire into the nature of morals, of taste, and, in the essay printed here, of tragedy. Like Aristotle and succeeding philosophers through the centuries, Hume speculates on why the sorrows of tragedy give us pleasure. No more than Aristotle's is Hume's the final answer, but it is a satisfying, closely reasoned, graceful exploration of an eternal problem.

Of Tragedy

It seems an unaccountable pleasure, which the spectators of a well-written tragedy receive from sorrow, terror, anxiety, and other passions, that are in themselves disagreeable and uneasy. The more they are touched and affected, the more are they delighted with the spectacle; and as soon as the uneasy passions cease to operate, the piece is at an end. One scene of full joy and contentment and security is the utmost that any composition of this kind can bear; and it is sure always to be the concluding one. If, in the texture of the piece, there be interwoven any scenes of satisfaction, they afford only faint gleams of pleasure, which are thrown in by way of variety, and in order to plunge the actors into deeper distress by means of that contrast and disappointment. The whole art of the poet is employed in rousing and supporting the compassion and indignation, the anxiety and resentment of his audience. They are pleased in proportion as they are afflicted and never are so happy as when they employ tears, sobs, and cries to give vent to their sorrow and relieve their heart, swollen with the tenderest sympathy and compassion.

The few critics who have had some tincture of philosophy have remarked this singular phenomenon and have endeavored to account for it.

L'Abbé Du Bos, in his reflections on poetry and painting, asserts that nothing is in general so disagreeable to the mind as the languid, listless state of indolence into which it falls upon the removal of all passion and occupation. To get rid of this painful situation, it seeks every amusement and pursuit; business, gaming, shows, executions; whatever will rouse the passions and take its attention from itself. No matter what the passion is: let it be disagreeable, afflicting, melancholy, disordered; it is still better than that insipid languor which arises from perfect tranquillity and repose.

It is impossible not to admit this account as being, at least in part, satisfactory. You may observe, when there are several tables of gaming, that all the company run to those where the deepest play is, even though they find not there the best players. The view, or at least imagination, of high passions arising from great loss or gain affects the spectator by sympathy, gives him some touches of the same passions, and serves him for a momentary entertainment. It makes the time pass the easier with him and is some relief to that oppression under which men commonly labour when left entirely to their own thoughts and meditations.

We find that common liars always magnify, in their narrations, all kinds of danger, pain, distress, sickness, deaths, murders, and cruelties; as well as joy, beauty, mirth, and magnificence. It is an absurd secret which they have for pleasing their company, fixing their attention, and attaching them to such marvellous relations by the passions and emotions which they excite.

There is, however, a difficulty in applying to the present subject, in its full extent, this solution, however ingenious and satisfactory it may appear. It is certain that the same object of distress which pleases in a tragedy, were it really set before us, would give the most unfeigned uneasiness, though it be then the most effectual cure to languor and indolence. Monsieur Fontenelle seems to have been sensible of this difficulty and accordingly attempts another solution of the phenomenon, at least makes some addition to the theory above mentioned.

"Pleasure and pain," says he, "which are two sentiments so different in themselves, differ not so much in their cause. From the instance of tickling, it appears that the movement of pleasure pushed a little too far becomes pain, and that the movement of pain a little moderated becomes pleasure. Hence it proceeds that there is such a thing as a sorrow soft and agreeable: it is a pain weakened and diminished. The heart likes naturally to be moved and affected. Melancholy objects suit it, and even disastrous and sorrowful, provided they are softened by some circumstance. It is certain that, on the theatre, the representation has almost the effect of reality; yet it has not altogether that effect. However we may be hurried away by the spectacle, whatever dominion the senses and imagination may usurp over the reason, there still lurks at the bottom a certain idea of falsehood in the whole of what we see. This idea, though weak and disguised, suffices to diminish the pain which we suffer from the misfortunes of those whom we love, and to reduce that affliction to such a pitch as converts it into a pleasure. We weep for the misfortune of a hero to whom we are attached. In the same instant we comfort ourselves by reflecting that it is nothing but a fiction. And it is precisely that mixture of sentiments, which composes an agreeable sorrow, and tears that delight us. But as that affliction which is caused by exterior and sensible objects is stronger than the consolation which arises from an internal reflection, they are the effects and symptoms of sorrow that ought to predominate in the composition."

This solution seems just and convincing, but perhaps it wants still some new addition in order to make it answer fully the phenomenon which we here examine. All the passions, excited by eloquence, are agreeable in the highest degree, as well as those which are moved by painting and the theatre. The epilogues of Cicero are, on this account chiefly, the delight of every reader of taste, and it is difficult to read some of them without the deepest sympathy and sorrow. His merit as an orator no doubt depends much on his success in this particular. When he had raised tears in his judges and all his audience, they were then the most highly delighted and expressed the greatest satisfaction with the pleader. The pathetic description of the butchery made by Verres of the Sicilian captains is a masterpiece of this kind. But I believe none will affirm that the being present at a melancholy scene of that nature would afford any entertainment. Neither is the sorrow here softened by fiction, for the audience were convinced of the reality of every circumstance. What is it then which in this case raises a pleasure from the bosom of uneasiness, so to speak, and a pleasure which still retains all the features and outward symptoms of distress and sorrow?

I answer: this extraordinary effect proceeds from that very eloquence with which the melancholy scene is represented. The genius required to paint objects in a lively manner, the art employed in collecting all the pathetic circumstances, the judgment displayed in disposing them: the exercise, I say, of these noble talents, together with the force of expression and beauty of oratorial numbers, diffuse the highest satisfaction on the audience and excite the most delightful movements. By this means, the uneasiness of the melancholy passions is not only overpowered and effaced by something stronger of an opposite kind, but the whole impulse of those passions is converted into pleasure and swells the delight which the eloquence raises in us. The same force of oratory, employed on an uninteresting subject, would not please half so much, or rather would appear altogether ridiculous; and the mind, being left in absolute calmness and indifference, would relish none of those beauties of imagination or expression which, if joined to passion, give it such exquisite entertainment. The impulse, or vehemence, arising from sorrow, compassion, indignation, receives a new direction from the sentiments of beauty. The latter, being the predominant emotion, seize the whole mind and convert the former into themselves, at least tincture them so strongly as totally to alter their nature. And the soul, being at the same time roused by passion and charmed by eloquence, feels on the whole a strong movement which is altogether delightful.

The same principle takes places in tragedy; with this addition, that tragedy is an imitation, and imitation is always of itself agreeable. This circumstance serves still further to smooth the motions of passion and convert the whole feeling into one uniform and strong enjoyment. Objects of the greatest terror and distress please in painting, and please more than most beautiful objects that appear calm and indifferent.[1]

[1] Painters make no scruple of representing distress and sorrow as well as any other passion, but they seem not to dwell so much on these melancholy

The affection, rousing the mind, excites a large stock of spirit and vehemence, which is all transformed into pleasure by the force of the prevailing movement. It is thus the fiction of tragedy softens the passion, by an infusion of a new feeling, not merely by weakening or diminishing the sorrow. You may by degrees weaken a real sorrow till it totally disappears; yet in none of its gradations will it ever give pleasure, except, perhaps, by accident to a man sunk under lethargic indolence, whom it rouses from that languid state.

To confirm this theory, it will be sufficient to produce other instances where the subordinate movement is converted into the predominant and gives force to it, though of a different, and even sometimes though of a contrary nature.

Novelty naturally rouses the mind and attracts our attention, and the movements which it causes are always converted into any passion belonging to the object and join their force to it. Whether an event excite joy or sorrow, pride or shame, anger or good-will, it is sure to produce a stronger affection when new or unusual. And though novelty of itself be agreeable, it fortifies the painful as well as agreeable passions.

Had you any intention to move a person extremely by the narration of any event, the best method of increasing its effect would be artfully to delay informing him of it and first to excite his curiosity and impatience before you let him into the secret. This is the artifice practised by Iago in the famous scene of Shakespeare, and every spectator is sensible that Othello's jealousy acquires additional force from his preceding impatience and that the subordinate passion is here readily transformed into the predominant one.

Difficulties increase passions of every kind; and by rousing our attention and exciting our active powers, they produce an emotion which nourishes the prevailing affection.

Parents commonly love that child most whose sickly, infirm frame of body has occasioned them the greatest pains, trouble, and anxiety in rearing him. The agreeable sentiment of affection here acquires force from sentiments of uneasiness.

Nothing endears so much a friend as sorrow for his death.

---

affections as the poets, who, though they copy every emotion of the human breast, yet pass very quickly over the agreeable sentiments. A painter represents only one instant, and if that be passionate enough, it is sure to affect and delight the spectator. But nothing can furnish to the poet a variety of scenes and incidents and sentiments except distress, terror, or anxiety. Complete joy and satisfaction is attended with security and leaves no further room for action.

The pleasure of his company has not so powerful an influence.

Jealousy is a painful passion; yet without some share of it, the agreeable affection of love has difficulty to subsist in its full force and violence. Absence is also a great source of complaint among lovers and gives them the greatest uneasiness; yet nothing is more favorable to their mutual passion than short intervals of that kind. And if long intervals often prove fatal, it is only because through time men are accustomed to them and they cease to give uneasiness. Jealousy and absence in love compose the *dolce peccante* of the Italians, which they suppose so essential to all pleasure.

There is a fine observation of the elder Pliny which illustrates the principle here insisted on. "It is very remarkable," says he, "that the last works of celebrated artists, which they left imperfect, are always the most prized, such as the Iris of Aristides, the Tyndarides of Nicomachus, the Medea of Timomachus, and the Venus of Appelles. These are valued even above their finished productions. The broken lineaments of the piece and the half-formed idea of the painter are carefully studied; and our very grief for that curious hand, which had been stopped by death, is an additional increase to our pleasure."[2]

These instances (and many more might be collected) are sufficient to afford us some insight into the analogy of Nature and to show us that the pleasure which poets, orators, and musicians give us, by exciting grief, sorrow, indignation, compassion, is not so extraordinary or paradoxical as it may at first sight appear. The force of imagination, the energy of expression, the power of numbers, the charms of imitation— all these are naturally, of themselves, delightful to the mind. And when the object presented lays hold also of some affection, the pleasure still rises upon us by the conversion of this subordinate movement into that which is predominant. The passion, though, perhaps, naturally, and when excited by the simple appearance of a real object, it may be painful, yet is so smoothed and softened and mollified when raised by the finer arts that it affords the highest entertainment.

To confirm this reasoning, we may observe that if the movements of the imagination be not predominant above those of the passion, a contrary effect follows, and the former, being now subordinate, is converted into the latter and still farther increases the pain and affliction of the sufferer.

Who could ever think of it as a good expedient for comforting an afflicted parent to exaggerate with all the force of elocution the irreparable loss which he has met with by the death of a favourite child? The more power of imagination and expression you here employ, the more you increase his despair and affliction.

The shame, confusion, and terror of Verres no doubt rose in proportion to the noble eloquence and vehemence of Cicero. So also did his pain and uneasiness. These former passions were too strong for the pleasure arising from the beauties of elocution and operated, though from the same principle, yet in a contrary manner to the sympathy, compassion, and indignation of the audience.

Lord Clarendon, when he approaches towards the catastrophe of the royal party, supposes that his narration must then become infinitely disagreeable, and he hurries over the king's death without giving us one circumstance of it. He considers it as too horrid a scene to be contemplated with any satisfaction, or even without the utmost pain and aversion. He himself, as well as the readers of that age, were too deeply concerned in the events and felt a pain from subjects which an historian and a reader of another age would regard as the most pathetic and most interesting, and, by consequence, the most agreeable.

An action represented in tragedy may be too bloody and atrocious. It may excite such movements of horror as will not soften into pleasure, and the greatest energy of expression bestowed on descriptions of that nature serves only to augment our uneasiness. Such is that action represented in *The Ambitious Stepmother* where a venerable old man, raised to the height of fury and despair, rushes against a pillar, and striking his head upon it, besmears it all over with mingled brains and gore. The English theatre abounds too much with such shocking images.

Even the common sentiments of compassion require to be softened by some agreeable affection in order to give a thorough satisfaction to the audience. The mere suffering of plaintive virtue under the triumphant tyranny and oppression of vice forms a disagreeable spectacle and is carefully avoided by all masters of the drama. In order to dismiss the audience with entire satisfaction and contentment, the virtue must either convert itself into a noble courageous despair, or the vice receive its proper punishment.

Most painters appear in this light to have been very unhappy in their subjects. As they wrought much for churches and convents, they have chiefly represented such horrible subjects as crucifixions and martyrdoms, where nothing appears but tortures, wounds, executions, and passive suffering, without any action or affection. When they turned their pencil from this ghastly mythology, they had commonly recourse to Ovid, whose fictions, though passionate and agreeable, are scarcely natural or probable enough for painting.

The same inversion of that principle which is here insisted on displays itself in common life as in the effects of oratory and poetry. Raise so the subordinate passion that it becomes the predominant, it swallows up that affection which it before nourished and increased. Too much jealousy extinguishes love. Too much difficulty renders us indifferent. Too much sickness and infirmity disgusts a selfish and unkind parent.

What so disagreeable as the dismal, gloomy, disastrous stories with which melancholy people entertain their companions? The uneasy passion being there raised alone, unaccompanied with any spirit, genius, or eloquence, conveys a pure uneasiness and is attended with nothing that can soften it into pleasure or satisfaction.

ALDOUS HUXLEY
1894–1963

Confronted with the manuscript for a bibliography of his works, and asked to write a foreword for the forthcoming publication, Aldous Huxley recalled what one of the sons of George III had said when Edward Gibbon presented him with a copy of the second volume of *The Decline and Fall:* "What, Mr. Gibbon, another thick, damned, square book? Nothing but scribble, scribble, scribble?" Yet Huxley defended what had been his way of life for two score years or more: "Scribble, scribble, scribble," he wrote, "is intrinsically no odder than sell, sell, sell, or preach, preach, preach, or play, play, play." The very act of scribbling, continues Huxley, "leaves behind a conspicuous and enduring residue." So tangible a monument is always available as evidence against a writer. But since the appearance in 1916 of *The Burning Wheel,* a book of verse, the many stories, novels, plays, reviews, translations, and essays of Aldous Huxley have usually placed readers in his debt rather than allied them against him. *Antic Hay, Brave New World, Ape and Essence,* and *Collected Essays* are only a few of the major contributions Aldous Huxley has made to thought, satire, and pleasure in our century.

Wordsworth in the Tropics

In the neighborhood of latitude fifty north, and for the last hundred years or thereabouts, it has been an axiom that Nature is divine and morally uplifting. For good Wordsworthians— and most serious-minded people are now Wordsworthians— either by direct inspiration or at second hand—a walk in the country is the equivalent of going to church, a tour through Westmorland is as good as a pilgrimage to Jerusalem. To commune with the fields and waters, the woodlands and the hills, is to commune, according to our modern and northern ideas, with the visible manifestations of the "Wisdom and Spirit of the Universe."

The Wordsworthian who exports this pantheistic worship of Nature to the tropics is liable to have his religious convictions somewhat rudely disturbed. Nature, under a vertical sun, and nourished by the equatorial rains, is not at all like that chaste, mild deity who presides over the *Gemütlichkeit,* the prettiness, the cozy sublimities of the Lake District. The worst that Wordsworth's goddess ever did to him was to make him hear

> Low breathings coming after me, and sounds
> Of undistinguishable motion, steps
> Almost as silent as the turf they trod;

was to make him realize, in the shape of "a huge peak, black and huge," the existence of "unknown modes of being." He seems to have imagined that this was the worst Nature *could* do. A few weeks in Malaya or Borneo would have undeceived him. Wandering in the hothouse darkness of the jungle, he would not have felt so serenely certain of those "Presences of Nature," those "Souls of Lonely Places," which he was in the habit of worshipping on the shores of Windermere and Rydal. The sparse inhabitants of the equatorial forest are all believers in devils. When one has visited, in even the most superficial manner, the places where they live, it is difficult not to share their faith. The jungle is marvelous, fantastic, beautiful; but it is also terrifying, it is also profoundly sinister. There is something in what, for lack of a better word, we must call the character of great forests—even in those of temperate lands—which is foreign, appalling, fundamentally and utterly inimical to intruding man. The life of those vast masses of swarming vegetation is alien to the human spirit and hostile to it. Meredith, in his "Woods of Westermaine," has tried reassuringly to persuade us that our terrors are unnecessary, that the hostility of these vegetable forces is more apparent than real, and that if we will but trust Nature we shall find our fears transformed into serenity, joy, and rapture. This may be sound philosophy in the neighborhood of Dorking; but it begins to be dubious even in the forests of Germany—there is too much of them for a human being to feel himself at ease within their enormous glooms; and when the woods of Borneo are substituted for those of Westermaine, Meredith's comforting doctrine becomes frankly ridiculous.

It is not the sense of solitude that distresses the wanderer in equatorial jungles. Loneliness is bearable enough—for a time, at any rate. There is something actually rather stimulating and exciting about being in an empty place where there is no life but one's own. Taken in reasonably small doses, the Sahara exhilarates, like alcohol. Too much of it, however (I speak, at any rate, for myself), has the depressing effect of the second bottle of Burgundy. But in any case it is not loneliness that oppresses the equatorial traveller: it is too much company; it is the uneasy feeling that he is an alien in the midst of an innumerable throng of hostile beings. To us who live beneath a temperate sky and in the age of Henry Ford, the worship of Nature comes almost naturally. It is easy to love a feeble and already conquered enemy. But an enemy with whom one is still at war, an unconquered, unconquerable, ceaselessly active enemy—no; one does not, one should not, love him. One respects him, perhaps; one has a salutary fear of him; and one goes on fighting. In our latitudes the hosts of Nature have mostly been vanquished and enslaved. Some few detachments, it is true, still hold the field against us. There are wild woods and mountains, marshes and heaths, even in England. But they are there only on sufferance, because we have chosen, out of our good pleasure, to leave them their freedom. It has not been worth our while to reduce them to slavery. We love them because we are the masters, because we know that at any moment we can overcome them as we overcame their fellows. The inhabitants of the tropics have no such comforting reasons for adoring the sinister forces which hem them in on every side. For us, the notion "river" implies (how obviously!) the notion "bridge." When we think of a plain, we think of agriculture, towns, and good roads. The corollary of mountain is tunnel; of swamp, an embankment; of distance, a railway. At latitude zero, however, the obvious is not the same as with us. Rivers imply wading, swimming, alligators. Plains mean swamps, forests, fevers. Mountains are either dangerous or impassable. To travel is to hack one's way laboriously through a tangled, prickly, and venomous darkness. "God made the country," said Cowper, in his rather too blank verse. In New Guinea he would have had his doubts; he would have longed for the man-made town.

The Wordsworthian adoration of Nature has two principal defects. The first, as we have seen, is that it is only possible in a country where Nature has been nearly or quite enslaved to man. The second is that it is only possible for those who are prepared to falsify their immediate intuitions of Nature. For Nature, even in the temperate zone, is always alien and in-

human, and occasionally diabolic. Meredith explicitly invites
us to explain any unpleasant experiences away. We are to
interpret them, Pangloss fashion, in terms of a preconceived
philosophy; after which, all will surely be for the best in the
best of all possible Westermaines. Less openly, Wordsworth
asks us to make the same falsification of immediate experience.
It is only very occasionally that he admits the existence in the
world around him of those "unknown modes of being" of
which our immediate intuitions of things make us so dis-
quietingly aware. Normally what he does is to pump the dangerous Unknown out of Nature and refill the emptied forms of
hills and woods, flowers and waters, with something more
reassuringly familiar—with humanity, with Anglicanism. He
will not admit that a yellow primrose is simply a yellow primrose—beautiful, but essentially strange, having its own alien
life apart. He wants it to possess some sort of soul, to exist
humanly, not simply flowerily. He wants the earth to be more
than earthy, to be a divine person. But the life of vegetation
is radically unlike the life of man: the earth has a mode of
being that is certainly not the mode of being of a person. "Let
Nature be your teacher," says Wordsworth. The advice is
excellent. But how strangely he himself puts it into practice!
Instead of listening humbly to what the teacher says, he shuts
his ears and himself dictates the lesson he desires to hear.
The pupil knows better than his master; the worshipper substitutes his own oracles for those of the god. Instead of accepting
the lesson as it is given to his immediate intuitions, he distorts
it rationalistically into the likeness of a parson's sermon or
a professorial lecture. Our direct intuitions of Nature tell us
that the world is bottomlessly strange: alien, even when it is
kind and beautiful; having innumerable modes of being that
are not our modes; always mysteriously not personal, not conscious, not moral; often hostile and sinister; sometimes even
unimaginably, because inhumanly, evil. In his youth, it would
seem, Wordsworth left his direct intuitions of the world un-
warped.

> The sounding cataract
> Haunted me like a passion: the tall rock,
> The mountain, and the deep and gloomy wood,
> Their colors and their forms, were then to me
> An appetite; a feeling and a love,
> That had no need of a remoter charm,
> By thought supplied, nor any interest
> Unborrowed from the eye.

As the years passed, however, he began to interpret them in terms of a preconceived philosophy. Procrustes-like, he tortured his feelings and perceptions until they fitted his system. By the time he was thirty,

> The immeasurable height
> Of woods decaying, never to be decayed,
> The stationary blasts of waterfalls—
> The torrents shooting from the clear blue sky,
> The rocks that muttered close upon our ears,
> Black drizzling crags that spake by the wayside
> As if a voice were in them, the sick sight
> And giddy prospect of the raving stream,
> The unfettered clouds and regions of the heavens,
> Tumult and peace, the darkness and the light—
> Were all like workings of one mind, the features
> Of the same face, blossoms upon one tree,
> Characters of the great Apocalypse,
> The types and symbols of eternity,
> Of first, and last, and midst, and without end.

"Something far more deeply interfused" had made its appearance on the Wordsworthian scene. The god of Anglicanism had crept under the skin of things, and all the stimulatingly inhuman strangeness of Nature had become as flatly familiar as a page from a textbook of metaphysics or theology. As familiar and as safely simple. Pantheistically interpreted, our intuitions of Nature's endless varieties of impersonal mysteriousness lose all their exciting and disturbing quality. It makes the world seem delightfully cozy, if you can pretend that all the many alien things about you are really only manifestations of one person. It is fear of the labyrinthine flux and complexity of phenomena that has driven men to philosophy, to science, to theology—fear of the complex reality driving them to invent a simpler, more manageable, and, therefore, consoling fiction. For simple, in comparison with the external reality of which we have direct intuitions, childishly simple is even the most elaborate and subtle system devised by the human mind. Most of the philosophical systems hitherto popular have not been subtle and elaborate even by human standards. Even by human standards they have been crude, bald, preposterously straightforward. Hence their popularity. Their simplicity has rendered them instantly comprehensible. Weary with much wandering in the maze of phenomena, frightened by the inhospitable strangeness of the world, men have rushed into the systems prepared for them by philosophers and founders of religions, as they would rush from a dark jungle into the haven of a well-lit, commodious house. With a sigh of relief and a thankful feeling that here at last is their true home, they settle down in their snug metaphysical villa and go to sleep. And how furious they are when any one comes rudely knocking at the door to tell them that their villa is jerry-built, dilapidated, unfit for human habitation, even non-existent! Men have been burnt at the stake for even venturing to criticize the color of the front door or the shape of the third-floor windows.

That man must build himself some sort of metaphysical shelter in the midst of the jungle of immediately apprehended reality is obvious. No practical activity, no scientific research, no speculation is possible without some preliminary hypothesis about the nature and the purpose of things. The human mind cannot deal with the universe directly, nor even with its own immediate intuitions of the universe. Whenever it is a question of thinking about the world or of practically modifying it, men can only work on a symbolic plan of the universe, only a simplified, two-dimensional map of things abstracted by the mind out of the complex and multifarious reality of immediate intuition. History shows that these hypotheses about the nature of things are valuable even when, as later experience reveals, they are false. Man approaches the unattainable truth through a succession of errors. Confronted by the strange complexity of things, he invents, quite arbitrarily, a simple hypothesis to explain and justify the world. Having invented, he proceeds to act and think in terms of this hypothesis, as though it were correct. Experience gradually shows him where his hypothesis is unsatisfactory and how it should be modified. Thus, great scientific discoveries have been made by men seeking to verify quite erroneous theories about the nature of things. The discoveries have necessitated a modification of the original hypotheses, and further discoveries have been made in the effort to verify the modifications—discoveries which, in their turn, have led to yet further modifications. And so on, indefinitely. Philosophical and religious hypotheses, being less susceptible of experimental verification than the hypotheses of science, have undergone far less modification. For example, the pantheistic hypothesis of Wordsworth is an ancient doctrine, which human experience has hardly modified throughout history. And rightly, no doubt. For it is obvious that there must be some sort of unity underlying the diversity of phenomena; for if there were not, the world would be quite unknowable.

Indeed, it is precisely in the knowableness of things, in the very fact that they are known, that their fundamental unity consists. The world which we know, and which our minds have fabricated out of goodness knows what mysterious things in themselves, possesses the unity which our minds have imposed upon it. It is part of our thought, hence fundamentally homogeneous. Yes, the world is obviously one. But at the same time it is no less obviously diverse. For if the world were absolutely one, it would no longer be knowable, it would cease to exist. Thought must be divided against itself before it can come to any knowledge of itself. Absolute oneness is absolute nothingness: homogeneous perfection, as the Hindus perceived and courageously recognized, is equivalent to non-existence, is nirvana. The Christian idea of a perfect heaven that is something other than a non-existence is a contradiction in terms. The world in which we live may be fundamentally one, but it is a unity divided up into a great many diverse fragments. A tree, a table, a newspaper, a piece of artificial silk are all made of wood. But they are, none the less, distinct and separate objects. It is the same with the world at large. Our immediate intuitions are of diversity. We have only to open our eyes to recognize a multitude of different phenomena. These intuitions of diversity are as correct, as well justified, as is our intellectual conviction of the fundamental homogeneity of the various parts of the world with one another and with ourselves. Circumstances have led humanity to set an ever-increasing premium on the conscious and intellectual comprehension of things. Modern man's besetting temptation is to sacrifice his direct perceptions and spontaneous feelings to his reasoned reflections; to prefer in all circumstances the verdict of his intellect to that of his immediate intuitions. "L'homme est visiblement fait pour penser," says Pascal; "c'est toute sa dignité et tout son mérite; et tout son devoir est de penser comme il faut." Noble words; but do they happen to be true? Pascal seems to forget that man has something else to do besides think: he must live. Living may not be so dignified or meritorious as thinking (particularly when you happen to be, like Pascal, a chronic invalid); but it is, perhaps unfortunately, a necessary process. If one would live well, one must live completely, with the whole being—with the body and the instincts, as well as with the conscious mind. A life lived, as far as may be, exclusively from the consciousness and in accordance with the considered judgments of the intellect, is a stunted life, a half-dead life. This is a fact that can be confirmed by daily observation. But consciousness, the intellect, the spirit, have acquired an inordinate prestige; and such is men's snobbish respect for authority, such is their pedantic desire to be consistent, that they go on doing their best to lead the exclusively conscious, spiritual, and intellectual life, in spite of its manifest disadvantages. To know is pleasant; it is exciting to be conscious; the intellect is a valuable instrument, and for certain purposes the hypotheses which it fabricates are of great practical value. Quite true. But, therefore, say the moralists and men of science, drawing conclusions only justified by their desire for consistency, therefore *all* life should be lived from the head, consciously, *all* phenomena should at *all* times be interpreted in terms of the intellect's hypotheses. The religious teachers are of a slightly different opinion. All life, according to them, should be lived spiritually, not intellectually. Why? On the grounds, as we discover when we push our analysis far enough, that certain occasional psychological states, currently called spiritual, are extremely agreeable and have valuable consequences in the realm of social behavior. The unprejudiced observer finds it hard to understand why these people should set such store by consistency of thought and action. Because oysters are occasionally pleasant, it does not follow that one should make of oysters one's exclusive diet. Nor should one take castor-oil every day because castor-oil is occasionally good for one. Too much consistency is as bad for the mind as it is for the body. Consistency is contrary to nature, contrary to life. The only completely consistent people are the dead. Consistent intellectualism and spirituality may be socially valuable, up to a point; but they make, gradually, for individual death. And individual death, when the slow murder has been consummated, is finally social death. So that the social utility of pure intellectualism and pure spirituality is only apparent and temporary. What is needed is as ever a compromise. Life must be lived in different ways at different moments. The only satisfactory way of existing in the modern, highly specialized world is to live with two personalities. A Dr. Jekyll that does the metaphysical and scientific thinking, that transacts business in the city, adds up figures, designs machines, and so forth. And a natural, spontaneous Mr. Hyde to do the physical, instinctive living in the intervals of work. The two personalities should lead their unconnected lives apart, without poaching on one another's preserves or inquiring too closely into one another's activities.

Only by living discreetly and inconsistently can we preserve both the man and the citizen, both the intellectual and the spontaneous animal being, alive within us. The solution may not be very satisfactory; but it is, I believe now (though once I thought differently), the best that, in the modern circumstances, can be devised.

The poet's place, it seems to me, is with the Mr. Hydes of human nature. He should be, as Blake remarked of Milton, "of the devil's party without knowing it"—or preferably with the full consciousness of being of the devil's party. There are so many intellectual and moral angels battling for rationalism, good citizenship, and pure spirituality; so many and such eminent ones, so very vocal and authoritative! The poor devil in man needs all the support and advocacy he can get. The artist is his natural champion. When an artist deserts to the side of the angels, it is the most odious of treasons. How unforgivable, for example, is Tolstoy! Tolstoy, the perfect Mr. Hyde, the complete embodiment, if ever there was one, of non-intellectual, non-moral, instinctive life—Tolstoy, who betrayed his own nature, betrayed his art, betrayed life itself, in order to fight against the devil's party of his earlier allegiances, under the standard of Dr. Jesus-Jekyll. Wordsworth's betrayal was not so spectacular: he was never so wholly of the devil's party as Tolstoy. Still, it was bad enough. It is difficult to forgive him for so utterly repenting his youthful passions and enthusiasms, and becoming, personally as well as politically, the anglican tory. One remembers B. R. Haydon's account of the poet's reactions to that charming classical sculpture of Cupid and Psyche. "The devils!" he said malignantly, after a long-drawn contemplation of their marble embrace. "The devils!" And he was not using the word in the complimentary sense in which I have employed it here: he was expressing his hatred of passion and life, he was damning the young man he had himself been—the young man who had hailed the French Revolution with delight and begotten an illegitimate child. From being an ardent lover of the nymphs, he had become one of those all too numerous

> woodmen who expel
> Love's gentle dryads from the haunts of life,
> And vex the nightingales in every dell.

Yes, even the nightingales he vexed. Even the nightingales, though the poor birds can never, like those all to human dryads, have led him into sexual temptation. Even the innocuous nightingales were moralized, spiritualized, turned into citizens and anglicans—and along with the nightingales, the whole of animate and inanimate Nature.

The change in Wordsworth's attitude toward Nature is symptomatic of his general apostasy. Beginning as what I may call a natural aesthete, he transformed himself, in the course of years, into a moralist, a thinker. He used his intellect to distort his exquisitely acute and subtle intuitions of the world, to explain away their often disquieting strangeness, to simplify them into a comfortable metaphysical unreality. Nature had endowed him with the poet's gift of seeing more than ordinarily far into the brick walls of external reality, of intuitively comprehending the character of the bricks, of feeling the quality of their being, and establishing the appropriate relationship with them. But he preferred to think his gifts away. He preferred, in the interests of a preconceived religious theory, to ignore the disquieting strangeness of things, to interpret the impersonal diversity of Nature in terms of a divine, anglican unity. He chose, in a word, to be a philosopher, comfortably at home with a man-made and, therefore, thoroughly comprehensible system, rather than a poet adventuring for adventure's sake through the mysterious world revealed by his direct and undistorted intuitions.

It is a pity that he never traveled beyond the boundaries of Europe. A voyage through the tropics would have cured him of his too easy and comfortable pantheism. A few months in the jungle would have convinced him that the diversity and utter strangeness of Nature are at least as real and significant as its intellectually discovered unity. Nor would he have felt so certain, in the damp and stifling darkness, among the leeches and the malevolently tangled rattans, of the divinely anglican character of that fundamental unity. He would have learned once more to treat Nature naturally, as he treated it in his youth; to react to it spontaneously, loving where love was the appropriate emotion, fearing, hating, fighting whenever Nature presented itself to his intuition as being, not merely strange, but hostile, inhumanly evil. A voyage would have taught him this. But Wordsworth never left his native continent. Europe is so well gardened that it resembles a work of art, a scientific theory, a neat metaphysical system. Man has re-created Europe in his own image. Its tamed and temperate Nature confirmed Wordsworth in his philosophizings. The poet, the devil's partisan were doomed; the angels triumphed. Alas!

THOMAS HENRY HUXLEY
1825–1895

Thomas Henry Huxley was a man of many skills and accomplishments. A distinguished scientist, President of the Royal Society and of the British Association for the Advancement of Science, he had the gift for translating difficult scientific concepts into simple, graceful language, intelligible and persuasive to the general public. And this gift was precisely what the times required. For a scientific revolution occurred in the middle of the nineteenth century, and in the process a good many old notions were upset or dangerously shaken. Most people, preferring their old notions, resisted the change. When Darwin's *Origin of Species* was published in 1859, indeed, their reaction was a scream of outrage. Darwin himself had no advocate's talents, but there was Huxley. And once Huxley was convinced of the theory of evolution, he made himself "Darwin's watchdog," to explain and defend that theory before the world. He defended not only Darwin, but all science, as in the following essay, "On the Advisableness of Improving Natural Knowledge"; he insisted on the essential relation of science to every human activity; and he campaigned for a revision in the English educational system that would bring science into the schools. Like Bertrand Russell today, he was a skeptic. He considered "blind faith the one unpardonable sin." But he had a faith for which he crusaded all his life; it was, of course, a faith in science.

On the Advisableness of Improving Natural Knowledge

This time two hundred years ago—in the beginning of January, 1666—those of our forefathers who inhabited this great and ancient city, took breath between the shocks of two fearful calamities: one not quite past, although its fury had abated; the other to come.

Within a few yards of the very spot on which we are assembled, so the tradition runs, that painful and deadly malady, the plague, appeared in the latter months of 1664; and, though no new visitor, smote the people of England, and especially of her capital, with a violence unknown before, in the course of the following year. The hand of a master has pictured what happened in those dismal months; and in that truest of fictions, "The History of the Plague Year," Defoe shows death, with every accompaniment of pain and terror, stalking through the narrow streets of old London, and changing their busy hum into a silence broken only by the wailing of the mourners of fifty thousand dead; by the woful denunciations and mad prayers of fanatics; and by the madder yells of despairing profligates.

But, about this time in 1666, the death-rate had sunk to nearly its ordinary amount; a case of plague occurred only here and there, and the richer citizens who had flown from the pest had returned to their dwellings. The remnant of the people began to toil at the accustomed round of duty, or of pleasure; and the stream of city life bid fair to flow back along its old bed, with renewed and uninterrupted vigour.

The newly-kindled hope was deceitful. The great plague, indeed, returned no more; but what it had done for the Londoners, the great fire, which broke out in the autumn of 1666, did for London; and, in September of that year, a heap of ashes and the indestructible energy of the people were all that remained of the glory of five-sixths of the city within the walls.

Our forefathers had their own ways of accounting for each of these calamities. They submitted to the plague in humility and in penitence, for they believed it to be the judgment of God. But, towards the fire they were furiously indignant, interpreting it as the effect of the malice of man,—as the work of the Republicans, or of the Papists, according as their prepossessions ran in favour of loyalty or of Puritanism.

It would, I fancy, have fared but ill with one who, standing where I now stand, in what was then a thickly-peopled and fashionable part of London, should have broached to our ancestors the doctrine which I now propound to you—that all their hypotheses were alike wrong; that the plague was no more, in their sense, Divine judgment, than the fire was the work of any political, or of any religious, sect; but that they were themselves the authors of both plague and fire, and that they must look to themselves to prevent the recurrence of calamities, to all appearance so peculiarly beyond the reach of human control—so evidently the result of the wrath of God, or of the craft and subtlety of an enemy.

And one may picture to one's self how harmoniously the holy cursing of the Puritan of that day would have chimed in with the unholy cursing and the crackling wit of the Rochesters and Sedleys, and with the revilings of the political fanatics, if my imaginary plain dealer had gone on to say that, if the return of such misfortunes were ever rendered impossible, it would not be in virtue of the victory of the faith of Laud, or of that of Milton; and, as little, by the triumph of republicanism, as by that of monarchy. But that the one thing needful for compassing this end was, that the people of England should second the efforts of an insignificant corporation, the establishment of which, a few years before the epoch of the great plague and the great fire, had been as little noticed, as they were conspicuous.

Some twenty years before the outbreak of the plague a few calm and thoughtful students banded themselves together for the purpose, as they phrased it, of "improving natural knowledge." The ends they proposed to attain cannot be stated more clearly than in the words of one of the founders of the organisation:—

"Our business was (precluding matters of theology and state affairs) to discourse and consider of philosophical enquiries, and such as related thereunto:—as Physick, Anatomy, Geometry, Astronomy, Navigation, Staticks, Magneticks, Chymicks, Mechanicks and Natural Experiments; with the state of these studies and their cultivation at home and abroad. We then discoursed of the circulation of the blood, the valves in the veins, the venæ lacteæ, the lymphatic vessels, the Copernican hypothesis, the nature of comets and new stars, the satellites of Jupiter, the oval shape (as it then appeared) of Saturn, the spots on the sun and its turning on its own axis, the inequalities and selenography of the moon, the several phases of Venus and Mercury, the improvement of telescopes and grinding of glasses for that purpose, the weight of air, the possibility or impossibility of vacuities and nature's abhorrence thereof, the Torricellian experiment in quicksilver, the descent of heavy bodies and the degree of acceleration, therein, with divers other things of like nature, some of which were then but new discoveries, and others not so generally known and embraced as now they are; with other things appertaining to what hath been called the New Philosophy, which from the times of Galileo at Florence, and Sir Francis Bacon (Lord Verulam) in England, hath been much cultivated in Italy, France, Germany, and other parts abroad, as well as with us in England."

The learned Dr. Wallis, writing in 1696, narrates in these words, what happened half a century before, or about 1645. The associates met at Oxford, in the rooms of Dr. Wilkins, who was destined to become a bishop; and subsequently coming together in London, they attracted the notice of the king. And it is a strange evidence of the taste for knowledge which the most obviously worthless of the Stuarts shared with his father and grandfather, that Charles the Second was not content with saying witty things about his philosophers, but did wise things with regard to them. For he not only bestowed upon them such attention as he could spare from his poodles and his mistresses, but, being in his usual state of impecuniosity, begged for them of the Duke of Ormond; and, that step being without effect, gave them Chelsea College, a charter, and a mace: crowning his favours in the best way they could be crowned, by burdening them no further with royal patronage or state interference.

Thus it was that the half-dozen young men, studious of the "New Philosophy," who met in one another's lodgings in Oxford or in London, in the middle of the seventeenth century, grew in numerical and in real strength, until, in its latter part, the "Royal Society for the Improvement of Natural Knowledge" had already become famous, and had acquired a claim upon the veneration of Englishmen, which it has ever since retained, as the principal focus of scientific activity in our islands, and the chief champion of the cause it was formed to support.

It was by the aid of the Royal Society that Newton published his "Principia." If all the books in the world, except the "Philosophical Transactions," were destroyed, it is safe to say that the foundations of physical science would remain unshaken, and that the vast intellectual progress of the last two centuries would be largely, though incompletely, recorded. Nor have any signs of halting or of decrepitude manifested themselves in our own times. As in Dr. Wallis's days, so in these, "our business is, precluding theology and state affairs, to discourse and consider of philosophical enquiries." But our "Mathematick" is one which Newton would have to go to school to learn; our "Staticks, Mechanicks, Magneticks, Chymicks, and Natural Experiments" constitute a mass of physical and chemical knowledge, a glimpse at which would compensate Galileo for the doings of a score of inquisitorial cardinals; our "Physick" and "Anatomy" have embraced such infinite varieties of being, have laid open such new worlds in time and space, have grappled, not unsuccessfully, with such complex problems, that the eyes of Vesalius and of Harvey might be dazzled by the sight of the tree that has grown out of their grain of mustard seed.

The fact is perhaps rather too much, than too little, forced upon one's notice, nowadays, that all this marvellous intellectual growth has a no less wonderful expression in practical life; and that, in this respect, if in no other, the movement symbolised by the progress of the Royal Society stands without a parallel in the history of mankind.

A series of volumes as bulky as the "Transactions of the Royal Society" might possibly be filled with the subtle speculations of the Schoolmen; not improbably, the obtaining a mastery over the products of mediæval thought might necessitate an even greater expenditure of time and of energy than the acquirement of the "New Philosophy;" but though such work engrossed the best intellects of Europe for a longer time than has elapsed since the great fire, its effects were "writ in water," so far as our social state is concerned.

On the other hand, if the noble first President of the Royal Society could revisit the upper air and once more gladden his eyes with a sight of the familiar mace, he would find himself in the midst of a material civilisation more different from that of his day, than that of the seventeenth was from that of the first century. And if Lord Brouncker's native sagacity had not deserted his ghost, he would need no long reflection to discover that all these great ships, these railways, these telegraphs, these factories, these printing-presses, without which the whole fabric of modern English society would collapse into a mass of stagnant and starving pauperism,— that all these pillars of our State are but the ripples and the bubbles upon the surface of that great spiritual stream, the springs of which only, he and his fellows were privileged to see; and seeing, to recognise as that which it behoved them above all things to keep pure and undefiled.

It may not be too great a flight of imagination to conceive our noble *revenant* not forgetful of the great troubles of his own day, and anxious to know how often London had been burned down since his time, and how often the plague had carried off its thousands. He would have to learn that, although London contains tenfold the inflammable matter that it did in 1666; though, not content with filling our rooms with woodwork and light draperies, we must needs lead inflammable and explosive gases into every corner of our streets and houses, we never allow even a street to burn down. And if he asked how this had come about, we should have to explain that the improvement of natural knowledge has furnished us with dozens of machines for throwing water upon fires, any one of which would have furnished the ingenious Mr. Hooke, the first "curator and experimenter" of the Royal Society, with ample materials for discourse before half a dozen meetings of that body; and that, to say truth, except for the progress of natural knowledge, we should not have been able to make even the tools by which these machines are constructed. And, further, it would be necessary to add, that although severe fires sometimes occur and inflict great damage, the loss is very generally compensated by societies, the operations of which have been rendered possible only by the progress of natural knowledge in the direction of mathematics, and the accumulation of wealth in virtue of other natural knowledge.

But the plague? My Lord Brouncker's observation would not, I fear, lead him to think that Englishmen of the nineteenth century are purer in life, or more fervent in religious faith, than the generation which could produce a Boyle, an Evelyn, and a Milton. He might find the mud of society at the bottom, instead of at the top, but I fear that the sum total would be as deserving of swift judgment as at the time of the Restoration. And it would be our duty to explain once more, and this time not without shame, that we have no reason to believe that it is the improvement of our faith, nor that of our morals, which keeps the plague from our city; but, again, that it is the improvement of our natural knowledge.

We have learned that pestilences will only take up their abode among those who have prepared unswept and ungarnished residences for them. Their cities must have narrow, unwatered streets, foul with accumulated garbage. Their houses must be ill-drained, ill-lighted, ill-ventilated. Their subjects must be ill-washed, ill-fed, ill-clothed. The London of 1665 was such a city. The cities of the East, where plague has an enduring dwelling, are such cities. We, in later times, have learned somewhat of Nature, and partly obey her. Because of this partial improvement of our natural knowledge and of that fractional obedience, we have no plague; because that knowledge is still very imperfect and that obedience yet incomplete, typhoid is our companion and cholera our visitor. But it is not presumptuous to express the belief that, when our knowledge is more complete and our obedience the expression of our knowledge, London will count her centuries of freedom from typhoid and cholera, as she now gratefully reckons her two hundred years of ignorance of that plague which swooped upon her thrice in the first half of the seventeenth century.

Surely, there is nothing in these explanations which is not fully borne out by the facts? Surely, the principles involved in them are now admitted among the fixed beliefs of all thinking men? Surely, it is true that our countrymen are less subject to fire, famine, pestilence, and all the evils which result from a want of command over and due anticipation of the course of Nature, than were the countrymen of Milton; and health, wealth, and well-being are more abundant with us than with them? But no less certainly is the difference due to the improvement of our knowledge of Nature, and the extent to which that improved knowledge has been incorporated with the household words of men, and has supplied the springs of their daily actions.

Granting for a moment, then, the truth of that which the depreciators of natural knowledge are so fond of urging, that its improvement can only add to the resources of our material civilisation; admitting it to be possible that the founders of the Royal Society themselves looked for no other reward than this, I cannot confess that I was guilty of exaggeration when I hinted, that to him who had the gift of distinguishing between prominent events and important events, the origin of a combined effort on the part of mankind to improve natural knowledge might have loomed larger than the Plague and have outshone the glare of the Fire, as a something fraught with a wealth of beneficence to mankind, in comparison with which the damage done by those ghastly evils would shrink into insignificance.

It is very certain that for every victim slain by the plague, hundreds of mankind exist and find a fair share of happiness in the world by the aid of the spinning jenny. And the great fire, at its worst, could not have burnt the supply of coal, the daily working of which, in the bowels of the earth, made possible by the steam pump, gives rise to an amount of wealth to which the millions lost in old London are but as an old song.

But spinning jenny and steam pump are, after all, but toys, possessing an accidental value; and natural knowledge creates multitudes of more subtle contrivances, the praises of which do not happen to be sung because they are not directly convertible into instruments for creating wealth. When I contemplate natural knowledge squandering such gifts among men, the only appropriate comparison I can find for her is, to liken her to such a peasant woman as one sees in the Alps, striding ever upward, heavily burdened, and with mind bent only on her home; but yet without effort and without thought, knitting for her children. Now stockings are good and comfortable things, and the children will undoubtedly be much the better for them; but surely it would be short-sighted, to say the least of it, to depreciate this toiling mother as a mere stocking-machine—a mere provider of physical comforts?

However, there are blind leaders of the blind, and not a few of them, who take this view of natural knowledge, and can see nothing in the bountiful mother of humanity but a sort of comfort-grinding machine. According to them, the improvement of natural knowledge always has been, and always must be, synonymous with no more than the improvement of the material resources and the increase of the gratifications of men.

Natural knowledge is, in their eyes, no real mother of mankind, bringing them up with kindness, and, if need be, with sternness, in the way they should go, and instructing them in all things needful for their welfare; but a sort of fairy godmother, ready to furnish her pets with shoes of swiftness, swords of sharpness, and omnipotent Aladdin's lamps, so that they may have telegraphs to Saturn, and see the other side of the moon, and thank God they are better than their benighted ancestors.

If this talk were true, I, for one, should not greatly care to toil in the service of natural knowledge. I think I would just as soon be quietly chipping my own flint axe, after the manner of my forefathers a few thousand years back, as be troubled with the endless malady of thought which now infests us all, for such reward. But I venture to say that such views are contrary alike to reason and to fact. Those who discourse in such fashion seem to me to be so intent upon trying to see what is above Nature, or what is behind her, that they are blind to what stares them in the face in her.

I should not venture to speak thus strongly if my justification were not to be found in the simplest and most obvious facts,—if it needed more than an appeal to the most notorious truths to justify my assertion, that the improvement of natural knowledge, whatever direction it has taken, and however low the aims of those who may have commenced it—has not only conferred practical benefits on men, but, in so doing, has effected a revolution in their conceptions of the universe and of themselves, and has profoundly altered their modes of thinking and their views of right and wrong. I say that natural knowledge, seeking to satisfy natural wants, has found the ideas which can alone still spiritual cravings. I say that natural knowledge, in desiring to ascertain the laws of comfort, has been driven to discover those of conduct, and to lay the foundations of a new morality.

Let us take these points separately; and first, what great ideas has natural knowledge introduced into men's minds?

I cannot but think that the foundations of all natural knowledge were laid when the reason of man first came face to face with the facts of Nature; when the savage first learned that the fingers of one hand are fewer than those of both; that it is shorter to cross a stream than to head it; that a stone stops where it is unless it be moved, and that it drops from the hand which lets it go; that light and heat come and go with the sun; that sticks burn away in a fire; that plants an animals grow and die; that if he struck his fellow savage a blow he would make him angry, and perhaps get a blow in return, while if he offered him a fruit he would please him, and perhaps receive a fish in exchange. When men had acquired this much knowledge, the outlines, rude though they were, of mathematics, of physics, of chemistry, of biology, of moral, economical, and political science, were sketched. Nor did the germ of religion fail when science began to bud. Listen to words which, though new, are yet three thousand years old:—

> ". . . When in heaven the stars about the moon
> Look beautiful, when all the winds are laid,
> And every height comes out, and jutting peak
> And valley, and the immeasurable heavens
> Break open to their highest, and all the stars

Shine, and the shepherd gladdens in his heart."[1]

If the half savage Greek could share our feelings thus far, it is irrational to doubt that he went further, to find as we do, that upon that brief gladness there follows a certain sorrow,—the little light of awakened human intelligence shines so mere a spark amidst the abyss of the unknown and unknowable; seems so insufficient to do more than illuminate the imperfections that cannot be remedied, the aspirations that cannot be realised, of man's own nature. But in this sadness, this consciousness of the limitation of man, this sense of an open secret which he cannot penetrate, lies the essence of all religion; and the attempt to embody it in the forms furnished by the intellect is the origin of the higher theologies.

Thus it seems impossible to imagine but that the foundations of all knowledge—secular or sacred—were laid when intelligence dawned, though the superstructure remained for long ages so slight and feeble as to be compatible with the existence of almost any general view respecting the mode of governance of the universe. No doubt, from the first, there were certain phænomena which, to the rudest mind, presented a constancy of occurrence, and suggested that a fixed order ruled, at any rate, among them. I doubt if the grossest of Fetish worshippers ever imagined that a stone must have a god within it to make it fall, or that a fruit had a god within it to make it taste sweet. With regard to such matters as these, it is hardly questionable that mankind from the first took strictly positive and scientific views.

But, with respect to all the less familiar occurrences which present themselves, uncultured man, no doubt, has always taken himself as the standard of comparison, as the centre and measure of the world; nor could he well avoid doing so. And finding that his apparently uncaused will has a powerful effect in giving rise to many occurrences, he naturally enough ascribed other and greater events to other and greater volitions, and came to look upon the world and all that therein is, as the product of the volitions of persons like himself, but stronger, and capable of being appeased or angered, as he himself might be soothed or irritated. Through such conceptions of the plan and working of the universe all mankind have passed, or are passing. And we may now consider what has been the effect of the improvement of natural knowledge on the views of men who have reached this stage, and who

[1] Need it be said that this is Tennyson's English for Homer's Greek?

have begun to cultivate natural knowledge with no desire but that of "increasing God's honour and bettering man's estate."

For example, what could seem wiser, from a mere material point of view, more innocent, from a theological one, to an ancient people, than that they should learn the exact succession of the seasons, as warnings for their husbandmen; or the position of the stars, as guides to their rude navigators? But what has grown out of this search for natural knowledge of so merely useful a character? You all know the reply. Astronomy,—which of all sciences has filled men's minds with general ideas of a character most foreign to their daily experience, and has, more than any other, rendered it impossible for them to accept the beliefs of their fathers. Astronomy,— which tells them that this so vast and seemingly solid earth is but an atom among atoms, whirling, no man knows whither, through illimitable space; which demonstrates that what we call the peaceful heaven above us, is but that space, filled by an infinitely subtle matter whose particles are seething and surging, like the waves of an angry sea; which opens up to us infinite regions where nothing is known, or ever seems to have been known, but matter and force, operating according to rigid rules; which leads us to contemplate phænomena the very nature of which demonstrates that they must have had a beginning, and that they must have an end, but the very nature of which also proves that the beginning was, to our conceptions of time, infinitely remote, and that the end is as immeasurably distant.

But it is not alone those who pursue astronomy who ask for bread and receive ideas. What more harmless than the attempt to lift and distribute water by pumping it; what more absolutely and grossly utilitarian? Yet out of pumps grew the discussions about Nature's abhorrence of a vacuum; and then it was discovered that Nature does not abhor a vacuum, but that air has weight; and that notion paved the way for the doctrine that all matter has weight, and that the force which produces weight is co-extensive with the universe, —in short, to the theory of universal gravitation and endless force. While learning how to handle gases led to the discovery of oxygen, and to modern chemistry, and to the notion of the indestructibility of matter.

Again, what simpler, or more absolutely practical, than the attempt to keep the axle of a wheel from heating when the wheel turns round very fast? How useful for carters and gig drivers to know something about this; and how good were it, if any ingenious person would find out the cause of such phænomena, and thence educe a general remedy for them. Such an ingenious person was Count Rumford; and he and his successors have landed us in the theory of the persistence, or indestructibility, of force. And in the infinitely minute, as in the infinitely great, the seekers after natural knowledge of the kinds called physical and chemical, have everywhere found a definite order and succession of events which seem never to be infringed.

And how has it fared with "Physick" and Anatomy? Have the anatomist, the physiologist, or the physician, whose business it has been to devote themselves assiduously to that eminently practical and direct end, the alleviation of the sufferings of mankind,—have they been able to confine their vision more absolutely to the strictly useful? I fear they are the worst offenders of all. For if the astronomer has set before us the infinite magnitude of space, and the practical eternity of the duration of the universe; if the physical and chemical philosophers have demonstrated the infinite minuteness of its constituent parts, and the practical eternity of matter and of force; and if both have alike proclaimed the universality of a definite and predicable order and succession of events, the workers in biology have not only accepted all these, but have added more startling theses of their own. For, as the astronomers discover in the earth no centre of the universe, but an eccentric speck, so the naturalists find man to be no centre of the living world, but one amidst endless modifications of life; and as the astronomer observes the mark of practically endless time set upon the arrangements of the solar system so the student of life finds the records of ancient forms of existence peopling the world for ages, which, in relation to human experience, are infinite.

Furthermore, the physiologist finds life to be as dependent for its manifestation on particular molecular arrangements as any physical or chemical phænomenon; and wherever he extends his researches, fixed order and unchanging causation reveal themselves, as plainly as in the rest of Nature.

Nor can I find that any other fate has awaited the germ of Religion. Arising, like all other kinds of knowledge, out of the action and interaction of man's mind, with that which is not man's mind, it has taken the intellectual coverings of Fetishism or Polytheism; of Theism or Atheism; of Superstition or Rationalism. With these, and their relative merits and demerits, I have nothing to do; but this it is needful for my purpose to say, that if the religion of the present differs from that of the past, it is because the theology of the present has become more scientific than that of the past; because it has not only renounced idols of wood and idols of stone, but begins to see the necessity of breaking in pieces the idols built up of books and traditions and fine-spun ecclesiastical cobwebs: and of cherishing the noblest and most human of man's emotions, by worship "for the most part of the silent sort" at the altar of the Unknown.

Such are a few of the new conceptions implanted in our minds by the improvement of natural knowledge. Men have acquired the ideas of the practically infinite extent of the universe and of its practical eternity; they are familiar with the conception that our earth is but an infinitesimal fragment of that part of the universe which can be seen; and that, nevertheless, its duration is, as compared with our standards of time, infinite. They have further acquired the idea that man is but one of innumerable forms of life now existing on the globe, and that the present existences are but the last of an immeasurable series of predecessors. Moreover, every step they have made in natural knowledge has tended to extend and rivet in their minds the conception of a definite order of the universe—which is embodied in what are called, by an unhappy metaphor, the laws of Nature—and to narrow the range and loosen the force of men's belief in spontaneity, or in changes other than such as arise out of that definite order itself.

Whether these ideas are well or ill founded is not the question. No one can deny that they exist, and have been the inevitable outgrowth of the improvement of natural knowledge. And if so, it cannot be doubted that they are changing the form of men's most cherished and most important convictions.

And as regards the second point—the extent to which the improvement of natural knowledge has remodelled and altered what may be termed the intellectual ethics of men,—what are among the moral convictions most fondly held by barbarous and semi-barbarous people.

They are the convictions that authority is the soundest basis of belief; that merit attaches to a readiness to believe; that the doubting disposition is a bad one, and scepticism a sin; that when good authority has pronounced what is to be believed, and faith has accepted it, reason has no further duty. There are many excellent persons who yet hold by these principles, and it is not my present business, or intention, to discuss their views. All I wish to bring clearly before your minds is the unquestionable fact, that the improvement of natural knowledge is effected by methods which directly give the lie to all these convictions, and assume the exact reverse of each to be true.

The improver of natural knowledge absolutely refuses to acknowledge authority, as such. For him, scepticism is the highest of duties; blind faith the one unpardonable sin. And it cannot be otherwise, for every great advance in natural knowledge has involved the absolute rejection of authority, the cherishing of the keenest scepticism, the annihilation of the spirit of blind faith; and the most ardent votary of science holds his firmest convictions, not because the men he most venerates hold them; not because their verity is testified by portents and wonders; but because his experience teaches him that whenever he chooses to bring these convictions into contact with their primary source, Nature—whenever he thinks fit to test them by appealing to experiment and to observation—Nature will confirm them. The man of science has learned to believe in justification, not by faith, but by verification.

Thus, without for a moment pretending to despise the practical results of the improvement of natural knowledge, and its beneficial influence on material civilisation, it must, I think, be admitted that the great ideas, some of which I have indicated, and the ethical spirit which I have endeavoured to sketch, in the few moments which remained at my disposal, constitute the real and permanent significance of natural knowledge.

If these ideas be destined, as I believe they are, to be more and more firmly established as the world grows older; if that spirit be fated, as I believe it is, to extend itself into all departments of human thought, and to become co-extensive with the range of knowledge; if, as our race approaches its maturity, it discovers, as I believe it will, that there is but one kind of knowledge and but one method of acquiring it; then we, who are still children, may justly feel it our highest duty to recognise the advisableness of improving natural knowledge, and so to aid ourselves and our successors in our course towards the noble goal which lies before mankind.

WASHINGTON IRVING
1783–1859

Washington Irving's is a name every adult American reader recalls from his early school days, when he studied "Rip Van Winkle" and learned that Irving was the "father of American literature." Since those days, he may well have encountered Irving only rarely, or not at all, for Irving has been out of fashion. He has been considered too moderate, too proper, too complacent. This moderation, however, was Irving's direct and legitimate heritage from the eighteenth century. His *Sketch Book* papers, published in 1819-20, continued in an unbroken line the great tradition of Addison, Steele, and Goldsmith. The wonder of it was that an American, dealing partly with American material, should have a place in that line. So to assert, not American literary independence, but American literary existence, was an enormous achievement at that time, which no changes of fashion should gloss over. For our time, moreover, Irving in his best sketches retains qualities of which we seem to have a very short supply: sanity, civility, and a healthy humor.

The Art of Book-Making

"If that severe doom of Synesius be true—'It is a greater offence to steal dead men's labor, than their clothes,' what shall become of most writers?"

—BURTON'S ANATOMY OF MELANCHOLY.

I have often wondered at the extreme fecundity of the press, and how it comes to pass that so many heads, on which nature seemed to have inflicted the curse of barrenness, should teem with voluminous productions. As a man travels on, however, in the journey of life, his objects of wonder daily diminish, and he is continually finding out some very simple cause for some great matter of marvel. Thus have I chanced, in my peregrinations about this great metropolis, to blunder upon a scene which unfolded to me some of the mysteries of the book-making craft, and at once put an end to my astonishment.

I was one summer's day loitering through the great saloons of the British Museum, with that listlessness with which one is apt to saunter about a museum in warm weather; sometimes lolling over the glass cases of minerals, sometimes studying the hieroglyphics on an Egyptian mummy, and sometimes trying, with nearly equal success, to comprehend the allegorical paintings on the lofty ceilings. Whilst I was gazing about in this idle way, my attention was attracted to a distant door, at the end of a suite of apartments. It was closed, but every now and then it would open, and some strange-favored being, generally clothed in black, would steal forth, and glide through the rooms, without noticing any of the surrounding objects. There was an air of mystery about this that piqued my languid curiosity, and I determined to attempt the passage of that strait, and to explore the unknown regions beyond. The door yielded to my hand, with that facility with which the portals of enchanted castles yield to the adventurous knight-errant. I found myself in a spacious chamber, surrounded with great cases of venerable books. Above the cases, and just under the cornice, were arranged a great number of black-looking portraits of ancient authors. About the room were placed long tables, with stands for reading and writing, at which sat many pale, studious personages, poring intently over dusty volumes, rummaging among mouldy manuscripts, and taking copious notes of their contents. A hushed stillness reigned through this mysterious apartment, excepting that you might hear the racing of pens over sheets of paper, or occasionally, the deep sigh of one of these sages, as he shifted his position to turn over the page of an old folio; doubtless arising from that hollowness and flatulency incident to learned research.

Now and then one of these personages would write something on a small slip of paper, and ring a bell, whereupon a familiar would appear, take the paper in profound silence, glide out of the room, and return shortly loaded with ponderous tomes, upon which the other would fall tooth and nail with famished voracity. I had no longer a doubt that I had happened upon a body of magi, deeply engaged in the study of occult sciences. The scene reminded me of an old Arabian tale, of a philosopher shut up in an enchanted library, in the bosom of a mountain, which opened only once a year; where he made the spirits of the place bring him books of all kinds of dark knowledge, so that at the end of the year, when the magic portal once more swung open on its hinges, he issued forth so versed in forbidden lore, as to be able to soar above the heads of the multitude, and to control the powers of nature.

My curiosity being now fully aroused, I whispered to one of the familiars, as he was about to leave the room, and begged an interpretation of the strange scene before me. A few words were sufficient for the purpose. I found that these mysterious personages, whom I had mistaken for magi, were principally authors, and in the very act of manufacturing books. I was, in fact, in the reading-room of the great British Library—an immense collection of volumes of all ages and languages, many of which are now forgotten, and most of which are seldom read: one of the sequestered pools of obsolete literature, to which modern authors repair, and draw buckets full of classic lore, or "pure English, undefiled," wherewith to swell their scanty rills of thought.

Being now in possession of the secret, I sat down in a corner, and watched the process of this book manufactory. I noticed one lean, bilious-looking wight, who sought none but the most worm-eaten volumes, printed in black-letter. He was evidently constructing some work of profound erudition, that would be purchased by every man who wished to be thought learned, placed upon a conspicuous shelf of his library, or laid open upon his table; but never read. I observed him, now and then, draw a large fragment of biscuit out of his pocket, and gnaw; whether it was his dinner, or whether he was endeavoring to keep off that exhaustion of the stomach produced by much pondering over dry works, I leave to harder students than myself to determine.

There was one dapper little gentleman in bright-colored clothes, with a chirping, gossiping expression of countenance, who had all the appearance of an author on good terms with his bookseller. After considering him attentively, I recognized in him a diligent getter-up of miscellaneous works, which bustled off well with the trade. I was curious to see how he manufactured his wares. He made more stir and show of business than any of the others; dipping into various books, fluttering over the leaves of manuscripts, taking a morsel out of one, a morsel out of another, "line upon line, precept upon precept, here a little and there a little." The contents of his book seemed to be as heterogeneous as those of the witches' caldron in "Macbeth." It was here a finger and there a thumb, toe of frog and blind-worm's sting, with his own gossip poured in like "baboon's blood," to make the medley "slab and good."

After all, thought I, may not this pilfering disposition be implanted in authors for wise purposes; may it not be the way in which Providence has taken care that the seeds of knowledge and wisdom shall be preserved from age to age, in spite of the inevitable decay of the works in which they were first produced? We see that nature has wisely, though whimsically, provided for the conveyance of seeds from clime to clime, in the maws of certain birds; so that animals, which, in themselves, are little better than carrion, and apparently the lawless plunderers of the orchard and the cornfield, are, in fact, nature's carriers to disperse and perpetuate her blessings. In like manner, the beauties and fine thoughts of ancient and obsolete authors are caught up by these flights of predatory writers, and cast forth again to flourish and bear fruit in a remote and distant tract of time. Many of their works, also, undergo a kind of metempsychosis, and spring up under new forms. What was formerly a ponderous history revives in the shape of a romance—an old legend changes into a modern play—and a sober philosophical treatise furnishes the body for a whole series of bouncing and sparkling essays. Thus it is in the clearing of our American woodlands; where we burn down a forest of stately pines, a progeny of dwarf oaks start up in their place; and we never see the prostrate trunk of a tree mouldering into soil, but it gives birth to a whole tribe of fungi.

Let us not, then, lament over the decay and oblivion into which ancient writers descend; they do but submit to the great law of nature, which declares that all sub-lunary shapes of matter shall be limited in their duration, but which decrees, also, that their elements shall never perish. Generation after generation, both in animal and vegetable life, passes away, but the vital principle is transmitted to posterity, and the species continue to flourish. Thus, also, do authors beget authors, and having produced a numerous progeny, in a good old age they sleep with their fathers, that is to say, with the authors who preceded them—and from whom they had stolen.

Whilst I was indulging in these rambling fancies, I had leaned my head against a pile of reverend folios. Whether it was owing to the soporific emanations from these works; or to the profound quiet of the room; or to the lassitude arising from much wandering; or to an unlucky habit of napping at improper times and places, with which I am grievously af-flicted, so it was, that I fell into a doze. Still, however, my imagination continued busy, and indeed the same scene remained before my mind's eye, only a little changed in some of the details. I dreamt that the chamber was still decorated with the portraits of ancient authors, but that the number was increased. The long tables had disappeared, and, in place of the sage magi, I beheld a ragged, threadbare throng, such as may be seen plying about the great repository of cast-off clothes, Monmouth-street. Whenever they seized upon a book, by one of those incongruities common to dreams, methought it turned into a garment of foreign or antique fashion, with which they proceeded to equip themselves. I noticed, however, that no one pretended to clothe himself from any particular suit, but took a sleeve from one, a cape from another, a skirt from a third, thus decking himself out piecemeal, while some of his original rags would peep out from among his borrowed finery.

There was a portly, rosy, well-fed parson, whom I observed ogling several mouldy polemical writers through an eye-glass. He soon contrived to slip on the voluminous mantle of one of the old fathers, and, having purloined the gray beard of another, endeavored to look exceedingly wise; but the smirking commonplace of his countenance set at naught all the trappings of wisdom. One sickly-looking gentleman was busied embroidering a very flimsy garment with gold thread drawn out of several old court-dresses of the reign of Queen Elizabeth. Another had trimmed himself magnificently from an illuminated manuscript, had stuck a nosegay in his bosom, culled from "The Paradise of Daintie Devices," and having put Sir Philip Sidney's hat on one side of his head, strutted off with an exquisite air of vulgar elegance. A third, who was but of puny dimensions, had bolstered himself out bravely with the spoils from several obscure tracts of philosophy, so that he had a very imposing front; but he was lamentably tattered in rear, and I perceived that he had patched his small-clothes with scraps of parchment from a Latin author.

There were some well-dressed gentlemen, it is true, who only helped themselves to a gem or so, which sparkled among their own ornaments, without eclipsing them. Some, too, seemed to contemplate the costumes of the old writers, merely to imbibe their principles of taste, and to catch their air and spirit; but I grieve to say, that too many were apt to array themselves from top to toe in the patchwork manner I have mentioned. I shall not omit to speak of one genius, in drab breeches and gaiters, and an Arcadian hat, who had a violent propensity to the pastoral, but whose rural wanderings had been confined to the classic haunts of Primrose Hill, and the solitudes of the Regent's Park. He had decked himself in wreaths and ribbons from all the old pastoral poets, and, hanging his head on one side, went about with a fantastical lack-a-daisical air, "babbling about green fields." But the personage that most struck my attention was a pragmatical old gentleman, in clerical robes, with a remarkably large and square, but bald head. He entered the room wheezing and puffing, elbowed his way through the throng, with a look of sturdy self-confidence, and having laid hands upon a thick Greek quarto, clapped it upon his head, and swept majestically away in a formidable frizzled wig.

In the height of this literary masquerade, a cry suddenly resounded from every side, of "Thieves! thieves!" I looked, and lo! the portraits about the wall became animated! The old authors thrust out, first a head, then a shoulder, from the canvas, looked down curiously, for an instant, upon the motley throng, and then descended with fury in their eyes, to claim their rifled property. The scene of scampering and hubbub that ensued baffles all description. The unhappy culprits endeavored in vain to escape with their plunder. On one side might be seen half a dozen old monks, stripping a modern professor; on another, there was sad devastation carried into the ranks of modern dramatic writers. Beaumont and Fletcher, side by side, raged round the field like Castor and Pollux, and sturdy Ben Jonson enacted more wonders than when a volunteer with the army in Flanders. As to the dapper little compiler of farragos, mentioned some time since, he had arrayed himself in as many patches and colors as Harlequin, and there was as fierce a contention of claimants about him, as about the dead body of Patroclus. I was grieved to see many men, to whom I had been accustomed to look up with awe and reverence, fain to steal off with scarce a rag to cover their nakedness. Just then my eye was caught by the pragmatical old gentleman in the Greek grizzled wig, who was scrambling away in sore affright with half a score of authors in full cry after him! They were close upon his haunches: in a twinkling off went his wig; at every turn some strip of raiment was peeled away; until in a few moments, from his domineering pomp, he shrunk into a little, pursy, "chopped bald shot," and made his exit with only a few tags and rags fluttering at his back.

There was something so ludicrous in the catastrophe of

this learned Theban, that I burst into an immoderate fit of laughter, which broke the whole illusion. The tumult and the scuffle were at an end. The chamber resumed its usual appearance. The old authors shrunk back into their picture-frames, and hung in shadowy solemnity along the walls. In short, I found myself wide awake in my corner, with the whole assemblage of book-worms gazing at me with astonishment. Nothing of the dream had been real but my burst of laughter, a sound never before heard in that grave sanctuary, and so abhorrent to the ears of wisdom, as to electrify the fraternity.

The librarian now stepped up to me, and demanded whether I had a card of admission. At first I did not comprehend him, but I soon found that the library was a kind of literary "preserve," subject to game-laws, and that no one must presume to hunt there without special license and permission. In a word, I stood convicted of being an arrant poacher, and was glad to make a precipitate retreat, lest I should have a whole pack of authors let loose on me.

SAMUEL JOHNSON
1709–1784

At the famous first meeting of Dr. Johnson and James Boswell
in Tom Davies' bookstore, Davies announced Johnson's approach
with Horatio's words to Hamlet on the appearance of his
father's ghost: "Look, my Lord, it comes." For although Johnson's
person was in no way ghostly, it was impressive and portentous;
and both Davies and Boswell seemed to sense that this encounter
was the first scene of a great drama. Yet that same hulking, over-
powering Johnson could be gentle, playful and affectionate. That
wielder of the polysyllabic word and the Latinate period, that
lexicographer and legislator of the English language, not only
could but most often did, write with humor, common sense, and
amazing psychological penetration. Rarely has the eternal problem of the conflict between the generations been probed more
acutely or more sanely than in this essay, "On Old Age," from
Johnson's periodical, the *Rambler,* published from 1750 to 1752.

On Old Age

Credebant hoc grande nefas, et morte piandum,
Si juvenis vetulo non assurrexerat, atque
Barbato cuicunque puer, licet ipse videret
Plura domi fraga, et majores glandis acervos.
—Juv. Sat. xiii. 54.

And had not men the hoary head rever'd,
And boys paid rev'rence when a man appear'd,
Both must have died, though richer skins they wore,
And saw more heaps of acorns in their store.
—Creech.

I have always thought it the business of those who turn their
speculations upon the living world, to commend the virtues,
as well as to expose the faults of their comtemporaries, and
to confute a false as well as to support a just accusation; not
only because it is peculiarly the business of a monitor to keep

his own reputation untainted, lest those who can once charge him with partiality, should indulge themselves afterwards in disbelieving him at pleasure; but because he may find real crimes sufficient to give full employment to caution or repentance, without distracting the mind by needless scruples and vain solicitudes.

There are certain fixed and stated reproaches that one part of mankind has in all ages thrown upon another, which are regularly transmitted through continued successions, and which he that has once suffered them is certain to use with the same undistinguishing vehemence, when he has changed his station, and gained the prescriptive right of inflicting on others what he had formerly endured himself.

To these hereditary imputations, of which no man sees the justice, till it becomes his interest to see it, very little regard is to be shewn; since it does not appear that they are produced by ratiocination or inquiry, but received implicitly, or caught by a kind of instantaneous contagion, and supported rather by willingness to credit, than ability to prove, them.

It has been always the practice of those who are desirous to believe themselves made venerable by length of time, to censure the new comers into life, for want of respect to grey hairs and sage experience, for heady confidence in their own understandings, for hasty conclusions upon partial views, for disregard of counsels, which their fathers and grandsires are ready to afford them, and a rebellious impatience of that subordination to which youth is condemned by nature, as necessary to its security from evils into which it would be otherwise precipitated, by the rashness of passion, and the blindness of ignorance.

Every old man complains of the growing depravity of the world, of the petulance and insolence of the rising generation. He recounts the decency and regularity of former times, and celebrates the discipline and sobriety of the age in which his youth was passed; a happy age, which is now no more to be expected, since confusion has broken in upon the world, and thrown down all the boundaries of civility and reverence.

It is not sufficiently considered how much he assumes who dares to claim the privilege of complaining; for as every man has, in his own opinion, a full share of the miseries of life, he is inclined to consider all clamorous uneasiness, as a proof of impatience rather than of affliction, and to ask, what merit has this man to show, by which he has acquired a right to repine at the distributions of nature? Or, why does he imagine that exemptions should be granted him from the general condition of man? We find ourselves excited rather to captiousness than pity, and instead of being in haste to soothe his complaints by sympathy and tenderness, we enquire, whether the pain be proportionate to the lamentation; and whether, supposing the affliction real, it is not the effect of vice and folly, rather than calamity.

The querulousness and indignation which is observed so often to disfigure the last scene of life, naturally leads us to enquiries like these. For surely it will be thought at the first view of things, that if age be thus contemned and ridiculed, insulted and neglected, the crime must at least be equal on either part. They who have had opportunities of establishing their authority over minds ductile and unresisting, they who have been the protectors of helplessness, and the instructors of ignorance, and who yet retain in their own hands the power of wealth, and the dignity of command, must defeat their influence by their own misconduct, and make use of all these advantages with very little skill, if they cannot secure to themselves an appearance of respect, and ward off open mockery, and declared contempt.

The general story of mankind will evince, that lawful and settled authority is very seldom resisted when it is well employed. Gross corruption, or evident imbecility, is necessary to the suppression of that reverence with which the majority of mankind look upon their governors, and on those whom they see surrounded by splendour, and fortified by power. For though men are drawn by their passions into forgetfulness of invisible rewards and punishments, yet they are easily kept obedient to those who have temporal dominion in their hands, till their veneration is dissipated by such wickedness and folly as can neither be defended nor concealed.

It may, therefore, very reasonably be suspected that the old draw upon themselves the greatest part of those insults which they so much lament, and that age is rarely despised but when it is contemptible. If men imagine that excess of debauchery can be made reverend by time, that knowledge is the consequence of long life, however idly or thoughtlessly employed, that priority of birth will supply the want of steadiness or honesty, can it raise much wonder that their hopes are disappointed, and that they see their posterity rather willing to trust their own eyes in their progress into life, than enlist themselves under guides who have lost their way?

There are, indeed, many truths which time necessarily and

certainly teaches, and which might, by those who have learned them from experience, be communicated to their successors at a cheaper rate: but dictates, though liberally enough bestowed, are generally without effect, the teacher gains few proselytes by instruction which his own behaviour contradicts; and young men miss the benefit of counsel, because they are not very ready to believe that those who fell below them in practice, can much excell them in theory. Thus the progress of knowledge is retarded, the world is kept long in the same state, and every new race is to gain the prudence of their predecessors by committing and redressing the same miscarriages.

To secure to the old that influence which they are willing to claim, and which might so much contribute to the improvement of the arts of life, it is absolutely necessary that they give themselves up to the duties of declining years; and contentedly resign to youth its levity, its pleasures, its frolicks, and its fopperies. It is a hopeless endeavour to unite the contrarieties of spring and winter; it is unjust to claim the privileges of age, and retain the playthings of childhood. The young always form magnificent ideas of the wisdom and gravity of men, whom they consider as placed at a distance from them in the ranks of existence, and naturally look on those whom they find trifling with long beards, with contempt and indignation, like that which women feel at the effeminacy of men. If dotards will contend with boys in those performances in which boys must always excel them; if they will dress crippled limbs in embroidery, endeavour at gaiety with faultering voices, and darken assemblies of pleasure with the ghastliness of disease, they may well expect those who find their diversions obstructed will hoot them away; and that if they descend to competition with youth, they must bear the insolence of successful rivals.

> *Lusisti satis, edisti satis atque bibisti:*
> *Tempus abire tibi est.*

> You've had your share of mirth, of meat and drink;
> 'Tis time to quit the scene—'tis time to think.
> —ELPHINSTON.

Another vice of age, by which the rising generation may be alienated from it, is severity and censoriousness, that gives no allowance to the failings of early life, that expects artfulness from childhood, and constancy from youth, that is peremptory in every command, and inexorable to every failure. There are many who live merely to hinder happiness, and whose descendants can only tell of long life, that it produces suspicion, malignity, peevishness, and persecution: and yet even these tyrants can talk of the ingratitude of the age, curse their heirs for impatience, and wonder that young men cannot take pleasure in their father's company.

He that would pass the latter part of life with honour and decency, must, when he is young, consider that he shall one day be old; and remember, when he is old, that he has once been young. In youth, he must lay up knowledge for his support, when his powers of acting shall forsake him; and in age forbear to animadvert with rigour on faults which experience only can correct.

CHARLES LAMB
1775–1834

A simplified history of the essay might run like this: Montaigne invented it; Bacon fathered it in English; Addison and Steele made it popular; but Charles Lamb made it synonymous with his own name. Whatever else the word "essay" may connote for the English reader, it inevitably raises up the shade of Charles Lamb, "the frolic and the gentle," the author of the *Essays of Elia*. Yet Lamb had considered himself at first a poet rather than a prose writer; and when, years later, he dedicated a volume of his early poetry to Coleridge, he apologized for having "dwindled into prose and criticism." To dwindle into prose like Lamb's, a significant number of poets would certainly forsake their Muse; but such prose is no more easily achieved than verse of equal excellence. For Lamb the achievement seemed easy only because in him all the rare yet essential elements were happily combined. His was the eighteenth-century heritage of clear, straightforward, if sometimes heavy exposition. The more varied, more resonant, more antique style of the seventeenth century was his too—the style of Sir Thomas Browne, of Burton and Fuller. And his— and only his—were the humor, the insight, the kindliness, the charm, which inform all the *Essays of Elia*. It is an amusing note that the following essay, "The Old and the New School-Master," makes a little gentle fun of the ideas on education proposed by no less a personage than John Milton, in his essay printed in this book.

The Old and the New School-Master

My reading has been lamentably desultory and immethodical. Odd, out of the way, old English plays and treatises, have supplied me with most of my notions and ways of feeling. In everything that relates to *science,* I am a whole Encyclopædia behind the rest of the world. I should have scarce-

ly cut a figure among the Franklins or country gentlemen in
King John's days. I know less geography than a school-boy
of six weeks' standing. To me a map of old Ortelius is as
authenthic as Arrowsmith. I do not know whereabout Africa
merges into Asia; whether Ethiopia lies in one or other of
those great divisions; nor can form the remotest conjecture of
the position of New South Wales, or Van Diemen's Land. Yet
do I hold a correspondence with a very dear friend in the first
named of these two Terræ Incognitæ. I have no astronomy.
I do not know where to look for the Bear, or Charles' Wain;
the place of any star; or the name of any of them at sight; I
guess at Venus only by her brightness—and if the sun on
some portentous morn were to make his first appearance in
the west, I verily believe, that, while all the world were gasp-
ing in apprehension about me, I alone should stand unterri-
fied, from sheer incuriosity and want of observation. Of
history and chronology I possess some vague points, such
as one cannot help picking up in the course of miscellaneous
study; but I never deliberately sat down to a chronicle, even
of my own country. I have most dim apprehensions of the
four great monarchies; and sometimes the Assyrian, sometimes the Persian, floats as *first* in my fancy. I make the
wildest conjectures concerning Egypt, and her shepherd kings.
My friend *M.*, with great painstaking, got me to think I understood the first proposition in Euclid, but gave me over in
despair at the second. I am entirely unacquainted with the
modern languages; and, like a better man than myself, have
"small Latin and less Greek." I am a stranger to the shapes
and texture of the commonest trees, herbs, flowers—not from
the circumstance of my being town-born—for I should have
brought the same inobservant spirit into the world with me,
had I first seen it "on Devon's leafy shores," and am no less
at a loss among purely town objects, tools, engines, mechanic
processes. Not that I affect ignorance—but my head has
not many mansions, nor spacious; and I have been obliged to
fill it with such cabinet curiosities as it can hold without
aching. I sometimes wonder how I have passed my probation
with so little discredit in the world, as I have done, upon so
meagre a stock. But the fact is, a man may do very well with
a very little knowledge, and scarce be found out, in mixed
company; everybody is so much more ready to produce his
own, than to call for a display of your acquisitions. But in a
tête-à-tête there is no shuffling. The truth will out. There is
nothing which I dread so much as the being left alone for a

quarter of an hour with a sensible, well-informed man that does not know me. I lately got into a dilemma of this sort.

In one of my daily jaunts between Bishopsgate and Shacklewell, the coach stopped to take up a staid-looking gentleman, about the wrong side of thirty, who was giving his parting direction (while the steps were adjusting), in a tone of mild authority, to a tall youth, who seemed to be neither his clerk, his son, nor his servant, but something partaking of all three. The youth was dismissed, and we drove on. As we were the sole passengers, he naturally enough addressed his conversation to me; and we discussed the merits of the fare; the civility and punctuality of the driver; the circumstance of an opposition coach having been lately set up, with the probabilities of its success—to all which I was enabled to return pretty satisfactory answers, having been drilled into this kind of etiquette by some years' daily practice of riding to and fro in the stage aforesaid—when he suddenly alarmed me by a startling question, whether I had seen the show of prize cattle that morning in Smithfield? Now, as I had not seen it, and do not greatly care for such sort of exhibitions, I was obliged to return a cold negative. He seemed a little mortified, as well as astonished at my declaration, as (it appeared) he was just come fresh from the sight and doubtless had hoped to compare notes on the subject. However, he assured me that I had lost a fine treat, as it far exceeded the show of last year. We were now approaching Norton Folgate, when the sight of some shop-goods *ticketed* freshened him up into a dissertation upon the cheapness of cottons this spring. I was now a little in heart, as the nature of my morning avocations had brought me into some sort of familiarity with the raw material, and I was surprised to find how eloquent I was becoming on the state of the India market, when presently he dashed my incipient vanity to the earth at once, by inquiring whether I had ever made any calculation as to the value of the rental of all the retail shops in London. Had he asked of men what song the Syrens sang, or what name Achilles assumed when he hid himself among women, I might, with Sir Thomas Browne, have hazarded a "wide solution."[1] My companion saw my embarrassment, and the almshouses beyond Shoreditch just coming in view, with great good nature and dexterity shifted his conversation to the subject of public charities, which led to the comparative merits of provision for the poor in past and present times, with observations on the old mo-

[1] *Urn Burial.*

nastic institutions, and charitable orders; but finding me rather
dimly impressed with some glimmering notions from old
poetic associations, than strongly fortified with any speculations reducible to calculation on the subject, he gave the
matter up, and, the country beginning to open more and
more upon us, as we approached the turnpike at Kingsland
(the destined termination of his journey), he put a home
thrust upon me, in the most unfortunate position he could
have chosen, by advancing some queries relative to the North
Pole Expedition. While I was muttering out something about
the Panorama of those strange regions (which I had actually
seen), by way of parrying the question, the coach stopping
relieved me from any further apprehensions. My companion
getting out, left me in the comfortable possession of my
ignorance, and I heard him, as he went off, putting questions
to an outside passenger who had alighted with him, regarding
an epidemic disorder that had been rife about Dalston, and
which my friend assured him had gone through five or six
schools in that neighborhood. The truth now flashed upon
me that my companion was a school-master, and that the
youth whom he had parted from at our first acquaintance,
must have been one of the bigger boys or the usher. He was
evidently a kind-hearted man, who did not seem so much
desirous of provoking discussion by the questions which he
put, as of obtaining information at any rate. It did not appear
that he took any interest, either, in such kind of inquiries,
for their own sake; but that he was in some way bound to
seek for knowledge. A greenish-colored coat, which he had
on, forbade me to surmise that he was a clergyman. The adventure gave birth to some reflections on the difference between persons of his profession in past and present times.

Rest to the souls of those fine old Pedagogues; the breed,
long since extinct, of the Lilys, and the Linacres; who believing that all learning was contained in the languages which
they taught, and despising every other acquirement as superficial and useless, came to their task as to a sport! Passing
from infancy to age, they dreamed away all their days as in a
grammar-school. Revolving in a perpetual cycle of declen-
sions, conjugations, syntaxes, and prosodies; renewing constantly the occupations which had charmed their studious
childhood; rehearsing continually the part of the past; life
must have slipped from them at last like one day. They were
always in their first garden, reaping harvests of their golden
time, among their *Flori* and their *Spici-legia;* in Arcadia still,

but kings; the ferule of their sway not much harsher, but of like dignity with that mild sceptre attributed to king Basileus; the Greek and Latin, their stately Pamela and their Philoclea; with the occasional duncery of some untoward tyro, serving for a refreshing interlude of a Mopsa, or a clown Damœtas!

With what a savor doth the Preface to Colet's, or (as it is sometimes called) Paul's Accidence, set forth! "To exhort every man to the learning of Grammar, that intendeth to attain the understanding of the tongues, wherein is contained a great treasury of wisdom and knowledge, it would seem but vain and lost labor; for so much as it is known, that nothing can surely be ended, whose beginning is either feeble or faulty; and no building be perfect whereas the foundation and groundwork is ready to fall, and unable to uphold the burden of the frame." How well doth this stately preamble (comparable to those which Milton commendeth as "having been the usage to prefix to some solemn law, then first promulgated by Solon or Lycurgus") correspond with and illustrate that pious zeal for conformity, expressed in a succeeding clause, which would fence about grammar-rules with the severity of faith-articles!—"as for the diversity of grammars, it is well profitably taken away by the King's Majesties wisdom, who foreseeing the inconvenience, and favorably providing the remedy, caused one kind of grammar by sundry learned men to be diligently drawn, and so to be set out, only everywhere to be taught for the use of learners, and for the hurt in changing of school-masters." What a *gusto* in that which follows: "wherein it is profitable that he (the pupil) can orderly decline his noun and his verb." *His* noun!

The fine dream is fading away fast: and the least concern of a teacher in the present day is to inculcate grammar rules.

The modern school-master is expected to know a little of everything, because his pupil is required not to be entirely ignorant of anything. He must be superficially, if I may say, omniscient. He is to know something of pneumatics; of chemistry; of whatever is curious or proper to excite the attention of the youthful mind; an insight into mechanics is desirable, with a touch of statistics; the quality of soils, etc, botany, the constitution of his country, *cum multis aliis*. You may get a notion of some part of his expected duties by consulting the famous Tractate on Education, addressed to Mr. Hartlib.

All these things—these, or the desire of them—he is expected to instil, not by set lessons from professors, which he may charge in the bill, but at school intervals, as he walks the

streets, or saunters through green fields (those natural instructors), with his pupils. The least part of what is expected
from him is to be done in school-hours. He must insinuate
knowledge at the *mollia tempora fandi*. He must seize every
occasion, the season of the year, the time of the day, a passing
cloud, a rainbow, a wagon of hay, a regiment of soldiers going
by, to inculcate something useful. He can receive no pleasure
from a casual glimpse of Nature, but must catch at it as an
object of instruction. He must interpret beauty into the picturesque. He cannot relish a beggar-man, or a gypsy, for thinking of the suitable improvement. Nothing comes to him, not
spoiled by the sophisticating medium of moral uses. The Universe—that Great Book, as it has been called—is to him,
indeed, to all intents and purposes, a book out of which he is
doomed to read tedious homilies to distasting school-boys.
Vacations themselves are none to him, he is only rather worse
off than before; for commonly he has some intrusive upper-
boy fastened upon him at such times; some cadet of a great
family; some neglected lump of nobility, or gentry; that he
must drag after him to the play, to the Panorama, to Mr.
Bartley's Orrery, to the Panopticon, or into the country, to a
friend's house, or his favorite watering-place. Wherever he
goes this uneasy shadow attends him. A boy is at his board,
and in his path, and in all his movements. He is boy-rid, sick
of perpetual boy.

Boys are capital fellows in their own way, among their
mates; but they are unwholesome companions for grown people. The restraint is felt no less on the one side than on the
other. Even a child, that "plaything for an hour," tires *always*. The noises of children, playing their own fancies—as I
now hearken to them, by fits, sporting on the green before my
window, while I am engaged in these grave speculations at
my neat suburban retreat at Shacklewell—by distance made
more sweet—inexpressibly take from the labor of my task.
It is like writing to music. They seem to modulate my periods.
They ought at least to do so—for in the voice of that tender
age there is a kind of poetry far unlike the harsh prose-
accents of man's conversation. I should but spoil their sport,
and diminish my own sympathy for them, by mingling in
their pastime.

I would not be domesticated all my days with a person of
very superior capacity to my own—not, if I know myself at
all, from any consideration of jealousy or self-comparison, for
the occasional communion with such minds has constituted

the fortune and felicity of my life—but the habit of too constant intercourse with spirits above you, instead of raising you, keeps you down. Too frequent doses of original thinking from others restrain what lesser portion of that faculty you may possess of your own. You get entangled in another man's mind, even as you lose yourself in another man's grounds. You are walking with a tall varlet, whose strides out-pace yours to lassitude. The constant operation of such potent agency would reduce me, I am convinced, to imbecility. You may derive thoughts from others; your way of thinking, the mould in which your thoughts are cast, must be your own. Intellect may be imparted, but not each man's intellectual frame.

As little as I should wish to be always thus dragged upward, as little (or rather still less) is it desirable to be stunted downward by your associates. The trumpet does not more stun you by its loudness than a whisper teases you by its provoking inaudibility.

Why are we never quite at our ease in the presence of a school-master? Because we are conscious that he is not quite at his ease in ours. He is awkward, and out of place in the society of his equals. He comes like Gulliver from among his little people, and he cannot fit the stature of his understanding to yours. He cannot meet you on the square. He wants a point given him, like an indifferent whist-player. He is so used to teaching, that he wants to be teaching *you*. One of these professors, upon my complaining that these little sketches of mine were anything but methodical, and that I was unable to make them otherwise, kindly offered to instruct me in the method by which young gentlemen in *his* seminary were taught to compose English themes. The jests of a school-master are coarse or thin. They do not *ell* out of school. He is under the restraint of a formal or didactive hypocrisy in company, as a clergyman is under a moral one. He can no more let his intellect loose in society than the other can his inclinations. He is forlorn among his coevals; his juniors cannot be his friends.

"I take blame to my self," said a sensible man of this profession writing to a friend respecting a youth who had quitted his school abruptly, "that your nephew was not more attached to me. But persons in my situation are more to be pitied than can well be imagined. We are surrounded by young, and, consequently, ardently affectionate hearts, but *we* can never hope to share an atom of their affections. The relation of master and scholar forbids this. *'How pleasing this must be to you, how I envy your feelings!'* my friends will sometimes say to me, when they see young men whom I have educated return after some years' absence from school, their eyes shining with pleasure, while they shake hands with their old master, bringing a present of game to me, or a toy to my wife, and thanking me in the warmest terms for my care of their education. A holiday is begged for the boys; the house is a scene of a happiness; I, only, am sad at heart. This fine-spirited and warm-hearted youth, who fancies he repays his master with gratitude for the care of his boyish years—this young man—in the eight long years I watched over him with a parent's anxiety, never could repay me with one look of genuine feeling. He was proud when I praised; he was submissive when I reproved him; but he did never *love* me— and what he now mistakes for gratitude and kindness for me, is but the pleasant sensation which all persons feel at revisiting the scenes of their boyish hopes and fears, and the seeing on equal terms the man they were accustomed to look up to with reverence. My wife, too," this interesting correspondent goes on to say, "my once darling Anna, is the wife of a schoolmaster. When I married her knowing that the wife of a schoolmaster ought to be a busy notable creature, and fearing that my gentle Anna would ill supply the loss of my dear bustling mother just then dead, who never sat still, was in every part of the house in a moment, and whom I was obliged sometimes to threaten to fasten down in a chair, to save her from fatiguing herself to death—I expressed my fears that I was bringing her into a way of life unsuitable to her; and she, who loved me tenderly, promised for my sake to exert herself to perform the duties of her new situation. She promised, and she has kept her word. What wonders will not woman's love perform? My house is managed with a propriety and decorum unknown in other schools; my boys are well fed, look healthy, and have every proper accommodation; and all this performed with a careful economy that never descends to meanness. But I have lost my gentle *helpless* Anna! When we sit down to enjoy an hour of repose after the fatigue of the day, I am compelled to listen to what have been her useful (and they are really useful) employments through the day, and what she proposes for her to-morrow's task. Her heart and her features are changed by the duties of her situation. To the boys, she never appears other than the *master's wife,* and she looks up to me as the *boys' master;* to whom all show of love and affection would be highly improper, and unbecoming the dignity of her situation and mine. Yet *this* my gratitude forbids me to hint to her. For my sake she submitted to be this altered creature, and can I reproach her for it?" For the communication of this letter I am indebted to my cousin Bridget.

WALTER SAVAGE LANDOR
1775–1864

Towards the end of his long life, Walter Savage Landor confessed: "I never did a single wise thing in the whole course of my existence, although I have written many which have been thought such"; and this confession aptly summarizes the two contradictory characters that warred in Landor until his death in 1864, in his ninetieth year. Impetuous, irritable, often arrogant in his behavior, he was at the same time classically calm and restrained in his writing, whether of poetry, drama, or those dramatic conversations, such as the selection printed below, which are essentially essays. Yet this paradox does not tell the whole story. There was a majesty about his wrath, and an underlying tenderness, which compelled love and admiration from a discriminating few. It was a discriminating few as well who were his readers, for he scorned to subscribe to any popular literary fashion; and the magnanimity of his thought, the perfection of his style, commanded only a limited audience. With the same candor, however, that he showed in admitting his frequent lack of wisdom, he was willing to acknowledge the scope of his achievement. He would not have early, easy fame, but fame would be his. "I shall dine late," he wrote, "but the dining-room will be well lighted, the guests few and select." Who two of those intimate guests will be, we now know from William Butler Yeats, who announced with all of Landor's assurance that he himself would eventually attend, in the company of another Worthy:

> And I may dine at journey's end
> With Landor and with Donne.

Henry VIII and Anne Boleyn: An Imaginary Conversation

Henry. Dost thou know me, Nanny, in this yeoman's dress? 'S blood! does it require so long and vacant a stare to recollect a husband after a week or two? No tragedy-tricks with me! a scream, a sob, or thy kerchief a trifle wetter, were enough. Why, verily the little fool faints in earnest. These whey faces, like their kinsfolk the ghosts, give us no warning. (*Sprinkling water over her.*) Hast had water enough upon thee? Take that, then: art thyself again?

Anne. Father of mercies! do I meet again my husband, as was my last prayer on earth? Do I behold my beloved lord— in peace—and pardoned, my partner in eternal bliss? It was his voice. I cannot see him: why cannot I? Oh why do these pangs interrupt the transports of the blessed?

Henry. Thou openest thy arms: faith! I came for that. Nanny, thou art a sweet slut. Thou groanest, wench: art in labour? Faith! among the mistakes of the night, I am ready to think almost that thou hast been drinking, and that I have not.

Anne. God preserve your Highness: grant me your forgiveness for one slight offence. My eyes were heavy; I fell asleep while I was reading. I did not know of your presence at first; and, when I did, I could not speak. I strove for utterance: I wanted no respect for my liege and husband.

Henry. My pretty warm nestling, thou wilt then lie! Thou wert reading, and aloud too, with thy saintly cup of water by thee, and—what! thou art still girlishly fond of those dried cherries!

Anne. I had no other fruit to offer your Highness the first time I saw you, and you were then pleased to invent for me some reason why they should be acceptable. I did not dry these: may I present them, such as they are? We shall have fresh next month.

Henry. Thou art always driving away from the discourse. One moment it suits thee to know me, another not.

Anne. Remember, it is hardly three months since I miscarried: I am weak, and liable to swoons.

Henry. Thou hast, however, thy bridal cheeks, with lustre upon them when there is none elsewhere, and obstinate lips resisting all impression; but, now thou talkest about miscarrying, who is the father of the boy?

Anne. The Father is yours and mine; he who hath taken him to his own home, before (like me) he could struggle or cry for it.

Henry. Pagan, or worse, to talk so! He did not come into the world alive: there was no baptism.

Anne. I thought only of our loss: my senses are confounded. I did not give him my milk, and yet I loved him tenderly; for I often fancied had he lived, how contented and joyful he would have made you and England.

Henry. No subterfuges and escapes. I warrant, thou canst not say whether at my entrance thou wert waking or wandering.

Anne. Faintness and drowsiness came upon me suddenly.

Henry. Well, since thou really and truly sleepedst, what didst dream of?

Anne. I begin to doubt whether I did indeed sleep.

Henry. Ha! false one—never two sentences of truth together! But come, what didst think about, asleep or awake?

Anne. I thought that God had pardoned me my offences, and had received me unto him.

Henry. And nothing more?

Anne. That my prayers had been heard and my wishes were accomplishing: the angels alone can enjoy more beatitude than this.

Henry. Vexatious little devil! she says nothing now about me, merely from perverseness. Hast thou never thought about me, nor about thy falsehood and adultery?

Anne. If I had committed any kind of falsehood, in regard to you or not, I should never have rested until I had thrown myself at your feet and obtained your pardon; but, if ever I had been guilty of that other crime, I know not whether I should have dared to implore it, even of God's mercy.

Henry. Thou hast heretofore cast some soft glances upon Smeaton; hast thou not?

Anne. He taught me to play on the virginals, as you know, when I was little, and thereby to please your Highness.

Henry. And Brereton and Norris, what have they taught thee?

Anne. They are your servants, and trusty ones.

Henry. Has not Weston told thee plainly that he loved thee?

Anne. Yes; and—

Henry. What didst thou?

Anne. I defied him.

Henry. Is that all?

Anne. I could have done no more if he had told me that he hated me. Then, indeed, I should have incurred more justly the reproaches of your Highness: I should have smiled.

Henry. We have proofs abundant: the fellows shall one and all confront thee.—Ay, clap thy hands and kiss thy sleeve, harlot!

Anne. Oh, that so great a favour is vouchsafed me. My honour is secure; my husband will be happy again; he will see my innocence.

Henry. Give me now an account of the moneys thou hast received from me within these nine months. I want them not back; they are letters of gold in record of thy guilt. Thou hast had no fewer than fifteen thousand pounds in that period, without even thy asking; what hast done with it, wanton?

Anne. I have regularly placed it out to interest.

Henry. Where? I demand of thee.

Anne. Among the needy and ailing. My Lord Archbishop has the account of it, sealed by him weekly. I also had a copy myself: those who took away my papers may easily find it; for there are few others, and they lie open.

Henry. Think on my munificence to thee; recollect who made thee. Dost sigh for what thou hast lost?

Anne. I do, indeed.

Henry. I never thought thee ambitious; but thy vices creep out one by one.

Anne. I do not regret that I have been a queen and am no longer one; nor that my innocence is called in question by those who never knew me: but I lament that the good people who loved me so cordially, hate and curse me; that those who pointed me out to their daughters for imitation, check them when they speak about me; and that he whom next to God I have served with most devotion is my accuser.

Henry. Wast thou conning over something in that dingy book for thy defence? Come, tell me, what wast thou reading?

Anne. This ancient chronicle. I was looking for some one in my own condition, and must have missed the page. Surely in so many hundred years there shall have been other young maidens, first too happy for exaltation, and after too exalted for happiness,—not, perchance, doomed to die upon a scaffold, by those they ever honoured and served faithfully: that, indeed, I did not look for nor think of; but my heart was bounding for any one I could love and pity. She would be unto me as a sister dead and gone; but hearing me, seeing me, consoling me, and being consoled. O my husband! it is so heavenly a thing—

Henry. To whine and whimper, no doubt, is vastly heavenly.

Anne. I said not so; but those, if there be any such, who never weep, have nothing in them of heavenly or of earthly. The plants, the trees, the very rocks and unsunned clouds, show us at least the semblances of weeping; and there is not an aspect of the globe we live on, nor of the waters and skies around it, without a reference and a similitude to our joys or sorrows.

Henry. I do not remember that notion anywhere. Take care no enemy rake out of it something of materialism. Guard well thy empty hot brain: it may hatch more evil. As for those odd words, I myself would fain see no great harm in them, knowing that grief and frenzy strike out many things which would else lie still, and neither spirt nor sparkle. I also know that thou hast never read any thing but Bible and history, —the two worst books in the world for young people, and the most certain to lead astray both prince and subject. For which reason I have interdicted and entirely put down the one, and will (by the blessing of the Virgin and of holy Paul) commit the other to a rigid censor. If it behooves us kings to enact what our people shall eat and drink,—of which the most unruly and rebellious spirit can entertain no doubt,— greatly more doth it behoove us to examine what they read and think. The body is moved according to the mind and will: we must take care that the movement be a right one, on pain of God's anger in this life and the next.

Anne. O my dear husband! it must be a naughty thing, indeed, that makes him angry beyond remission. Did you ever try how pleasant it is to forgive any one? There is nothing else wherein we can resemble God perfectly and easily.

Henry. Resemble God perfectly and easily! Do vile creatures talk thus of the Creator?

Anne. No, Henry, when his creatures talk thus of him, they are no longer vile creatures! When they know that he is good, they love him; and, when they love him, they are good themselves. O Henry! my husband and King! the judgments of our Heavenly Father are righteous: on this, surely, we must think alike.

Henry. And what, then? Speak out: again I command thee, speak plainly! thy tongue was not so torpid but this moment. Art ready? must I wait?

Anne. If any doubt remains upon your royal mind of your equity in this business; should it haply seem possible to you that passion or prejudice, in yourself or another, may have warped so strong an understanding,—do but supplicate the Almighty to strengthen and enliven it, and he will hear you.

Henry. What! thou wouldst fain change thy quarters, ay?

Anne. My spirit is detached and ready, and I shall change them shortly, whatever your Highness may determine. Ah! my native Bickling is a pleasant place. May I go back to it? Does that kind smile say, *Yes*? Do the hounds ever run that way now? The fruit-trees must be all in full blossom, and the gorse on the hill above quite dazzling. How good it was in you to plant your park at Greenwich after my childish notion, tree for tree, the very same as at Bickling! Has the hard winter killed them, or the winds loosened the stakes about them?

Henry. Silly child! as if thou shouldst see them any more.

Anne. Alas, what strange things happen! But they and I are nearly of the same age; young alike, and without hold upon any thing.

Henry. Yet thou appearest hale and resolute, and (they tell me) smirkest and smilest to everybody.

Anne. The withered leaf catches the sun sometimes, little as it can profit by it; and I have heard stories of the breeze in other climates that sets in when daylight is about to close, and how constant it is, and how refreshing. My heart, indeed, is now sustained strangely: it became the more sensibly so from that time forward, when power and grandeur and all things terrestrial were sunk from sight. Every act of kindness in those about me gives me satisfaction and pleasure, such as I did not feel formerly. I was worse before God chastened me; yet I was never an ingrate. What pains have I taken to find out the village-girls who placed their posies in my chamber ere I arose in the morning! How gladly would I have recompensed the forester who lit up a brake on my birthnight, which else had warmed him half the winter! But these are times past: I was not Queen of England.

Henry. Nor adulterous, nor heretical.

Anne. God be praised!

Henry. Learned saint! thou knowest nothing of the lighter, but perhaps canst inform me about the graver, of them.

Anne. Which may it be, my liege?

Henry. Which may it be? Pestilence! I marvel that the walls of this tower do not crack around thee at such impiety.

Anne. I would be instructed by the wisest of theologians: such is your Highness.

Henry. Are the sins of the body, foul as they are, comparable to those of the soul?

Anne. When they are united, they must be worse.

Henry. Go on, go on: thou pushest thy own breast against the sword. God hath deprived thee of thy reason for thy punishment. I must hear more: proceed, I charge thee.

Anne. An aptitude to believe one thing rather than another, from ignorance or weakness, or from the more persuasive manner of the teacher, or from his purity of life, or from the strong impression of a particular text at a particular time, and various things beside, may influence and decide our opinion; and the hand of the Almighty, let us hope, will fall gently on human fallibility.

Henry. Opinion in matters of faith! rare wisdom! rare religion! Troth, Anne! thou hast well sobered me. I came rather warmly and lovingly; but these light ringlets, by the holy rood, shall not shade this shoulder much longer. Nay, do not start; I tap it for the last time, my sweetest. If the Church permitted it, thou shouldst set forth on thy long journey with the eucharist between thy teeth, however loath.

Anne. Love your Elizabeth, my honoured lord, and God bless you! She will soon forget to call me. Do not chide her: think how young she is.

Could I, could I kiss her, but once again! it would comfort my heart,—or break it.

D. H. LAWRENCE
1885–1930

"Whatever else it is," commented D. H. Lawrence on his novel, *The Rainbow,*" it is a voyage of discovery towards the real and eternal and unknown land." That voyage of discovery went on, more or less openly, in everything Lawrence wrote, whether novels, poetry, travel pieces, or criticism. He was always trying to find a way through the dead clutter—as he considered it— of our modern, over-intellectualized society, to an underlying natural yet mysterious power. He did not expect to arrive. "Life," he acknowledged, "will *not* be known." The important thing was to recognize the existence of the mystery, to submit to it and live in harmony with it. Lawrence's proclamation of this doctrine understandably shocked the upholders of the *status quo,* who responded by banning his books, even closing an exhibition of his paintings. But the shock has diminished since Lawrence's death. Book buyers at last may legally purchase *Lady Chatterley's Lover,* and book readers increasingly recognize the importance of what Lawrence had to say and his mastery in saying it. Even in the few following pages, originally published three years before his death, he communicates the enormous terror and wonder of elemental forces, and the insignificance of civilized man beside them. Interesting to compare with this electric "Mercury" is Santayana's essay on "Hermes the Interpreter" on pages 332–337. Hermes, the same god by his Greek name, is a much pleasanter fellow; yet a similar sense of ultimate mystery informs both selections.

Mercury

It was Sunday, and very hot. The holiday-makers flocked to the hill of Mercury, to rise two thousand feet above the steamy haze of the valleys. For the summer had been very wet, and the sudden heat covered the land in hot steam.

Every time it made the ascent, the funicular was crowded.

It hauled itself up the steep incline, that towards the top looked almost perpendicular, the steel thread of the rails in the gulf of pine-trees hanging like an iron rope against a wall. The women held their breath, and didn't look. Or they looked back towards the sinking levels of the river, steamed and dim, far-stretching over the frontier.

When you arrived at the top, there was nothing to do. The hill was a pine-covered cone; paths wound between the high tree-trunks, and you could walk round and see the glimpses of the world all round, all round: the dim, far river-plain, with a dull glint of the great stream, to westwards; southwards the black, forest-covered, agile-looking hills, with emerald-green clearings and a white house or two; east, the inner valley, with two villages, factory chimneys, pointed churches, and hills beyond; and north, the steep hills of forest, with reddish crags and reddish castle ruins. The hot sun burned overhead, and all was in steam.

Only on the very summit of the hill there was a tower, an outlook tower; a long restaurant with its beer-garden, all the little yellow tables standing their round disks under the horse-chestnut trees; then a bit of a rock-garden on the slope. But the great trees began again in wilderness a few yards off.

The Sunday crowd came up in waves from the funicular. In waves they ebbed through the beer-garden. But not many sat down to drink. Nobody was spending any money. Some paid to go up the outlook tower, to look down on a world of vapours and black, agile crouching hills, and half-cooked towns. Then everybody dispersed along the paths, to sit among the trees in the cool air.

There was not a breath of wind. Lying and looking upwards at the shaggy, barbaric middle-world of the pine-trees, it was difficult to decide whether the pure high trunks supported the upper thicket of darkness, or whether they descended from it like great cords stretched downwards. Anyhow, in between the tree-top world and the earth-world went the wonderful clean cords of innumerable proud tree-trunks, clear as rain. And as you watched, you saw that the upper world was faintly moving, faintly, most faintly swaying, with a circular movement, though the lower trunks were utterly motionless and monolithic.

There was nothing to do. In all the world, there was nothing to do, and nothing to be done. Why have we all come to the top of the Merkur? There is nothing for us to do.

What matter? We have come a stride beyond the world. Let it steam and cook its half-baked reality below there. On the hill of Mercury we take no notice. Even we do not trouble to wander and pick the fat, blue, sourish bilberries. Just lie and see the rain-pure tree-trunks like chords of music between two worlds.

The hours pass by: people wander and disappear and re-appear. All is hot and quiet. Humanity is rarely boisterous any more. You go for a drink: finches run among the few people at the tables: everybody glances at everybody, but with re-moteness.

There is nothing to do but to return and lie down under the pine trees. Nothing to do. But why do anything, anyhow? The desire to do anything has gone. The tree-trunks, living like rain, they are quite active enough.

At the foot of the obsolete tower there is an old table-stone with a very much battered Mercury, in relief. There is also an altar, or votive stone, both from the Roman times. The Romans are supposed to have worshipped Mercury on the summit. The battered god, with his round sun-head, looks very hollow-eyed and unimpressive in the purplish-red sand-stone of the district. And no one any more will throw grains of offering in the hollow of the votive stone: also common, purplish-red sandstone, very local and un-Roman.

The Sunday people do not even look. Why should they? They keep passing on into the pine-trees. And many sit on the benches; many lie upon the long chairs. It is very hot, in the afternoon, and very still.

Till there seems a faint whistling in the tops of the pine-trees, and out of the universal semi-consciousness of the after-noon arouses a bristling uneasiness. The crowd is astir, look-ing at the sky. And sure enough, there is a great flat blackness reared up in the western sky, curled with white wisps and loose breast-feathers. It looks very sinister, as only the ele-ments still can look. Under the sudden weird whistling of the upper pine trees, there is a subdued babble and calling of frightened voices.

They want to get down; the crowd want to get down off the hill of Mercury, before the storm comes. At any price to get off the hill! They stream towards the funicular, while the sky blackens with incredible rapidity. And as the crowd presses down towards the little station, the first blaze of lightning opens out, followed immediately by a crash of thunder, and great darkness. In one strange movement, the crowd takes refuge in the deep veranda of the restaurant, pressing among the little tables in silence. There is no rain, and no definite wind, only a sudden coldness which makes the crowd press closer.

They press closer, in the darkness and the suspense. They have become curiously unified, the crowd, as if they had fused into one body. As the air sends a chill waft under the veranda the voices murmur plaintively, like birds under leaves, the bodies press closer together, seeking shelter in contact.

The gloom, dark as night, seems to continue a long time. Then suddenly the lightning dances white on the floor, dances and shakes upon the ground, up and down, and lights up the white striding of a man, lights him up only to the hips, white and naked and striding, with fire on his heels. He seems to be hurrying, this fiery man whose upper half is invisible, and at his naked heels white little flames seem to flutter. His flat, powerful thighs, his legs white as fire stride rapidly across the open, in front of the veranda, dragging little white flames at the ankles, with the movement. He is going somewhere, swiftly.

In the great bang of the thunder the apparition disappears. The earth moves, and the house jumps in complete darkness. A faint whimpering of terror comes from the crowd, as the cold air swirls in. But still, upon the darkness, there is no rain. There is no relief: a long wait.

Brilliant and blinding, the lightning falls again; a strange bruising thud comes from the forest, as all the little tables and the secret tree-trunks stand for one unnatural second exposed. Then the blow of the thunder, under which the house and the crowd reel as under an explosion. The storm is playing directly upon the Merkur. A belated sound of tearing branches comes out of the forest.

And again the white splash of the lightning on the ground: but nothing moves. And again the long, rattling, instantaneous volleying of the thunder, in the darkness. The crowd is panting with fear, as the lightning again strikes white, and something again seems to burst, in the forest, as the thunder crashes.

At last, into the motionlessness of the storm, in rushes the wind, with the fiery flying of bits of ice and the sudden sea-like roaring of the pine trees. The crowd winces and draws back, as the bits of ice hit in the face like fire. The roar of the trees is so great, it becomes like another silence. And through it is heard the crashing and splintering of timber, as the hurricane concentrates upon the hill.

Down comes the hail, in a roar that covers every other sound, threshing ponderously upon the ground and the roofs and the trees. And as the crowd surges irresistibly into the interior of the building, from the crushing of this ice-fall, still amid the sombre hoarseness sounds the tinkle and crackle of things breaking.

After an eternity of dread, it ends suddenly. Outside is a faint gleam of yellow light, over the snow and the endless debris of twigs and things broken. It is very cold, with the atmosphere of ice and deep winter. The forest looks wan, above the white earth, where the ice-balls lie in their myriads, six inches deep, littered with all the twigs and things they have broken.

"Yes! Yes!" say the men, taking sudden courage as the yellow light comes into the air. "Now we can go!"

The first brave ones emerge, picking up the big hailstones, pointing to the overthrown tables. Some, however, do not linger. They hurry to the funicular station, to see if the apparatus is still working.

The funicular station is on the north side of the hill. The men come back, saying there is no one there. The crowd begins to emerge upon the wet, crunching whiteness of the hail, spreading around in curiosity, waiting for the men who operate the funicular.

On the south side of the outlook tower two bodies lay in the cold but thawing hail. The dark-blue of the uniforms showed blackish. Both men were dead. But the lightning had completely removed the clothing from the legs of one man, so that he was naked from the hips down. There he lay, his face sideways on the snow, and two drops of blood running from his nose into his big, blond, military moustache. He lay there near the votive stone of the Mercury. His companion, a young man, lay face downwards, a few yards behind him.

The sun began to emerge. The crowd gazed in dread, afraid to touch the bodies of the men. Why had they, the dead funicular men, come round to this side of the hill anyhow?

The funicular would not work. Something had happened to it in the storm. The crowd began to wind down the bare hill, on the sloppy ice. Everywhere the earth bristled with broken pine boughs and twigs. But the bushes and the leafy trees were stripped absolutely bare, to a miracle. The lower earth was leafless and naked as in winter.

"Absolute winter!" murmured the crowd, as they hurried, frightened, down the steep, winding descent, extricating themselves from the fallen pine-branches.

Meanwhile the sun began to steam in great heat.

ABRAHAM LINCOLN
1809–1865

Abraham Lincoln, best-known and best-loved of all American presidents, needs no introduction here. Most of us have the words of his Gettysburg Address by heart; their simplicity and strength are part of our heritage. Almost equally familiar is the Second Inaugural Address, printed on the following pages. But nothing Lincoln ever wrote or said can become too familiar. This address, delivered more than a hundred years ago, speaks to us of problems which concern us still. We have not done paying for "the bondman's two hundred and fifty years of unrequited toil," nor for "every drop of blood drawn with the lash." We still have need "to finish the work we are in; to bind up the nation's wounds." And we still have need of "malice toward none," of "charity for all."

Second Inaugural Address

At this second appearing to take the oath of the presidential office, there is less occasion for an extended address than there was at the first. Then a statement, somewhat in detail, of a course to be pursued, seemed fitting and proper. Now, at the expiration of four years, during which public declarations have been constantly called forth on every point and phase of the great contest which still absorbs the attention, and engrosses the energies of the nation, little that is new could be presented. The progress of our arms, upon which all else chiefly depends, is as well known to the public as to myself; and it is, I trust, reasonably satisfactory and encouraging to all. With high hope for the future, no prediction in regard to it is ventured.

On the occasion corresponding to this four years ago, all thoughts were anxiously directed to an impending civil war. All dreaded it—all sought to avert it. While the inaugural address was being delivered from this place, devoted altogether to *saving* the Union without war, insurgent agents were in the city seeking to *destroy* it without war—seeking to dissolve the Union, and divide effects, by negotiation. Both parties deprecated war; but one of them would *make* war rather than let the nation survive; and the other would *accept* war rather than let it perish. And the war came.

One-eighth of the whole population were colored slaves, not distributed generally over the Union, but localized in the Southern part of it. These slaves constituted a peculiar and powerful interest. All knew that this interest was, somehow, the cause of the war. To strengthen, perpetuate, and extend this interest was the object for which the insurgents would rend the Union, even by war; while the government claimed no right to do more than to restrict the territorial enlargement of it. Neither party expected for the war, the magnitude, or the duration, which it has already attained. Neither anticipated that the *cause* of the conflict might cease with, or even before, the conflict itself should cease. Each looked for an easier triumph, and a result less fundamental and astounding. Both read the same Bible, and pray to the same God; and each invokes His aid against the other. It may seem strange that any men should dare to ask a just God's assistance in wringing their bread from the sweat of other men's faces; but let us judge not that we be not judged. The prayers of both could not be answered; that of neither has been answered fully. The Almighty has His own purposes. "Woe unto the world because of offenses! for it must needs be that offenses come; but woe to that man by whom the offense cometh!" If we shall suppose that American slavery is one of those offenses which, in the providence of God, must needs come, but which, having continued through His appointed time, He now wills to remove, and that He gives to both North and South, this terrible war, as the woe due to those by whom the offense came, shall we discern therein any departure from those divine attributes which the believers in a Living God always ascribe to Him? Fondly do we hope—fervently do we pray—that this mighty scourge of war may speedily pass away. Yet, if God wills that it continue, until all the wealth piled by the bondman's two hundred and fifty years of unrequited toil shall be sunk, and until every drop of blood drawn with the lash, shall be paid by another drawn with the sword, as was said three thousand years ago, so still it must be said "the judgments of the Lord, are true and righteous altogether."

With malice toward none; with charity for all; with firmness in the right, as God gives us to see the right, let us strive on to finish the work we are in; to bind up the nation's wounds; to care for him who shall have borne the battle, and for his widow, and his orphan—to do all which may achieve and cherish a just, and a lasting peace, among ourselves, and with all nations.

ROBERT LYND
1879–1949

To most Americans the name of Robert Lynd has not yet
become familiar, but British readers have had the pleasure of
his acquaintance for a long time. When the first issue of the
weekly *New Statesman* appeared in London in April, 1913, it
contained an article by Lynd; and soon thereafter his essays,
signed always with the initials "Y. Y.", became a regular *New
Statesman* feature. From time to time collections of these essays
were published, with such names as *The Blue Lion, The Green
Man, The Cockleshell,* and other pleasant echoes of the signs at
British inns. As literary editor of the London *News Chronicle*
and a contributor to *John O'London's Weekly,* Lynd reached a
still wider audience, that waited eagerly each week to see what
had struck his fancy now. For like Lamb, whom he much resembled in wit and wisdom, Lynd wrote about everything, because
he was interested in everything: people, books, birds, Ireland
(he was born in Belfast and was a passionate Irish nationalist),
and even delinquent Dutch sailors guilty of the "un-English" crime
of biting! He wrote always with reason, order, and clarity; and
through these transparent qualities invariably shone the richness
of his own personality: his kindness, his humor, his abiding faith
in humanity and in humanism. Of him it seems to be universally
agreed that both as man and as writer he was universally loved.

Un-English

Nothing better in the way of comic drama in real life has
been produced for some time than the scene recently reported
in the *New Statesman and Nation,* in which we were told of
the trial of a number of Dutch sailors, who, after arriving in
Belfast, went to a dance hall in York Street, became drunk,
and were arrested on a charge of disorderly behaviour—which
took the form not only of fighting but of biting people. The

captain of the Dutch ship came forward to interpret the evidence given by his men, and at the end of the trial the magistrate addressed him gravely and said: 'It is very un-English to bite people, and I would like you to impress it on your men.' To which the Dutch captain replied, equally gravely: 'It is very un-Dutch, too, your worship.' That, I think, is one of the great retorts of history.

I confess, when I read the story, my first feeling was that the magistrate, remembering the proud province to which he belonged, ought to have said to the Dutch captain: 'It is very un-Northern-Irish to bite people.' After all, we all like to boast about the virtues of our native soil, and Northern Ireland—the home of Partick Murphy, of County Down, and his V. C. lifeboat—is no more a part of England than the Canadian province of Saskatchewan. A moment's reflection, however, told me that England was the only unit in these islands in which bad conduct is reprobated in a local adjective beginning with 'un.' Even the most ardent Welsh patriot would never think of telling a foreigner that 'It is very un-Welsh to bite people.' I asked a Scotchman whether he had ever heard any one using the adjective 'un-Scotch'; and he said he could not imagine it except in reference to Irish whisky.

For a time I wondered whether the English were the only people who had ever used the prefix 'un' before their national designation to register their disapproval of something or other. I remembered vaguely from my school days that the Greeks used to call foreigners 'barbarians,' but I could not remember any instance of their having condemned any practice as 'un-Athenian,' 'un-Spartan,' or 'un-Macedonian.' Nor through the centuries could I find a trace of any incident in which the misbehaviour of some drunken sailor had been described with racial pride as 'un-Visigothic' or 'un-Ostrogothic.' America has left us no record of an enemy of the Palefaces who described some unpleasant white man's practice as 'un-Red-Indian.' Were the English, then, the only race that ever condemned habits they disliked by epithets formed on the model of 'un-English,' and, if so, when did they begin to use this boastful adjective? Did Englishmen in Shakespeare's day, for example, say to themselves with pride that 'it is very un-English to bite people,' taking for granted that all foreigners bit people? Or did the adjective 'un-English' come in about the same time as the phrase: 'It isn't cricket'?

I could scarcely believe that it was older than the Victorian era and the now withered white flower of a blameless life.

Turning to the *New English Dictionary*, however, I discovered to my surprise that the use of the word 'un-English' is as old as 1633 when Prynne—wasn't it he who lost his ears?—wrote: 'So unmanly, degenerous, and un-English (if I may so speak) in their whole conversation.' There has been, I fear, a great deal of conversation since then that Prynne would have described as un-English. The next reference to the word comes from Horace Walpole who wrote in 1743: 'This is so un-English, or so unheroic, that I despair of you!' That has the smack of the modern usage. Then we find the word used in a more restricted sense by a writer who in 1848 commented on the secret ballot in the despondent sentence: 'The un-English practice of secret voting will be resorted to.' No doubt to a good Tory every innovation has at first seemed un-English—income tax, health insurance, and all the rest of it. The *New English Dictionary*, unfortunately, gives us no examples of the use of the word 'un-English' after 1872, when someone wrote of 'a false patriotism that thought it un-English to wear foreign fabrics.'

Lest you should think, however, that the English are the only people who believe that everything right is a home product and that everything wrong is something done or produced by foreigners, it would be well for you to take note of the fact that the dictionary also contains the adjective 'un-American.' Even under the early date, 1818, we have the entry: 'Ninety marble capitals have been imported at vast cost from Italy . . . and show how un-American is the whole plan.' One would like to know the context of this, as of the next entry (from the *Daily News,* in 1894): 'However it came about, it is un-American and should be repudiated by the people.' There we see the perfect use of the 'un' adjective which should suggest that anything not practised by one's own people is wrong.

I have been told by an expert in language that all nations have this method of depreciating the customs of foreigners, but I can find little evidence of this in the dictionary. The word un-Irish appears, it is true, but only in such sentences as 'The youth endeavoured to become un-Irish in everything,' 'An awkward effort at enjoyment and amusement, un-Irish and lamentable in the extreme,' and (adverbially) 'They wisely and un-Irishly chose the money.'

This last sentence, by the way, is as modest as it is boastful.

On the whole, however, it must be admitted that, when nations describe something as uncharacteristic of themselves, they do so with a boastful implication. When an Englishman tells you that it is un-English to boast, is he not boasting that he alone among civilized men is guiltless of the sin of boasting? When he tells you that it is un-English to hit a man when he is down, is he not announcing his superiority to foreigners among whom hitting a man when he is down is the common practice? Similarly, if he says that it is un-English to strike a woman, he suggests that only in this other Eden, demi-Paradise, is wife-beating looked on as a vice. I wish someone would compile a complete list of the things that are un-English. They would include, I fancy, besides those I have mentioned, lying, bearing malice, hitting below the belt, kicking, and all forms of unsportsmanlike behaviour.

To me it seems that this indirect boastfulness has its uses. Not only does it assert the superiority of the chosen people—and every people is a chosen people in its own eyes—but it proclaims a code of behaviour below which none of its citizens should fall. Men cannot live without some code or other, and even the code implied in the phrase, 'It isn't cricket,' is better than no code at all. Hence I think that the more crimes, vices, and unpleasant forms of conduct are catalogued as un-English, the better it will be for England. If every Englishman could be persuaded, for example, that it was un-English to steal or to profiteer, or to enter the black market, what a sunburst of honesty would suddenly illuminate the country! But no one ever says even that 'it is un-English to wangle.' A common phrase about the wangler is, indeed: 'You can't blame him, can you?' Yet it is vastly more important to discourage Englishmen from wangling extra rations in war-time than to discourage them from biting people. After all, how many Englishmen since their nursery days have fixed their teeth in the flesh of a fellow human being? I have never met a grown-up Englishman who bit people. Or, for that matter, a grown-up Frenchman, or a grown-up Italian, or a grown-up Japanese.

In most countries, I feel pretty sure, biting people is the hobby only of the few. The fact that one lives in a country in which people do not bite people seems to me scarcely worth boasting about. To use the vainglorious adjective 'un-English' as a description of such abstinence is surely a waste of a good word.

Still, however it may be used, the adjective 'un-English' does express an ideal. It is no small achievement to have made 'un-English' a synonym for (according to the dictionary definition) 'not straightforward; unfair; unsportsmanlike.' Foreigners may not be impressed, but the word may help to keep Englishmen up to the mark. Human beings perhaps need to praise themselves in order to make themselves worthy of their praise. Let a people begin to boast of its virtues, and it may end by practising them. That may account for the almost complete disappearance of the inhuman custom of biting people, not only in Great Britain and Northern Ireland but, as we now know, in Holland too.

H. L. MENCKEN
1880–1956

A flamboyant critic of American culture, a sagacious humorist, H. L. Mencken throughout his long career (5,000,000 words) wrote with gusto and enthusiasm, whether or not his readers were willing to accept his ideas. Whatever his subject, from politics, religion, education, or sex, en route to his impressive work in describing the American language, the "Sage of Baltimore" enjoyed a great belly laugh at the expense of "the booboisie of the hinterland." "Moronia" was his favorite word for Hollywood. His "Boobus americanus" requires no explanation. Journalist since the age of seventeen, editor of *Smart Set* and *The American Mercury,* master of an incisive wit, a self-confessed man of "fixed and invariable ideas," Mencken has at various times and for an assortment of reasons been compared to Rabelais, Swift, Voltaire, and Samuel Johnson. The essay reprinted here from *A Mencken Chrestomathy* appeared originally in *In Defense of Women* (really no defense at all), published in 1918 while Mencken, chafing under wartime censorship, "refused to engage in patriotic whooping" and decided to devote himself to what he called "neutral matters." But Mencken is never neutral; that is why it is such fun to read him. Those who may bristle a little at "The Feminine Mind" should be aware of two related points. First, Mencken declared that he was taking pains "to make this brochure upon the woman question extremely *pianissimo* in tone." Second, before he was married in 1930, at the age of fifty, to Sara Haardt, he had declared: "Bachelors know more about women than married men. If they didn't they'd be married, too." When people, either friendly or inimical, raised eyebrows at his shift in policy, Mencken had the ready retort: "I was formerly not as wise as I am now."

The Feminine Mind

A man's women folk, whatever their outward show of respect for his merit and authority, always regard him secretly as an ass, and with something akin to pity. His most gaudy sayings and doings seldom deceive them; they see the actual man within, and know him for a shallow and pathetic fellow. In this fact, perhaps, lies one of the best proofs of feminine intelligence, or, as the common phrase makes it, feminine intuition. The marks of that so-called intuition are simply a sharp and accurate perception of reality, a habitual immunity to emotional enchantment, a relentless capacity for distinguishing clearly between the appearance and the substance. The appearance, in the normal family circle, is a hero, a magnifico, a demigod. The substance is a poor mountebank.

A man's wife, true enough, may envy her husband certain of his more soothing prerogatives and sentimentalities. She may envy him his masculine liberty of movement and occupation, his impenetrable complacency, his peasant-like delight in petty vices, his capacity for hiding the harsh face of reality behind the cloak of romanticism, his general innocence and childishness. But she never envies him his shoddy and preposterous soul.

This shrewd perception of masculine bombast and make-believe, this acute understanding of man as the eternal tragic comedian, is at the bottom of that compassionate irony which passes under the name of the maternal instinct. A woman wishes to mother a man simply because she sees into his helplessness, his need of an amiable environment, his touching self-delusion. That ironical note is not only daily apparent in real life; it sets the whole tone of feminine fiction. The woman novelist, if she be skillful enough to be taken seriously, never takes her heroes so. From the day of Jane Austen to the day of Selma Lagerlöf she has always got into her character study a touch of superior aloofness, of ill-concealed derision. I can't recall a single masculine figure created by a woman who is not, at bottom, a booby.

That it should be necessary, at this late stage in the senility of the human race, to argue that women have a fine and fluent intelligence is surely an eloquent proof of the defective observation, incurable prejudice, and general imbecility of their lords and masters. Women, in fact, are not only intelligent; they have almost a monopoly of certain of the subtler and more utile forms of intelligence. The thing itself, indeed, might be reasonably described as a special feminine character; there is in it, in more than one of its manifestations, a femaleness as palpable as the femaleness of cruelty, masochism or rouge. Men are strong. Men are brave in physical combat. Men are romantic, and love what they conceive to be virtue and beauty. Men incline to faith, hope and charity. Men know how to sweat and endure. Men are amiable and fond. But in so far as they show the true fundamentals of intelligence—in so far as they reveal a capacity for discovering the kernel of eternal verity in the husk of delusion and hallucination and a passion for bringing it forth—to that extent, at least, they are feminine, and still nourished by the milk of their mothers. The essential traits and qualities of the male, the hall-marks of the unpolluted masculine, are at the same time the hall-marks of the numskull. The caveman is all muscles and mush. Without a woman to rule him and think for him, he is a truly lamentable spectacle: a baby with whiskers, a rabbit with the frame of an aurochs, a feeble and preposterous caricature of God.

Here, of course, I do not mean to say that masculinity contributes nothing whatsoever to the complex of chemicophysiological reactions which produces what we call superior ability; all I mean to say is that this complex is impossible without the feminine contribution—that it is a product of the interplay of the two elements. In women of talent we see the opposite picture. They are commonly somewhat mannish, and shave as well as shine. Think of George Sand, Catherine the Great, Elizabeth of England, Rosa Bonheur, Teresa Carreño or Cosima Wagner. Neither sex, without some fertilization of the complementary characters of the other, is capable of the highest reaches of human endeavor. Man, without a saving touch of woman in him, is too doltish, too naïve and romantic, too easily deluded and lulled to sleep by his imagination to be anything above a cavalryman, a theologian or a corporation director. And woman, without some trace of that divine innocence which is masculine, is too harshly the realist for those vast projections of the fancy which lie at the heart of what we call genius. The wholly manly man lacks the wit necessary to give objective form to his soaring and secret dreams, and the wholly womanly woman is apt to be too cynical a creature to dream at all.

What men, in their egotism, constantly mistake for a deficiency of intelligence in woman is merely an incapacity for mastering that mass of small intellectual tricks, that complex of petty knowledges, that collection of cerebral rubber-stamps, which constitute the chief mental equipment of the average male. A man thinks that he is more intelligent than his wife because he can add up a column of figures more accurately, or because he is able to distinguish between the ideas of rival politicians, or because he is privy to the minutiæ of some sordid and degrading business or profession. But these empty talents, of course, are not really signs of intelligence; they are, in fact, merely a congeries of petty tricks and antics, and their acquirement puts little more strain on the mental powers than a chimpanzee suffers in learning how to catch a penny or scratch a match.

The whole mental baggage of the average business man, or even the average professional man, is inordinately childish. It takes no more actual sagacity to carry on the everyday hawking and haggling of the world, or to ladle out its normal doses of bad medicine and worse law, than it takes to operate a taxicab or fry a pan of fish. No observant person, indeed, can come into close contact with the general run of business and professional men—I confine myself to those who seem to get on in the world, and exclude the admitted failures—without marveling at their intellectual lethargy, their incurable ingenuousness, their appalling lack of ordinary sense. The late Charles Francis Adams, a grandson of one American President and a great-grandson of another, after a long life-time in intimate association with some of the chief business "geniuses" of the United States, reported in his old age that he had never heard a single one of them say anything worth hearing. These were vigorous and masculine men, and in a man's world they were successful men, but intellectually they were all blank cartridges.

There is, indeed, fair ground for arguing that, if men of that kidney were genuinely intelligent, they would never succeed at their gross and driveling concerns—that their very capacity to master and retain such balderdash as constitutes their stock in trade is proof of their inferior mentality. The notion is certainly supported by the familiar incompetency of admittedly first-rate men for what are called practical concerns. One could not think of Aristotle multiplying 3,472,701 by 99,999 without making a mistake, nor could one think of him remembering the range of this or that railway share for two years, or the number of tenpenny nails in a hundred-weight, or the freight on lard from Galveston to Rotterdam. And by the same token one could not imagine him expert at bridge, or at golf, or at any other of the idiotic games at which what are called successful men commonly divert themselves. In his great study of British genius, Havelock Ellis found that an incapacity for such shabby expertness is visible in almost all first-rate men. They are bad at tying cravats. They are puzzled by bookkeeping. They know nothing of party politics. In brief, they are inert and impotent in the very fields of endeavor that see the average men's highest performances, and are easily surpassed by men who, in actual intelligence, are about as far below them as the *Simidæ*.

This lack of skill at manual and mental tricks of a trivial character—which must inevitably appear to a barber as stupidity, and to a successful haberdasher as downright imbecility—is a character that men of the first class share with women of the first, second and even third classes. One seldom hears of women succeeding in the occupations which bring out such expertness most lavishly—for example, tuning pianos, practising law, or writing editorials for newspapers—despite the circumstance that the great majority of such occupations are well within their physical powers, and that few of them offer any very formidable social barriers to female entrance. There is no external reason why they should not prosper at the bar, or as editors of magazines, or as managers of factories, or in the wholesale trade, or as hotel-keepers. The taboos that stand in the way are of very small force; various adventurous women have defied them with impunity, and once the door is entered there remains no special handicap within. But, as everyone knows, the number of women actually practising these trades and professions is very small, and few of them have attained to any distinction in competition with men.

The cause thereof, as I say, is not external, but internal. It lies in the same disconcerting apprehension of the larger realities, the same impatience with the paltry and meretricious, the same disqualification for mechanical routine and empty technic which one finds in the higher varieties of men. Even in the pursuits which, by the custom of Christendom, are especially their own, women seldom show any of that elaborately conventionalized and half automatic proficiency which

is the pride and boast of most men. It is a commonplace of
observation that a housewife who actually knows how to cook,
or who can make her own clothes with enough skill to conceal the fact from the most casual glance, or who is competent
to instruct her children in the elements of morals, learning
and hygiene—it is a platitude that such a woman is very rare
indeed, and that when she is encountered she is not usually
esteemed for her general intelligence.

This is particularly true in the United States, where the
position of women is higher than in any other civilized or
semi-civilized country, and the old assumption of their intellectual inferiority has been most successfully challenged.
The American bourgeois dinner-table becomes a monument
to the defective technic of the American housewife. The guest
who respects his esophagus, invited to feed upon its discordant
and ill-prepared victuals, evades the experience as long and
as often as he can, and resigns himself to it as he might resign
himself to being shaved by a paralytic. Nowhere else in the
world have women more leisure and freedom to improve their
minds, and nowhere else do they show a higher level of intelligence, but nowhere else is there worse cooking in the
home, or a more inept handling of the whole domestic
economy, or a larger dependence upon the aid of external
substitutes, by men provided, for the skill that is wanting
where it theoretically exists. It is surely no mere coincidence
that the land of the emancipated and enthroned woman is also
the land of canned soup, of canned pork and beans, of whole
meals in cans, and of everything else ready made. And nowhere else is there a more striking tendency to throw the whole
business of training the minds of children upon professional
pedagogues, mostly idiots, and the whole business of develop-
ing and caring for their bodies upon pediatricians, playground
"experts," sex hygienists and other such professionals, mostly
frauds.

In brief, women rebel—often unconsciously, sometimes
even submitting all the while—against the dull, mechanical
tricks of the trade that the present organization of society
compels so many of them to practise for a living, and that
rebellion testifies to their intelligence. If they enjoyed and
took pride in those tricks, and showed it by diligence and
skill, they would be on all fours with such men as are head
waiters, accountants, school-masters or carpetbeaters, and
proud of it. The inherent tendency of any woman above the
most stupid is to evade the whole obligation, and, if she can-

not actually evade it, to reduce its demands to the minimum. And when some accident purges her, either temporarily or permanently, of the inclination to marriage, and she enters into competition with men in the general business of the world, the sort of career that she commonly carves out offers additional evidence of her mental superiority. In whatever calls for no more than an invariable technic and a feeble chicanery she usually fails; in whatever calls for independent thought and resourcefulness she usually succeeds. Thus she is almost always a failure as a lawyer, for the law requires only an armament of hollow phrases and stereotyped formulæ, and a mental habit which puts these phantasms above sense, truth and justice; and she is almost always a failure in business, for business, in the main, is so foul a compound of trivialities and rogueries that her sense of intellectual integrity revolts against it. But she is usually a success as a sick-nurse, for that profession requires ingenuity, quick comprehension, courage in the face of novel and disconcerting situations, and above all, a capacity for penetrating and dominating character; and whenever she comes into competition with men in the arts, particularly on those secondary planes where simple nimbleness of mind is unaided by the master strokes of genius, she holds her own invariably. In the *demi-monde* one will find enough acumen and daring, and enough resilience in the face of special difficulties, to put the equipment of any exclusively male profession to shame. If the work of the average man required half the mental agility and readiness of resource of the work of the average brothel-keeper, the average man would be constantly on the verge of starvation.

Men, as everyone knows, are disposed to question this superior intelligence of women; their egoism demands the denial, and they are seldom reflective enough to dispose of it by logical and evidential analysis. Moreover, there is a certain specious appearance of soundness in their position; they have forced upon women an artificial character which well conceals their real character, and women have found it profitable to encourage the deception. But though every normal man thus cherishes the soothing unction that he is the intellectual superior of all women, and particularly of his wife, he constantly gives the lie to his pretension by consulting and deferring to what he calls her intuition. That is to say, he knows by experience that her judgment in many matters of capital concern is more subtle and searching than his own, and,

being disinclined to accredit this great sagacity to a more
competent intelligence, he takes refuge behind the doctrine
that it is due to some impenetrable and intangible talent for
guessing correctly, some half mystical supersense, some vague
(and, in essence, infra-human) instinct.

The true nature of this alleged instinct, however, is revealed
by an examination of the situations which inspire a man to
call it to his aid. These situations do not arise out of the purely technical problems that are his daily concern, but out of
the rarer and more fundamental, and hence enormously more
difficult problems which beset him only at long and irregular
intervals, and so offer a test, not of his mere capacity for
being drilled, but of his capacity for genuine ratiocination.
No man, I take it, save one consciously inferior and hen-
pecked, would consult his wife about hiring a clerk, or about
extending credit to some paltry customer, or about some
routine piece of tawdry swindling; but not even the most
egoistic man would fail to sound the sentiment of his wife
about taking a partner into his business, or about standing for
public office, or about marrying off their daughter. Such
things are of massive importance; they lie at the foundation
of well-being; they call for the best thought that the man
confronted by them can muster; the perils hidden in a wrong
decision overcome even the clamors of vanity. It is in such
situations that the superior mental grasp of women is of
obvious utility, and has to be admitted. It is here that they rise
above the insignificant sentimentalities, superstitions and formulæ of men, and apply to the business their singular talent
for separating the appearance from the substance, and so
exercise what is called their intuition.

Intuition? Bosh! Women, in fact, are the supreme realists of
the race. Apparently illogical, they are the possessors of a rare
and subtle super-logic. Apparently whimsical, they hang to the
truth with a tenacity which carries them through every phase
of its incessant, jelly-like shifting of form. Apparently un-
observant and easily deceived, they see with bright and
horrible eyes. . . . In men, too, the same merciless perspicacity
sometimes shows itself—men recognized to be more aloof and
uninflammable than the general—men of special talent for the
logical—sardonic men, cynics. Men, too, sometimes have
brains. But that is a rare, rare man, I venture, who is as
steadily intelligent, as constantly sound in judgment, as little
put off by appearances, as the average multipara of forty-eight.

JOHN MILTON
1608–1674

"Thy soul was like a Star, and dwelt apart," wrote Wordsworth in his sonnet to Milton; and to us, too, Milton seems apart: an inhabitant of the empyrean, an associate of the archangels. We forget that until his blindness and retirement, he was ardently engaged in the affairs of this world. An official of Cromwell's Commonwealth, he was responsible for defending its policies against criticism at home and abroad. A scholar who was not happy with the English educational system as he had experienced it at Cambridge, he put his ideas of reform into practice for a few years by instructing "the sons of some gentlemen who were his intimate friends." But it was in his essay "Of Education" that he gave the fullest formulation to his unorthodox scheme for producing young men "such as shall deserve the regard and honor of all men where they pass." Here, in prose surprisingly rugged for the author of *Paradise Lost,* yet direct and powerful, Milton makes a plea for "a complete and generous education" which will fit "a man to perform justly, skilfully, and magnanimously all the offices, both private and public, of peace and war."

Of Education
To Master Samuel Hartlib

I am long since persuaded, Master Hartlib, that to say or do aught worth memory and imitation, no purpose or respect should sooner move us than simply the love of God, and of mankind. Nevertheless to write now the reforming of education, though it be one of the greatest and noblest designs that can be thought on, and for the want whereof this nation perishes, I had not yet at this time been induced, but by your earnest entreaties and serious conjurements; as having my mind for the present half diverted into the pursuance of some other assertions, the knowledge and the use of which cannot but be a great furtherance both to the enlargement of truth, and honest living with much more peace. Nor should the laws of any private friendship have prevailed with me to divide thus, or transpose my former thoughts, but that I see those aims, those actions, which have won you with me the esteem of a person sent hither by some good providence from a far country to be the occasion and incitement of great good to this island.

And, as I hear, you have obtained the same repute with men of most approved wisdom, and some of the highest authority among us; not to mention the learned correspondence which you hold in foreign parts, and the extraordinary pains and diligence which you have used in this matter, both here and beyond the seas; either by the definite will of God so ruling, or the peculiar sway of nature, which also is God's working. Neither can I think that so reputed and so valued as you are, you would, to the forfeit of your own discerning ability, impose upon me an unfit and over-ponderous argument; but that the satisfaction which you profess to have received, from those incidental discourses which we have wandered into, hath pressed and almost constrained you into a persuasion, that what you require from me in this point, I neither ought nor can in conscience defer beyond this time both of so much need at once, and so much opportunity to try what God hath determined.

I will not resist, therefore, whatever it is, either of divine or human obligement, that you lay upon me; but will forthwith set down in writing, as you request me, that voluntary idea, which hath long, in silence, presented itself to me, of a better education, in extent and comprehension far more large, and yet of time far shorter, and of attainment far more certain, than hath been yet in practice. Brief I shall endeavour to be; for that which I have to say, assuredly this nation hath extreme need should be done sooner than spoken. To tell you, therefore, what I have benefited herein among old renowned authors, I shall spare; and to search what many modern Januas and Didactics, more than ever I shall read, have projected, my inclination leads me not. But if you can accept of these few observations which have flowered off, and are as it were the burnishing of many studious and contemplative years, altogether spent in the search of religious and civil knowledge, and such as pleased you so well in the relating, I here give you them to dispose of.

The end then of learning is to repair the ruins of our first parents by regaining to know God aright, and out of that knowledge to love him, to imitate him, to be like him, as we may the nearest by possessing our souls of true virtue, which being united to the heavenly grace of faith, makes up the highest perfection. But because our understanding cannot in this body found itself but on sensible things, nor arrive so clearly to the knowledge of God and things invisible, as by orderly conning over the visible and inferior creature, the same method is necessarily to be followed in all discreet teaching. And seeing every nation affords not experience and tradition enough for all kinds of learning, therefore we are chiefly taught the languages of those people who have at any time been most industrious after wisdom; so that language is but the instrument conveying to us things useful to be known. And though a linguist should pride himself to have all the tongues that Babel cleft the world into, yet if he have not studied the solid things in them, as well as the words and lexicons, he were nothing so much to be esteemed a learned man, as any yeoman or tradesman competently wise in his mother dialect only.

Hence appear the many mistakes which have made learning generally so unpleasing and so unsuccessful; first, we do amiss to spend seven or eight years merely in scraping together so much miserable Latin and Greek, as might be learned otherwise easily and delightfully in one year. And that which casts our proficiency therein so much behind, is our time lost partly in too oft idle vacancies given both to schools and universities; partly in a preposterous exaction, forcing the empty wits of children to compose themes, verses, and orations, which are the acts of ripest judgment, and the final work of a head filled by long reading and observing, with elegant maxims and copious invention. These are not matters to be wrung from poor striplings, like blood out of the nose, or the plucking of untimely fruit. Besides the ill habit which they get of wretched barbarising against the Latin and Greek idiom, with their untutored Anglicisms, odious to be read, yet not to be avoided without a well-continued and judicious conversing among pure authors digested, which they scarce taste. Whereas, if after some preparatory grounds of speech by their certain forms got into memory, they were led to the praxis thereof in some chosen short book lessoned thoroughly to them, they might then forthwith proceed to learn the substance of good things, and arts in due order, which would bring the whole language quickly into their power. This I take to be the most rational and most profitable way of learning languages, and whereby we may best hope to give account to God of our youth spent herein.

And for the usual method of teaching arts, I deem it to be an old error of universities, not yet well recovered from the scholastic grossness of barbarous ages, that instead of beginning with arts most easy (and those be such as are most obvious to the sense), they present their young unmatriculated novices, at first coming, with the most intellective abstractions of logic and metaphysics; so that they having but newly left those grammatic flats and shallows, where they stuck unreasonably to learn a few words with lamentable construction, and now on the sudden transported under another climate, to be tossed and turmoiled with their unballasted wits in fathomless and unquiet deeps of controversy, do for the most part grow into hatred and contempt of learning, mocked and deluded all this while with ragged notions and babblements, while they expected worthy and delightful knowledge; till poverty or youthful years call them importunately their several ways, and hasten them, with the sway of friends, either to an ambitious and mercenary, or ignorantly zealous divinity: some allured to the trade of law, grounding their purposes not on the prudent and heavenly contemplation of justice and equity, which was never taught them, but on the promising and pleasing thoughts of litigious terms, fat contentions, and flowing fees; others betake them to state affairs, with souls so unprincipled in virtue and true generous breeding, that flattery and court-shifts and tyrannous aphorisms appear to them the highest points of wisdom; instilling their barren hearts with a conscientious slavery; if, as I rather think, it be not feigned. Others, lastly, of a more delicious and airy spirit, retire themselves (knowing no better) to the enjoyments of ease and luxury, living out their days in feast and jollity; which indeed is the wisest and safest course of all these, unless they were with more integrity undertaken. And these are the errors, and these are the fruits of misspending our prime youth at the schools and universities as we do, either in learning mere words, or such things chiefly as were better unlearned.

I shall detain you now no longer in the demonstration of what we should not do, but straight conduct you to a hillside, where I will point you out the right path of a virtuous and noble education; laborious indeed at the first ascent, but else so smooth, so green, so full of goodly prospect, and melodious sounds on every side, that the harp of Orpheus was not more charming. I doubt not but ye shall have more ado to drive our dullest and laziest youth, our stocks and stubs, from the infinite desire of such a happy nurture, than we have now to hale and drag our choicest and hopefullest wits to that asinine feast of sowthistles and brambles, which is commonly set before them as all the food and entertainment of their tenderest and most docible age. I call therefore a complete and generous education, that which fits a man to perform justly, skilfully, and magnanimously all the offices, both private and public, of peace and war. And how all this may be done between twelve and one-and-twenty, less time than is now bestowed in pure trifling at grammar and sophistry, is to be thus ordered.

First, to find out a spacious house and ground about it fit for an academy, and big enough to lodge a hundred and fifty persons, whereof twenty or thereabout may be attendants, all under the government of one, who shall be thought of desert sufficient, and ability either to do all, or wisely to direct and oversee it done. This place should be at once both school and university, not needing a remove to any other house of scholarship, except it be some peculiar college of law, or physic, where they mean to be practitioners; but as for those general studies which take up all our time from Lily to commencing, as they term it, master of art, it should be absolute. After this pattern, as many edifices may be converted to this use as shall be needful in every city throughout this land, which would tend much to the increase of learning and civility everywhere. This number, less or more thus collected, to the convenience of a foot company, or interchangeably two troops of cavalry, should divide their day's work into three parts as it lies orderly: their studies, their exercise, and their diet.

For their studies: first, they should begin with the chief and necessary rules of some good grammar, either that now used, or any better; and while this is doing, their speech is to be fashioned to a distinct and clear pronunciation, as near as may be to the Italian, especially in the vowels. For we Englishmen being far northerly, do not open our mouths in the cold air wide enough to grace a southern tongue; but are observed by all other nations to speak exceeding close and inward, so that to smatter Latin with an English mouth, is as ill a hearing as law French. Next, to make them expert in the usefullest points of grammar, and withal to season them and win them early to the love of virtue and true labour, ere any flattering seducement or vain principle seize them wandering, some easy and delightful book of education would be read to them, whereof the Greeks have store, as Cebes, Plutarch, and other Socratic discourses. But in Latin we have none of classic authority extant, except the two or three first books of Quintilian, and some select pieces elsewhere.

But here the main skill and groundwork will be, to temper them such lectures and explanations, upon every opportunity, as may lead and draw them in willing obedience, inflamed with the study of learning and the admiration of virtue; stirred up with high hopes of living to be brave men, and worthy patriots, dear to God, and famous to all ages. That they may despise and scorn all their childish and ill-taught qualities, to delight in manly and liberal exercises, which he who hath the art and proper eloquence to catch them with, what with mild and effectual persuasions, and what with the intimation of some fear, if need be, but chiefly by his own example, might in a short space gain them to an incredible diligence and courage, infusing into their young breasts such an ingenuous and noble ardour, as would not fail to make many of them renowned and matchless men. At the same time, some other hour of the day, might be taught them the rules of arithmetic; and soon after the elements of geometry, even playing, as the old manner was. After evening repast, till bedtime, their thoughts would be best taken up in the easy grounds of religion, and the story of scripture.

The next step would be to the authors of agriculture, Cato, Varro and Columella, for the matter is most easy; and, if the language be difficult, so much the better, it is not a difficulty above their years. And here will be an occasion of inciting, and enabling them hereafter to improve the tillage of their country, to recover the bad soil, and to remedy the waste that is made of good; for this was one of Hercules' praises. Ere half these authors be read (which will soon be with plying hard and daily) they cannot choose but be masters of any ordinary prose. So that it will be then seasonable for them to learn in any modern author the use of the globes, and all the maps, first, with the old names, and then with the new; or they might be then capable to read any compendious method of natural philosophy.

And at the same time might be entering into the Greek tongue, after the same manner as was before prescribed in the

Latin; whereby the difficulties of grammar being soon over-come, all the historical physiology of Aristotle and Theophrastus are open before them, as I may say, under contribution. The like access will be to Vitruvius, to Seneca's natural questions, to Mela, Celsus, Pliny, or Solinus. And having thus passed the principles of arithmetic, geometry, astronomy, and geography, with a general compact of physics, they may descend in mathematics to the instrumental science of trigonometry, and from thence to fortification, architecture, enginery, or navigation. And in natural philosophy they may proceed leisurely from the history of meteors, minerals, plants, and living creatures, as far as anatomy.

Then also in course might be read to them, out of some not tedious writer, the institution of physic, that they may know the tempers, the humours, the seasons, and how to manage a crudity; which he who can wisely and timely do, is not only a great physician to himself and to his friends, but also may, at some time or other, save an army by this frugal and expenseless means only; and not let the healthy and stout bodies of young men rot away under him for want of this discipline; which is a great pity, and no less a shame to the commander. To set forward all these proceedings in nature and mathematics, what hinders but that they may procure, as oft as shall be needful, the helpful experience of hunters, fowlers, fishermen, shepherds, gardeners, apothecaries; and in the other sciences, architects, engineers, mariners, anatomists; who doubtless would be ready, some for reward, and some to favour such a hopeful seminary. And this will give them such a real tincture of natural knowledge, as they shall never forget, but daily augment with delight. Then also those poets which are now counted most hard, will be both facile and pleasant, Orpheus, Hesiod, Theocritus, Aratus, Nicander, Oppian, Dionysius; and in Latin, Lucretius, Manilius, and the rural part of Virgil.

By this time, years and good general precepts will have furnished them more distinctly with that act of reason which in ethics is called Proairesis; that they may with some judgment contemplate upon moral good and evil. Then will be required a special reinforcement of constant and sound indoctrinating, to set them right and firm, instructing them more amply in the knowledge of virtue and the hatred of vice; while their young and pliant affections are led through all the moral works of Plato, Xenophon, Cicero, Plutarch, Laertius, and those Locrian remnants; but still to be reduced in their night-

ward studies wherewith they close the day's work, under the
determinate sentence of David or Solomon, or the evangelists
and apostolic scriptures. Being perfect in the knowledge of
personal duty, they may then begin the study of economics.
And either now or before this, they may have easily learned,
at any odd hour, the Italian tongue. And soon after, but with
wariness and good antidote, it would be wholesome enough to
let them taste some choice comedies, Greek, Latin, or Italian;
those tragedies also, that treat of household matters, as
Trachiniæ, Alcestis, and the like.

The next removal must be to the study of politics; to know
the beginning, end, and reasons of political societies; that they
may not, in a dangerous fit of the commonwealth, be such
poor, shaken, uncertain reeds, of such a tottering conscience,
as many of our great counsellors have lately shown themselves, but steadfast pillars of the state. After this, they are to
dive into the grounds of law, and legal justice; delivered first
and with best warrant by Moses; and as far as human prudence can be trusted, in those extolled remains of Grecian
lawgivers, Lycurgus, Solon, Zaleucus, Charondas, and thence
to all the Roman edicts and tables with their Justinian; and
so down to the Saxon and common laws of England, and the
statutes.

Sundays also and every evening may be now understand-
ingly spent in the highest matters of theology, and church
history, ancient and modern; and ere this time the Hebrew
tongue at a set hour might have been gained, that the scriptures may be now read in their own original; whereto it would
be no impossibility to add the Chaldee and the Syrian dialect.
When all these employments are well conquered, then will
the choice histories, heroic poems, and Attic tragedies of
stateliest and most regal argument, with all the famous political orations, offer themselves; which if they were not only
read, but some of them got by memory, and solemnly pronounced with right accent and grace, as might be taught,
would endue them even with the spirit and vigour of Demos-
thenes or Cicero, Euripides or Sophocles.

And now, lastly, will be the time to read with them those
organic arts, which enable men to discourse and write per-
spicuously, elegantly, and according to the fittest style, of lofty,
mean, or lowly. Logic, therefore, so much as is useful, is to be
referred to this due place with all her well-couched heads and
topics, until it be time to open her contracted palm into a
graceful and ornate rhetoric, taught out of the rule of Plato,

Aristotle, Phalereus, Cicero, Hermogenes, Longinus. To which poetry would be made subsequent, or indeed rather precedent, as being less subtile and fine, but more simple, sensuous, and passionate. I mean not here the prosody of a verse, which they could not but have hit on before among the rudiments of grammar; but that sublime art which in Aristotle's poetics, in Horace, and the Italian commentaries of Castelvetro, Tasso, Mazzoni, and others, teaches what the laws are of a true epic poem, what of a dramatic, what of a lyric, what decorum is, which is the grand masterpiece to observe. This would make them soon perceive what despicable creatures our common rhymers and play-writers be; and show them what religious, what glorious and magnificent use might be made of poetry, both in divine and human things.

From hence, and not till now, will be the right season of forming them to be able writers and composers in every excellent matter, when they shall be thus fraught with an universal insight into things. Or whether they be to speak in parliament or council, honour and attention would be waiting on their lips. There would then also appear in pulpits other visage, other gestures, and stuff otherwise wrought than what we now sit under, ofttimes to as great a trial of our patience as any other that they preach to us. These are the studies wherein our noble and our gentle youth ought to bestow their time, in a disciplinary way, from twelve to one-and-twenty: unless they rely more upon their ancestors dead, than upon themselves living. In which methodical course it is so supposed they must proceed by the steady pace of learning onward, as at convenient times, for memory's sake, to retire back into the middle ward, and sometimes into the rear of what they have been taught, until they have confirmed and solidly united the whole body of their perfected knowledge, like the embattling of a Roman legion. Now will be worth the seeing, what exercises and recreations may best agree, and become these studies.

The course of study hitherto briefly described is, what I can guess by reading, likest to those ancient and famous schools of Pythagoras, Plato, Isocrates, Aristotle, and such others, out of which were bred such a number of renowned philosophers, orators, historians, poets, and princes all over Greece, Italy, and Asia, besides the flourishing studies of Cyrene and Alexandria. But herein it shall exceed them, and supply a defect as great as that which Plato noted in the commonwealth of Sparta; whereas that city trained up their youth most for war, and these in their academies and Lycæum all for the gown, this institution of breeding which I here delineate shall be equally good both for peace and war. Therefore about an hour and a half ere they eat at noon should be allowed them for exercise, and due rest afterwards; but the time for this may be enlarged at pleasure, according as their rising in the morning shall be early.

The exercise which I commend first, is the exact use of their weapon, to guard, and to strike safely with edge or point; this will keep them healthy, nimble, strong, and well in breath; is also the likeliest means to make them grow large and tall, and to inspire them with a gallant and fearless courage, which being tempered with seasonable lectures and precepts to them of true fortitude and patience, will turn into a native and heroic valour, and make them hate the cowardice of doing wrong. They must be also practised in all the locks and gripes of wrestling, wherein Englishmen were wont to excel, as need may often be in fight to tug, to grapple, and to close. And this perhaps will be enough, wherein to prove and heat their single strength.

The interim of unsweating themselves regularly, and convenient rest before meat, may, both with profit and delight, be taken up in recreating and composing their travailed spirits with the solemn and divine harmonies of music, heard or learned; either whilst the skilful organist plies his grave and fancied descant in lofty fugues, or the whole symphony with artful and unimaginable touches adorn and grace the well-studied chords of some choice composer; sometimes the lute or soft organ-stop waiting on elegant voices, either to religious, martial, or civil ditties; which, if wise men and prophets be not extremely out, have a great power over dispositions and manners, to smooth and make them gentle from rustic harshness and distempered passions. The like also would not be inexpedient after meat, to assist and cherish nature in her first concoction, and send their minds back to study in good tune and satisfaction. Where having followed it close under vigilant eyes, till about two hours before supper, they are, by a sudden alarum or watchword, to be called out to their military motions, under sky or covert, according to the season, as was the Roman wont; first on foot, then, as their age permits, on horseback, to all the art of cavalry; that having in sport, but with much exactness and daily muster, served out the rudiments of their soldiership, in all the skill of embattling, marching, encamping, fortifying, besieging, and battering, with all the helps of ancient and modern stratagems, tactics, and warlike maxims, they may as it were out of a long war come forth renowned and perfect commanders in the service of their country. They would not then, if they were trusted with fair and hopeful armies, suffer them, for want of just and wise discipline, to shed away from about them like sick feathers, though they be never so oft supplied; they would not suffer their empty and unrecruitable colonels of twenty men in a company, to quaff out or convey into secret hoards, the wages of a delusive list, and a miserable remnant; yet in the meanwhile to be overmastered with a score or two of drunkards, the only soldiery left about them, or else to comply with all rapines and violences. No, certainly, if they knew aught of that knowledge that belongs to good men or good governors, they would not suffer these things.

But to return to our own institute: besides these constant exercises at home, there is another opportunity of gaining experience to be won from pleasure itself abroad; in those vernal seasons of the year when the air is calm and pleasant, it were an injury and sullenness against nature, not to go out and see her riches, and partake in her rejoicing with heaven and earth. I should not therefore be a persuader to them of studying much then, after two or three years that they have well laid their grounds, but to ride out in companies, with prudent and staid guides, to all the quarters of the land: learning and observing all places of strength, all commodities of building and of soil, for towns and tillage, harbours and ports for trade. Sometimes taking sea as far as to our navy, to learn there also what they can in the practical knowledge of sailing and of sea-fight.

These ways would try all their peculiar gifts of nature; and if there were any secret excellence among them would fetch it out, and give it fair opportunities to advance itself by, which could not but mightily redound to the good of this nation, and bring into fashion again those old admired virtues and excellencies, with far more advantage now in this purity of Christian knowledge. Nor shall we then need the monsieurs of Paris to take our hopeful youth into their slight and prodigal custodies, and send them over, back again, transformed into mimics, apes, and kickshaws. But if they desire to see other countries at three or four and twenty years of age, not to learn principles, but to enlarge experience, and make wise observation, they will by that time be such as shall deserve the regard and honour of all men where they pass, and the society and friendship of those in all places who are best and most eminent. And, perhaps, then other nations will be glad to visit us for their breeding, or else to imitate us in their own country.

Now, lastly, for their diet there cannot be much to say, save only that it would be best in the same house; for much time else would be lost abroad, and many ill habits got; and that it should be plain, healthful, and moderate, I suppose is out of controversy. Thus, Mr. Hartlib, you have a general view in writing, as your desire was, of that which at several times I had discoursed with you concerning the best and noblest way of education; not beginning, as some have done, from the cradle, which yet might be worth many considerations, if brevity had not been my scope; many other circumstances also I could have mentioned, but this, to such as have the worth in them to make trial, for light and direction may be enough. Only I believe that this is not a bow for every man to shoot in, that counts himself a teacher; but will require sinews almost equal to those which Homer gave Ulysses; yet I am withal persuaded that it may prove much more easy in the assay, than it now seems at distance, and much more illustrious; howbeit, not more difficult than I imagine, and that imagination presents me with nothing but very happy, and very possible according to best wishes; if God have so decreed, and this age have spirit and capacity enough to apprehend.

MICHEL EYQUEM DE MONTAIGNE
1533–1592

"I am myself the subject of my book." Those famous words, which Michel Eyquem de Montaigne addressed "To the Reader" of his essays in 1580, are still accurate commentary. We do not know, of course, what recesses of the mind he may have hidden from us, nor what sores and scars may be glossed over. But as we follow his introspections and digressions, smile at his homely examples, gasp at his sudden mental leaps, we cannot resist the conviction that he is hiding nothing. This is his whole self that Montaigne lays before us with such painstaking honesty. Yet he is not self-centered; for although he dissects himself, it is all mankind, as revealed in himself, to whom his attention is ultimately directed. We ourselves, we find, are included with Montaigne as the subjects of his book.

Of Repentance

Others form man; I only report him; and represent a particular one, ill fashioned enough, and whom, if I had to model him anew, I should certainly make something else than what he is: but that's past recalling. Now, though the features of my picture alter and change, 'tis not, however, unlike: the world eternally turns round; all things therin are incessantly moving, the earth, the rocks of Caucasus, and the pyramids of Egypt, both by the public motion and their own. Even constancy itself is no other but a slower and more languishing motion. I cannot fix my object; 'tis always tottering and reeling by a natural giddiness: I take it as it is at the instant I consider it; I do not paint its being, I paint its passage; not a passing from one age to another, or, as the people say, from seven to seven years, but from day to day, from minute to minute. I must accommodate my history to the hour: I may presently change, not only by fortune, but also by intention.

243

'Tis a counterpart of various and changeable accidents, and
of irresolute imaginations, and, as it falls out, sometimes
contrary; whether it be that I am then another self, or that I
take subjects by other circumstances and considerations: so it
is, that I may peradventure contradict myself, but, as Demades
said, I never contradict the truth. Could my soul once take
footing, I would not essay but resolve: but it is always learning and making trial.

I propose a life ordinary and without lustre: 'tis all one; all
moral philosophy may as well be applied to a common and
private life, as to one of richer composition: every man
carries the entire form of human condition. Authors communicate themselves to the people by some especial and
extrinsic mark; I, the first of any, by my universal being; as
Michel de Montaigne, not as a grammarian, a poet, or a
lawyer. If the world find fault that I speak too much of myself, I find fault that they do not so much as think of themselves. But is it reason, that being so particular in my way of
living, I should pretend to recommend myself to the public
knowledge? And is it also reason that I should produce to
the world, where art and handling have so much credit and
authority, crude and simple effects of nature, and of a weak
nature to boot? Is it not to build a wall without stone or brick,
or some such thing, to write books without learning and without art? The fancies of music are carried on by art; mine by
chance. I have this, at least, according to discipline, that
never any man treated of a subject he better understood and
knew, than I what I have undertaken, and that in this I am
the most understanding man alive: secondly, that never any
man penetrated farther into his matter, nor better and more
distinctly sifted the parts and sequences of it, nor ever more
exactly and fully arrived at the end he proposed to himself.
To perfect it, I need bring nothing but fidelity to the work;
and that is there, and the most pure and sincere that is anywhere to be found. I speak truth, not so much as I would,
but as much as I dare; and I dare a little the more, as I
grow older; for, methinks, custom allows to age more liberty
of prating, and more indiscretion of talking of a man's self.
That cannot fall out here, which I often see elsewhere, that
the work and the artificer contradict one another: "Can a
man of such sober conversation have written so foolish a
book?" Or "Do so learned writings proceed from a man of so
weak conversation?" He who talks at a very ordinary rate, and
writes rare matter, 'tis to say that his capacity is borrowed

and not his own. A learned man is not learned in all things: but a sufficient man is sufficient throughout, even to ignorance itself; here my book and I go hand in hand together. Elsewhere men may commend or censure the work, without reference to the workman; here they cannot: who touches the one, touches the other. He who shall judge of it without knowing him, will more wrong himself than me; he who does know him, gives me all the satisfaction I desire. I shall be happy beyond my desert, if I can obtain only thus much from the public approbation, as to make men of understanding perceive that I was capable of profiting by knowledge, had I had it; and that I deserved to have been assisted by a better memory.

Be pleased here to excuse what I often repeat, that I very rarely repent, and that my conscience is satisfied with itself, not as the conscience of an angel, or that of a horse, but as the conscience of a man, always adding this clause, not one of ceremony, but a true and real submission, that I speak inquiring and doubting, purely and simply referring myself to the common and accepted beliefs for the resolution. I do not teach, I only relate.

There is no vice that is absolutely a vice which does not offend, and that a sound judgment does not accuse; for there is in it so manifest a deformity and inconvenience, that, peradventure, they are in the right who say that it is chiefly begotten by stupidity and ignorance: so hard is it to imagine that a man can know without abhorring it. Malice sucks up the greatest part of its own venom, and poisons itself. Vice leaves repentance in the soul, like an ulcer in the flesh, which is always scratching and lacerating itself; for reason effaces all other grief and sorrows, but it begets that of repentance, which is so much the more grievous, by reason it springs within, as the cold and heat of fevers are more sharp than those that only strike upon the outward skin. I hold for vices (but every one according to its proportion), not only those which reason and nature condemn, but those also which the opinion of men, though false and erroneous, have made such, if authorized by law and custom.

There is likewise no virtue which does not rejoice a well-descended nature; there is a kind of, I know not what, congratulation in well doing that gives us an inward satisfaction, and a generous boldness that accompanies a good conscience: a soul daringly vicious may, peradventure, arm itself with security, but it cannot supply itself with this complacency and satisfaction. 'Tis no little satisfaction to feel a man's self preserved from the contagion of so depraved an age, and to say to himself: "Whoever could penetrate into my soul would not there find me guilty either of the affliction or ruin of any one, or of revenge or envy, or any offense against the public laws, or of innovation or disturbance, or failure of my word; and though the license of the time permits and teaches every one so to do, yet have I not plundered any Frenchman's goods, or taken his money, and have lived upon what is my own, in war as well as in peace; neither have I set any man to work without paying him his hire." These testimonies of a good conscience please, and this natural rejoicing is very beneficial to us, and the only reward that we can never fail of.

To ground the recompense of virtuous actions upon the approbation of others is too uncertain and unsafe a foundation, especially in so corrupt and ignorant an age as this, wherein the good opinion of the vulgar is injurious: upon whom do you rely to show you what is recommendable? God defend me from being an honest man, according to the descriptions of honor I daily see every one make of himself. *"Quæ feurant vitia, mores sunt."* Some of my friends have at times schooled and scolded me with great sincerity and plainness, either of their own voluntary motion, or by me entreated to it as to an office, which to a well-composed soul surpasses not only in utility, but in kindness all other offices of friendship: I have always received them with the most open arms, both of courtesy and acknowledgment; but, to say the truth, I have often found so much false measure, both in their reproaches and praises, that I had not done much amiss, rather to have done ill, than to have done well according to their notions. We, who live private lives, not exposed to any other view than our own, ought chiefly to have settled a pattern within ourselves by which to try our actions; and according to that, sometimes to encourage and sometimes to correct ourselves. I have my laws and my judicature to judge of myself, and apply myself more to these than to any other rules: I do, indeed, restrain my actions according to others; but extend them not by any other rule than my own. You yourself only know if you are cowardly and cruel, loyal and devout: others see you not, and only guess at you by uncertain conjectures, and do not so much see your nature as your art: rely not therefore upon their opinions, but stick to your own: *"Tuo tibi judicio est utendum . . . Virtutis et vitiorum grave ipsius conscientiæ pondus est: qua sublata, jacent omnia."*

But the saying that repentance immediately follows the sin seems not to have respect to sin in its high estate, which is lodged in us as in its own proper habitation. One may disown and retract the vices that surprise us, and to which we are hurried by passions; but those which by a long habit are rooted in a strong and vigorous will are not subject to contradiction. Repentance is no other but a recanting of the will and an opposition to our fancies, which lead us which way they please. It makes this person disown his former virtue and continency:

"Quæ mens est hodie, cur eadem non puero fuit?
Vel cur his animis incolumes non redeunt genæ?"

'Tis an exact life that maintains itself in due order in private. Every one may juggle his part, and represent an honest man upon the stage: but within, and in his own bosom, where all may do as they list, where all is concealed, to be regular—there's the point. The next degree is to be so in his house, and in his ordinary actions, for which we are accountable to none, and where there is no study nor artifice. And therefore Bias, setting forth the excellent state of a private family, says: "of which the master is the same within, by his own virtue and temper, that he is abroad, for fear of the laws and report of men." And it was a worthy saying of Julius Drusus, to the masons who offered him, for three thousand crowns, to put his house in such a posture that his neighbours should no longer have the same inspection into it as before; "I will give you," said he, "six thousand to make it so that everybody may see into every room." 'Tis honorably recorded of Agesilaus, that he used in his journeys always to take up his lodgings in temples, to the end that the people and the gods themselves might pry into his most private actions. Such a one has been a miracle to the world, in whom neither his wife nor servant has ever seen anything so much as remarkable; few men have been admired by their own domestics; no one was ever a prophet, not merely in his own house, but in his own country, says the experience of histories: 'tis the same in things of naught, and in this low example the image of a greater is to be seen. In my country of Gascony, they look upon it as a drollery to see me in print; the further off I am read from my own home, the better I am esteemed. I am fain

to purchase printers in Guienne; elsewhere they purchase me.
Upon this it is that they lay their foundation who conceal
themselves present and living, to obtain a name when they are
absent and dead. I had rather have a great deal less in hand,
and do not expose myself to the world upon any other account
than my present share; when I leave it I quit the rest. See this
functionary whom the people escort in state, with wonder and
applause, to his very door; he puts off the pageant with his
robe, and falls so much the lower by how much he was higher
exalted: in himself within, all is tumult and degraded. And
though all should be regular there, it will require a vivid and
well-chosen judgment to perceive it in these low and private
actions; to which may be added, that order is a dull, somber
virtue. To enter a breach, conduct an embassy, govern a
people, are actions of renown: to reprehend, laugh, sell, pay,
love, hate, and gently and justly converse with a man's own
family, and with himself; not to relax, not to give a man's
self the lie is more rare and hard, and less remarkable. By
which means, retired lives, whatever is said to the contrary,
undergo duties of as great or greater difficulty than the others
do; and private men, says Aristotle, serve virtue more painfully and highly, than those in authority do: we prepare ourselves for eminent occasions, more out of glory than conscience. The shortest way to arrive at glory, would be to do
that for conscience which we do for glory: and the virtue of
Alexander appears to me of much less vigor in his great
theater, than that of Socrates in his mean and obscure employment. I can easily conceive Socrates in the place of Alexander, but Alexander in that of Socrates, I cannot. Who shall
ask the one what he can do, he will answer, "Subdue the
world:" and who shall put the same question to the other,
he will say, "Carry on human life conformably with its natural condition;" a much more general, weighty, and legitimate
science than the other.

The virtue of the soul does not consist in flying high, but
in walking orderly; its grandeur does not exercise itself in
grandeur, but in mediocrity. As they who judge and try us
within, make no great account of the luster of our public
actions, and see they are only streaks and rays of clear water
springing from a slimy and muddy bottom: so, likewise, they
who judge of us by this gallant outward appearance, in like
manner conclude of our internal constitution; and cannot
couple common faculties, and like their own, with the other
faculties that astonish them, and are so far out of their sight.

Therefore it is, that we give such savage forms to demons: and who does not give Tamerlane great eyebrows, wide nostrils, a dreadful visage, and a prodigious stature, according to the imagination he has conceived by the report of his name? Had any one formerly brought me to Erasmus, I should hardly have believed but that all was adage and apothegm he spoke to his man or his hostess. We much more aptly imagine an artisan upon his close-stool, or upon his wife, than a great president venerable by his port and sufficiency: we fancy that they, from their high tribunals, will not abase themselves so much as to live. As vicious souls are often incited by some foreign impulse to do well, so are virtuous souls to do ill; they are therefore to be judged by their settled state, when they are at home, whenever that may be; and, at all events, when they are nearer repose, and in their native station.

Natural inclinations are much assisted and fortified by education: but they seldom alter and overcome their institution: a thousand natures of my time have escaped toward virtue or vice, through a quiet contrary discipline;

> "Sic ubi desuetæ silvis in carcere clausæ
> Mansuevere feræ, et vultus posuere minaces,
> Atque hominem didicere pati, si torrida parvus
> Venit in ora cruor, redeunt rabiesque furorque,
> Admonitæque tument gustato sanguine fauces;
> Fervet, et a trepido vix abstinet ira magistro;"

these original qualities are not to be rooted out; they may be covered and concealed. The Latin tongue is as it were natural to me; I understand it better than French; but I have not been used to speak it, nor hardly to write it these forty years. Yet, upon extreme and sudden emotions which I have fallen into twice or thrice in my life, and once, seeing my father in perfect health fall upon me in a swoon, I have always uttered my first outcries and ejaculations in Latin; nature starting up, and forcibly expressing itself, in spite of so long a discontinuation; and this example is said of many others.

They who in my time have attempted to correct the manners of the world by new opinions, reform seeming vices, but the essential vices they leave as they were, if indeed, they do not augment them; and augmentation is, therein, to be feared; we defer all other well doing upon the account of these external reformations, of less cost and greater show, and thereby expiate cheaply, for the other natural consubstantial and intestine vices. Look a little into our experience: there is no man, if he listen to himself, who does not in himself discover a particular and governing form of his own, that jostles his education, and wrestles with the tempest of passions that are contrary to it. For my part, I seldom find myself agitated with surprises; I always find myself in my place, as heavy and unwieldly bodies do; if I am not at home, I am always near at hand; my dissipations do not transport me very far, there is nothing strange nor extreme in the case; and yet I have sound and vigorous turns.

The true condemnation, and which touches the common practice of men, is, that their very retirement itself is full of filth and corruption; the idea of their reformation composed; their repentance sick and faulty, very nearly as much as their sin. Some, either from having been linked to vice by a natural propension, or long practice, cannot see its deformity. Others (of which constitution I am) do indeed feel the weight of vice, but they counterbalance it with pleasure, or some other occasion; and suffer, and lend themselves to it, for a certain price, but viciously and basely. Yet there might, haply, be imagined so vast a disproportion of measure, where with justice the pleasure might excuse the sin, as we say of utility; not only if accidental, and out of sin, as in thefts, but the very exercise of sin, as in the enjoyment of women, where the temptation is violent, and 'tis said, sometimes not to be overcome.

Being the other day at Armaignac, on the estate of a kinsman of mine, I there saw a country fellow who was by every one nicknamed the thief. He thus related the story of his life; that being born a beggar, and finding that he should not be able, so as to be clear of indigence, to get his living by the sweat of his brow, he resolved to turn thief, and by means of his strength of body, had exercised this trade all the time of his youth in great security; for he ever made his harvest and vintage in other men's grounds, but a great way off, and in so great quantities, that it was not to be imagined one man could have carried away so much in one night upon his shoulders; and, moreover, was careful equally to divide and distribute the mischief he did, that the loss was of less importance to every particular man. He is now grown old, and rich for a man of his condition, thanks to his trade, which he openly confesses to every one. And to make his peace with God, he says, that he is daily ready by good offices to make satisfaction to the successors of those he has robbed, and if he do not finish (for to do it all at once he is not able) he will then leave it in charge to his heirs to perform the rest, proportionably to the wrong he himself only knows he has done to each. By this description, true or false, this man looks upon theft as a dishonest action, and hates it, but less than poverty, and simply repents; but to the extent he has thus recompensed, he repents not. This is not that habit which incorporates us into vice, and conforms even our understanding itself to it; nor is it that impetuous whirlwind that by gusts troubles and blinds our souls and for the time precipitates us, judgment and all, into the power of vice.

I customarily do what I do thoroughly and make but one step on't; I have rarely any movement that hides itself and steals away from my reason, and that does not proceed in the matter by the consent of all my faculties, without division or intestine sedition; my judgment is to have all the blame or all the praise; and the blame it once has, it has always; for almost from my infancy it has ever been one; the same inclination, the same turn, the same force; and as to universal opinions, I fixed myself from my childhood in the place where I resolved to stick. There are some sins that are impetuous, prompt, and sudden; let us set them aside; but in these other sins so often repeated, deliberated, and contrived, whether sins of complexion or sins of profession and vocation, I cannot conceive that they should have so long been settled in the same resolution, unless the reason and conscience of him who has them, be constant to have them; and the repentance he boasts to be inspired with on a sudden, is very hard for me to imagine or form. I follow not the opinion of the Pythagorean sect, "that men take up a new soul when they repair to the images of the gods to receive their oracles," unless he mean that it must needs be extrinsic, new, and lent for the time; our own showing so little sign of purification and cleanness, fit for such an office.

They act quite contrary to the stoical precepts, who do indeed, command us to correct the imperfections and vices we know ourselves guilty of, but forbid us therefore to disturb the repose of our souls; these make us believe that they have great grief and remorse within; but of amendment, correction, or interruption, they make nothing appear. It cannot be a cure if the malady be not wholly discharged; if repentance were laid upon the scale of the balance, it would weigh down sin. I find no quality so easy to counterfeit as devotion, if men do not conform their manners and life to the profession; its essence is abstruse and occult; the appearances easy and ostentatious.

For my own part, I may desire in general to be other than
I am; I may condemn and dislike my whole form, and beg of
Almighty God for an entire reformation, and that He will
please to pardon my natural infirmity: but I ought not to call
this repentance, methinks, no more, than the being dissatisfied
that I am not an angel or Cato. My actions are regular, and
conformable with what I am, and to my condition; I can do
no better; and repentance does not properly touch things
that are not in our power; sorrow does. I imagine an infinite
number of natures more elevated and regular than mine; and
yet I do not for all that improve my faculties, no more than
my arm or will grow more strong and vigorous for con-
ceiving those of another to be so. If to conceive and wish a
nobler way of acting than that we have, should produce a repentance of our own, we must then repent us of our most
innocent actions, forasmuch as we may well suppose that in a
more excellent nature they would have been carried on with
greater dignity and perfection; and we would that ours were
so. When I reflect upon the deportments of my youth, with
that of my old age, I find that I have commonly behaved
myself with equal order in both, according to what I understand: this is all that my resistance can do. I do not flatter
myself; in the same circumstances I should do the same
things. It is not a patch, but rather an universal tincture, with
which I am stained. I know no repentance, superficial, halfway and ceremonious; it must sting me all over before I can
call it so, and must prick my bowels as deeply and universally
as God sees into me.

As to business, many excellent opportunities have escaped
me for want of good management; and yet my deliberations
were sound enough, according to the occurrences presented to
me: 'tis their way to choose always the easiest and safest
course. I find that, in my former resolves, I have proceeded
with discretion, according to my own rule, and according to
the state of the subject proposed, and should do the same a
thousand years hence in like occasions; I do not consider what
it is now, but what it was then, when I deliberated on it: the
force of all counsel consists in the time; occasions and things
eternally shift and change. I have in my life committed some
important errors, not for want of good understanding, but for
want of good luck. There are secret, and not to be foreseen,
parts in matters we have in hand, especially in the nature
of men; mute conditions, that make no show, unknown sometimes even to the possessors themselves, that spring and start

up by incidental occasions; if my prudence could not penetrate into nor foresee them, I blame it not: 'tis commissioned no further than its own limits; if the event be too hard for me, and take the side I have refused, there is no remedy; I do not blame myself, I accuse my fortune, and not my work; this cannot be called repentance.

Phocion, having given the Athenians an advice that was not followed, and the affair nevertheless succeeding contrary to his opinion, some one said to him; "Well, Phocion, art thou content that matters go so well?" "I am very well content," replied he, "that this has happened so well, but I do not repent that I counseled the other." When any of my friends address themselves to me for advice, I give it candidly and clearly, without sticking, as almost all other men do, at the hazard of the thing's falling out contrary to my opinion, and that I may be reproached for my counsel; I am very indifferent as to that, for the fault will be theirs for having consulted me, and I could not refuse them that office.

I, for my own part, can rarely blame any one but myself for my oversights and misfortunes, for indeed I seldom solicit the advice of another, if not by honor of ceremony, or excepting where I stand in need of information, special science, or as to matter of fact. But in things wherein I stand in need of nothing but judgment, other men's reasons may serve to fortify my own, but have little power to dissuade me; I hear them all with civility and patience: but to my recollection, I never made use of any but my own. With me, they are but flies and atoms, that confound and distract my will; I lay no great stress upon my opinions; but I lay as little upon those of others, and fortune rewards me accordingly: if I receive but little advice, I also give but little. I am seldom consulted, and still more seldom believed, and know no concern, either public or private, that has been mended or bettered by my advice. Even they whom fortune had in some sort tied to my direction, have more willingly suffered themselves to be governed by any other counsels than mine. And as a man who am as jealous of my repose as of my authority, I am better pleased that it should be so; in leaving me there, they humor what I profess, which is to settle and wholly contain myself within myself. I take a pleasure in being uninterested in other men's affairs, and disengaged from being their warranty, and responsible for what they do.

In all affairs that are past, be it how it will, I have very little regret; for this imagination puts me out of my pain, that they were so to fall out; they are in the great revolution of the world, and in the chain of stoical causes: your fancy cannot, by wish and imagination, move one tittle, but that the great current of things will not reverse both the past and the future.

As to the rest, I abominate that incidental repentance which old age brings along with it. He, who said of old, that he was obliged to his age for having weaned him from pleasure, was of another opinion than I am; I can never think myself beholden to impotency, for any good it can do to me; *"Nec tam aversa unquam videbitur ab opere suo providentia, ut debilitas inter optima inventa sit."* Our appetites are rare in old age; a profound satiety seizes us after the act; in this I see nothing of conscience; chagrin and weakness imprint in us a drowsy and rheumatic virtue. We must not suffer ourselves to be so wholly carried away by natural alterations, as to suffer our judgments to be imposed upon by them. Youth and pleasure have not formerly so far prevailed with me, that I did not well enough discern the face of vice in pleasure; neither does the distaste that years have brought me, so far prevail with me now, that I cannot discern pleasure in vice. Now that I am no more in my flourishing age, I judge as well of these things as if I were. I, who narrowly and strictly examine it, find my reason the very same it was in my most licentious age, except, perhaps, that 'tis weaker and more decayed by being grown older; and I find that the pleasure it refuses me upon the account of my bodily health, it would no more refuse now, in consideration of the health of my soul, than at any time heretofore. I do not repute it the more valiant for not being able to combat; my temptations are so broken and mortified, that they are not worth its opposition; holding but out my hands, I repel them. Should one present the old concupiscence before it, I fear it would have less power to resist it than heretofore; I do not discern that in itself it judges anything otherwise now, than it formerly did, nor that it has acquired any new light: wherefore, if there be convalescence, 'tis an enchanted one. Miserable kind of remedy, to owe one's health to one's disease! 'Tis not that our misfortune should perform this office, but the good fortune of our judgment. I am not to be made to do anything by persecutions and afflictions, but to curse them: that is for people who cannot be roused but by a whip. My reason is much more free in prosperity, and much more distracted, and put to't to digest pains than pleasures: I see best in a clear sky; health admonishes me more cheerfully, and to better purpose, than sickness. I did all that in me lay to reform and regulate myself from pleasures, at a time when I had health and vigor to enjoy them; I should be ashamed and envious, that the misery and misfortune of my old age should have credit over my good, healthful, sprightly, and vigorous years; and that men should estimate me, not by what I have been, but by what I have ceased to be.

In my opinion, 'tis the happy living, and not (as Antisthenes said) the happy dying, in which human felicity consists. I have not made it my business to make a monstrous addition of a philosopher's tail to the head and body of a libertine; nor would I have this wretched remainder give the lie to the pleasant, sound, and long part of my life: I would present myself uniformly throughout. Were I to live my life over again, I should live it just as I have lived it; I neither complain of the past, nor do I fear the future; and if I am not much deceived, I am the same within that I am without. 'Tis one main obligation I have to my fortune, that this succession of my bodily estate has been carried on according to the natural seasons; I have seen the grass, the blossom, and the fruit; and now see the withering; happily, however, because naturally. I bear the infirmities I have the better, because they came not till I had reason to expect them, and because also they make me with greater pleasure remember that long felicity of my past life. My wisdom may have been just the same in both ages; but it was more active, and of better grace while young and sprightly, than now it is when broken, peevish and uneasy. I repudiate, then, these casual and painful reformations. God must touch our hearts; our consciences must amend of themselves, by the aid of our reason, and not by the decay of our appetites; pleasure is, in itself, neither pale nor discolored, to be discerned by dim and decayed eyes.

We ought to love temperance for itself, and because God has commanded that and chastity; but that which we are reduced to by catarrhs, and for which I am indebted to the stone, is neither chastity nor temperance; a man cannot boast that he despises and resists pleasure, if he cannot see it, if he knows not what it is, and cannot discern its graces, its force, and most alluring beauties; I know both the one and the other, and may therefore the better say it. But, methinks, our souls, in old age, are subject to more troublesome maladies and imperfections than in youth; I said the same when young and when I was reproached with the want of a beard; and I say so now that my gray hairs give me some authority. We call the difficulty of our humors and the disrelish of present things wisdom; but, in truth, we do not so much forsake vices as we change them, and, in my opinion, for worse. Besides a foolish and feeble pride, an impertinent prating, froward and insociable humors, superstition, and a ridiculous desire of riches when we have lost the use of them, I find there more envy, injustice and malice. Age imprints more wrinkles in the mind than it does on the face; and souls are never, or very rarely seen, that in growing old do not smell sour and musty. Man moves all together, both toward his perfection and decay. In observing the wisdom of Socrates, and many circumstances of his condemnation, I should dare to believe, that he in some sort himself purposely, by collusion, contributed to it, seeing that, at the age of seventy years, he might fear to suffer the lofty motions of his mind to be cramped, and his wonted luster obscured. What strange metamorphoses do I see age every day make in many of my acquaintance! 'Tis a potent malady, and that naturally and imperceptibly steals into us; a vast provision of study and great precaution are required to evade the imperfections it loads us with, or at least, to weaken their progress. I find that, notwithstanding all my entrenchments, it gets foot by foot upon me; I make the best resistance I can, but I do not know to what at last it will reduce me. But fall out what will, I am content the world may know, when I am fallen, from what I fell.

JOHN HENRY NEWMAN
1801–1890

John Henry, Cardinal Newman, bore a striking resemblance
in face and figure to Julius Caesar, and there are interesting
contrasts and correspondences in the lives of the two men.
Caesar, the victorious Roman, came to England to meet failure;
Newman, the Englishman, came in defeat to the Church of Rome,
to gain eventual victory and the crimson hat of a Cardinal. Before
that final triumph, however, there were years such as Caesar
never knew: years of loneliness when Newman was cut off from
his old friends in the Anglican Church, yet still not trusted by his
new Catholic associates; and it was in this period that he wrote
the essay printed below, "What Is a University?" Appointed
Rector in 1851 of a new Catholic University projected for Dublin,
he delivered a series of great statements on the nature of university
education. Against both sectarian and utilitarian objections, he
maintained the value of seeking knowledge for its own sake; and
here in this essay he employs his customary eloquence to defend
the university as "a place of concourse, whither students come
from every quarter for every kind of knowledge," a place "in
which the intellect may safely range and speculate, sure to find
its equal in some antagonist activity, and its judge in the tribunal
of truth."

What Is a University?

If I were asked to describe as briefly and popularly as I
could, what a University was, I should draw my answer from
its ancient designation of a *Studium Generale,* or "School of
Universal Learning." This description implies the assemblage
of strangers from all parts in one spot;—*from all parts;* else,
how will you find professors and students for every department of knowledge? and *in one spot;* else, how can there be
any school at all? Accordingly, in its simple and rudimental

form, it is a school of knowledge of every kind, consisting of teachers and learners from every quarter. Many things are requisite to complete and satisfy the idea embodied in this description; but such as this a University seems to be in its essence, a place for the communication and circulation of thought, by means of personal intercourse, through a wide extent of country.

There is nothing far-fetched or unreasonable in the idea thus presented to us; and if this be a University, then a University does but contemplate a necessity of our nature, and is but one specimen in a particular medium, out of many which might be adduced in others, of a provision for that necessity. Mutual education, in a large sense of the word, is one of the great and incessant occupations of human society, carried on partly with set purpose, and partly not. One generation forms another; and the existing generation is ever acting and reacting upon itself in the persons of its individual members. Now, in this process, books, I need scarcely say, that is, the *litera scripta,* are one special instrument. It is true; and emphatically so in this age. Considering the prodigious powers of the press, and how they are developed at this time in the never-intermitting issue of periodicals, tracts, pamphlets, works in series, and light literature, we must allow there never was a time which promised fairer for dispensing with every other means of information and instruction. What can we want more, you will say, for the intellectual education of the whole man, and for every man, than so exuberant and diversified and persistent a promulgation of all kinds of knowledge? Why, you will ask, need we go up to knowledge, when knowledge comes down to us? The Sibyl wrote her prophecies upon the leaves of the forest, and wasted them; but here such careless profusion might be prudently indulged, for it can be afforded without loss, in consequence of the almost fabulous fecundity of the instrument which these latter ages have invented. We have sermons in stones, and books in the running brooks; works larger and more comprehensive than those which have gained for ancients an immortality, issue forth every morning, and are projected onwards to the ends of the earth at the rate of hundreds of miles a day. Our seats are strewed, our pavements are powered, with swarms of little tracts; and the very bricks of our city walls preach wisdom, by informing us by their placards where we can at once cheaply purchase it.

I allow all this, and much more; such certainly is our popular education, and its effects are remarkable. Nevertheless, after all, even in this age, whenever men are really serious about getting what, in the language of trade, is called "a good article," when they aim at something precise, something refined, something really luminous, something really large, something choice, they go to another market; they avail themselves in some shape or other, of the rival method, the ancient method, of oral instruction, of present communication between man and man, of teachers instead of learning, of the personal influence of a master, and the humble initiation of a disciple, and, in consequence, of great centres of pilgrimage and throng, which such a method of education necessarily involves. This, I think, will be found to hold good in all those departments or aspects of society, which possess an interest sufficient to bind men together, or to constitute what is called "a world." It holds in the political world, and in the high world, and in the religious world; and it holds also in the literary and scientific world.

If the actions of men may be taken as any test of their convictions, then we have reason for saying this, viz.:—that the province and the inestimable benefit of the *litera scripta* is that of being a record of truth, and an authority of appeal, and an instrument of teaching in the hands of a teacher; but that, if we wish to become exact and fully furnished in any branch of knowledge which is diversified and complicated, we must consult the living man and listen to his living voice. I am not bound to investigate the cause of this, and anything I may say will, I am conscious, be short of its full analysis;— perhaps we may suggest, that no books can get through the number of minute questions which it is possible to ask on any extended subject, or can hit upon the very difficulties which are severally felt by each reader in succession. Or again, that no book can convey the special spirit and delicate peculiarities of its subject with that rapidity and certainty which attend on the sympathy of mind with mind, through the eyes, the look, the accent, and the manner, in casual expressions thrown off at the moment, and the unstudied turns of familiar conversation. But I am already dwelling too long on what is but an incidental portion of my main subject. Whatever be the cause, the fact is undeniable. The general principles of any study you may learn by books at home; but the detail, the colour, the tone, the air, the life which makes it live in us, you must catch all these from those in whom it lives already. You must imitate the student in French or German, who is not content with his grammar, but goes to Paris or Dresden: you must take example from the young artist, who aspires to visit the great Masters in Florence and in Rome. Till we have discovered some intellectual daguerreotype, which takes off the course of thought, and the form, lineaments, and features of truth, as completely and minutely as the optical instrument reproduces the sensible object, we must come to the teachers of wisdom to learn wisdom, we must repair to the fountain, and drink there. Portions of it may go from thence to the ends of the earth by means of books; but the fulness is in one place alone. It is in such assemblages and congregations of intellect that books themselves, the masterpieces of human genius, are written, or at least originated.

The principle on which I have been insisting is so obvious, and instances in point are so ready, that I should think it tiresome to proceed with the subject, except that one or two illustrations may serve to explain my own language about it, which may not have done justice to the doctrine which it has been intended to enforce.

For instance, the polished manners and high-bred bearing which are so difficult of attainment, and so strictly personal when attained,—which are so much admired in society, from society are acquired. All that goes to constitute a gentleman, —the carriage, gait, address, gestures, voice; the ease, the self-possession, the courtesy, the power of conversing, the talent of not offending; the lofty principle, the delicacy of thought, the happiness of expression, the taste and propriety, the generosity and forbearance, the candour and consideration, the openness of hand;—these qualities, some of them come by nature, some of them may be found in any rank, some of them are a direct precept of Christianity; but the full assemblage of them, bound up in the unity of an individual character, do we expect they can be learned from books? are they not necessarily acquired, where they are to be found, in high society? The very nature of the case leads us to say so; you cannot fence without an antagonist, nor challenge all comers in disputation before you have supported a thesis; and in like manner, it stands to reason, you cannot learn to converse till you have the world to converse with; you cannot unlearn your natural bashfulness, or awkwardness, or stiffness, or other besetting deformity, till you serve your time in some school of manners. Well, and is it not so in matter of fact? The metropolis, the court, the great houses of the land, are the centres to which at stated times the country comes up, as to shrines of refinement and good taste; and then in due time the country goes back again home, enriched with a portion of the social accomplishments, which those very visits serve to call out and heighten in the gracious dispensers of them. We are unable to conceive how the "gentlemanlike" can otherwise be maintained; and maintained in this way it is.

And now a second instance: and here too I am going to speak without personal experience of the subject I am introducing. I admit I have not been in Parliament, any more than I have figured in the *beau monde;* yet I cannot but think that statesmanship, as well as high breeding, is learned, not by books, but in certain centres of education. If it be not presumption to say so, Parliament puts a clever man *au courant* with politics and affairs of state in a way surprising to himself. A member of the Legislature, if tolerably observant, begins to see things with new eyes, even though his views undergo no change. Words have a meaning now, and ideas a reality, such as they had not before. He hears a vast deal in public speeches and private conversation, which is never put into print. The bearings of measures and events, the action of parties, and the persons of friends and enemies, are brought out to the man who is in the midst of them with a distinctness, which the most diligent perusal of newspapers will fail to impart to them. It is access to the fountain-heads of political wisdom and experience, it is daily intercourse, of one kind or another, with the multitude who go up to them, it is familiarity with business, it is access to the contributions of fact and opinion thrown together by many witnesses from many quarters, which does this for him. However, I need not account for a fact, to which it is sufficient to appeal; that the Houses of Parliament and the atmosphere around them are a sort of University of politics.

As regards the world of science, we find a remarkable instance of the principle which I am illustrating, in the periodical meetings for its advance, which have arisen in the course of the last twenty years, such as the British Association. Such gatherings would to many persons appear at first sight simply preposterous. Above all subjects of study, Science is conveyed, is propagated, by books, or by private teaching; experiments and investigations are conducted in silence; discoveries are made in solitude. What have philosophers to do with festive celebrities, and panegyrical solemnities with mathematical and physical truth? Yet on a closer attention to the subject, it is found that not even scientific thought can dispense with the suggestions, the instruction, the stimulus, the sympathy, the intercourse with mankind on a large scale, which such meetings secure. A fine time of year is chosen, when days are long, skies are bright, the earth smiles, and all nature rejoices; a city or town is taken by turns, of ancient name or modern opulence, where buildings are spacious and hospitality hearty. The novelty of place and circumstance, the excitement of strange, or the refreshment of well-known faces, the majesty of rank or of genius, the amiable charities of men pleased both with themselves and with each other; the elevated spirits, the circulation of thought, the curiosity; the morning sections, the outdoor exercise, the well-furnished, well-earned board, the not ungraceful hilarity, the evening circle; the brilliant lecture, the discussions or collisions or guesses of great men one with another, the narratives of scientific processes, of hopes, disappointments, conflicts, and successes, the splendid eulogistic orations; these and the like constituents of the annual celebration, are considered to do something real and substantial for the advance of knowledge which can be done in no other way. Of course they can but be occasional; they answer to the annual Act, or Commencement, or Commemoration of a University, not to its ordinary condition; but they are of a University nature; and I can well believe in their utility. They issue in the promotion of a certain living and, as it were, bodily communication of knowledge from one to another, of a general interchange of ideas, and a comparison and adjustment of science with science, of an enlargement of mind, intellectual and social, of an ardent love of the particular study, which may be chosen by each individual, and a noble devotion to its interests.

Such meetings, I repeat, are but periodical, and only partially represent the idea of a University. The bustle and whirl which are their usual concomitants, are in ill keeping with the order and gravity of earnest intellectual education. We desiderate means of instruction which involve no interruption of our ordinary habits; nor need we seek it long, for the natural course of things brings it about, while we debate over it. In every great country, the metropolis itself becomes a sort of necessary University, whether we will or no. As the chief city is the seat of the court, of high society, of politics, and of law, so as a matter of course is it the seat of letters also; and at this time, for a long term of years, London and Paris are in fact and in operation Universities, though in Paris its

famous University is no more, and in London a University
scarcely exists except as a board of administration. The newspapers, magazines, reviews, journals, and periodicals of all
kinds, the publishing trade, the libraries, museums, and academies there found, the learned and scientific societies, necessarily invest it with the functions of a University; and that atmosphere of intellect, which in a former age hung over Oxford or Bologna or Salamanca, has, with the change of times,
moved away to the centre of civil government. Thither come
up youths from all parts of the country, the students of law,
medicine, and the fine arts, and the *employés and attachés* of
literature. There they live, as chance determines; and they
are satisfied with their temporary home, for they find in it all
that was promised to them there. They have not come in vain,
as far as their own object in coming is concerned. They have
not learned any particular religion, but they have learned
their own particular profession well. They have, moreover, become acquainted with the habits, manners, and opinions of
their place of sojourn, and done their part in maintaining the
tradition of them. We cannot then be without virtual Universities; a metropolis is such: the simple question is, whether the
education sought and given should be based on principle,
formed upon rule, directed to the highest ends, or left to the
random succession of masters and schools, one after another,
with a melancholy waste of thought and an extreme hazard of
truth.

Religious teaching itself affords us an illustration of our subject to a certain point. It does not indeed seat itself merely
in centres of the world; this is impossible from the nature of
the case. It is intended for the many, not the few; its subject
matter is truth necessary for us, not truth recondite and rare;
but it concurs in the principle of a University so far as this,
that its great instrument, or rather organ, has ever been that
which nature prescribes in all education, the personal presence
of a teacher, or, in theological language, Oral Tradition. It is
the living voice, the breathing form, the expressive countenance, which preaches, which catechizes. Truth, a subtle, invisible, manifold spirit, is poured into the mind of the scholar
by his eyes and ears through his affections, imagination, and
reason; it is poured into this mind and is sealed up there in
perpetuity, by propounding and repeating it, by questioning
and requestioning, by correcting and explaining, by progress-
ing and then recurring to first principles, by all those ways
which are implied in the word "catechizing." In the first ages,

it was a work of long time; months, sometimes years, were devoted to the arduous task of disabusing the mind of the incipient Christian of its pagan errors, and of moulding it upon the Christian faith. The Scriptures indeed were at hand for the study of those who could avail themselves of them; but St. Irenæus does not hesitate to speak of whole races, who had been converted to Christianity, without being able to read them. To be unable to read or write was in those times no evidence of want of learning: the hermits of the deserts were, in the sense of the word, illiterate; yet the great St. Anthony, though he knew not letters, was a match in disputation for the learned philosophers who came to try him. Didymus again, the great Alexandrian theologian, was blind. The ancient discipline, called the *Disciplina Arcani,* involved the same principle. The more sacred doctrines of Revelation were not committed to books but passed on by successive tradition. The teaching on the Blessed Trinity and the Eucharist appears to have been so handed down for some hundred years; and when at length reduced to writing, it has filled many folios, yet has not been exhausted.

But I have said more than enough in illustration; I end as I began;—a University is a place of concourse, whither students come from every quarter for every kind of knowledge. You cannot have the best of every kind everywhere; you must go to some great city or emporium for it. There you have all the choicest productions of nature and art all together, which you find each in its own separate place elsewhere. All the riches of the land, and of the earth, are carried up thither; there are the best markets, and there the best workmen. It is the centre of trade, the supreme court of fashion, the umpire of rival talents, and the standard of things rare and precious. It is the place for seeing galleries of first-rate pictures, and for hearing wonderful voices and performers of transcendent skill. It is the place for great preachers, great orators, great nobles, great statesmen. In the nature of things, greatness and unity go together; excellence implies a centre. And such, for the third or fourth time, is a University; I hope I do not weary out the reader by repeating it. It is the place to which a thousand schools make contributions; in which the intellect may safely range and speculate, sure to find its equal in some antagonist activity, and its judge in the tribunal of truth. It is a place where inquiry is pushed forward, and discoveries verified and perfected, and rashness rendered innocuous, and error exposed, by the collision of mind with mind, and knowledge with knowledge. It is the place where the professor becomes eloquent, and is a missionary and a preacher, displaying his science in its most complete and most winning form, pouring it forth with the zeal of enthusiasm, and lighting up his own love of it in the breasts of his hearers. It is the place where the catechist makes good his ground as he goes, treading in the truth day by day into the ready memory, and wedging and tightening it into the expanding reason. It is a place which wins the admiration of the young by its celebrity, kindles the affections of the middle-aged by its beauty, and rivets the fidelity of the old by its associations. It is a seat of wisdom, a light of the world, a minister of the faith, an Alma Mater of the rising generation. It is this and a great deal more, and demands a somewhat better head and hand than mine to describe it well.

Such is a University in its idea and in its purpose; such in good measure has it before now been in fact. Shall it ever be again? We are going forward in the strength of the Cross, under the patronage of the Blessed Virgin, in the name of St. Patrick, to attempt it.

SEAN O'CASEY
1880–1964

Sean O'Casey, in the judgment of New York *Times* critic
Brooks Atkinson, "is writing the most glorious English prose of
his time. It has the gusto of the Elizabethan, and the music of
the Irish." It has more, as a reading of the following essay, "The
Power of Laughter," will verify; it has a wild imagination and
a strict honesty, a scorn of pedantry and a love for the "low
fellows" of life, the "low fellows" that all of us sometimes are.
Readers of *The Green Crow,* the collection from which this essay
is taken, will discover further virtues in O'Casey's prose, as will
those who look into his six magnificent autobiographical volumes,
beginning with *I Knock at the Door.* But to feel directly the
scorching heat of O'Casey, his indignation as "savage" as Swift's,
his compassion, his humor, readers must buy theatre tickets and
go to see one of his plays — *Juno and the Paycock, The Plough
and the Stars, The Silver Tassie.* Here are all the wretchedness and
the gallantry of the swarming Dublin tenements where O'Casey
grew up, worked, and fought for a free Ireland. Here is the nest
that feathered the "Green Crow," as O'Casey calls himself; where
he learned that inimitable "caw" now known as "glorious prose,"
and where, too, in spite of hardship, he acquired the furious joy
of the crow tribe, who are "tumblers in the sky."

The Power of Laughter:
Weapon Against Evil

Laughter is wine for the soul—laughter soft, or loud and
deep, tinged through with seriousness. Comedy and tragedy
step through life together, arm in arm, all along, out along,
down along lea. A laugh is the loud echo of a sigh; a sigh the
faint echo of a laugh. A laugh is a great natural stimulator,
a pushful entry into life; and once we can laugh, we can
live. It is the hilarious declaration made by man that life is

worth living. Man is always hopeful of, always pushing towards, better things; and to bring this about, a change must be made in the actual way of life; so laughter is brought in to mock at things as they are so that they may topple down, and make room for better things to come.

People are somewhat afraid of laughing. Many times, when laughter abounded, I have heard the warning remark, "Oh, give it a rest, or it'll end in a cry." It is odd how many seem to be curiously envious of laughter, never of grief. You can have more than your fill of grief, and nobody minds: they never grudge your grief to you. You are given the world to grieve in; laughter is more often confined to a corner. We are more afraid of laughter than we are of grief. The saying is all wrong—it should be "Grieve, and the world grieves with you; laugh, and you laugh alone." Laughter may be a bad thing; grief is invariably a good or a harmless one.

Laughter tends to mock the pompous and the pretentious; all man's boastful gadding about, all his pretty pomps, his hoary customs, his wornout creeds, changing the glitter of them into the dullest hue of lead. The bigger the subject, the sharper the laugh. No one can escape it: not the grave judge in his robe and threatening wig; the parson and his saw; the general full of his sword and his medals; the palled prelate, tripping about, a blessing in one hand, a curse in the other; the politician carrying his magic wand of Wendy windy words; they all fear laughter, for the quiet laugh or the loud one upends them, strips them of pretense, and leaves them naked to enemy and friend.

Laughter is allowed when it laughs at the foibles of ordinary men, but frowned on and thought unseemly when it makes fun of superstitions, creeds, customs, and the blown-up importance of brief authority of those going in velvet and fine linen. The ban on laughter stretches back to the day when man wore skins and defended himself with the stone hammer. Many enemies have always surrounded laughter, have tried to banish it from life; and many have perished on the high gallows tree because they laughed at those who had been given power over them. Hell-fire tried to burn it, and the weeping for sins committed did all that was possible to drown it; but laughter came safely through the ordeals of fire and water; came smiling through. The people clung to laughter, and held it safe, holding both its sides, in their midst; out in the field, at home in the mud hovel, under the castle wall, at the very gateway of the Abbey.

Every chance of leisure the medieval peasant and worker
snatched from his fearsome and fiery labor was spent in low
revelry, banned by the church, deprecated by the grandees;
the hodden gray put on gay and colorful ribbons, and the
hours went in making love, listening to and singing ditties
mocking spiritual pastor and master, and whirling rapturously
and riotously round the beribboned maypole. The bawl of
the ballad came into the Abbey or Priory Church, and poured
through the open windows of the Castle Hall, irritating and
distracting the lord and his lady poring over the pictured book
of hours. In story whispered from ear to ear, in song sung
at peasant gatherings, they saw themselves as they were seen
by their people, and they didn't like it; they weren't amused,
for these things ate into their dignity, made them nearer to the
common stature of common men, who learned that the
grand and the distant ones were but a hand's span away from
themselves.

Nothing could kill or stay laughter, or hold it fast in one
place. It spread itself out all over the world, for, though men
show their thoughts in many different manners and modes,
they all laugh the same way.

When Christianity became a power, and took the place of
the Roman Empire, they closed the theaters, deeming them
places of surly rioting and brazen infamy, destroying souls,
displeasing God, and hindering holiness on its dismal way.
Bang, bang went the doors, shutting poor Satan in with the
shadows. The dispersed actors became wandering minstrels,
and whereas before they had been thorns in the Church's
fingers, now, in songs of laughter, satire, and ridicule, they
shot arrows into her breast and into her two thighs. A lot of
the minor clergy joined them, and added their songs, too, to
the ballads of the ministrels, ridiculing and damaging the
rulers of both Church and State. Footsore, tired, hungry,
and ragged, they laughed their way along the highway of
lord and bishop; they put a laughable ban on everything they
knew, all they had heard of, laughing on though the end
of many was a drear death in a ditch, with the curse of the
Church as a hard pillow for a stiffening head.

Nothing seems too high or low for the humorist; he is above
honor, above faith, preserving sense in religion and sanity in
life. The minstrels thought (as we should think, too) that
"The most completely lost of all days is that on which one
hasn't laughed." So, if you get a chance in the hurry and

complexity of life, laugh when the sun shines, when the rain falls, or even when the frost bites the skin or touches the heart with a chill.

Laughter has always been a puzzle to the thinker, a kind of a monkey-puzzle, a tree that doesn't look like a tree at all, but is as much a tree as any other one. Philosophers and sages have stopped up many and many a night, seeking an explanation, trying out a definition of comedy; but have gone to bed no wiser, and dead tired, while man kept on laughing, content to enjoy it, and never bothering his head as to what it was. Crowds of thinkers have set down big theories about laughter and comedy, among them the great Aristotle, Plato, Socrates, Jamblichus, and Kant; but though all of them were often blue in the face thinking it out, none of them got to the bottom of its mystery.

One American writer has connected laughter with Salvation; and maybe he isn't far wrong. He says: "The Church will prosper not through diminishing its requirements upon its members, nor in punishing them too severely for their delinquencies, but in showing mercy and kindness. Mercy is a flexible connective between the ideal and the real; it is a proper manifestation of the comic spirit. God, too, has a sense of humor: is He not revealed unto us as full of compassion, long-suffering, and merciful?" That is Dudley Zuver's opinon, and a new and odd one it will be to many. Not to David Lyndsay, the Scottish poet of the sixteenth century, who saw God near breaking his sides laughing at a rogue of an old woman who got past the indignant St. Peter by the use of her ready and tricky tongue.

It is high time and low time that we made a sense of humor an attribute of whatever God there may be. Why, at times, the whole earth must present a comic picture to whatever deity may be watching its antics. There's the United Nations, for instance, never more divided than now in conference, sub-conference, committee, sub-committee, this council and that council, trying out one question, and making a thousand more questions out of their discussions. What fools these mortals be!

It is odd—significant, too—that in any litany whatsoever, Catholic or Protestant, Methodist or Baptist, there isn't a single petition for a sense of humor. There are petitions for everything, ideal conditions and real conditions; for everything except a sense of humor. If they petitioned for this, and got it, then the other petitions wouldn't be so many, for they would understand themselves more clearly, and cease to pester God to do things for them that they could do in an easier and better way for themselves. They would become more tolerant, would priest and parson, more understanding, more sociable, and, in many ways, more worthy of heaven and of earth. So let all who pray ask for what most of them need badly, a sense of humor to lighten their way through life, making it merrier for themselves and easier for others. Then there will be something in the carol's greeting—God rest you merry, gentlemen!

Even Shakespeare seems to be somewhat shy of laughter; even he. He rarely—save in the play, *Troilus and Cressida*— goes all out for the mockery of the heroic and the nobility. He often dismisses his clowns with a scornful gesture, as if half apologizing for their existence. He gives a semi-comic and partly-pathetic touch to the death of Falstaff, his supreme comic character, and makes poor Bardolph swing by the neck from the end of a rope for stealing a silver pyx out of a church during the campaign in France. Mistress Quickly and Doll Tearsheet suddenly become shadows; so does Poins. Only the ranting Pistol is left to eat the leek, and then creep away from life forever. Shakespeare kept ridicule warm for the lower class, recognizing in his middle-class way that to criticize the nobility by comic characterization might be dangerous, by letting the peasant and poor worker know what they really looked like. Yet, by and large, we can warmly feel how Shakespeare loved his rascals, a love so deep that, in their drawing, he made them live forever.

Where was laughter born, and when was it first heard? No one seems to know. We don't even know what it is. A baby knows how to cry before it learns to laugh. Its first smile is regarded as a miracle. So it is—the greatest and most valuable miracle born amongst men, though one thinker, Vico, says that "laughter is an attribute of second-rate minds." Let it be, then, for it is a lovely humor. It is so intensely human: however we may differ in color, in thought, in manners, in ideologies, we all laugh the same way; it is a golden chain binding us all together. The human mind will always be second-rate in the sense of still having to learn. To rise above humor is to rise above partiality, and no human being can do this; we are all partial, one way or another. We do not seek to be gods; we are content to be good men and good women; useful, neighborly, and fond of life, rounding it off with a big laugh and a little sleep.

The conscious humorist, said Vico, is a very low fellow. We're all very low fellows, for all of us, some time or another, are conscious humorists. And well we are, for our souls' sake, and for the sake of man's sanity. We couldn't live without comedy. Let us pray: Oh, Lord, give us a sense of humor with courage to manifest it forth, so that we may laugh to shame the pomps, the vanities, the sense of self-importance of the Big Fellows that the world sometimes sends among us, and who try to take our peace away. Amen.

J. ROBERT OPPENHEIMER
1904——

J. Robert Oppenheimer, under whose wartime direction the atom bomb was developed at Los Alamos, was one of the first to assess the consequences of the bomb. Even while what was going on at Los Alamos was top secret to the rest of the world, Dr. Oppenheimer led his colleagues in discussing how to control this terrifying new force on a world scale. And when, after Hiroshima, the secret was out, Dr. Oppenheimer was one of the first to answer the inevitable question: "Is there any defense against the atom bomb?" His reply was the one word: "Peace." For Dr. Oppenheimer's horizons have never been limited by laboratory walls. He has continually seen beyond, to all the other areas of man's activity, and he has been aware of the urgent need for communication among them. As professor of physics at the University of California and the California Institute of Technology, as adviser to the Atomic Energy Commission, and since 1947 as Director of the Institute for Advanced Study at Princeton, Dr. Oppenheimer has devoted a significant proportion of his skill and energy to achieving this communication. In the following essay, which was delivered as an address at the international symposium honoring Columbia University's Bicentennial in 1954, he explores once more, in thoughtful and lucid language, the paths which connect the different "villages" where man's work in art and science is quietly carried on. And he argues persuasively for a cultivation of these intimate paths, as an antidote to the superhighways of the mass media which are creating all around us "a great, open, windy world."

Prospects in the Arts and Sciences

The words "prospects in the arts and sciences" mean two quite different things to me. One is prophecy: What will the scientists discover and the painters paint, what new forms will alter music, what parts of experience will newly yield to objective description? The other meaning is that of a view: What do we see when we look at the world today and compare it with the past? I am not a prophet; and I cannot very well speak to the first subject, though in many ways I should like to. I shall try to speak to the second, because there are some features of this view which seem to me so remarkable, so new and so arresting, that it may be worth turning our eyes to them; it may even help us to create and shape the future better, though we cannot foretell it.

In the arts and in the sciences, it would be good to be a prophet. It would be a delight to know the future. I had thought for a while of my own field of physics and of those nearest to it in the natural sciences. It would not be too hard to outline the questions which natural scientists today are asking themselves and trying to answer. What, we ask in physics, is matter, what is it made of, how does it behave when it is more and more violently atomized, when we try to pound out of the stuff around us the ingredients which only violence creates and makes manifest? What, the chemists ask, are those special features of nucleic acids and proteins which make life possible and give it its characteristic endurance and mutability? What subtle chemistry, what arrangements, what reactions and controls make the cells of living organisms differentiate so that they may perform functions as oddly diverse as transmitting information throughout our nervous systems or covering our heads with hair? What happens in the brain to make a record of the past, to hide it from consciousness, to make it accessible to recall? What are the physical features which make consciousness possible?

All history teaches us that these questions that we think the pressing ones will be transmuted before they are answered, that they will be replaced by others, and that the very process of discovery will shatter the concepts that we today use to describe our puzzlement.

It is true that there are some who profess to see in matters of culture, in matters precisely of the arts and sciences, a certain macrohistorical pattern, a grand system of laws which determines the course of civilization and gives a kind of inevitable quality to the unfolding of the future. They would, for instance, see the radical, formal experimentation which characterized the music of the last half century as an inevitable consequence of the immense flowering and enrichment of natural science; they would see a necessary order in the fact that innovation in music precedes that in painting and that in turn in poetry, and point to this sequence in older cultures. They would attribute the formal experimentation of the arts to the dissolution, in an industrial and technical society, of authority, of secular, political authority, and of the catholic authority of the church. They are thus armed to predict the future. But this, I fear, is not my dish.

If a prospect is not a prophecy, it is a view. What does the world of the arts and sciences look like? There are two ways of looking at it: One is the view of the traveler, going by horse or foot, from village to village to town, staying in each to talk with those who live there and to gather something of the quality of its life. This is the intimate view, partial, somewhat accidental, limited by the limited life and strength and curiosity of the traveler, but intimate and human, in a human compass. The other is the vast view, showing the earth with its fields and towns and valleys as they appear to a camera carried in a high altitude rocket. In one sense this prospect will be more complete; one will see all branches of knowledge, one will see all the arts, one will see them as part of the vastness and complication of the whole of human life on earth. But one will miss a great deal; the beauty and warmth of human life will largely be gone from that prospect.

It is in this vast high altitude survey that one sees the general surprising quantitative features that distinguish our time. This is where the listings of science and endowments and laboratories and books published show up; this is where we learn that more people are engaged in scientific research today than ever before, that the Soviet world and the free world are running neck and neck in the training of scientists, that more books are published per capita in England than in the United States, that the social sciences are pursued actively in America, Scandinavia, and England, that there are more people who hear the great music of the past, and more music composed and more paintings painted. This is where we learn that the arts and sciences are flourishing. This great map, showing the world from afar and almost as to a stranger, would show more: It would show the immense diversity of culture and life, diversity in place and tradition for the first time clearly manifest on a world-wide scale, diversity in technique and language, separating science from science and art from art, and all of one from all of the other. This great map, world-wide, culture-wide, remote, has some odd features. There are innumerable villages. Between the villages there appear to be almost no paths discernible from this high altitude. Here and there passing near a village, sometimes through its heart, there will be a superhighway, along which windy traffic moves at enormous speed. The superhighways seem to have little connection with villages, starting anywhere, ending anywhere, and sometimes appearing almost by design to disrupt the quiet of the village. This view gives us no sense of order or of unity. To find these we must visit the villages, the quiet, busy places, the laboratories and studies and studios. We must see the paths that are barely discernible; we must understand the superhighways, and their dangers.

In the natural sciences these are and have been and are likely to continue to be heroic days. Discovery follows discovery, each both raising and answering questions, each ending a long search, and each providing the new instruments for a new search. There are radical ways of thinking unfamiliar to common sense and connected with it by decades or centuries of increasingly specialized and unfamiliar experience. There are lessons of how limited, for all its variety, the common experience of man has been with regard to natural phenomena, and hints and analogies as to how limited may be his experience with man. Every new finding is a part of the instrument kit of the sciences for further investigation and for penetrating into new fields. Discoveries of knowledge fructify technology and the practical arts, and these in turn pay back refined techniques, new possibilities of observation and experiment.

In any science there is harmony between practitioners. A man may work as an individual, learning of what his colleagues do through reading or conversation; he may be working as a member of a group on problems whose technical equipment is too massive for individual effort. But whether he is a part of a team or solitary in his own study, he, as a professional, is a member of a community. His colleagues in his own branch of science will be grateful to him for the inventive or creative thoughts he has, will welcome his criticism. His world and work will be objectively communicable; and he will be quite sure that if there is error in it, that error will not long be undetected. In his own line of work he lives in a community where common understanding combines with common purpose and interest to bind men together both in freedom and in cooperation.

This experience will make him acutely aware of how limited, how inadequate, how precious is this condition of his life; for in his relations with a wider society, there will be neither the sense of community nor of objective understanding. He will sometimes find, in returning to practical undertakings, some sense of community with men who are not expert in his science, with other scientists whose work is remote from his, and with men of action and men of art. The frontiers of science are separated now by long years of study, by specialized vocabularies, arts, techniques, and knowledge from the common heritage even of a most civilized society; and anyone working at the frontier of such science is in that sense a very long way from home, a long way too from the practical arts that were its matrix and origin, as indeed they were of what we today call art.

The specialization of science is an inevitable accompaniment of progress; yet it is full of dangers, and it is cruelly wasteful, since so much that is beautiful and enlightening is cut off from most of the world. Thus it is proper to the role of the scientist that he not merely find new truth and communicate it to his fellows, but that he teach, that he try to bring the most honest and intelligible account of new knowledge to all who will try to learn. This is one reason—it is the decisive organic reason —why scientists belong in universities. It is one reason why the patronage of science by and through universities is its most proper form; for it is here, in teaching, in the association of scholars, and in the friendships of teachers and taught, of men who by profession must themselves be both teachers and taught, that the narrowness of scientific life can best be moderated, and that the analogies, insights, and harmonies of scientific discovery can find their way into the wider life of man.

In the situation of the artist today there are both analogies to and differences from that of the scientist; but it is the differences which are the most striking, and which raise the problems that touch most on the evil of our day. For the artist it is not enough that he communicate with others who are expert in his own art. Their fellowship, their understanding, and their appreciation may encourage him; but that is not the end of his work, nor its nature. The artist depends on a common sensibility and culture, on a common meaning of symbols, on a community of experience and common ways of describing and interpreting it. He need not write for everyone or paint or play for everyone. But his audience must be man; it must be man, and not a specialized set of experts among his fellows. Today that is very difficult. Often the artist has an aching sense of great loneliness, for the community to which he addresses himself is largely not there; the traditions and the culture, the symbols and the history, the myths and the common experience, which it is his function to illuminate, to harmonize, and to portray, have been dissolved in a changing world.

There is, it is true, an artificial audience maintained to moderate between the artist and the world for which he works: the audience of the professional critics, popularizers, and advertisers of art. But though, as does the popularizer and promoter of science, the critic fulfills a necessary present function and introduces some order and some communication between the artist and the world, he cannot add to the intimacy and the directness and the depth with which the artist addresses his fellow men.

To the artist's loneliness there is a complementary great and terrible barrenness in the lives of men. They are deprived of the illumination, the light and tenderness and insight of an intelligible interpretation, in contemporary terms, of the sorrows and wonders and gaieties and follies of man's life. This may be in part offset, and is, by the great growth of technical means for making the art of the past available. But these provide a record of past intimacies between art and life; even when they are applied to the writing and painting and composing of the day, they do not bridge the gulf between a society, too vast and too disordered, and the artist trying to give meaning and beauty to its parts.

In an important sense this world of ours is a new world, in which the unity of knowledge, the nature of human communities, the order of society, the order of ideas, the very notions of society and culture have changed and will not return to what they have been in the past. What is new is new not because it has never been there before, but because it has changed in quality. One thing that is new is the prevalence of newness, the changing scale and scope of change itself, so that the world alters as we walk in it, so that the years of man's life measure not some small growth or rearrangement or moderation of what he learned in childhood, but a great upheaval. What is new is that in one generation our knowledge of the natural world engulfs, upsets, and complements all knowledge of the natural world before. The techniques, among and by which we live, multiply and ramify, so that the whole world is bound together by communication, blocked here and there by the immense synapses of political tyranny.

The global quality of the world is new; our knowledge of and sympathy with remote and diverse peoples, or involvement with them in practical terms, and our commitment to them in terms of brotherhood. What is new in the world is the massive character of the dissolution and corruption of authority, in belief, in ritual, and in temporal order. Yet this is the world that we have come to live in. The very difficulties which it presents derive from growth in understanding, in skill, in power. To assail the changes that have unmoored us from the past is futile, and in a deep sense, I think, it is wicked. We need to recognize the change and learn what resources we have.

Again I will turn to the schools and, as their end and as their center, the universities. For the problem of the scientist is in this respect not different from that of the artist or of the historian. He needs to be a part of the community, and the community can only with loss and peril be without him. Thus it is with a sense of interest and hope that we see a growing recognition that the creative artist is a proper charge on the university, and the university a proper home for him; that a composer or a poet or a playwright or painter needs the toleration, understanding, the rather local and parochial patronage that a university can give; and that this will protect him from the tyranny of man's communication and professional promotion. For here there is an honest chance that what the artist has of insight and of beauty will take root in the community, and that some intimacy and some human bonds can mark his relations with his patrons. For a university rightly and inherently is a place where the individual man can form new syntheses, where the accidents of friendship and association can open a man's eyes to a part of science or art which he had not known before, where parts of human life, remote and perhaps superficially incompatible, can find in men their harmony and their synthesis.

These then, in rough and far too general words, are some of the things we see as we walk through the villages of the arts and of the sciences and notice how thin are the paths that lead from one to another, and how little in terms of human understanding and pleasure the work of the villages comes to be shared outside.

The superhighways do not help. They are the mass media— from the loud speakers in the deserts of Asia Minor and the cities of Communist China to the organized professional theater of Broadway. They are the purveyors of art and science and culture for the millions upon millions—the promotors who represent the arts and sciences to humanity and who represent humanity to the arts and sciences; they are the means by which we are reminded of the famine in remote places or of war or trouble or change; they are the means by which this great earth and its peoples have become one to one another, the means by which the news of discovery or honor and the stories and songs of today travel and resound throughout the world. But they are also the means by which the true human community, the man knowing man, the neighbor understanding neighbor, the school boy learning a poem, the woman dancing, the individual curiosity, the individual sense of beauty are being blown dry and issueless, the means by which the passivity of the disengaged spectator presents to the man of art and science the bleak face of unhumanity.

For the truth is that this is indeed, inevitably and increasingly, an open and, inevitably and increasingly, an eclectic world. We know too much for one man to know much, we live too variously to live as one. Our histories and traditions—the very means of interpreting life—are both bonds and barriers among us. Our knowledge separates us as well as it unites; our orders disintegrate as well as bind; our art brings us together and sets us apart. The artist's loneliness, the scholar despairing, because no one will any longer trouble to learn what he can teach, the narrowness of the scientist— these are not unnatural insignia in this great time of change.

For what is asked of us is not easy. The openness of this world derives its character from the irreversibility of learning; what is once learned is part of human life. We cannot close our minds to discovery. We cannot stop our ears so that the voices of far-off and strange people can no longer reach them. The great cultures of the East cannot be walled off from ours by impassible seas and defects of understanding based on ignorance and unfamiliarity. Neither our integrity as men of learning nor our humanity allows that. In this open world, what is there any man may try to learn.

This is no new problem. There has always been more to know than one man could know; there have always been modes of feeling that could not move the same heart; there have always been deeply held beliefs that could not be composed into a synthetic union. Yet never before today has the diversity, the complexity, the richness so clearly defied hierachical order and simplification, never before have we had to understand the complementary, mutually not compatible ways of life and recognize choice between them as the only course of freedom. Never before today has the integrity of the intimate, the detailed, the true art, the integrity of craftsmanship and the preservation of the familiar, of the humorous and the beautiful stood in more massive contrast to the vastness of life, the greatness of the globe, the otherness of people, the otherness of ways, and the all-encompassing dark.

This is a world in which each of us, knowing his limitations, knowing the evils of superficiality and the terrors of fatigue, will have to cling to what is close to him, to what he knows, to what he can do, to his friends and his tradition and his love, lest he be dissolved in a universal confusion and know nothing and love nothing. It is at the same time a world in which none of us can find hieratic prescription or general sanction for any ignorance, any insensitivity, and indifference. When a friend tells us of a new discovery we may not understand, we may not be able to listen without jeopardizing the work that is ours and closer to us; but we cannot find in a book or canon—and we should not seek—grounds for hallowing our ignorance. If a man tells us that he sees differently than we or that he finds beautiful what we find ugly, we may have to leave the room, from fatigue or trouble; but that is our weakness and our default. If we must live with a perpetual sense that the world and the men in it are greater than we and too much for us, let it be the measure of our virtue that we know this and seek no comfort. Above all let us not proclaim that the limits of our powers correspond to some special wisdom in our choice of life, of learning, or of beauty.

This balance, this perpetual, precarious, impossible balance between the infinitely open and the intimate, this time—our twentieth century—has been long in coming; but it has come. It is, I think, for us and our children, our only way.

This is for all men. For the artist and for the scientist there is a special problem and a special hope, for in their extraordinarily different ways, in their lives that have increasingly divergent character, there is still a sensed bond, a sensed analogy. Both the man of science and the man of art live always at the edge of mystery, surrounded by it; both always, as the measure of their creation, have had to do with the harmonization of what is new with what is familiar, with the balance between novelty and synthesis, with the struggle to make partial order in total chaos. They can, in their work and in their lives, help themselves, help one another, and help all men. They can make the paths that connect the villages of arts and sciences with each other and with the world at large the multiple, varied, precious bonds of a true and world-wide community.

This cannot be an easy life. We shall have a rugged time of it to keep our minds open and to keep them deep, to keep our sense of beauty and our ability to make it, and our occasional ability to see it in places remote and strange and unfamiliar; we shall have a rugged time of it, all of us in keeping these gardens in our villages, in keeping open the manifold, intricate, casual paths, to keep these flourishing in a great, open, windy world; but this, as I see it, is the condition of man; and in this condition we can help, because we can love, one another.

FRANCIS PARKMAN
1823–1893

Francis Parkman, properly Boston born and bred, spent four childhood years outside of the city, on the edge of the Medford Fells, then a rocky, unconquerable wilderness; and from that time on the wilderness haunted his dreams. On vacations from Harvard, he took strenuous camping trips, and in his eighteenth year he decided on his life's work: to write the story of the conflict between England and France on the American continent. "For here . . . the forest drama was more stirring and the forest stage more thronged with appropriate actors than in any other passage of our history." To know more intimately some of the actors in that drama, he passed some time in a European monastery, and he spent a dangerous summer traveling in the Dakotas with a tribe of Sioux Indians. Years of overexertion culminated now in a breakdown, but in spite of incredible physical disabilities, Parkman persisted in his work. Sometimes writing only six lines a day, he nevertheless succeeded in publishing, between 1851 and 1892, eight masterly volumes that told the story he had set out to tell. From these labors, Parkman had little time to spare for other writing, but he did publish in the *Nation* in 1869 an article called "The Tale of the 'Ripe Scholar'", reprinted here. The occasion was the movement taking shape at Harvard, where Parkman was an Overseer, and in other colleges, to change the pattern of higher education to meet the needs of a changing America. But in an America altered far beyond Parkman's vision, the need for educational reform still persists; his eloquent plea for a "class of strong thinkers" to guide democracy is still provocative and timely.

The Tale of the "Ripe Scholar"

Not many years ago, a certain traditional prestige, independent of all considerations of practical utility, attached to the scholastic character, at least in New England, where the clergy long held a monopoly of what passed for learning. New England colleges were once little more than schools for making ministers. As the clergyman has lost in influence, so the scholar has lost in repute, and the reasons are not hard to find. The really good scholars were exceptions, and very rare ones. In the matter of theology some notable results were produced, but secular scholarship was simply an exotic and a sickly one. It never recovered from its transplantation and drew on vital juices from the soul. The climate was hostile to it. All the vigor of the country drifted into practical pursuits, and the New England man of letters, when he happened not to be a minister, was usually some person whom constitutional defects, bodily or mental, had unfitted for politics or business. He was apt to be a recluse, ignorant of the world, bleached by a close room and an iron stove, never breathing the outer air when he could help it, and resembling a mediæval monk in his scorn of the body, or rather in his utter disregard of it. Sometimes he was reputed a scholar merely because he was nothing else. The products of his mind were as pallid as the hue of his face, and, like their parent, void of blood, bone, sinew, muscle, and marrow. That he should be provincial was for a long time, inevitable, but that he was emasculate was chiefly his own fault. As his scholarship was not fruitful of any very valuable results, as it did not make itself felt in the living world that ranged around it, as, in short, it showed no vital force, it began at length to be regarded as a superfluous excrescence. Nevertheless, like the monkish learning of the middle ages, it served a good purpose in keeping alive the tradition of liberal culture against a future renaissance. We shall be told that we exaggerate, and, in one sense, this is true, for we describe not an individual, but a type, from which, however, the reality was rarely very remote, and with which it was sometimes identified. The most finished and altogether favorable example of this devitalized scholarship, with many graceful additions, was Edward Everett, and its echoes may still be heard in the halls of Congress, perplexing Western members with Latin quotations, profuse, if not always correct.

As the nation grew in importance and in sensitiveness, the want of intellectual productiveness began to trouble the popular pride, and an impatient public called on its authors to be "original." Spasmodic efforts were made to respond, and the results were such as may be supposed. The mountain went into convulsions of labor and produced a mouse, or something as ridiculous. After an analogous fashion some of the successors of our pallid, clerical scholars raise the cry, "Let us be strong," and fall into the moral and physical gymnastics of muscular Christianity. This, certainly, is no bad sign, in so far as it indicates the consciousness of a want; but neither originality nor force can be got up to order. They must spring from a deeper root and grow by laws of their own. Happily our soil has begun to put forth such a growth, promising in quality, but as yet, in quantity and in maturity, wholly inadequate to the exigent need.

In times of agitation, alive with engrossing questions of pressing moment, when all is astir with pursuit and controversy, when some are mad for gold, and some are earnest and some rabid for this cause or for that, the scholarship of the past is naturally pronounced not up with the times. Despite his manifold failings, "the self-made man," with his palatial mansion, his exploits in the gold-room, in the caucus, on the stump, in Congress, and in the presidential chair, flatters popular self-love and fills the public eye. Only a slight reason is wanted for depreciating the scholar, and a strong one is offered. Because the culture which our colleges supplied and which too many of them still supply, was weak, thin, and unsuitable, it was easy to depreciate all culture. By culture we mean development, not polish or adornment, though these are its natural and by no means useless belongings. Using the word, then, in this sense, culture is with us a supreme necessity, not for the profit of a few but of all. The presence of minds highly and vigorously developed is the most powerful aid to popular education, and the necessary condition of its best success. In a country where the ruling power is public opinion, it is above all things necessary that the best and maturest thought should have a fair share in forming it. Such thought cannot exist in any force in the community without propagating its own image, and a class of strong thinkers is the palladium of democracy. They are the natural enemies of ignorant, ostentatious, and aggressive wealth, and the natural friends of all that is best in the popular heart. They are sure of the hatred of charlatans, demagogues, and political sharpers. They are the only hope of our civilization; without them it is a failure, a mere platitude of mediocrity, stagnant or turbid, as the case may be. The vastest aggregate of average intelligences can do nothing to supply their place, and even material growth is impeded by an ignorance of its conditions and laws. If we may be forgiven the metaphor, our civilization is at present a creature with a small and feeble head, a large, muscular, and active body, and a tail growing at such a rate that it threatens to become unmanageable and shake the balance of the vital powers.

The tendency of a partial education, such as the best popular education must of necessity be, is to produce an excess of self-confidence; and one of its results in this country is a prodigious number of persons who think, and persuade others to think, that they know everything necessary to be known, and are fully competent to form opinions and make speeches upon all questions whatever. As these are precisely the persons who make the most noise on the most momentous questions of the day, who have the most listeners and admirers, and who hold each other up as shining examples for imitation, their incompetency becomes a public evil of the first magnitude. If rash and ignorant theorizing, impulsive outcries, and social and political charlatanry of all sorts are to have the guiding of our craft, then farewell to the hope that her voyage will be a success. The remedy is to infuse into the disordered system the sedative and tonic of a broad knowledge and a vigorous reason. This means to invigorate and extend the higher education; to substitute for the effete and futile scholasticism which the popular mind justly holds in slight account, an energetic and manly development, trained to grapple with the vast questions of the present, and strong enough in numbers as well as quality to temper with its mature thought the rashness of popular speculation. Our best colleges are moving hopefully in this direction; none of them with more life and vigor than the oldest of them all. The present generation will see an increase in the number of our really efficient thinkers, but it is a positive, not a relative increase, and is far behind the fast increasing need. Powerful causes are at work against it, and we will try to explain what, to our thinking, some of these causes are.

Perhaps the most obvious of them is the ascendency of material interests among us. To the great mass of our population, the clearing of lands, the acquiring of new territory, the building of cities, the multiplication of railroads, steamboats, and telegraph lines, the growth of trade and manufactures, the opening of mines, with the resulting fine houses, fine clothes, and sumptuous fare, constitute the real sum and substance of progress and civilization. Art, literature, philosophy, and science—so far as science has no direct bearing on material interests—are regarded as decorations, agreeable and creditable, but not essential. In other words, the material basis of civilization is accepted for the entire structure. A prodigious number of persons think that money-making is the only serious business of life, and there is no corresponding number who hold a different faith. There are not a few among us who would "improve" our colleges into schools of technology, where young men may be trained with a view mainly to the production of more steamboats, railroads, and telegraphs; more breadstuffs; more iron, copper, silver, and gold; more cottons and woolens; and, consequently, more fine houses and fine clothes. All this is very well, but it does not answer the great and crying need of the time. The truth is, our material growth so greatly exceeds our other growth that the body politic suffers from diseases of repletion. A patient bloated with generous living, and marked already with the eruptions of a perverted, diseased blood, is not to be cured solely by providing him with more food.

The drift towards material activity is so powerful among us that it is very difficult for a young man to resist it; and the difficulty increases in proportion as his nature is active and energetic. Patient and devoted study is rarely long continued in the vortex of American life. The dusty arena of competition and strife has fascinations almost irresistible to one conscious of his own vigor. Intellectual tastes may, however, make a compromise. Journalism and the lecture-room offer them a field midway between the solitude of the study and the bustle of the world of business; but the journal and the lecture-room have influences powerfully adverse to solid, mature, and independent thinking. There, too, is the pulpit, for those who have a vocation that way; but in this, also, a mighty and increasing temptation besets the conscientious student. As for politics, they have fallen to such a pass that the men are rare who can mingle in them without deteriorating.

Paradoxical as it may seem, the diffusion of education and intelligence is at present acting against the free development of the highest education and intelligence. Many have hoped and still hope that by giving a partial teaching to great numbers of persons, a stimulus would be applied to the best minds among them, and a thirst for knowledge awakened which would lead to high results; but thus far these results have not equalled the expectation. There has been a vast expenditure of brick and mortar for educational purposes, and, what is more to the purpose, many excellent and faithful teachers of both sexes have labored diligently in their vocation; but the system of competitive cramming in our public schools has not borne fruits on which we have much cause to congratulate ourselves. It has produced an immense number of readers; but what thinkers are to be found may be said to exist in spite of it. The public school has put money in abundance into the pockets of the dealers in sensation stories, sensation illustrated papers, and all the swarm of trivial, sickly, and rascally literature. From this and cheap newspapers thousands—nay, millions—draw all their mental improvement, and pamper their mental stomachs with adulterated, not to say poisoned, sweetmeats, till they have neither desire nor digestion for strong and wholesome food. But we would speak rather of that truly intelligent and respectable public which forms the auditories of popular preachers and popular lecturers, which is the lavish patron of popular periodical literature, which interests itself in the questions of the day, and has keen mental appetites of a certain kind. This public is strong in numbers and very strong in collective wealth. Its voice can confer celebrity, if not reputation; and it can enrich those who win its favor. In truth, it is the American people. Now, what does this great public want? It is, in the main, busied with the active work of life, and though it thinks a little and feels a great deal on matters which ought to engage the attention of every self-governing people, yet it is impatient of continuous and cool attention to anything but its daily business, and sometimes even to that. Indeed, the exciting events of the last ten years, joined to the morbid stimulus applied to all departments of business, have greatly increased this tendency; and to-day there are fewer serious and thoughtful readers than in the last decade. More than ever before, the public demands elocution rather than reason of those who address it; something to excite the feelings and captivate the fancy rather than something to instruct the understanding. It rejoices in sweeping statements, confident assertions, bright lights and black shadows alternating with something funny. Neither does it care much for a terse, idiomatic, and pointed diction, but generally prefers the flatulent periods of the ready writers. On matters of the greatest interest it craves to be excited or amused. Lectures professing to instruct are turned to a tissue of jokes, and the pulpit itself is sometimes enlivened after a similar fashion. The pill must be sugared and the food highly seasoned, for the public mind is in a state of laxity and needs a tonic. But the public taste is very exacting, and it offers great and tempting rewards to those who please it.

That which pleases it pays so much better in money and notoriety, and is so much cheaper of production, than the better article which does not please it, that the temptation to accept light work and high wages in place of hard work and low wages is difficult to resist. Nothing but a deep love of truth or of art can stand unmoved against it. In our literary markets, educated tastes are completely outridden by uneducated or half-educated tastes, and the commodity is debased accordingly. Thus, the editor of a magazine may be a man of taste and talents; but his interests as a man of letters and his interests as a man of business are not the same. "Why don't you make your magazine what it ought to be?" we once asked of a well-known editor. "Because," he replied, "if we did, we should lose four-fifths of our circulation." A noted preacher not long ago confessed to us that the temptation to give his audience the sort of preaching which they liked to hear, instead of that which it was best that they should hear, was almost irresistible.

The amount of what we have been saying is, that the public which demands a second-rate article is so enormously large in comparison with the public which demands a first-rate article that it impairs the quality of literary production, and exercises an influence adverse to the growth of intellectual eminence. Now, what is the remedy? It seems to us to be two-fold. First, to direct popular education, not to stuffing the mind with crude aggregations of imperfect knowledge, but rather to the development of its powers of observation, comparison, analysis, and reasoning; to strengthening and instructing its moral sense, and leading it to self-knowledge and consequent modesty. All this, no doubt, is vastly more difficult and far less showy in its results than the present system of competitive cramming, and requires in its teachers a high degree of good sense and sound instruction. The other remedy consists in a powerful re-enforcement of the higher education, and the consequent development of a class of persons, whether rich or poor, so well instructed and so numerous as to hold their ground against charlatanry, and propagate sound and healthy thought through the community. He who gives or bequeaths money to a well-established and wisely-conducted university confers a blessing which radiates through all the ranks of society. He does a service eminently practical, and constitutes himself the patron of the highest and best utilitarianism.

GERARD PIEL
1915——

Winner of the international Kalinga Prize for achievement in the popularization of science, recipient of honorary doctorates from Lawrence, Colby, Rutgers, and Columbia, Fellow of the American Academy of Arts and Sciences, and publisher of *Scientific American,* Gerard Piel explores "various corners of the large and small questions" that intrigue and trouble man in the current Atom and Space Age. His book, *Science in the Cause of Man,* and his essays (in *Science, Bulletin of the Atomic Scientists, New Statesman,* and *Atlantic Monthly*) have demonstrated his profound concern with the relevance of science to every area of human activity. The essay reprinted here, in which Henry Adams and the relation of science to the history of society serve as appropriate touchstones, carries forward Mr. Piel's belief in "the need to bring into the framing of private and public policy the scientific understanding and the scientific attitude that have profoundly transformed man's relationship to nature." This essay, "The Acceleration of History," is the address delivered in April, 1963, at the dedication of the Thomas M. Evans Hall, Phillips Academy at Andover.

The Acceleration of History

These days, in the common discourse of our country, science and technology have come to be "thing" words, describing human activities that are concerned with ways and means. By contrast, freedom, culture, and civilization are "value" words, freighted with the higher concerns of ends, goals, and purpose.

It is against this compartmentation of human life and action that I speak here. From history, I shall show that the time has come—most urgently—to heal this mutilation of the thinking process of society.

The truth-seeking and tool-making enterprise of science by no means encompasses all of the concerns of man. Remote recesses of the interior experience of life and distant reaches of the exterior universe will remain always to lure and defy the enquirer. Today, however, there are few realms of human concern to which science is not relevant. An understanding of science is essential to each man's orientation in the world as it is known to the mind of man. Both as knowledge and as process, science responds to the troubling questions: Who are we? Whence have we come? Whither do we go? Moreover, science shows us how to ask such questions in a more productive form. Beneath the surfaces of things accessible to the unaided senses, science discloses forces, dynamics and transformations, symmetries and diversities, order, precision, and grandeur unknown to previous generations.

These are some of the considerations—philosophical, moral, and esthetic—that assert the identity and continuity of science with the spectrum of human activities and concerns. Truth cannot be sought in the absence of concern for value; nor can value be cherished without courage to face the truth. No division of logic or of labor permits one portion of the community to delegate the custody and understanding of science to another. There is still another consideration that presses for the closing of this breach in our culture. An understanding of science becomes increasingly essential to the exercise of citizenship in a civilization that is being transformed by science. The peril we live in now—the shameful catastrophe

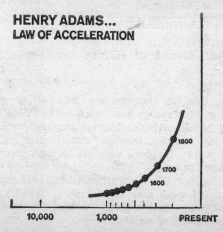

**HENRY ADAMS...
LAW OF ACCELERATION**

1800

1700

1600

10,000   1,000   PRESENT

that overhangs civilization—places each of us under responsibility we cannot delegate to others.

Our peril was prophesied at the turn of the century by one of the few historians who has ever undertaken to explore the relations between science and the history of society. Henry Adams knew something of the work of Faraday and Maxwell in electromagnetism; he comprehended the main theme of the thermodynamics of Josiah Willard Gibbs; in his private speculations, he attempted to deal with the dilemma in which physics was placed by Michelson and Morley, and he was ready for Becquerel's discovery of radioactivity. Looking back over the tumult of modern history, he plotted the rising curves of the rate of scientific discovery, of coal output, of steam power, of the transition from mechanical to electrical power. Any schoolboy, he said, could plot such curves and see that "arithmetical ratios were useless"; the curves followed "the old familiar law of squares." That is, they rose more steeply as they ascended from the time baseline. The logarithmic scale of the time baseline of Adams' chart gives equal space to the last millennium and to the preceding 10,000 years. It thus not only serves geometrical

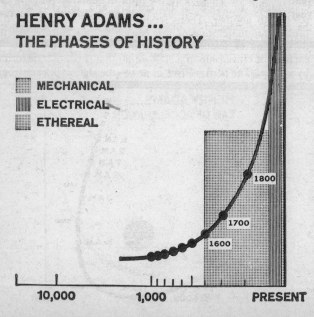

HENRY ADAMS...
THE PHASES OF HISTORY

MECHANICAL
ELECTRICAL
ETHEREAL

1800

1700

1600

10,000   1,000   PRESENT

convenience but also reflects the compression of the past in our memory.

"The acceleration of the seventeenth century," Adams observed, "was rapid, and that of the eighteenth was startling. The acceleration even became measurable, for it took the form of utilizing heat as force, through the steam engine, and this addition of power was measurable in the coal-output." Acceleration was the law of history.

From his acquaintance with Gibbs's historic work, Adams was prepared to recognize that such changes in quantity amounted to changes in quality—changes in "phase," in the language of thermodynamics. The history of thought was in passage through three phases, each with a duration in years that was the inverse square of the duration of the preceding phase. "Supposing the Mechanical Phase to have lasted 300 years, from 1600 to 1900, the next, or Electric Phase would have a life equal to $\sqrt{300}$, or about seventeen years and a half, when—that is, in 1917—it would pass into another, or Ethereal Phase, which, for half a century, science has been promising, and which would last only $\sqrt{17.5}$, or about four years, and bring Thought to the limit of its possibilities in the year 1921. It may well be! Nothing whatever is beyond the range of possibility; but even if the life of the previous phase, 1600-1900, were extended another hundred years, the

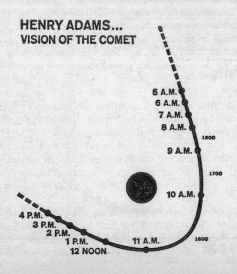

HENRY ADAMS...
VISION OF THE COMET

5 A.M.
6 A.M.
7 A.M.
8 A.M.
1800
9 A.M.
1700
10 A.M.
1600
4 P.M.
3 P.M.
2 P.M.
1 P.M.   11 A.M.
12 NOON

difference to the last term of the series would be negligible. In that case, the Ethereal Phase would last till about 2025."

By Adams' calculations our lives are on probation: we are living in the grace period between 1921 and 2025. Adams despaired of our capacity to withstand the overriding force of acceleration. In 1905, he declared, "Yet it is quite sure, according to my score of ratios and curves, that, at the accelerated rate of progression since 1600, it will not need another century or half-century to turn thought upside down. Law, in that case, would disappear . . . and give place to force. Morality would become police. Explosives would reach cosmic violence. Disintegration would overcome integration."

He likened the life of thought to the passage of a comet: "If not a Thought, the comet is a sort of brother of Thought, an early condensation of the ether itself, as the human mind may be another, traversing the infinite without origin or end, and attracted by a sudden object of curiosity that lies by chance near its path. If the calculated curve of deflection of Thought in 1600-1900 were put on that of the planet, it would show that man's evolution had passed perihelion, and that his movement was already retrograde."

The same nightmare vision of the comet has recurred more recently to another man. That man, of all men, was H. G. Wells. In the last year of his life, within twelve months after the first public demonstration of the new explosives of cosmic violence, he wrote: "Events now follow one another in an entirely untrustworthy sequence. . . . Spread out and examine the pattern of events and you will find yourself face to face with a new scheme of being, hitherto unimaginable by the human mind. This new cold glare mocks and dazzles the human intelligence . . . no matter how this intelligence under its cold urgency contrives to seek some way out or round or through the impasse. . . . The writer has come to believe that the congruence of mind, which man has attributed to the secular process, is not really there at all. . . . The two processes have run parallel for what we call Eternity and now abruptly they swing off at a tangent from one another— just as a comet at its perihelion hangs portentous in the heavens for a season and then rushes away for ages or for ever."

Most of us are less well-prepared than Adams and Wells to explore the relevance of science to history. Yet we may charge to their personal circumstances the despair to which each man came at the end of his exploration; for each had come as well to the end of life. I am not here to urge their despair upon you.

On the contrary, it is my thesis that the dilemma of our age—the catatonic indecision of men and nations in their present perilous confrontation with the choice of life or death —follows directly from the general failure to understand that science is relevant to history. That failure is compounded by another: the failure to comprehend the lesson that is pointed by the relevance of science to history.

I shall state the lesson in didactic terms in the hope to state it plainly: Science is the ultimate source of value in the life of mankind.

Man's ascending mastery over the forces of nature has progessively transformed not only the relationship of man to nature, but the relationship of man to man. From age to age, discovery and invention have opened new scope and possibility to human life. With each new possibility has come the necessity to choose. In the succession of choices, the moral and the social order—men's ideas of good and evil and the institutions that embody them—have evolved. The now steeply accelerating advance of science allows no time for evolution. We are compelled to an immediate re-examination and deliberate overhaul of the values and institutions that we have carried into the present from the swiftly receding past.

Let us spread out the pattern of events and see how it sustains this thesis. In the chart, I have projected Henry Adams' curve backward to the classical period, 2000 years

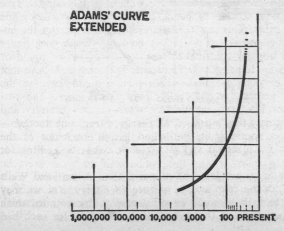

ADAMS' CURVE
EXTENDED

1,000,000   100,000   10,000   1,000   100 PRESENT

ago, and forward 50 years to the present. A wealth of
statistical data supports the ascent of the curve to twice the
height at which Adams charted it at the turn of the century.
Every index, from the consumption of energy *per caput* in
the U. S. to the volume of scientific publication, has more
than doubled in this period. Since few statistical series reach
beyond 150 or 200 years into the past, the projection of the
curve back before 1600 must be regarded as largely symbolic.
The projection is documented, however, by a number of cru-
cial indexes, especially if one may reverse the rule of phase
and count changes in quality as accumulations in quantity.

Consider, for example, the shrinking time-intervals shown
here from the discovery of one primary force of nature to the
next. At the outset, there had to be the notion of a natural
or inanimate force, as distinguished from the animistic *genius*
of the place, thing, or process; this elementary idea was first
propounded in the science of the Greeks two millennia ago.
Then 300 years ago, came the Galilean-Newtonian great world

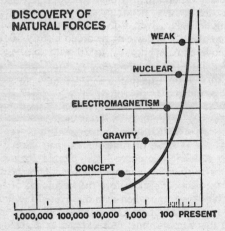

system ordered by the force of gravity. Next, only 100 years
ago, came the Franklin-Faraday-Maxwell discovery of the
electromagnetic force. Then, only 50 years ago, Einstein,
Planck, Rutherford, and Bohr uncovered the most energetic
of the forces, that which binds the nucleus of the atom. Last,
at this very moment, physics is comprehending the presence of
the fourth primary force of the universe: the so-called weak
force observed in the decay of elementary particles.

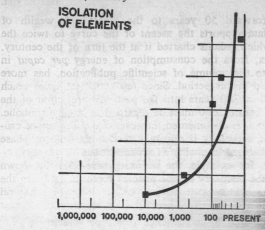

**ISOLATION
OF ELEMENTS**

1,000,000 100,000 10,000 1,000   100 PRESENT

Consider, alternatively, the curve that is plotted by the successive isolations of the 92 elements into which matter is chemically differentiated. Perhaps as many as five elements—carbon, copper, gold, silver, iron—had come into use in more or less pure form at the dawn of recorded history 10,000 years ago. The number rose abruptly to 20 with the beginning of modern chemistry 200 years ago. By the time Mendeleyev laid out the table of elements, a century ago, the number of elements isolated had more than doubled again, to 60-odd. Today physics has carried the series out beyond the bounty of nature, adding 10 so-called synthetic elements to the table —and the curve might be extended indefinitely by grafting on the lengthening table of fundamental particles.

Consider still another curve—that plotted by the mastery of the major sources of inanimate power. The starting point carries our projection back before the beginning of history to at least 50,000 years ago when man discovered the first uses of fire. With his own vital energy amplified by fire, man must already, in that remote time, be reckoned as a geologic force. He used fire not only to warm his body and to cook his food, but more significantly to burn forests and extend the grasslands over which he could hunt more safely and productively. The next point on the curve marks the harnessing of water power in the Bronze Age, 5,000 years ago. It was only 800 years ago that man began to make comparable use of the wind; the invention of the windmill in twelfth-century Europe was something of a technological revolution, spreading in a

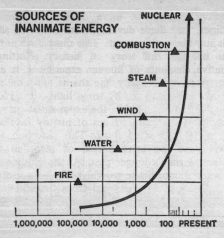

SOURCES OF INANIMATE ENERGY

century from Normandy to the Black Sea. The industrial revolution itself began, of course, with the harnessing of steam, 200 years ago. Direct or internal combustion—which generates as much mechanical and electrical energy as steam in contemporary technology—dates back only a century. And now the first nuclear reactors are delivering electricity to the power networks of the world.

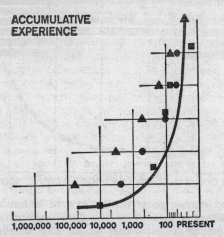

ACCUMULATIVE EXPERIENCE

The pattern of events, therefore, shows history on a course of accelerating acceleration. The major developments in man's accumulative experience have occurred within the most recent times, and these developments occur at shorter time-intervals into the very present. This chart does not, of course, begin to tell the full story of history. Plotting only the accumulative elements of human experience, it excludes the rest—the glory and tragedy, the shame and honor, the bestial and the humane—and so, by some lights, it excludes all that gives meaning to history. Yet the exponential curve of science, I believe, plots the main stream of history insofar as history has not merely repeated itself. This assertion is confirmed when we place the brief period of recorded time in the perspective of man's longer past. At the giddy vantage point on the vertical coordinate to which we have ascended in our lifetime, we are as far removed from the nineteenth century as from pre-historic time.

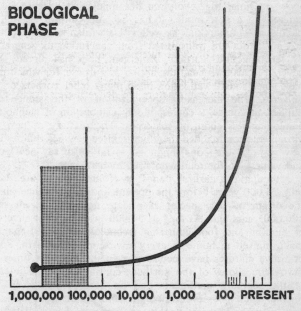

BIOLOGICAL PHASE

1,000,000 100,000 10,000 1,000 100 PRESENT

The starting point of the plot of history may now be established as far back as 1.7 million years before the present, and proportionately closer to the time baseline. At a site reliably dated to that distant time, on a buried lakeshore in the Rift country of Africa, anthropologists have recently unearthed an assemblage of stone tools. With these tools they found fragments of the bones of the hands that had made them. The hands are not human hands—not our hands. They are the hands of a primate who still used them at times for walking. In the old taxonomy of primates it was supposed that man had made the first tools: tool-making was the status symbol of membership in our species. Now, it would appear, tools made man. Certainly, tool-making conferred a competitive advantage on the maker of better tools. But the meaning of this phase of history goes deeper. The truth is: man made himself.

The record as to bones of hands and skulls is scanty. There is an abundance, however, of the fossils of behavior—the stone tools. In their increasing diversity, specialization, and refinement, they give evidence of the evolution of the hand and of the brain, of which the hand is an extension. The tools show, in time, that evolution has quickened because it has entered on a new mode. It has become cultural as well as biological—Lamarckian as well as Darwinian in that acquired characteristics are transmitted from generation to generation by teaching and learning. Emergent man has already discovered in his own head the notion of purpose, for which men have since sought validation in so many other corners of the universe. The increasing specialization of the stone tools implies, of course, a corresponding elaboration of technology employing less enduring materials. The mastery of new environments commanded thereby disclosed new possibilities and new ways of life—one might go so far as to say new goals and values—to the men who sired modern man.

Although the earliest bones of *Homo sapiens* are dated only 25,000 years before the present, indirect evidence places the origin of our species at a date no more recent than 100,000 years ago. As long as 50,000 years ago, the diversity of hunting and food-gathering technologies enabled man to make himself at home in every environment on earth. Some primitive cultures have persisted even into modern times on the Arctic shores of the northern continents, in the interior of the southern continents and on oceanic islands in the Pacific. These peoples have taught us to use the term primitive with respect. There is no human language that is primitive; each has a grammar as well as a vocabulary. The esthetics of these cultures is the more compelling because it so directly articulates the experience of life. Typically, their social order is the extended family, and the code of law and custom

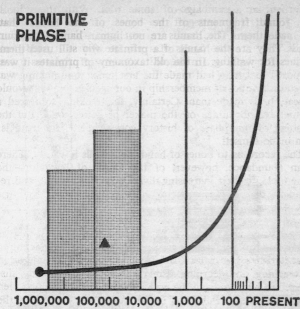

PRIMITIVE PHASE

1,000,000 100,000 10,000 1,000 100 PRESENT

submerges the individual in the common identity and destiny of the group.

It has been shown that even in a continental environment as favorable as that of North America, primitive technology could not sustain more than one person per 10 square miles of territory. The aboriginal population, of course, never approached the limiting density. This may be taken as a measure of the hazard and uncertainty of the hunting and food-gathering way of life that is the common theme of primitive religion and art. Imperceptibly, over tens of thousands of years, as certain of these peoples came into possession of more intimate understanding of their environment, they found a more secure way of life, as herdsmen and cultivators of the soil. By 10,000 years ago they had domesticated all of the plants and animals now grown on the world's farms. There could be no doubt about the progressive nature of this development. It multiplied by 100 the potential size of the population that could be sustained on the land. As history was soon to show, the labor of four families in the field could now support a fifth family in the city.

The transition of agricultural civilization was made in the

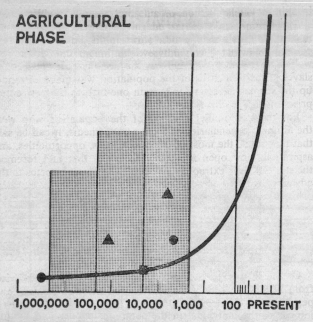

AGRICULTURAL PHASE

1,000,000 100,000 10,000 1,000 100 PRESENT

same 2,000-3,000-year period in Asia Minor, in the valley of the Nile, in the Indus Valley in India, and in China; the transition was made more recently in pre-Columbian America, but in entire independence of events in the Old World. Wherever this revolution occurred, it gave rise to essentially the same social and economic institutions. The function of these institutions was to secure the inequitable distribution of the product of the soil. Law and custom speedily legitimized the necessary measures of coercion. But the primary compulsion, as we can now see, was supplied by the slant of the curve of discovery and invention. Over millennia or centuries, progress was substantial; in the lifetime of a man, however, it brought no appreciable increase in the product of his labor. Population tended always to increase faster than production, maintaining a constant equilibrium of scarcity. Bertrand de Jouvenel has described the situation with precision: "As long as there is a fairly constant limit to production *per caput*, one man can gain wealth only by making use of another man's labor; only a few members of society can gain wealth, therefore, and at the expense of the rest. All ancient civilizations rested upon the inexplicit premise that the productivity of labor is constant."

The inexplicit premise of scarcity is stated plainly enough in the plan of the ancient cities. Invariably it shows the palace, the temple, and the garrison within the ruin of the walls and, outside, the traces in the soil of the hovels of the slaves. Thus four-fifths of the population was made to render up the surplus necessary to sustain one-fifth in the new enterprises of high civilization.

For the still smaller fraction of the population who were the ultimate beneficiaries of these arrangements, it can be said that they made the most of the possibilities, opportunities, and aspirations now open to them. History is first and foremost the story of their extraordinary lives. They gave impetus to the advance of invention and discovery; they explored new realms of esthetic experience, enriching the lives of all men with their vitality and sensibility; they pondered deeply on questions of justice and equity, setting their reflections down in codes of law and treatises on moral philosophy; they developed the arts of government and administration; they led their countrymen on bold adventures in politics, war, and conquest.

Of the 80 per cent of the population who were excluded from history—except when war loosed murder, famine, and pestilence on the land—history has little to say. It has even less to say about the underlying inequity of the social and economic institutions—whether slavery, serfdom, taxes, rent, or interest—that laid the burden of history on their backs. Laws were passed to regulate the treatment of slaves and serfs, but the gross immorality of these institutions was never called in question until modern times—not until, that is, the inexplicit premise of scarcity itself had been overturned.

It is easy now to mark the turning point of history. But even in the seventeenth century people sensed the accelerative force of the contemporary deflection of thought. Without doubt, the most revolutionary idea in the life of man was the concept of inertia advanced in 1638 by Galileo—then already past the age of seventy and writing in secret under house arrest for the lesser heresy of advocating the Copernican revolution. Galileo's great insight comprehended at once the swinging of a pendulum and the motion of the planets on their orbits. The idea of inertia not only changed men's view of nature; it placed a primary force of nature in their hands. Within a few generations they were setting much else besides pendulums in motion.

The surplus gathered in by the institutions of scarcity

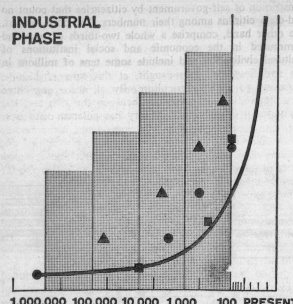

**INDUSTRIAL
PHASE**

1,000,000 100,000 10,000 1,000 100 PRESENT

found a new historic function. It became the wealth of nations
to be invested in the increase of capacity to produce wealth.
Though hindsight encourages us to place emphasis on the
acceleration of the rate of discovery and invention in this
period, we must not fail to credit the role of the institutions
of political economy. In 1802, looking in satisfaction on the
ascendance of Britain, then in the vanguard of the industrial
revolution, Sir Humphry Davy astutely observed: "The unequal division of property and of labour, the difference of
rank and condition amongst mankind, are the sources of power
in civilized life, its moving causes and even its very soul."

Today, after two centuries of industrial revolution, we
have come to speak of two kinds of nations: developed and
underdeveloped, or, in plainer language, rich and poor. Some
20-odd nations, comprising about one-third of the world's
population, have joined in the industrial revolution. To one or
another degree, their entire populations are entrained in the
heady experience of increasing well-being. It is no accident
that the nations that set out first on this course and have
come farthest have also given the world the most favorable

demonstration of self-government by citizenries that count no second-class citizens among their numbers. The poor nations, on the other hand, comprise a whole two-thirds of mankind still immured in the economic and social institutions of agricultural civilization and include some tens of millions in Africa and Southeast Asia caught, at this turn of history, in transition to settled agriculture. By all the quantitative indexes that measure the contrast between the rich and the poor nations, it is plain that history has entered on a new phase.

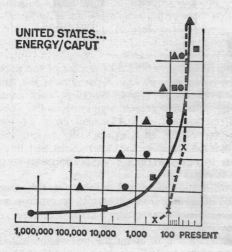

**UNITED STATES...
ENERGY/CAPUT**

1,000,000 100,000 10,000 1,000 100 PRESENT

The signs of change in quality as well as quantity can best be seen in the life of our own country. In the United States we behold the contemporary climax of the industrial revolution. Our standard of living serves as the usual index of our revolutionary leadership. Actually this well-advertised story obscures the crux of the change. Americans, it is true, consume three times as much in goods and services *per caput* as their fellow inhabitants of industrial civilization and more than twenty times as much as the denizens of contemporary agricultural civilization. It is also true that this represents a gain of seven times over the American standard of living of 120 years ago. And the curve even runs ahead of the curve of history we have plotted here. But the triumph fades somewhat when it is observed that our famous miracle was achieved at a rate of less than 2 per cent per year per person. Contemporary industrial economies are advancing at two and three times this rate! The American celebration is dampened further when we are compelled to admit that the average hides poverty that withers the lives of a third of our people. We have cause for downright alarm when we learn from the 1960 census that the middle-income groups are shrinking upward from the bottom, losing increasing numbers to the sink below the poverty line.

No, it is not our success as consumers, but rather as producers that opens the new phase in history. Strangely, perhaps, it is the agriculture of our industrial system that most clearly exposes the nature of the change technology has brought and portends in man's way of life. In contrast with agricultural civilization, where 80 per cent of the people are bound to the land, no more than 8 per cent of the American labor force work on the farm. Working fewer acres each year, they produce still greater yields; presently, enough to feed 12,000 calories to each American every day—enough to feed a billion people an adequate daily ration. Suffice to say, we cannot eat all of it, and, after giving and throwing a great deal of it away, we still have a surplus to keep compulsively in storage.

In the American agricultural surplus we behold a very different kind of surplus from that which was gathered by the lash in Mesopotamia 6,000 years ago. It is a true granary-bursting, physical surplus; it may be taken as symbolic of the surpluses generated elsewhere and everywhere in our industrial system. From these surpluses our economy adds to its capital at no visible cost to current consumption, maintains a vast military establishment, and still accumulates unsold inventories that periodically throttle its channels of distribution. The industrial surplus is the opposite of the scarcity surplus: it is abundance.

America's capacity to produce abundance has long since been freed from the limitations of human muscles and nervous systems. The exponential increase in the flow of mechanical energy through our economy has placed the equivalent of more than 100 human slaves at the disposal, on the average, of every man, woman, and child. Less than half our labor force are employed as producers of goods; not much more than 40 per cent, if the production or armaments is subtracted from the total output. Factory workers will be as scarce as

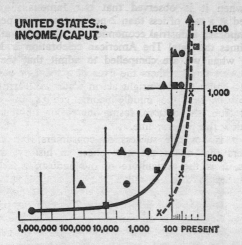

UNITED STATES...
INCOME/CAPUT

1,500

1,000

500

1,000,000 100,000 10,000 1,000 100 PRESENT

farmers in another generation. Our abundance is freed equally from the constraint of resources. The industrial order does not discover resources; it literally creates them. Nor does the system waste and lie idle for lack of demand on its capacity. In addition to our private, family poverty, already reckoned here, our land presents an appalling landscape of public poverty: of blighted cities, polluted rivers, wasting natural resources, neglected schools, bankrupt health services, to mention a few of the demands outstanding.

I could go on and cite the demand of increased investment coming now from the underdeveloped nations that have begun their industrial revolutions; they will carry their revolutions forward without our help and at our greater cost in that event. I would close by wondering aloud why the extravagant demands of the space and military captains should have such exclusive claim on our surplus, especially since they can't use it all!

The constraints on the distribution of adundance, it is apparent, originate elsewhere. Inevitably, the transition to the latest phase of history, which I have called the humane phase, must confront us with a crisis in our institutions and values. The old regime of scarcity is at an end; the time has come to repeal the iron law that says one man's well-being can be increased only at the expense of his brothers. In its place we must frame our values and institutions to respond to

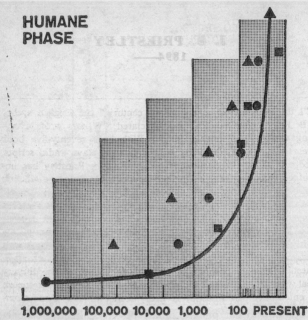

HUMANE
PHASE

1,000,000   100,000   10,000   1,000   100 PRESENT

the new dispensation of abundance: the well-being of each
man increases with increase in the well-being of all.

The menace of the power man has taken in his hands from
nature has been all too well popularized. Statesmen and
citizens alike have learned to reckon with it in all their
calculations about the future. There are signs, in fact, that they
have become used to reckoning with it. The promise of the
power in our hands ought to have an equal place in the public
and private consciousness. The realization of that promise
must begin with the understanding that truth-seeking and tool-
making have disclosed the noblest and most generous ends to
human life, and have given us the means to accomplish them
here on this earth.

J. B. PRIESTLEY
1894——

"I think of myself as eighteenth century," the English author
J. B. Priestley has several times declared. "Writers wrote everything then, essays, novels, plays." With over seventy-five book
titles to his credit, including essays, novels, plays, radio scripts,
accounts of his travels, and an opera libretto, Priestley has undoubtedly equaled any eighteenth-century record for production
and versatility. Further, he has equaled the clarity of that century.
"Too simple," some critics have termed this clarity, but Priestley
disagrees. He has aimed at simplicity, he has cultivated a prose
style "like an easy persuasive voice," for he wants to communicate
with the public. "Art to me," he writes, "is not synonymous with
introversion." It is outward-going, other-directed; and here again
Priestley speaks as of the eighteenth century, when the literary
ideal was to entertain and to instruct—the public. How superb
an entertainer Mr. Priestley is, every reader of *The Good Companions* can tell. How well he instructs, while still entertaining,
the following report of the mythical "Hesperides Conference" is
here to testify.

The Hesperides Conference

The Hesperides Conference was on the highest level and
of exceptional size. Not only were all the leaders of the
Great Powers there but also all their Foreign Ministers,
Chiefs of Staffs, and top busybodies. Experts on foreign affairs and leading political commentators from America, Russia, Britain, and France descended upon the island, to grum-
ble about the small back bedrooms that had been allotted to
them. Articles discussing the possible results of the Conference appeared in the world's Press. They were as usual quite
futile but at least provided their writers with a fair living.
Highly paid reporters, flown to the island at enormous ex-

pense, told their readers, at an overall cost of about ten
pounds a word, that the cigars smoked by the British Prime
Minister seemed half an inch longer than usual, that the
President of the United States was already playing golf, that
the members of the Soviet Delegation had been seen eating
caviare and drinking vodka. Newsreel men took the usual
shots of bigwigs meeting and greeting other bigwigs at the
airport. The F.B.I. investigated the salad chef of the Hotel
Bristol. The Russians installed two microphones (which did
not work) into the smoke-room of the Savoy-Plaza Hotel.
A member of the French Delegation plunged into a rapturous
affair with a honey-coloured American secretary. An oldish
member of the British Delegation began taking a strong interest in the piano-accordion player at the Beach Café-Bar.
Two American correspondents, after four hours of bourbon-
on-the-rocks, swung punches at each other and broke twelve
glasses. The weather was beautiful. The Conference began.

It was during the third morning, when the head of the
Russian Delegation was making a speech about everything,
that several high-level personages first lost consciousness. As
usual there had been plenty of yawns and several men had
dropped off, but that was only to be expected. When, however, the session was adjourned for lunch, and the French
Foreign Minister, among others, refused to wake up, it was
realised that this was no ordinary bout of somnolence. By
nightfall, after the British Delegation's cocktail party had
been abandoned, all the leaders and Foreign Ministers had
succumbed to this mysterious malady and had lost consciousness. Most of the Chiefs of Staffs and junior Ministers and
expert advisers crawled to their beds during the following
twenty-four hours. On the fifth day, the Hesperides Conference was in a coma.

Lord Ward and Sir Thomas Tittlemouse arrived by special
plane from London. Doctors Elmer K. Jefferson and Herman
Funf were rushed from Johns Hopkins to the American Delegation. Professor Oskarvitz, from Moscow, and Professor
Nicolia, of Erivan, came to look after the Soviet representatives. Paris, Lyons, and Marseilles sent their finest specialists
to examine the unconscious French politicians, soldiers, and
officials. The games room of the Savoy-Plaza was turned over
to the medical men, who began to hold a sort of conference
themselves, and once they felt certain that their distinguished
patients were in no immediate danger, began to enjoy themselves. The best resources of these hotels were now at their

disposal. They were able to compare notes on this and other medical problems. The weather was still beautiful. The young Frenchman and the honey-coloured American secretary were still highly conscious, at least of each other, and had a glorious time.

Most of the foreign affairs experts, who had already begun sketching out articles called *After Hesperides—What?*, were victims of the strange sleeping sickness, remaining motionless in their little back bedrooms, now as good as any other. But the reporters in general had escaped the malady, and now they despatched hundreds of thousands of words to the astonished world, giving the verdicts of the assembled medical men and describing the amazing scene with all the wealth of adjectives at their command. The newsreel men were not allowed to film the unconscious great, but some excellent shots were made of less important victims and it was clearly indicated that if you had seen one you had seen, in effect, the lot. With the result that newsreel theatres in every capital city did wonderful business.

Bulletins were broadcast and published in the Press every few hours during the first days, and then daily after a week or two. There were as many theories as there were doctors on the spot. What was certain, after a week or so, was that nobody was in immediate danger, all pulses and respiration being excellent, that all the victims were in something more than a sound long sleep but in nothing more than a very light coma, and that there seemed no reason why they should not wake up as suddenly as they fell asleep. It was generally agreed too that the older delegates, who had existed under a severe strain for years and had made far too many journeys by plane, would probably benefit from this enforced immobility and lack of consciousness. One theory, indeed, took as its basis the idea that the root cause was mental rather than physical, taking the form of a group regression of libido.

Meanwhile, in all the countries concerned, no new appointments were made to places of power. The highest Offices of State remained vacant. Foreign Ministries, robbed of their most influential and forceful personalities and much of their authority, limited themselves to modest routine work. The various Governments, not feeling themselves competent to deal on a high level with foreign relations, concentrated upon home affairs, and even here tended to act with caution and restraint. The international situation remained as it was when the Hesperides Conference first assembled. And as most of the experts and leading commentators were themselves still unconscious on the island, and editors shrank from asking other writers to occupy their space, the more serious newspapers and periodicals in the chief capitals of the world devoted more and more of their columns to the discussion of non-political subjects, such as the arts, sciences, philosophy, travel, and the relations between men and women. And the discovery of two new fascinating games to be played on TV at once captured the more popular papers of the U.S., Britain, and France. In Russia, the Press, uncertain what line to take on any subject, dwindled until it almost disappeared.

As weeks passed into months, however, and the Hesperides Conference still remained unconscious, it was only in theory that the international situation stayed the same. As the Conference was officially still in progress, and had not yet announced its decisions, no action, no bold pronouncement in foreign affairs, was considered possible. This state of things soon brought about its own changes. For the first time for many years no important speeches were made, denouncing the West from the East, the East from the West. No new crusade against Communism was mentioned. World revolution was placed in cold storage. Neither God nor the historic destiny of mankind was loudly proclaimed an ally. No threats, no jeers, were exchanged. Even Anglo-American and Franco-British relations, being no longer examined and commented on at a high level, now failed to reach any crises. The Press no longer warned its readers that the hour was at hand. No radio talks asked listeners to stand firm.

Millions of people who had been weighed down with feelings of fear, hate, horror, and guilt now found themselves living in a different world. At last they could breathe freely. They began to make sensible long-term plans for the future. Many groups of scientists, freed temporarily from their researches into the possibilities of atomic and biological warfare, ventured, timidly at first but then with growing confidence, to divert their research into harmless and possibly useful channels. Having a chance at last to mind their own business, the countries represented at the Conference began making some effort to improve the conditions of life, to lighten the burdens of their citizens. Diplomats and minor officials, able for the time being to ignore time-old foreign policies that had never brought anything but disaster, often converted the very scenes of recurring crises into friendly meeting-places. As the chief representatives of the power motive were still unconscious, the power motive itself rapidly lost force and momentum. All the machinery of ideological and national propaganda, lacking the guiding hand, fell into disuse, and plans were eagerly made to spend the vast sums of money now saved, chiefly on various amenities that the over-taxed citizens had hitherto been unable to afford. Without Presidents, Prime Ministers, Foreign Secretaries, the Americans, British, and French did not know what was happening to Anglo-American and Franco-British relations; and for the first time for years began to get along quite nicely. There was even talk of temporarily suspending the rules and regulations about visas and passports. The easy freedom of the pre-1914 world was almost in sight.

It was then that a brilliant young pathologist from Barcelona arrived at the Hesperides. He had a theory, which he explained to the assembled doctors. He also had a small supply of a new and very powerful antibiotic, which he begged to be allowed to inject into three or four of the unconscious men. He was certain it would bring them out of their coma. Finally, he was given permission to treat one Chief of Staff, one Under-Secretary for Foreign Affairs, and one economic adviser. Within an hour, all three were not only awake but beginning to make angry speeches or to demand secretaries to attend them so that they could dictate aggressive memos. It was a triumph for the young man from Barcelona, who declared that if he were given the necessary facilities, he could return within two or three weeks with a sufficient supply of his remedy to revivify the whole Conference. As he announced this, through the long corridors where peace and quiet had reigned for many months, loud angry voices were heard. The medical men exchanged long inquiring glances. They were well aware of what had been happening in the world during the time the Conference had slept.

They escorted the young man back to their headquarters, the former games room of the hotel, securely barred from the Press. They looked thoughtfully at him. They exchanged more dubious glances. *What was their decision?* No prizes are offered for the best replies.

RAINER MARIA RILKE
1875–1926

Although Rainer Maria Rilke is best known as a poet (for his *Duino Elegies* and the *Sonnets to Orpheus*), he was also a superlative essayist. When he was born in Prague in 1875, his mother was disappointed. She had wanted a girl, to take the place of her first girl baby, who had died. She did not reject the new child, however; she treated him as a girl—dressed him like one, combed his hair in long curls, and gave him dolls. These dolls recur in many guises throughout Rilke's poetry and prose, but it is in this essay, "Some Reflections on Dolls," that they assume their most monstrous aspect. Here Rilke is full of resentment against dolls, because they refuse to absorb any of the tenderness lavished upon them. They remain impervious, silent, with a silence that gives a child for the first time "that emptiness of feeling, that heart-pause, in which we should perish did not the whole, gently persisting Nature then lift us across abysses like some lifeless thing." And because affection spent on them is wasted, they teach the uselessness of love; they destroy love by destroying the belief in it. Nor is this all. But this was enough, when Rilke was reading the essay to Benvenuta, one of the women with whom he hoped to recover the love wrecked by the dolls, to make her cry out: "I cannot listen any more. . . . I find it horrifying." And from that moment dated the decline of their relationship.

Some Reflections on Dolls
(Occasioned by the Wax Dolls of Lotte Pritzel)

In order to define the sphere within which the existence of these dolls falls, one might conjecture concerning them that there are no children in their lives: this would be, in a certain sense, the condition of their origin, that the world of children was past and over. In these figures the doll has at last outgrown the understanding, the sympathy, the pleasure, and the sorrow of the child, it has become independent, grown-up, prematurely old, it has entered upon all the unrealities of its own life.

Have we not asked ourselves a thousand times anent the plump, unchanging dolls of childhood, as we do in the case of certain students, what will they be later? Are these then the grown-up versions of those doll-childhoods, which were pampered to excess by real and enacted emotions? Are these the fruits which they fleetingly reflected in humanly saturated atmosphere? The sham fruits, the germ of which knew no rest, being now almost washed away by tears, and now exposed to the arid heat of anger or to the void of forgetfulness; planted in the softest depth of a tenderness infinitely experimental and torn out again a hundred times, flung into a corner amongst sharp-edged broken objects, scorned, spurned, done with.

Fed like the "Ka" on imaginary food, when it seemed absolutely essential that they should be given real food, they messed themselves with it like spoiled children, being impenetrable and incapable of absorbing, at any point, even a drop of water in their extreme state of well-enough known solidity; without any judgment of their own, acquiescent towards every rag, and yet, once it was theirs, possessing it in their own careless, complacent, unclean manner; awake only at the moment of opening their eyes, then immediately continuing to sleep with their disproportionate, mobile eyes open, scarcely capable, indeed, of distinguishing whether it was the mechanical lid or that other thing, the air, which lay upon them; indolent, dragged about through the changing emotions of the day, remaining where they lie; made a confidant, a confederate, like a dog, not, however, receptive and forgetful like a dog, but in both cases a burden; initiated into the first, nameless experiences of their owners, lying about in their earliest uncanny lonelinesses, as in the midst of empty rooms, as if all they had to do was to exploit unfeelingly the new spaciousness with all their limbs—taken into cots, dragged into the heavy folds of illnesses, present in dreams, involved in the fatalities of nights of fever: such were these dolls. For they themselves never made any effort in all this; they lay there on the border of the children's sleep, filled, at most, with the rudimentary idea of falling down, allowing them-

selves to *be dreamed*; as it was their habit, during the day, to
be lived unwearyingly with energies not their own.

When one thinks how grateful other things are for tender
treatment, how they recover under it, indeed, how they feel
even the hardest usage to be a consuming caress, provided
only that they are loved, a caress which, no doubt, wears
them away, but beneath which they take, as it were, courage
which permeates them the more strongly, the more their
body gives way (it makes them almost mortal, in a higher
sense, so that they are able to share with us that grief which
is our greatest possession); when we consider this and recall
the sensitive beauty that certain things have been able to
appropriate, which have been thoroughly and intimately incorporated in human life; I am not saying even that it is
necessary to visit the rooms of the *Armeria* in Madrid and to
admire the suits of armour, helmets, daggers, and two-handed
swords, in which the pure, clever art of the armourer is immeasurably excelled by that something which the proud and
fiery use of them has added to these weapons; I am not
thinking of the smiling and the weeping which lie hidden in
much-worn jewels; I do not dare to think of a certain pearl,
in which the uncertain nature of its subaqueous world had
gained such heightened spiritual significance that the whole
inscrutability of destiny seemed to utter its lament in that
innocent pearl-drop; I pass over the intimate, the touching,
the deserted, thoughtful aspect of many things, which, as I
passed them, moved me deeply by their beautiful participa-
tion in human living; I will only cite in passing quite simple
things: a sewing clamp, a spinning-wheel, a domestic loom,
a bridal glove, a cup, the binding and the leaves of a Bible;
not to speak of the mighty will of a hammer, the self-surrender
of a violin, the friendly eagerness of horn spectacles,—
indeed, only throw that pack of cards on the table, with which
patience has been played so often, and it forms at once the
centre of melancholy hopes, which have long since been
realized in ways not hoped for. If we were to bring all this
to mind again and at the same moment to find one of these
dolls—pulling it out from a pile of more responsive things—it
would almost anger us with its frightful obese forgetfulness,
the hatred, which undoubtedly has always been a part of our
relationship to it unconsciously, would break out, it would
lie before us unmasked as the horrible foreign body on which
we had wasted our purest ardour; as the externally painted

watery corpse, which floated and swam on the flood-tides of our affection, until we were on dry land again and left it lying forgotten in some undergrowth. I know, I know it was necessary for us to have things of this kind, which acquiesced in everything. The simplest love relationships were quite beyond our comprehension, we could not possibly have lived and had dealings with a person who *was* something; at most, we could only have entered into such a person and have lost ourselves there. With the doll we were forced to assert ourselves, for, had we surrendered ourselves to it, there would then have been no one there at all. It made no response whatever, so that we were put in the position of having to take over the part it should have played, of having to split our gradually enlarging personality into part and counterpart; in a sense, through it to keep the world, which was entering into us on all sides, at a distance. The things which were happening to us incomprehensibly we mixed in the doll, as in a test tube, and saw them there change colour and boil up. That is to say, we *invented* that also, it was so abysmally devoid of phantasy, that our imagination became inexhaustible in dealing with it. For hours together, for whole weeks we were content to lay the first downlike silk of our hearts in folds against this motionless mannequin, but I cannot help thinking that there were certain all too lengthy afternoons in which our twofold inspirations flagged, and suddenly we sat facing it, expecting something from it. It may be that there was then one of those things lying near, which are ugly and shabby by nature and consequently full of their own opinions, the head of an indestructible Casper, a half-broken horse, or something that made a noise and that could hardly wait to submerge us and the whole room by exerting its full powers. But even if this was not so; if there was nothing lying there to suggest other thoughts to us, if that creature without occupation continued, in its stupid stolidity, to put on airs, ignorant, like a peasant Danaë, of everything but the ceaseless golden rain of our inventiveness: I wish I could remember if we inveighed against it, flew into a passion and let the monster know that our patience was at an end? If, standing in front of it and trembling with rage, we did not demand to know, item by item, what actual use it was making of all these riches. It was silent then, not deliberately, it was silent because that was its constant mode of evasion, because it was made of useless and entirely irresponsible material, was silent, and the idea did not occur to it to take some credit to itself

on that score, although it could not but gain great importance
thereby in a world in which Destiny, and even God Himself,
have become famous above all because they answer us with
silence. At a time when everyone was still intent on giving
us a quick and reassuring answer, the doll was the first to
inflict on us that tremendous silence (larger than life) which
was later to come to us repeatedly out of space, whenever we
approached the frontiers of our existence at any point. It was
facing the doll, as it stared at us, that we experienced for
the first time (or am I mistaken?) that emptiness of feeling,
that heart-pause, in which we should perish did not the whole,
gently persisting Nature then lift us across abysses like some
lifeless thing. Are we not strange creatures to let ourselves go
and to be induced to place our earliest affections where they
remain hopeless? So that everywhere there was imparted to
that most spontaneous tenderness the bitterness of knowing
that it was in vain? Who knows if such memories have not
caused many a man afterwards, out there in life, to suspect
that he is not lovable? If the influence of their doll does not
continue to work disastrously in this and that person, so that
they pursue vague satisfactions, simply in opposition to the
state of unsatisfied desire by which it ruined their lives? I
remember seeing, in the hands of the children of a manor
house on a lonely Russian estate, an old inherited doll which
the whole family resembled. A poet might succumb to the
domination of a marionette, for the marionette has only imagination. The doll has none, and is precisely so much less than
a thing as the marionette is more. But this being-less-than-a-
thing, in its utter irremediability, is the secret of its superiority.
The child must accustom itself to things, it must accept them,
each thing has its pride. Things put up with the doll, none of
them love it, we might imagine that the table throws it down,
scarcely have we withdrawn our glance, before it is lying
once more on the floor. Beginners in the world, as we were,
we could not feel superior to any thing except, at most, to
such a half-object as this, given to us the way some broken
fragment is given to the creatures in aquariums, so that it
may serve them as a measure and landmark in the world
around them. We took our bearings from the doll. It was by
nature on a lower level than ourselves, so that we could flow
towards it imperceptibly, find ourselves in it and recognize
our new surroundings in it, even if a little dimly. But we
soon realized that we could not make a person or a thing of
it, and at such moments it became a stranger to us, and all

the confidences we had poured into and over it became foreign to us.

But that, in spite of all this, we did not make an idol of you, you sack, and did not perish in the fear of you, that was, I tell you, because we were not thinking of *you* at all. We were thinking of something quite different, an invisible Something, which we held high above you and ourselves, secretly and with foreboding, and for which both we and you were, so to say, merely pretexts, we were thinking of a soul: the doll-soul.

Great, courageous soul of the rocking-horse, you rocking breakers tossing the boy's heart, soul that agitated the air of the play-room until it frenzied as over the world's famous battlefields, proud, credible, almost visible soul. How you made the walls, the cross-work of the windows, the daily horizons tremble, as though the storms of the future were already shaking these most provisional conventions, which, in the stationariness of the afternoons, could appear so invisible. Ah! how you swept one away, you rocking-horse soul, away and into the realm of the irresistibly heroic, where one perished gloriously and glowingly with one's hair in the most frightful disorder. And there you lay, doll, and had not enough innocence to understand that your St. George was rolling beneath him the beast of your stupidity, the dragon that turned the most surging tides of our emotions into a solid mass within you, into a perfidious, indifferent unbreakableness. Or you, convinced soul of the tramway, that was almost able to get the better of us when we travelled round the room, believing even only a little in our tram nature. You, souls of all these solitary games and adventures; ingenuously complaisant soul of the ball, soul in the smell of the domino pieces, inexhaustible soul of the picture book. Soul of the school satchel, towards which we felt a little distrustful because it was often so obviously on the side of the grown-ups; dumb soul of the tube of the good little trumpet: how amiable you all were and almost comprehensible. Only you, doll's soul, one could never say exactly where you really were. Whether you were in oneself or in the sleepy creature over there, whom one constantly endowed with you; undoubtedly we often relied upon one another, and in the end neither of us had you, and you were trodden under foot. When were you ever really present? On a birthday morning perhaps, when a new doll sat there and seemed almost to appropriate some bodily warmth from the still warm cake beside it? Or on the eve of Christmas, when the dolls we already possessed felt the over-ruling proximity of our future dolls through the door of the room which had been closed to us for days? Or— what is more probable—when a doll suddenly fell down and became ugly: then, for a second, it was as if you were taken off your guard. And you were, I believe, capable of giving pain as indefinite as the beginning of toothache, when we don't yet know just where it is going to be, when the favourite doll, Anna, was suddenly lost, not to be found again for ever: was gone. But fundamentally one was so busy keeping you alive that one had no time to determine what you were. I cannot say what it is like, when a little girl dies and re- fuses, even at the very end, to let go one of her dolls (per- haps one which had always been quite neglected), so that the poor thing is completely dry and withered in the consum- ing heat of her feverish hand, caught up into the Serious, the Ultimate: does a little bit of soul then form within it, curious to see a real soul?

O doll-soul, not made by God, you soul, asked for capri- ciously from some thoughtless fairy, thing-soul breathed forth by an idol with mighty effort, which we have all, half timidly, half magnanimously received and from which no one can entirely withdraw himself, O soul, that has never been really worn, that has only been kept always stored up (like furs in summer), protected by all kinds of old-fashioned odours: look, now the moths have got into you. You have been left untouched too long, now a hand both careful and mischievous is shaking you—look, look, all the little woebe- gone moths are fluttering out of you, indescribably mortal, beginning, even at the moment when they find themselves, to bid themselves farewell.

And so, in the end, we have quite destroyed you, doll-soul, whilst thinking to care for you in our dolls; they were, after all, the maggots which ate you away—that is the explanation why they were so fat and inert and why they could not be got to take any more food.

Now this new, timid race escapes and flutters through our subconscious feeling. Perceiving it, we are tempted to say that they are little sighs, so tenuous that our hearing is not sufficient for them; they appear, as they vanish, on the quiveringmost borders of our vision. For this is their only concern: to fade away. Sexless as the dolls of childhood were, they can find no decease in their stagnant ecstasy, which has neither inflow nor outflow. It is as if they were consumed with the desire for a beautiful flame, into which they might fling themselves after the manner of moths (and then the immediate smell of their burning would inundate us with limitless, hitherto unknown emotions). Reflecting thus and looking up, one is confronted and almost overwhelmed by their waxen nature.

BERTRAND RUSSELL
1872——

Bertrand Russell, philosopher, mathematician, Nobel Prize winner, and tireless preacher of the skeptical doctrine, "It is undesirable to believe a proposition when there is no good ground whatever for supposing it true," is now past his ninetieth year, and as indefatigable and irrepressible as ever. Logician that he is, he has always been exercised by the lack of logic in human affairs; and therefore, in addition to writing such great philosophical works as *The Principles of Mathematics,* definitely not for the layman, he has published for the ordinary reader *The Conquest of Happiness, Marriage and Morals, Roads to Freedom, Has Man a Future?* and many more volumes all intended to alert irrational mankind to the consequences of its irrationality. In performing this work of redemption, Russell has obviously taken extreme pleasure in pricking society's favorite pretensions. His style, as the following essay makes clear, is not calculated to soothe, but to raise the blood pressure; it is like a powerful cocktail full of clinking ice—sharp, shocking, chilling, but stimulating. Equally stimulating, and to many equally shocking, have been Russell's public acts of logic in the course of his long life. He dared to be a pacifist in World War I, and spent six months in a British jail in consequence. He dared to question the accepted customs of matrimony, and was nearly mobbed by angry mothers outside the College of the City of New York. He has dared now to question the desirability of blowing up the world with hydrogen bombs, and all of us have seen pictures of his lank frame firmly seated on London pavements as he led thousands of his fellow citizens in anti-bomb demonstrations. As Russell has observed of himself, "His principles were curious, but such as they were they governed his actions." He has been a grand fighter, and he has enjoyed the fight.

The Harm That Good Men Do

I

A hundred years ago there lived a philosopher named Jeremy Bentham, who was universally recognized to be a very wicked man. I remember to this day the first time that I came across his name when I was a boy. It was in a statement by the Rev. Sydney Smith to the effect that Bentham thought people ought to make soup of their dead grandmothers. This practice appeared to me as undesirable from a culinary as from a moral point of view, and I therefore conceived a bad opinion of Bentham. Long afterwards, I discovered that the statement was one of those reckless lies in which respectable people are wont to indulge in the interests of virtue. I also discovered what was the really serious charge against him. It was no less than this: that he defined a "good" man as a man who does good. This definition, as the reader will perceive at once if he is right-minded, is subversive of all true morality. How much more exalted is the attitude of Kant, who lays it down that a kind action is not virtuous if it springs from affection for the beneficiary, but only if it is inspired by the moral law, which is, of course, just as likely to inspire unkind actions. We know that the exercise of virtue should be its own reward, and it seems to follow that the enduring of it on the part of the patient should be its own punishment. Kant, therefore, is a more sublime moralist than Bentham, and has the suffrages of all those who tell us that they love virtue for its own sake.

It is true that Bentham fulfilled his own definition of a good man: he did much good. The forty middle years of the nineteenth century in England were years of incredibly rapid progress, materially, intellectually, and morally. At the begining of the period comes the Reform Act, which made Parliament representative of the middle-class, not, as before, of the aristocracy. This Act was the most difficult of the steps towards democracy in England, and was quickly followed by other important reforms, such as the abolition of slavery in Jamaica. At the beginning of the period the penalty for petty theft was death by hanging; very soon the death penalty was confined to those who were guilty of murder or high treason. The Corn Laws, which made food so dear as to cause atrocious poverty, were abolished in 1846. Compulsory education was introduced in 1870. It is the fashion to decry the Victorians, but I wish our age had half as good a record as theirs. This, however, is beside the point. My point is that a very large proportion of the progress during those years must be attributed to the influence of Bentham. There can be no doubt that nine-tenths of the people living in England in the latter part of last century were happier than they would have been if he had never lived. So shallow was his philosophy that he would have regarded this as a vindication of his activities. We, in our more enlightened age, can see that such a view is preposterous; but it may fortify us to review the grounds for rejecting a groveling utilitarianism such as that of Bentham.

II

We all know what we mean by a "good" man. The ideally good man does not drink or smoke, avoids bad language, converses in the presence of men only exactly as he would if there were ladies present, attends church regularly, and holds the correct opinions on all subjects. He has a wholesome horror of wrongdoing, and realizes that it is our painful duty to castigate Sin. He has a still greater horror of wrong thinking, and considers it the business of the authorities to safeguard the young against those who question the wisdom of the views generally accepted by middle-aged successful citizens. Apart from his professional duties, at which he is assiduous, he spends much time in good works: he may encourage patriotism and military training; he may promote industry, sobriety, and virtue among wage-earners and their children by seeing to it that failures in these respects receive due punishment; he may be a trustee of a university and prevent an ill-judged respect for learning from allowing the employment of professors with subversive ideas. Above all, of course, his "morals," in the narrow sense, must be irreproachable.

It may be doubted whether a "good" man, in the above sense, does, on the average, any more good than a "bad" man. I mean by a "bad" man the contrary of what we have been describing. A "bad" man is one who is known to smoke and to drink occasionally, and even to say a bad word when some one treads on his toe. His conversation is not always such as could be printed, and he sometimes spends fine Sundays out-of-doors instead of at church. Some of his opinions are subversive; for instance, he may think that if you desire peace you should prepare for peace, not for war. Towards wrongdoing he takes a scientific attitude, such as he would take towards his motor-car if it misbehaved; he argues that sermons and prison will no more cure vice than mend a broken tire. In the matter of wrong thinking he is even more perverse. He maintains that what is called "wrong thinking" is simply thinking, and what is called "right thinking" is repeating words like a parrot; this gives him a sympathy with all sorts of undesirable cranks. His activities outside his working hours may consist merely in enjoyment, or, worse still, in stirring up discontent with preventable evils which do not interfere with the comfort of the men in power. And it is even possible that in the matter of "morals" he may not conceal his lapses as carefully as a truly virtuous man would do, defending himself by the perverse contention that it is better to be honest than to pretend to set a good example. A man who fails in any or several of these respects will be thought ill of by the average respectable citizen, and will not be allowed to hold any position conferring authority, such as that of a judge, a magistrate, or a schoolmaster. Such positions are open only to "good" men.

This whole state of affairs is more or less modern. It existed in England during the brief reign of the Puritans in the time of Cromwell, and by them it was transplanted to America. It did not reappear in force in England till after the French Revolution, when it was thought to be a good method of combating Jacobinism (*i.e.*, what we should now call Bolshevism). The life of Wordsworth illustrates the change. In his youth he sympathized with the French Revolution, went to France, wrote good poetry, and had a natural daughter. At this period he was a "bad" man. Then he became "good," abandoned his daughter, adopted correct principles, and wrote bad poetry. Coleridge went through a similar change: when he was wicked he wrote *Kubla Khan*, and when he was good he wrote theology.

It is difficult to think of any instance of a poet who was "good" at the times when he was writing good poetry. Dante was deported for subversive propaganda; Shakespeare, to judge by the Sonnets, would not have been allowed by American immigration officers to land in New York. It is of the essence of a "good" man that he supports the Government; therefore, Milton was good during the reign of Cromwell, and bad before and after; but it was before and after that he wrote his poetry—in fact most of it was written after he had narrowly escaped hanging as a Bolshevik. Donne was virtuous after he became Dean of St. Paul's, but all his poems were written before that time, and on account of them his appointment caused a scandal. Swinburne was wicked in his youth, when he wrote *Songs Before Sunrise* in praise of those who fought for freedom; he was virtuous in his old age, when he wrote savage attacks on the Boers for defending their liberty against wanton aggression. It is needless to multiply examples; enough has been said to suggest that the standards of virtue now prevalent are incompatible with the production of good poetry.

In other directions the same thing is true. We all know that Galileo and Darwin were bad men; Spinoza was thought dreadfully wicked until a hundred years after his death; Descartes went abroad for fear of persecution. Almost all the Renaissance artists were bad men. To come to humbler matters, those who object to preventable mortality are necessarily wicked. I lived in a part of London which is partly very rich, partly very poor; the infant death-rate is abnormally high, and the rich, by corruption and intimidation, control the local government. They use their power to cut down the expenditure on infant welfare and public health and to engage a medical officer at less than the standard rate on condition that he gives only half his time to the work. No one can win the respect of the important local people unless he considers that good dinners for the rich are more important than life for the children of the poor. The corresponding thing is true in every part of the world with which I am acquainted. This suggests that we may simplify our account of what constitutes a good man: a good man is one whose opinions and activities are pleasing to the holders of power.

III

It has been painful to have to dwell upon the bad men who, in the past, have unfortunately achieved eminence. Let us turn to the more agreeable contemplation of the virtuous.

A typically virtuous man was George III. When Pitt wanted him to emancipate the Catholics (who at that time were not allowed to vote), he would not agree, on the ground that to do so would be contrary to his coronation oath. He righteously refused to be misled by the argument that it would do good to emancipate them; the question, for him, was not whether it would do good, but whether it was "right" in the abstract. His interference in politics was largely responsible for the régime which caused America to claim independence; but his interference was always dictated by the most lofty motives. The same may be said of the ex-Kaiser, a deeply religious man, sincerely convinced, until his fall, that God was on his side, and (so far as I know) wholly free from personal vices. Yet it would be hard to name any man of our time who has done more to cause human misery.

Among politicians good men have their uses, the chief of which is to afford a smoke-screen behind which others can carry on their activities unsuspected. A good man will never suspect his friends of shady actions: this is part of his goodness. A good man will never be suspected by the public of using his goodness to screen villains: this is part of his utility. It is clear that this combination of qualities makes a good man extremely desirable wherever a somewhat narrow-minded public objects to the transference of public funds into the hands of the deserving rich. I am told—though far be it from me to endorse this statement—that at a not very distant period in history there was an American President who was a good man and served this purpose. In England, Whittaker Wright, at the height of his fame, surrounded himself with blameless peers, whose virtue made them incapable of understanding his arithmetic, or of knowing that they did not.

Another of the uses of good men is that any undesirables can be kept out of politics by means of scandals. Ninety-nine men out of a hundred commit breaches of the moral law, but in general this fact does not become public. And when in the ninety-ninth case it becomes known in relation to any individual, the one man in the hundred who is genuinely innocent expresses genuine horror, while the other ninety-eight are compelled to follow suit for fear of being suspected. When, therefore, any man of obnoxious opinions ventures into politics, it is only necessary for those who have the preservation of our ancient institutions at heart to keep track of his private activities until they discover something which, if exposed, will ruin his political career. They then have three courses open to them: to make the facts known and cause him to disappear in a cloud of obloquy; or to compel him to retire into private life by threats of exposure; or to derive for themselves a comfortable income by means of blackmail. Of these three courses the first two protect the public, while the third protects those who protect the public. All three, therefore, are to be commended, and all three are only rendered possible through the existence of good men.

Consider, again, such a matter as venereal disease: it is known that this can be almost entirely prevented by suitable precautions taken in advance, but owing to the activities of good men this knowledge is disseminated as little as possible, and all kinds of obstacles are placed in the way of its utilization. Consequently sin still secures its "natural" punishment, and the children are still punished for the sins of the fathers, in accordance with Biblical precept. How dreadful it would be if this were otherwise, for, if sin were no longer punished, there might be people so abandoned as to pretend that it was no longer sin, and if the punishment did not fall also upon the innocent, it would not seem so dreadful. How grateful we ought to be, therefore, to those good men who ensure that the stern laws of retribution decreed by Nature during our days of ignorance can still be made to operate in spite of the impious knowledge rashly acquired by scientists. All right-thinking people know that a bad act is bad quite regardless of the question whether it causes any suffering or not, but since men are not all capable of being guided by the pure moral law, it is highly desirable that suffering should follow from sin in order to secure virtue. Men must be kept in ignorance of all ways of escaping the penalties which were incurred by sinful actions in pre-scientific ages. I shudder when I think how much we should all know about the preservation of mental and physical health if it were not for the protection against this dangerous knowledge which our good men so kindly provide.

Another way in which good men can be useful is by getting themselves murdered. Germany acquired the province of Shantung in China by having the good fortune to have two missionaries murdered there. The Archduke who was murdered at Sarajevo was, I believe, a good man; and how grateful we ought to be to him! If he had not died as he did, we might not have had the war, and then the world would not have been made safe for democracy, nor would militarism have been overthrown, nor should we be now enjoying military despotisms in Spain, Italy, Hungary, Bulgaria, and Russia.

To speak seriously: the standards of "goodness" which are

generally recognized by public opinion are not those which are calculated to make the world a happier place. This is due to a variety of causes, of which the chief is tradition, and the next most powerful is the unjust power of dominant classes. Primitive morality seems to have developed out of the notion of taboo; that is to say, it was originally purely superstitious, and forbade certain perfectly harmless acts (such as eating out of the chief's dish) on the supposed ground that they produced disaster by magical means. In this way there came to be prohibitions, which continued to have authority over people's feelings when the supposed reasons for them were forgotten. A considerable part of current morals is still of this sort: certain kinds of conduct produce emotions of horror, quite regardless of the question whether they have bad effects or not. In many cases the conduct which inspires horror is in fact harmful; if this were not the case, the need for a revision of our moral standards would be more generally recognized. Murder, for example, can obviously not be tolerated in a civilized society; yet the origin of the prohibition of murder is purely superstitious. It was thought that the murdered man's blood (or, later, his ghost) demanded vengeance, and might punish not only the guilty man, but any one who showed him kindness. The superstitious character of the prohibition of murder is shown by the fact that it was possible to be purified from blood-guiltiness by certain ritual ceremonies, which were apparently designed, originally, to disguise the murderer so that the ghost would not recognize him. This, at least, is the theory of Sir J. G. Frazer. When we speak of repentance as "washing out" guilt we are using a metaphor derived from the fact that long ago actual washing was used to remove bloodstains. Such notions as "guilt" and "sin" have an emotional background connected with this source in remote antiquity. Even in the case of murder a rational ethic will view the matter differently: it will be concerned with prevention and cure, as in the case of illness, rather than with guilt, punishment, and expiation.

Our current ethic is a curious mixture of superstition and rationalism. Murder is an ancient crime, and we view it through a mist of age-long horror. Forgery is a modern crime, and we view it rationally. We punish forgers, but we do not feel them strange beings set apart, as we do murderers. And we still think in social practice, whatever we may hold in theory, that virtue consists in not doing rather than in doing. The man who abstains from certain acts labeled "sin" is a good man, even though he never does anything to further the welfare of others. This, of course, is not the attitude inculcated in the Gospels: "Love thy neighbor as thyself" is a positive precept. But in all Christian communities the man who obeys this precept is persecuted, suffering at least poverty, usually imprisonment, and sometimes death. The world is full of injustice, and those who profit by injustice are in a position to administer rewards and punishments. The rewards go to those who invent ingenious justifications for inequality, the punishments to those who try to remedy it. I do not know of any country where a man who has a genuine love for his neighbor can long avoid obloquy. In Paris, just before the outbreak of the war, Jean Jaurès, the best citizen of France, was murdered; the murderer was acquitted, on the ground that he had performed a public service. This case was peculiarly dramatic, but the same sort of thing happens everywhere.

Those who defend traditional morality will sometimes admit that it is not perfect, but contend that any criticism will make all morality crumble. This will not be the case if the criticism is based upon something positive and constructive, but only if it is conducted with a view to nothing more than momentary pleasure. To return to Bentham: he advocated, as the basis of morals, "the greatest happiness of the greatest number." A man who acts upon this principle will have a much more arduous life than a man who merely obeys conventional precepts. He will necessarily make himself the champion of the oppressed, and so incur the enmity of the great. He will proclaim facts which the powers that be wish to conceal; he will deny falsehoods designed to alienate sympathy from those who need it. Such a mode of life does not lead to a collapse of genuine morality. Official morality has always been oppressive and negative: it has said "thou shalt not," and has not troubled to investigate the effect of activities not forbidden by the code. Against this kind of morality all the great mystics and religious teachers have protested in vain: their followers ignored their most explicit pronouncements. It seems unlikely, therefore, that any large-scale improvements will come through their methods.

More is to be hoped, I think, from the progress of reason and science. Gradually men will come to realize that a world whose institutions are based upon hatred and injustice is not the one most likely to produce happiness. The late war taught this lesson to a few, and would have taught it to many more if it had ended in a draw. We need a morality based upon love of life, upon pleasure in growth and positive achievement, not upon repression and prohibition. A man should be regarded as "good" if he is happy, expansive, generous, and glad when others are happy; if so, a few peccadillos should be regarded as of little importance. But a man who acquires a fortune by cruelty and exploitation should be regarded as at present we regard what is called an "immoral" man; and he should be so regarded even if he goes to church regularly and gives a portion of his ill-gotten gains to public objects. To bring this about, it is only necessary to instill a rational attitude towards ethical questions, instead of the mixture of superstition and oppression which still passes muster as "virtue" among important personages. The power of reason is thought small in these days, but I remain an unrepentant rationalist. Reason may be a small force, but it is constant, and works always in one direction, while the forces of unreason destroy one another in futile strife. Therefore every orgy of unreason in the end strengthens the friends of reason, and shows afresh that they are the only true friends of humanity.

GEORGE SANTAYANA
1863–1952

Philosopher, poet, novelist, George Santayana is too complex a personality to characterize in a paragraph. Even his parentage and nationality were complex, and he added to his mingled Spanish and American heritage a cosmopolitan European experience. *The World My Host* was a fitting title of one of his volumes of recollections. But something can be said of his essay "Hermes the Interpreter," which is printed below. This is the concluding Soliloquy in a volume Santayana wrote in England during and immediately after the first World War. Tramping through the fields and the "willowed paths" about Oxford, he found his thoughts driven by the tragedy of the time "even deeper than they would otherwise have ventured into the maze of reflection and of dreams." Out of this maze and out of the incongruous peace of the English landscape, he drew his Soliloquies —"but poor wild symbols," he confessed, just as words are, "for their unfathomed objects." And he added: "I should be the first to hate their verbiage, if a certain spiritual happiness did not seem to breathe through it, and redeem its irrelevance." That "spiritual happiness" shines with particular brightness in "Hermes," and there are subsidiary gleams as well, of delicate mischief and of consummate verbal grace. The tremendous scope of Santayana's philosophical writing is certainly not suggested here, but here, in small compass, is all his felicity of style, and here is the quiet elegance of his poetry.

Hermes the Interpreter

A traveller should be devout to Hermes, and I have always loved him above the other gods for that charming union which is found in him of youth with experience, alacrity with prudence, modesty with laughter, and a ready tongue with a sound heart. In him the first bubblings of mockery subside

at once into courtesy and helpfulness. He is the winged
Figaro of Olympus, willing to yield to others in station and to
pretend to serve them, but really wiser and happier than any
of them. There is a certain roguery in him, and the habit of
winking at mischief. He has a great gift for dissertation, and
his abundant eloquence, always unimpeachable in form and in
point, does not hug the truth so closely as pious people might
expect in a god who, as they say sagaciously, can have no
motive for lying. But gods do not need motives. The lies of
Hermes are jests; they represent things as they might have
been, and serve to show what a strange accident the truth is.
The reproach which Virgil addresses to his Juno, "Such malignity in minds celestial?" could never apply to this amiable
divinity, who, if he is a rascal at all (which I do not admit),
is a disinterested rascal. He has given no pawns to fortune,
he is not a householder, he is not pledged against his will to
any cause. Homer tells us that Hermes was a thief; but
the beauty of mythology is that every poet can recast it
according to his own insight and sense of propriety; as, in
fact, our solemn theologians do also, although they pretend
that their theology is a science, and are not wide awake
enough to notice the dreamful, dramatic impulse which
leads them to construct it. Now, in my vision, the thievery
of Hermes, and the fact that he was the patron of robbers,
merchants, rhetoricians, and liars, far from being unworthy
of his divine nature, are a superb and humorous expression
of it. He did not steal the cattle of Apollo for profit.
Apollo himself—a most exquisite young god—did not give
a fig for his cattle nor for his rustic employment; in
adopting it he was doing a kind turn to a friend, or had
a love-lorn scheme or a wager afoot, or merely wished for
the moment to be idyllic. It was a pleasant *scherzo* (after
the *andante* which he played in the heavens, in his capacity
of sun-god and inspirer of all prophets) to lean gracefully
here on his herdsman's staff, or to lie under a tuft of trees
on some mossy hillock, in the midst of his pasturing kine,
and to hold the poor peeping dryads spellbound by the
operatic marvels of his singing. In purloining those oxen,
Hermes, who was a very little boy at the time, simply
wanted to mock these affectations of his long-haired elder
brother; and Apollo, truly an enraptured artist and not
a prig, and invulnerable like Hermes in his godlike freedom,
did not in the least mind the practical joke, nor the ridicule,
but was the first to join in the laugh.

When Hermes consents to be the patron of thieves and money-lenders it is in the same spirit. Standing, purse in hand, in his little shrine above their dens, he smiles as if to remind them that everything is trash which mortals can snatch from one another by thieving or bargaining, and that the purpose of all their voyages, and fairs, and highway robberies is a bauble, such as the dirty children playing in the street set up as a counter in their game. But Hermes is not impatient even of the gutter-snipes, with their cries and their shrill quarrels. He laughs at their grimaces; their jests do not seem emptier to him than those of their elders; he is not offended at their rags, but sends sleep to them as they lie huddled under some archway or stretched in the sun upon the temple steps. He presides no less benignly over thieves' kitchens and over the shipyards and counting-houses of traders; not that he cares at all who makes the profit or who hoards the treasure, but that sagacity and the hum of business are delightful to him in themselves. He likes to cull the passion and sparkle out of the most sordid life, and the confused rumble of civilization is pleasant to his senses, like a sweet vapour rising from the evening sacrifice.

His admirable temper and mastery of soul appear in nothing more clearly than in his love-affair with the beautiful Maia. She is ill-spoken of, but he is very, very fond of her, and deeply happy in her love. It is a secret relation, although everybody has heard of it; but the nymph is a mystery; in fact, although everybody has seen her at one time or another, no one has ever known then that it was she. Hermes alone recognizes and loves her in her own person, and calls her by her name; but privately. Sometimes, with that indiscretion and over-familiarity which the young allow themselves in their cups, his brothers ask him where he meets her; and he only smiles a little and is silent. She is said to be a wild unmanageable being, half maenad and half shrew; a waif always appearing and disappearing without any reason, and in her fitful temper at once exacting and tedious. Her eyes are sometimes blue and sometimes black, like heaven. Empty-headed and too gay, some people think her; but others understand that she is constitutionally melancholy and quite mad. They say she often sits alone, hardly distinguishable in the speckled sunshine of the forest, or else by the sea, spreading her hair to the wind and moaning: and then Hermes flies to her and comforts her, for she is an exile everywhere and he is everywhere at home. It is rumoured that in the East she has had a great position, and has been Queen of the Universe; but in Europe she has no settled metaphysical status, and it is not known whether she is really a goddess, mistress over herself, or only a fay or a phantom at other people's beck and call; and she has nowhere any temple or rustic sanctuary or respectable oracle. Moreover, she has inexpressibly shocked the virtuous, who think so much of genealogy, by saying, as is reported, that she has no idea who is the father of her children. Hermes laughs merrily at this, calling it one of her harmless sallies, which she indulges in simply because they occur to her, and because she likes to show her independence and to flout the sober censors of this world. He is perfectly confident she has never had any wooer but himself, nor would dream of accepting any other. Even with him she is always reverting to stubborn refusals and denials and calling him names; but when the spitfire is raging most angrily, he has only to gaze at her steadily and throw his arm gaily about her, as much as to say, "Don't be a fool," for her to be instantly mollified and confess that it was all make-believe, but that she couldn't help it. Then it is wonderful how reasonable she becomes, how perfectly trustful and frank, so that no companion could be more deeply delightful. She is as light as a feather, then, in his arms. The truth is, she lives only for him; she really has no children, only young sisters who are also more or less in love with him and he with them; and she sleeps her whole life long in his absence. In all those strange doings and wanderings reported of her she is only walking in her sleep. The approach of Hermes awakes her and lends her life—the only life she has. Her true name is Illusion; and it is very characteristic of him, so rich in pity, merriment, and shrewdness, to have chosen this poor child, Illusion, for his love.

Hermes is the great interpreter, the master of riddles. I should not honour him for his skill in riddles if I thought he invented them wantonly, because he liked to puzzle himself with them, or to reduce other people to a foolish perplexity without cause. I hate enigmas; and if I believed that Hermes was the inspirer of those odious persons who are always asking conundrums and making puns I should renounce him altogether, break his statue, turn his picture to the wall, and devote myself exclusively to the cult of some sylvan deity, all silence and simple light. But I am sure Hermes loves riddles only because they are no riddles to him; he is never caught in the tangle, and he laughs to see how unnecessarily poor opinionated mortals befool themselves, wilfully following any devious scent once they are on it by chance, and missing the obvious for ever. He gives them what sly hints he can to break the spell of their blindness; but they are so wedded to their false preconceptions that they do not understand him, and are only the more perplexed. Sometimes, however, they take the hint, their wit grows nimble, their thoughts catch fire, and insight, solving every idle riddle, harmonizes the jarring cords of the mind.

The wand of Hermes has serpents wound about it, but is capped with wings, so that at its touch the sting and the coil of care may vanish, and that we may be freed from torpor and dull enchantment, and may see, as the god does, how foolish we are. All these mysteries that befog us are not mysteries really; they are the mother-tongue of nature. Rustics, and also philosophers, think that any language but theirs is gibberish; they are sorry for the stranger who can speak only an unintelligible language, and are sure he will be damned unless the truth is preached to him speedily by some impertinent missionary from their own country. They even argue with nature, trying to convince her that she cannot move, or cannot think, or cannot have more dimensions than those of their understanding. Oh for a touch of the healing wand of Hermes the Interpreter, that we might understand the language of the birds and the stars, and, laughing first at what they say of us, might then see our image in the mirror of infinity, and laugh at ourselves! Here is a kindly god indeed, humane though superhuman, friendly though inviolate, who does not preach, who does not threaten, who does not lay new, absurd, or morose commands on our befuddled souls, but who unravels, who relieves, who shows us the innocence of the things we hated and the clearness of the things we frowned on or denied. He interprets us to the gods, and they accept us; he interprets us to one another, and we perceive that the foreigner, too, spoke a plain language: happy he if he was wise in his own tongue. It is for the divine herald alone to catch the meaning of all, without subduing his merry voice to any dialect of mortals. He mocks our stammerings and forgives them; and when we say anything to the purpose, and reach any goal which, however wantonly, we had proposed to ourselves, he applauds and immensely enjoys our little achievement; for it is inspired by him and like his own. May he be my guide: and not in this world only, in which the way before me seems to descend gently, quite straight and

clear, towards an unruffled sea; but at the frontiers of
eternity let him receive my spirit, reconciling it, by his
gracious greeting, to what had been its destiny. For he
is the friend of the shades also, and makes the greatest
interpretation of all, that of life into truth, translating the
swift words of time into the painted language of eternity.
That is for the dead; but for living men, whose feet must
move forward whilst their eyes see only backward, he
interprets the past to the future, for its guidance and
ornament. Often, too, he bears news to his father and brothers
in Olympus, concerning any joyful or beautiful thing that is
done on earth, lest they should despise or forget it. In that
fair inventory and chronicle of happiness let my love of him
be remembered.

RICHARD STEELE
1672–1729

Steele's prose in the *Tatler,* which he initiated in 1709, is so direct, easy, and graceful, it seems to mirror an age of equal ease, grace, and equanimity. Yet Dr. Johnson wrote that the purpose of the *Tatler* was "to divert the attention of the people from public discontent"; to apply "cooler and more inoffensive reflections" to "minds heated with political contest." And this in fact was Steele's object: to tame a raw and boisterous populace; to teach a new and rapidly growing middle class how to act and speak, even how to feel. He succeeded magnificently because he taught not so much by precept as by charm, by sharp character sketch and amusing anecdote, and by such affectionate warmth as he shows in this *Tatler* paper on the death of his father.

The First Sense of Sorrow

Dies, ni fallor, adest, quem semper acerbum,
Semper honoratum; sic, Dii, voluistis, habebo.

—Virg.

And now the rising day renews the year,
A day for ever sad, for ever dear.

—Dryden

FROM MY OWN APARTMENT, JUNE 5

There are those among Mankind, who can enjoy no Relish of their Being, except the World is made acquainted with all that relates to them, and think every Thing lost that passes unobserved; but others find a solid Delight in stealing by the Crowd, and modelling their Life after such a Manner, as is as much above the Approbation as the practice of the Vulgar. Life being too short to give Instances great enough of true Friendship or Good-Will, some Sages have thought it pious to preserve a certain Reverence for the Manes of their deceased Friends, and have withdrawn themselves from the

338

rest of the World at certain Seasons, to commemorate in their own Thoughts such of their Acquaintance who have gone before them out of this Life: And indeed, when we are advanced in Years, there is not a more pleasing Entertainment, than to recollect in a gloomy Moment the many we have parted with that have been dear and agreeable to us, and to cast a melancholy Thought or Two after those with whom, perhaps, we have indulged our selves in whole Nights of Mirth and Jollity. With such Inclinations in my Heart I went to my Closet Yesterday in the Evening, and resolved to be sorrowful; upon which Occasion, I could not but look with Disdain upon my self, that though all the Reasons which I had to lament the Loss of many of my Friends are now as forcible as at the Moment of their Departure, yet did not my Heart swell with the same Sorrow which I felt at that Time; but I could, without Tears, reflect upon many pleasing Adventures I have had with some who have long been blended with common Earth. Though it is by the Benefit of Nature that Length of Time thus blots out the Violence of Afflictions; yet with Tempers too much given to Pleasure, it is almost necessary to revive the old Places of Grief in our Memory, and ponder Step by Step on past Life, to lead the Mind into that Sobriety of Thought which poises the Heart, and makes it beat with due Time, without being quickened with Desire, or retarded with Despair, from its proper and equal Motion. When we wind up a Clock that is out of Order, to make it go well for the future, we do not immediately set the Hand to the present Instant, but we make it strike the Round of all its Hours, before it can recover the Regularity of its Time. Such, thought I, shall be my Method this Evening; and since it is that Day of the Year which I dedicate to the Memory of such in another Life as I much delighted in when living, an Hour or Two shall be sacred to Sorrow and their Memory, while I run over all the melancholy Circumstances of this Kind which have occurred to me in my whole Life.

The first Sense of Sorrow I ever knew was upon the Death of my Father, at which Time I was not quite Five Years of Age; but was rather amazed at what all the House meant, than possessed with a real Understanding why no Body was willing to play with me. I remember I went into the Room where his Body lay, and my Mother sat weeping alone by it. I had my Battledore in my Hand, and fell a beating the Coffin, and calling Papa; for I know not how I had some slight Idea that he was locked up there. My Mother catched

me in her Arms, and transported beyond all Patience of the
silent Grief she was before in, she almost smothered me in
her Embrace, and told me in a Flood of Tears, Papa could
not hear me, and would play with me no more, for they were
going to put him under Ground, whence he could never come
to us again. She was a very beautiful Woman, of a noble
Spirit, and there was a Dignity in her Grief amidst all the
Wildness of her Transport, which, methought, struck me with
an Instinct of Sorrow, which, before I was sensible of what it
was to grieve, seized my very Soul, and has made Pity the
Weakness of my Heart ever since. The Mind in Infancy is,
methinks, like the Body in Embrio, and receives Impressions
so forcible, that they are as hard to be removed by Reason,
as any Mark with which a Child is born is to be taken away
by any future Application. Hence it is, that Good-Nature in
me is no Merit; but having been so frequently over-whelmed
with her Tears before I knew the Cause of any Affliction, or
could draw Defences from my own Judgment, I imbibed
Commiseration, Remorse, and an unmanly Gentleness of
Mind, which has since insnared me into Ten Thousand
Calamities, and from whence I can reap no Advantage, except
it be, that in such an Humour as I am now in, I can the
better indulge my self in the Softnesses of Humanity, and
enjoy that sweet Anxiety which arises from the Memory of
past Afflictions.

We that are very old, are better able to remember Things
which befel us in our distant Youth, than the Passages of
later Days. For this Reason it is, that the Companions of my
strong and vigorous Years present themselves more immediately to me in this Office of Sorrow. Untimely or unhappy
Deaths are what we are most apt to lament, so little are we
able to make it indifferent when a Thing happens, though we
know it must happen. Thus we groan under Life, and bewail
those who are relieved from it. Every Object that returns to
our Imagination raises different Passions, according to the
Circumstance of their Departure. Who can have lived in an
Army, and in a serious Hour reflect upon the many gay and
agreeable Men that might long have flourished in the Arts of
Peace, and not join with the Imprecations of the Fatherless
and Widow on the Tyrant to whose Ambition they fell
Sacrifices? But gallant Men, who are cut off by the Sword,
move rather our Veneration than our Pity, and we gather Relief enough from their own Contempt of Death, to make it no
Evil, which was approached with so much Chearfulness, and

attended with so much Honour. But when we turn our
Thoughts from the great Parts of Life on such Occasions, and
instead of lamenting those who stood ready to give Death to
those from whom they had the Fortune to receive it; I say,
when we let our Thoughts wander from such noble Objects,
and consider the Havock which is made among the Tender
and the Innocent, Pity enters with an unmixed Softness, and
possesses all our Souls at once.

Here (were there Words to express such Sentiments with
proper Tenderness) I should record the Beauty, Innocence,
and untimely Death, of the first Object my Eyes ever beheld
with Love. The beauteous Virgin! How ignorantly did she
charm, how carelessly excel? Oh Death! Thou hast Right to
the Bold, to the Ambitious, to the High, and to the Haughty;
but why this Cruelty to the Humble, to the Meek, to the Un-
discerning, to the Thoughtless? Nor Age, nor Business, nor
Distress, can erase the dear Image from my Imagination. In
the same Week, I saw her dressed for a Ball, and in a Shrowd.
How ill did the Habit of Death become the Pretty Trifler? I
still behold the smiling Earth—A large Train of Disasters
were coming on to my Memory, when my Servant knocked at
my Closet Door, and interrupted me with a Letter, attended
with a Hamper of Wine, of the same Sort with that which is
to be put to Sale on *Thursday* next at Garraway's Coffee-
house. Upon the Receipt of it, I sent for Three of my Friends.
We are so intimate, that we can be Company in whatever
State of Mind we meet, and can entertain each other without
expecting always to rejoice. The Wine we found to be generous and warming, but with such an Heat as moved us rather
to be chearful than frolicksome. It revived the Spirits without
firing the Blood. We commended it till Two of the Clock this
Morning, and having to Day met a little before Dinner, we
found, that though we drank Two Bottles a Man, we had
much more Reason to recollect than forget what had passed
the Night before.

ROBERT LOUIS STEVENSON
1850–1894

His was a continuing struggle for health against death, a passionate determination to lead, in Scotland, on the Continent, in America, in Samoa, or wherever necessary, a full and creative working life despite every obstacle. Such toughening experiences, superimposed upon his native genius and his close study of Montaigne, Sir Thomas Browne, Hazlitt, Lamb, and other writers possessed of "some conspicuous force or some happy distinction in the style," lent strength and variety to the natural grace and charm of Stevenson's work as an essayist. These are the qualities so clearly visible in the essay printed here, "Æs Triplex," plus an understated but inescapable note of fortitude. For Æs Triplex stands for triple brass, the three-fold armor which supported Dr. Johnson's courageous heart as he toured in old age through the Highlands (see p. 188), and the same armor which Stevenson wore in the continual presence of death. The pathos and excitement of Stevenson's fight for life, indeed, combined with the controversy and special pleading frequently occasioned by his work, have had the result that throughout the twentieth century the author of *Treasure Island, The Strange Case of Dr. Jekyll and Mr. Hyde,* and *A Child's Garden of Verses* has been a most popular subject for biographers and critics. "My fame will not last more than four years," lamented Stevenson to his wife shortly before his death. But as we go to press, almost eighteen times four years have elapsed, and "R. L. S." is still very much an author people are both reading and reading about.

Æs Triplex

The changes wrought by death are in themselves so sharp and final, and so terrible and melancholy in their consequences, that the thing stands alone in man's experience, and has no parallel upon earth. It outdoes all other accidents because it is the last of them. Sometimes it leaps suddenly upon its victims like a Thug; sometimes it lays a regular siege and creeps upon their citadel during a score of years. And when the business is done, there is sore havoc made in other people's lives, and a pin knocked out by which many subsidiary friendships hung together. There are empty chairs, solitary walks, and single beds at night. Again, in taking away our friends, death does not take them away utterly, but leaves behind a mocking, tragical, and soon intolerable residue, which must be hurriedly concealed. Hence a whole chapter of sights and customs striking to the mind, from the pyramids of Egypt to the gibbets and dule trees of mediæval Europe. The poorest persons have a bit of pageant going toward the tomb; memorial stones are set up over the least memorable; and, in order to preserve some show of respect for what remains of our old loves and friendships, we must accompany it with much grimly ludicrous ceremonial, and the hired undertaker parades before the door. All this, and much more of the same sort, accompanied by the eloquence of poets, has gone a great way to put humanity in error; nay, in many philosophies the error has been embodied and laid down with every circumstance of logic; although in real life the bustle and swiftness, in leaving people little time to think, have not left them enough to go dangerously wrong in practice.

As a matter of fact, although few things are spoken of with more fearful whisperings than this prospect of death, few have less influence on conduct under healthy circumstances. We have all heard of cities in South America built upon the side of fiery mountains, and how, even in this tremendous neighborhood, the inhabitants are not a jot more impressed by the solemnity of mortal conditions than if they were delving gardens in the greenest corner of England. There are serenades and suppers and much gallantry among the myrtles overhead; and meanwhile the foundation shudders underfoot, the bowels of the mountain growl, and at any moment living ruin may leap sky-high into the moonlight, and tumble man and his merry-making in the dust. In the eyes of very young people, and very dull old ones, there is something indescribably reckless and desperate in such a picture. It seems not credible that respectable married people, with umbrellas, should find appetite for a bit of supper within quite a long distance of a fiery mountain; ordinary life begins to smell of high-handed *debauch* when it is carried on so close to a catastrophe; and even cheese and salad, it seems, could hardly be relished in

such circumstances without something like a defiance of the
Creator. It should be a place for nobody but hermits dwelling
in prayer and *maceration*, or mere born-devils drowning care
in a perpetual carouse.

And yet, when one comes to think upon it calmly, the situation of these South American citizens forms only a very pale
figure for the state of ordinary mankind. This world itself,
travelling blindly and swiftly in overcrowded space, among
a million other worlds travelling blindly and swiftly in contrary directions, may very well come by a knock that would
set it into explosion like a penny squib. And what, *patho-
logically* looked at, is the human body with all its organs, but
a mere bagful of *petards?* The least of these is as dangerous
to the whole economy as the ship's powder-magazine to the
ship; and with every breath we breathe, and every meal we
eat, we are putting one or more of them in peril. If we clung
as devotedly as some philosophers pretend we do to the
abstract idea of life, or were half as frightened as they make
out we are, for the subversive accident that ends it all, the
trumpets might sound by the hour and no one would follow
them into battle—the blue peter might fly at the truck, but who
would climb into a seagoing ship? Think (if these philosophers
were right) with what a preparation of spirit we should affront
the daily peril of the dinner-table: a deadlier spot than any
battle-field in history, where the far greater proportion of
our ancestors have miserably left their bones! What woman
would ever be lured into marriage, so much more dangerous
than the wildest sea? And what would it be to grow old? For,
after a certain distance, every step we take in life we find
the ice growing thinner below our feet, and all around us and
behind us we see our contemporaries going through. By the
time a man gets well into the seventies, his continued existence
is a mere miracle; and when he lays his old bones in bed for
the night, there is an overwhelming probability that he will
never see the day. Do the old men mind it, as a matter of
fact? Why, no. They were never merrier; they have their
grog at night, and tell the raciest stories; they hear of the
death of people about their own age, or even younger, not as
if it was a grisly warning, but with a simple childlike pleasure
at having outlived some one else; and when a draught might
puff them out like a guttering candle, or a bit of a stumble
shatter them like so much glass, their old hearts keep sound
and unaffrighted, and they go on, bubbling with laughter,
through years of man's age compared to which the valley of

Balaclava was as safe and peaceful as a village cricket-green on Sunday. It may fairly be questioned (if we look to the peril only) whether it was a much more daring feat for Curtius to plunge into the gulf, than for any old gentleman of ninety to doff his clothes and clamber into bed.

Indeed, it is a memorable subject for consideration, with what unconcern and gaiety mankind pricks on along the Valley of the Shadow of Death. The whole way is one wilderness of snares, and the end of it, for those who fear the last pinch, is irrevocable ruin. And yet we go spinning through it all, like a party for the Derby. Perhaps the reader remembers one of the humorous devices of the deified Caligula: how he encouraged a vast concourse of holiday-makers on to his bridge over Baiæ bay; and when they were in the height of their enjoyment, turned loose the Prætorian guards among the company, and had them tossed into the sea. This is no bad miniature of the dealings of nature with the transitory race of man. Only, what a checkered picnic we have of it, even while it lasts! and into what great waters, not to be crossed by any swimmer, God's pale Prætorian throws us over in the end!

We live the time that a match flickers; we pop the cork of a ginger-beer bottle, and the earthquake swallows us on the instant. Is it not odd, is it not incongruous, is it not, in the highest sense of human speech, incredible, that we should think so highly of the ginger-beer, and regard so little the devouring earthquake? The love of Life and the fear of Death are two famous phrases that grow harder to understand the more we think about them. It is a well-known fact that an immense proportion of boat accidents would never happen if people held the sheet in their hands instead of making it fast; and yet, unless it be some martinet of a professional mariner or some landsman with shattered nerves, every one of God's creatures makes it fast. A strange instance of man's unconcern and brazen boldness in the face of death!

We confound ourselves with metaphysical phrases, which we import into daily talk with noble inappropriateness. We have no idea of what death is, apart from its circumstances and some of its consequences to others; and although we have some experience of living, there is not a man on earth who has flown so high into abstraction as to have any practical guess at the meaning of the word *life*. All literature, from Job and Omar Khayyam to Thomas Carlyle or Walt Whitman, is but an attempt to look upon the human state with such

largeness of view as shall enable us to rise from the consideration of living to the Definition of Life. And our sages give
us about the best satisfaction in their power when they say
that it is a vapor, or a show, or made of the same stuff with
dreams. Philosophy, in its more rigid sense, has been at the
same work for ages; and after a myriad bald heads have
wagged over the problem, and piles of words have been heaped
one upon another into dry and cloudy volumes without end,
philosophy has the honor of laying before us, with modest
pride, her contribution toward the subject: that life is a
Permanent Possibility of Sensation. Truly a fine result! A man
may very well love beef, or hunting, or a woman; but surely,
surely, not a Permanent Possibility of Sensation! He may be
afraid of a precipice, or a dentist, or a large enemy with a
club, or even an undertaker's man; but not certainly of abstract
death. We may trick with the word life in its dozen senses until
we are weary of tricking; we may argue in terms of all the
philosophies on earth, but one fact remains true throughout—
that we do not love life, in the sense that we are greatly
preoccupied about its conservation—that we do not, properly
speaking, love life at all, but living. Into the views of the least
careful there will enter some degree of providence; no man's
eyes are fixed entirely on the passing hour; but although we
have some anticipation of good health, good weather, wine,
active employment, love, and self-approval, the sum of these
anticipations does not amount to anything like a general view
of life's possibilities and issues; nor are those who cherish
them most vividly, at all the most scrupulous of their personal
safety. To be deeply interested in the accidents of our existence, to enjoy keenly the mixed texture of human experience,
rather leads a man to disregard precautions, and risk his neck
against a straw. For surely the love of living is stronger in an
Alpine climber roping over a peril, or a hunter riding merrily
at a stiff fence, than in a creature who lives upon a diet and
walks a measured distance in the interest of his constitution.

There is a great deal of very vile nonsense talked upon both
sides of the matter: tearing divines reducing life to the dimensions of a mere funeral procession, so short as to be hardly
decent; and melancholy unbelievers yearning for the tomb
as if it were a world too far away. Both sides must feel a
little ashamed of their performances now and again when
they draw in their chairs to dinner. Indeed, a good meal and
a bottle of wine is an answer to most standard works upon
the question. When a man's heart warms to his viands, he

forgets a great deal of sophistry, and soars into a rosy zone of contemplation. Death may be knocking at the door, like the Commander's statue; we have something else in hand, thank God, and let him knock. Passing bells are ringing all the world over. All the world over, and every hour, some one is parting company with all his aches and ecstasies. For us also the trap is laid. But we are so fond of life that we have no leisure to entertain the terror of death. It is a honeymoon with us all through, and none of the longest. Small blame to us if we give our whole hearts to this glowing bride of ours, to the appetites, to honor, to the hungry curiosity of the mind, to the pleasure of the eyes in nature, and the pride of our own nimble bodies.

We all of us appreciate the sensations; but as for caring about the Permanence of the Possibility, a man's head is generally very bald, and his senses very dull, before he comes to that. Whether we regard life as a lane leading to a dead wall—a mere bag's end, as the French say—or whether we think of it as a vestibule or gymnasium, where we wait our turn and prepare our faculties for some more noble destiny; whether we thunder in a pulpit, or pule in little atheistic poetry-books, about its vanity and brevity; whether we look justly for years of health and vigor, or are about to mount into a Bath chair, as a step toward the hearse; in each and all of these views and situations there is but one conclusion possible: that a man should stop his ears against paralyzing terror, and run the race that is set before him with a single mind. No one surely could have recoiled with more heartache and terror from the thought of death than our respected lexicographer; and yet we know how little it affected his conduct, how wisely and boldly he walked, and in what a fresh and lively vein he spoke of life. Already an old man, he ventured on his Highland tour; and his heart, bound with triple brass, did not recoil before twenty-seven individual cups of tea. As courage and intelligence are the two qualities best worth a good man's cultivation, so it is the first part of intelligence to recognize our precarious estate in life, and the first part of courage to be not at all abashed before the fact. A frank and somewhat headlong carriage, not looking too anxiously before, not dallying in maudlin regret over the past, stamps the man who is well armored for this world.

And not only well armored for himself, but a good friend and a good citizen to boot. We do not go to cowards for tender dealing; there is nothing so cruel as panic; the man who has

least fear for his own carcass, has most time to consider
others. That eminent chemist who took his walks abroad in
tin shoes, and subsisted wholly upon tepid milk, had all his
work cut out for him in considerate dealings with his own
digestion. So soon as prudence has begun to grow up in the
brain, like a dismal fungus, it finds its first expression in a
paralysis of generous acts. The victim begins to shrink spiritually; he develops a fancy for parlors with a regulated temperature, and takes his morality on the principle of tin shoes
and tepid milk. The care of one important body or soul
becomes so engrossing, that all noises of the outer world
begin to come thin and faint into the parlor with the regulated
temperature; and the tin shoes go equably forward over blood
and rain. To be overwise is to ossify; and the scruple-monger
ends by standing stock-still. Now the man who has his heart
on his sleeve, and a good whirling weathercock of a brain,
who reckons his life as a thing to be dashingly used and
cheerfully hazarded, makes a very different acquaintance of
the world, keeps all his pulses going true and fast, and gathers
impetus as he runs, until, if he be running toward anything
better than wildfire, he may shoot up and become a constella-
tion in the end. Lord, look after his health; Lord, have a care
of his soul, says he; and he has at the key of the position, and
swashes through incongruity and peril toward his aim. Death
is on all sides of him with pointed batteries, as he is on all
sides of all of us; unfortunate surprises gird him round; mim-
mouthed friends and relations hold up their hands in quite
a little elegiacal synod about his path: and what cares he for
all this? Being a true lover of living, a fellow with something
pushing and spontaneous in his inside, he must, like any other
soldier, in any other stirring, deadly warfare, push on at his
best pace until he touch the goal. "A peerage or Westminster
Abbey!" cried Nelson in his bright, boyish, heroic manner.
These are great incentives; not for any of these, but for the
plain satisfaction of living, of being about their business in
some sort or other, do the brave, serviceable men of every
nation tread down the nettle danger, and pass flyingly over
all the stumbling-blocks of prudence. Think of the heroism
of Johnson, think of that superb indifference to mortal limitation that set him upon his dictionary, and carried through
triumphantly until the end! Who, if he were wisely considerate
of things at large, would ever embark upon any work much
more considerable than a half penny post card? Who would
project a serial novel, after Thackeray and Dickens had each

fallen in mid-course? Who would find heart enough to begin to live, if he dallied with the consideration of death?

And, after all, what sorry and pitiful quibbling all this is! To forego all the issues of living in a parlor with the regulated temperature—as if that were not to die a hundred times over, and for ten years at a stretch! As if it were not to die in one's own lifetime, and without even the sad immunities of death! As if it were not to die, and yet be the patient spectators of our own pitiable change! The Permanent Possibility is preserved, but the sensations carefully held at arm's length, as if one kept a photographic plate in a dark chamber. It is better to lose health like a spendthrift than to waste it like a miser. It is better to live and be done with it, than to die daily in the sickroom. By all means begin your folio; even if the doctor does not give you a year, even if he hesitates about a month, make one brave push and see what can be accomplished in a week. It is not only in finished undertakings that we ought to honor useful labor. A spirit goes out of the man who means execution, which outlives the most untimely ending. All who have meant good work with their whole hearts, have done good work, although they may die before they have the time to sign it. Every heart that has beat strong and cheerfully has left a hopeful impulse behind it in the world, and bettered the tradition of mankind. And even if death catch people, like an open pitfall, and in mid-career, laying out vast projects, and planning monstrous foundations, flushed with hope, and their mouths full of boastful languages, they should be at once tripped up and silenced: is there not something brave and spirited in such a termination? and does not life go down with a better grace, foaming in full body over a precipice, than miserably straggling to an end in sandy deltas? When the Greeks made their fine saying that those whom the gods love die young, I cannot help believing they had this sort of death also in their eye. For surely at whatever age it overtake the man, this is to die young. Death has not been suffered to take so much as an illusion from his heart. In the hot-fit of life, a-tiptoe on the highest point of being, he passes at a bound on to the other side. The noise of the mallet and chisel is scarcely quenched, the trumpets are hardly done blowing, when, trailing with him clouds of glory, this happy-starred, full-blooded spirit shoots into the spiritual land.

JONATHAN SWIFT
1667–1745

"Where savage indignation can no longer tear his heart," are the words inscribed in Latin on Jonathan Swift's grave in St. Patrick's Cathedral, Dublin, where he was Dean for thirty-two years. That savage indignation, shaped and controlled by art, underlies the disarming simplicity of "A Modest Proposal," as it erupts in the biting satire of *Gulliver's Travels*. But Swift addressed *Gulliver* to the human race; "A Modest Proposal" he intended "for this one individual kingdom of Ireland, and for no other that ever was, is, or I think, can ever be upon Earth." It was to lighten the oppression of the Irish people, whom he saw "living in Filth and Nastiness . . . without . . . a House so convenient as an English-Hog-sty to receive them," that he wrote a series of pamphlets, culminating in "A Modest Proposal" in 1728.

A Modest Proposal for Preventing the Children of Poor People in Ireland from Being a Burden to Their Parents or Country, and for Making Them Beneficial to the Public

It is a melancholy object to those who walk through this great town, or travel in the country, when they see the streets, the roads and cabin-doors crowded with beggars of the female sex, followed by three, four, or six children, all in rags, and importuning every passenger for an alms. These mothers, instead of being able to work for their honest livelihood, are forced to employ all their time in strolling, to beg sustenance for their helpless infants, who, as they grow up, either turn thieves for want of work, or leave their dear native country to fight for the Pretender in Spain, or sell themselves to the Barbadoes.

I think is is agreed by all parties that this prodigious number of children, in the arms, or on the backs, or at the heels of their mothers, and frequently of their fathers, is in the present deplorable state of the kingdom a very great additional grievance; and therefore whoever could find out a fair, cheap, and easy method of making these children sound and useful members of the commonwealth would deserve so well of the public as to have his statue set up for a preserver of the nation.

But my intention is very far from being confined to provide only for the children of professed beggars; it is of a much greater extent, and shall take in the whole number of infants at a certain age who are born of parents in effect as little able to support them as those who demand our charity in the streets.

As to my own part, having turned my thoughts for many years upon this important subject, and maturely weighed the several schemes of other projectors, I have always found them grossly mistaken in their computation. It is true a child just dropped from its dam may be supported by her milk for a solar year with little other nourishment, at most not above the value of two shillings, which the mother may certainly get, or the value in scraps, by her lawful occupation of begging, and it is exactly at one year old that I propose to provide for them, in such a manner as, instead of being a charge upon their parents, or the parish, or wanting food and raiment for the rest of their lives, they shall, on the contrary, contribute to the feeding and partly to the clothing of many thousands.

There is likewise another great advantage in my scheme, that it will prevent those voluntary abortions, and that horrid practice of women murdering their bastard children, alas, too frequent among us, sacrificing the poor innocent babes, I doubt, more to avoid the expense than the shame, which would move tears and pity in the most savage and inhuman breast.

The number of souls in Ireland being usually reckoned one million and a half, of these I calculate there may be about two hundred thousand couples whose wives are breeders, from which number I subtract thirty thousand couples who are able to maintain their own children, although I apprehend there cannot be so many under the present distresses of the kingdom, but this being granted, there will remain an hundred and seventy thousand breeders. I again subtract fifty thousand for those women who miscarry, or whose children die by accident or disease within the year. There only remain an hundred and twenty thousand children of poor parents annually born: the question therefore is, how this number shall be reared, and provided for, which, as I have already said, under the present situation of affairs is utterly impossible by all the methods hitherto proposed, for we can neither employ them in handicraft or agriculture; we neither build houses (I mean in the country), nor cultivate land: they can very seldom pick up a livelihood by stealing until they arrive at six years old, except where they are of towardly parts, although I confess they learn the rudiments much earlier, during which time they can however be properly looked upon only as probationers, as I have been informed by a principal gentleman in the County of Cavan, who protested to me that he never knew above one or two instances under the age of six, even in a part of the kingdom so renowned for the quickest proficiency in that art.

I am assured by our merchants that a boy or a girl before twelve years old, is no saleable commodity, and even when they come to this age, they will not yield above three pounds, or three pounds and half-a-crown at most on the Exchange, which cannot turn to account either to the parents or the kingdom, the charge of nutriment and rags having been at least four times that value.

I shall now therefore humbly propose my own thoughts, which I hope will not be liable to the least objection.

I have been assured by a very knowing American of my acquaintance in London, that a young healthy child well nursed is at a year old a most delicious, nourishing and wholesome food, whether stewed, roasted, baked, or boiled, and I make no doubt that it will equally serve in a fricassee, or a ragout.

I do therefore humbly offer it to public consideration, that of the hundred and twenty thousand children already computed, twenty thousand may be reserved for breed, whereof only one fourth part to be males, which is more than we allow to sheep, black-cattle, or swine, and my reason is that these children are seldom the fruits of marriage, a circumstance not much regarded by our savages, therefore one male will be sufficient to serve four females. That the remaining hundred thousand may at a year old be offered in sale to the persons of quality, and fortune, through the kingdom, always advising the mother to let them suck plentifully in the last month, so as to render them plump, and fat for a good table. A child will make two dishes at an entertainment for friends, and when the family dines alone, the fore or hind quarter will make a reasonable dish, and seasoned with a little pepper or salt will be very good boiled on the fourth day, especially in winter.

I have reckoned upon a medium, that a child just born will weigh twelve pounds, and in a solar year if tolerably nursed increaseth to twenty-eight pounds.

I grant this food will be somewhat dear, and therefore very proper for landlords, who, as they have already devoured most of the parents, seem to have the best title to the children.

Infant's flesh will be in season throughout the year, but more plentiful in March, and a little before and after, for we are told by a grave* author, an eminent French physician, that fish being a prolific diet, there are more children born in Roman Catholic countries about nine months after Lent than at any other season; therefore reckoning a year after Lent, the markets will be more glutted than usual, because the number of Popish infants is at least three to one in this kingdom, and therefore it will have one other collateral advantage by lessening the number of Papists among us.

I have already computed the charge of nursing a beggar's child (in which list I reckon all cottagers, labourers, and four-fifths of the farmers) to be about two shillings *per annum*, rags included, and I believe no gentleman would repine to give ten shillings for the carcass of a good fat child, which, as I have said, will make four dishes of excellent nutritive meat, when he hath only some particular friend or his own family to dine with him. Thus the Squire will learn to be a good landlord and grow popular among his tenants, the mother will have eight shillings net profit, and be fit for work until she produces another child.

Those who are more thrifty (as I must confess the times require) may flay the carcass; the skin of which artificially dressed, will make admirable gloves for ladies, and summer boots for fine gentlemen.

As to our city of Dublin, shambles may be appointed for this purpose, in the most convenient parts of it, and butchers we may be assured will not be wanting, although I rather recommend buying the children alive, and dressing them hot from the knife, as we do roasting pigs.

A very worthy person, a true lover of his country, and whose virtues I highly esteem, was lately pleased, in discours-

* Rabelais

ing on this matter to offer a refinement upon my scheme. He said that many gentlemen of this kingdom, having of late destroyed their deer, he conceived that the want of venison might be well supplied by the bodies of young lads and maidens, not exceeding fourteen years of age, nor under twelve, so great a number of both sexes in every county being now ready to starve, for want of work and service: and these to be disposed of by their parents if alive, or otherwise by their nearest relations. But with due deference to so excellent a friend, and so deserving a patriot, I cannot be altogether in his sentiments. For as to the males, my American acquaintance assured me from frequent experience that their flesh was generally tough and lean, like that of our schoolboys, by continual exercise, and their taste disagreeable, and to fatten them would not answer the charge. Then as to the females, it would, I think with humble submission, be a loss to the public, because they soon would become breeders themselves: and besides, it is not improbable that some scrupulous people might be apt to censure such a practice (although indeed very unjustly) as a little bordering upon cruelty, which I confess, hath always been with me the strongest objection against any project, howsoever well intended.

But in order to justify my friend, he confessed that this expedient was put into his head by the famous Psalmanazar, a native of the island Formosa, who came from thence to London, above twenty years ago, and in conversation told my friend that in his country when any young person happened to be put to death, the executioner sold the carcass to persons of quality, as a prime dainty, and that, in his time, the body of a plump girl of fifteen, who was crucified for an attempt to poison the emperor, was sold to his Imperial Majesty's Prime Minister of State, and other great Mandarins of the Court, in joints from the gibbet, at four hundred crowns. Neither indeed can I deny that if the same use were made of several plump young girls in this town who, without one single groat to their fortunes, cannot stir abroad without a chair, and appear at the playhouse and assemblies in foreign fineries, which they never will pay for, the kingdom would not be the worse.

Some persons of a desponding spirit are in great concern about that vast number of poor people, who are aged, diseased, or maimed, and I have been desired to employ my thoughts what course may be taken to ease the nation of so grievous an encumbrance. But I am not in the least pain upon that matter, because it is very well known that they are every day dying, and rotting, by cold, and famine, and filth, and vermin, as fast as can be reasonably expected. And as to the younger labourers they are now in almost as hopeful a condition. They cannot get work, and consequently pine away from want of nourishment, to a degree that if at any time they are accidentally hired to common labour, they have not strength to perform it; and thus the country and themselves are in a fair way of being soon delivered from the evils to come.

I have too long disgressed, and therefore shall return to my subject. I think the advantages by the proposal which I have made are obvious and many, as well as of the highest importance.

For first, as I have already observed, it would greatly lessen the number of Papists, with whom we are yearly over-run, being the principal breeders of the nation, as well as our most dangerous enemies, and who stay at home on purpose with a design to deliver the kingdom to the Pretender, hoping to take their advantage by the absence of so many good Protestants, who have chosen rather to leave their country than stay at home and pay tithes against their conscience to an idolatrous Episcopal curate.

Secondly, the poorer tenants will have something valuable of their own, which by law may be made liable to distress, and help to pay their landlord's rent, their corn and cattle being already seized, and money a thing unknown.

Thirdly, whereas the maintenance of an hundred thousand children, from two years old, and upwards, cannot be computed at less than ten shillings a piece *per annum,* the nation's stock will be thereby increased fifty thousand pounds *per annum,* besides the profit of a new dish, introduced to the tables of all gentlemen of fortune in the kingdom, who have any refinement in taste, and the money will circulate among ourselves, the goods being entirely of our own growth and manufacture.

Fourthly, the constant breeders, besides the gain of eight shillings sterling *per annum,* by the sale of their children, will be rid of the charge of maintaining them after the first year.

Fifthly, this food would likewise bring great custom to taverns, where the vintners will certainly be so prudent as to procure the best receipts for dressing it to perfection, and consequently have their houses frequented by all the fine gentlemen, who justly value themselves upon their knowledge in good eating; and a skilful cook, who understands how to oblige his guests, will contrive to make it as expensive as they please.

Sixthly, this would be a great inducement to marriage, which all wise nations have either encouraged by rewards, or enforced by laws and penalties. It would increase the care and tenderness of mothers towards their children, when they were sure of a settlement for life, to the poor babes, provided in some sort by the public to their annual profit instead of expense. We should soon see an honest emulation among the married women, which of them could bring the fattest child to the market. Men would become as fond of their wives, during the time of their pregnancy, as they are now of their mares in foal, their cows in calf, or sows when they are ready to farrow, nor offer to beat or kick them (as it is too frequent a practice) for fear of a miscarriage.

Many other advantages might be enumerated. For instance, the addition of some thousand carcasses in our exportation of barrelled beef; the propagation of swine's flesh, and improvement in the art of making good bacon, so much wanted among us by the great destruction of pigs, too frequent at our tables, are no way comparable in taste or magnificence to a well-grown, fat yearling child, which roasted whole will make a considerable figure at a Lord Mayor's feast, or any other public entertainment. But this and many others I omit, being studious of brevity.

Supposing that one thousand families in this city would be constant customers for infants flesh, besides others who might have it at merry meetings, particularly weddings and christenings; I compute that Dublin would take off annually about twenty thousand carcasses, and the rest of the kingdom (where probably they will be sold somewhat cheaper) the remaining eighty thousand.

I can think of no one objection that will possibly be raised against this proposal, unless it should be urged that the number of people will be thereby much lessened in the kingdom. This I freely own, and it was indeed one principal design in offering it to the world. I desire the reader will observe, that I calculate my remedy *for this one individual Kingdom of* Ireland, *and for no other that ever was, is, or, I think, ever can be upon earth.* Therefore let no man talk to me of other expedients: *Of taxing our absentees at five shillings a pound: Of using neither clothes, nor household furniture, except what is of our own growth and manufacture: Of utterly rejecting the materials and instruments that promote foreign* luxury: *Of curing the expensiveness of pride, vanity, idleness, and gaming in our women: Of introducing a vein of parsimony, prudence, and temperance: Of learning to love our country, wherein we differ even from* Laplanders, *and the inhabitants of* Topinamboo: *Of quitting our animosities and factions, nor act any longer like the* Jews, *who were murdering one another at the very moment their city was taken: Of being a little cautious not to sell our country and consciences for nothing: Of teaching landlords to have at least one degree of mercy towards their tenants.* Lastly, *of putting a spirit of honesty, industry, and skill into our shopkeepers, who, if a resolution could now be taken to buy only our native goods, would immediately unite to cheat and exact upon us in the price, the measure and the goodness, nor could ever yet be brought to make one fair proposal of just dealing, though often and earnestly invited to it.*

Therefore I repeat, let no man talk to me of these and the like expedients, till he hath at least a glimpse of hope that there will ever be some hearty and sincere attempt to put them in practice.

But as to myself, having been wearied out for many years with offering vain, idle, visionary thoughts, and at length utterly despairing of success, I fortunately fell upon this proposal, which as it is wholly new, so it hath something solid and real, of no expense and little trouble, full in our own power, and whereby we can incur no danger in disobliging England. For this kind of commodity will not bear exportation, the flesh being of too tender a consistence to admit a long continuance in salt, *although perhaps I could name a country which would be glad to eat up our whole nation without it.*

After all I am not so violently bent upon my own opinion as to reject any offer, proposed by wise men, which shall be found equally innocent, cheap, easy and effectual. But before some thing of that kind shall be advanced in contradiction to my scheme, and offering a better, I desire the author, or authors, will be pleased maturely to consider two points. First, as things now stand, how they will be able to find food and raiment for a hundred thousand useless mouths and backs? And secondly, there being a round million of creatures in human figure, throughout this kingdom, whose whole subsistence put into a common stock would leave them in debt two millions of pounds sterling; adding those who are beggars by profession, to the bulk of farmers, cottagers, and labourers with their wives and children, who are beggars in effect; I desire those politicians who dislike my overture, and may perhaps be so bold to attempt an answer, that they will first ask the parents of these mortals whether they would not at this day think it a great happiness to have been sold for food at a year old, in the manner I prescribe, and thereby have avoided such a perpetual scene of misfortunes as they have since gone through, by the oppression of landlords, the impossibility of paying rent without money or trade, the want of common sustenance, with neither house nor clothes to cover them from the inclemencies of weather, and the most inevitable prospect of entailing the like, or greater miseries upon their breed for ever.

I profess in the sincerity of my heart that I have not the least personal interest in endeavouring to promote this necessary work, having no other motive than the *public good of my country, by advancing our trade, providing for infants, relieving the poor, and giving some pleasure to the rich.* I have no children by which I can propose to get a single penny; the youngest being nine years old, and my wife past childbearing.

JEREMY TAYLOR
1613–1667

Because the main stream of our thinking today is so largely secular, it is hard for us to realize the extent to which religious concerns dominated the thinking of the seventeenth century. Laity and clergy, tinkers and scholars, merchants and lords, all pondered, discussed, argued, and bloodily fought over doctrinal questions that have long since been settled or forgotten. Religious writings of all kinds poured from the presses. "Why, sir," commented Dr. Johnson in the next century, "you are to consider that sermons make a considerable branch of English literature"; and sermons had already made a considerable branch a hundred years earlier. In addition, there were controversial tracts and books of prayers, meditations, and moral advice. Under these circumstances, many of the most gifted writers of the times naturally took religion for their subject, with the result that they are less widely read today than their talents would justify. So noted a preacher as Jeremy Taylor, for instance, is now almost forgotten; unlike Donne, he wrote no poems for the twentieth century to rediscover. Yet the magnificent periods of Taylor's sermons still enchant the ear; and the "rules and exercises" he framed in his *Holy Living,* to guide men to a virtuous life, still have the impress of art and the ring of incontestable truth.

Of Modesty

Modesty is the appendage of sobriety, and is to chastity, to temperance, and to humility, as the fringes are to a garment. It is a grace of God, that moderates the over-activeness and curiosity of the mind, and orders the passions of the body and external actions, and is directly opposed to curiosity, to boldness, to indecency. The practice of modesty consists in these following rules.

ACTS AND DUTIES OF MODESTY, AS IT IS OPPOSED TO CURIOSITY

1. Inquire not into the secrets of God, but be content to learn thy duty according to the quality of thy person or employment: that is, plainly, if thou beest not concerned in the conduct of others; but if thou beest a teacher, learn it so as may best enable thee to discharge thy office. God's commandments were proclaimed to all the world; but God's counsels are to himself and to his secret ones, when they are admitted within the veil.

2. Inquire not into the things which are too hard for thee, but learn modestly to know thy infirmities and abilities; and raise not thy mind up to inquire into mysteries of state, or the secrets of government, or difficulties theological, if thy employment really be, or thy understanding be judged to be, of a lower rank.

3. Let us not inquire into the affairs of others that concern us not, but be busied within ourselves and our own spheres; ever remembering that to pry into the actions or interests of other men not under our charge, may minister to pride, to tyranny, to uncharitableness, to trouble, but can never consist with modesty; unless where duty or the mere intentions of charity and relation do warrant it.

4. Never listen at the doors or windows: for, besides that it contains in it danger and a snare, it is also an invading my neighbor's privacy, and a laying that open which he therefore enclosed that it might not be open. Never ask what he carries covered so curiously; for it is enough that it is covered curiously. Hither, also, is reducible that we never open letters without public authority, or reasonable presumed leave, or great necessity, or charity.

Every man hath in his own life sins enough, in his own mind trouble enough, in his own fortune evils enough, and in performance of his offices failings more than enough, to entertain his own inquiry; so that curiosity after the affairs of others cannot be without envy and an evil mind. What is it to me, if my neighbor's grandfather were a Syrian, or his grandmother illegitimate; or that another is indebted five thousand pounds, or whether his wife be expensive? But commonly curious persons, or (as the apostle's phrase is) "busy-bodies," are not solicitous or inquisitive into the beauty and order of a well-governed family, or after the virtues of an excellent person; but if there be any thing for which men keep locks, and bars, and porters, things that blush to see the light, and either are shameful in manners, or private in nature, these things are their care and their business. But if great things will satisfy our inquiry, the course of the sun and moon, the spots in their faces, the firmament of heaven, and the supposed orbs, the ebbing and flowing of the sea, are work enough for us: or if this be not, let him tell me whether the number of the stars be even or odd, and when they began to be so; since some ages have discovered new stars which the former knew not, but might have seen if they had been where now they are fixed. If these be too troublesome, search lower, and tell me why this turf this year brings forth a daisy, and the next year a plantain, why the apple bears his seed in his heart, and wheat bears it in his head: let him tell why a graft, taking nourishment from a crab-stock, shall have a fruit more noble than its nurse and parent: let him say why the best of oil is at the top, the best of wine in the middle, and the best of honey at the bottom, otherwise than it is in some liquors that are thinner, and in some that are thicker. But these things are not such as please busy-bodies; they must feed upon tragedies, and stories of misfortunes and crimes: and yet tell them ancient stories of the ravishment of chaste maidens, or the debauchment of nations, or the extreme poverty of learned persons, or the persecutions of the old saints, or the changes of government, and sad accidents happening in royal families among the Arsacidæ, the Cæsars, the Ptolemies, these were enough to scratch the itch of knowing sad stories; but unless you tell them something sad and new, something that is done within the bounds of their own knowledge or relation, it seems tedious and unsatisfying; which shows plainly, it is an evil spirit; envy and idleness married together, and begot curiosity. Therefore Plutarch rarely well compares curious and inquisitive ears to the execrable gates of cities, out of which only malefactors and hangmen and tragedies pass—nothing that is chaste or holy. If a physician should go from house to house unsent for, and inquire what woman hath a cancer in her bowels, or what man hath a fistula in his colic-gut, though he could pretend to cure it, he would be almost as unwelcome as the disease itself; and therefore it is inhuman to inquire after crimes and disasters without pretence of amending them, but only to discover them. We are not angry with searchers and publicans, when they look only on public merchandise; but when they break open trunks, and pierce vessels, and unrip packs, and open sealed letters.

Curiosity is the direct incontinency of the spirit; and adultery itself, in its principle, is many times nothing but a curious inquisition after, and envying of another man's enclosed pleasures; and there have been many who refused fairer objects that they might ravish an enclosed woman from her retirement and single possessor. But these inquisitions are seldom without danger, never without baseness; they are neither just, nor honest, nor delightful, and very often useless to the curious inquirer. For men stand upon their guards against them, as they secure their meat against harpies and cats, laying all their counsels and secrets out of their way; or as men clap their garments close about them, when the searching and saucy winds would discover their nakedness; as knowing that what men willingly hear they do willingly speak of. Knock, therefore, at the door before you enter upon your neighbor's privacy; and remember, that there is no difference between entering his house and looking into it.

ACTS OF MODESTY AS IT IS OPPOSED TO BOLDNESS

1. Let us always bear about us such impressions of reverence and fear of God as to tremble at his voice, to express our apprehensions of his greatness in all great accidents, in popular judgments, loud thunders, tempests, earthquakes; not only for fear of being smitten ourselves, or that we are concerned in the accident, but also that we may humble ourselves before his Almightiness, and express that infinite distance between his infiniteness and our weaknesses, at such times especially when he gives such visible arguments of it. He that is merry and airy at shore when he sees a sad and a loud tempest on the sea, or dances briskly when God thunders from heaven, regards not when God speaks to all the world, but is possessed with a firm immodesty.

2. Be reverent, modest, and reserved in the presence of thy betters, giving to all according to their quality, their titles of honor, keeping distance, speaking little, answering pertinently, not interposing without leave or reason, not answering to a question propounded to another; and ever present to thy superiors the fairest side of thy discourse, of thy temper, of thy ceremony, as being ashamed to serve excellent persons with unhandsome intercourse.

3. Never lie before a king or a great person, nor stand in a lie, when thou art accused; nor offer to justify what is indeed a fault, but modestly be ashamed of it, ask pardon, and make amends.

4. Never boast of thy sin, but at least lay a veil upon thy

nakedness and shame, and put thine hand before thine eyes, that thou mayest have this beginning of repentance, to believe thy sin to be thy shame. For he that blushes not at his crime, but adds shamelessness to his shame, hath no instrument left to restore him to the hopes of virtue.

5. Be not confident and affirmative in an uncertain matter, but report things modestly and temperately, according to the degree of that persuasion which is, or ought to be, begotten in thee by the efficacy of the authority, or the reason inducing thee.

6. Pretend not to more knowledge than thou hast, but be content to seem ignorant where thou art so, lest thou beest either brought to shame, or retirest into shamelessness.

ACTS OF MODESTY AS IT IS OPPOSED TO INDECENCY

1. In your prayers, in churches and places of religion, use reverent postures, great attention, grave ceremony, the lowest gestures of humility, remembering that we speak to God, in our reverence to whom we cannot possibly exceed; but that the expression of this reverence be according to law or custom; and the example of the most prudent and pious persons; that is, let it be the best in its kind to the best of essences.

2. In all public meetings, private addresses, in discourses, in journeys, use those forms of salutation, reverence, and decency, which the custom prescribes, and is usual amongst the most sober persons; giving honor to whom honor belongeth, taking place of none of thy betters, and in all cases of question concerning civil precedency, giving it to any one that will take it, if it be only thy own right that is in question.

3. Observe the proportion of affections in all meetings and to all persons: be not merry at a funeral, nor sad upon a festival; but rejoice with them that rejoice, and weep with them that weep.

4. Abstain from wanton and dissolute laughter, petulant and uncomely jests, loud talking, jeering, and all such actions, which in civil account are called indecencies and incivilities.

5. Towards your parents use all modesty of duty and humble carriage; towards them and all your kindred, be severe in the modesties of chastity; ever fearing lest the freedoms of natural kindness should enlarge into any neighborhood of unhandsomeness. For all incestuous mixtures, and all circumstances and degrees towards it, are the highest violations of modesty in the world: for therefore incest is grown to be so high a crime, especially in the last periods of

the world, because it breaks that reverence which the consent of all nations and the severity of human laws hath enjoined towards our parents and nearest kindred, in imitation of that law which God gave to the Jews in prosecution of modesty in this instance.

6. Be a curious observer of all those things which are of good report, and are parts of public honesty. For public fame, and the sentence of prudent and public persons, is the measure of good and evil in things indifferent; and charity requires us to comply with those fancies and affections which are agreeable to nature, or the analogy of virtue, or public laws, or old customs. It is against modesty for a woman to marry a second husband as long as she bears a burden by the first; or to admit a second love while the funeral tears are not wiped from her cheeks. It is against public honesty to do some lawful actions of privacy in public theatres, and therefore in such cases retirement is a duty of modesty.

7. Be grave, decent, and modest, in thy clothing and ornament: never let it be above thy condition, not always equal to it, never light or amorous, never discovering a nakedness through a thin veil, which thou pretendest to hide, never to lay a snare for a soul; but remember what becomes a Christian, professing holiness, chastity, and the discipline of the Holy Jesus: and the first effect of this let your servants feel by your gentleness and aptness to be pleased with their usual diligence, and ordinary conduct. For the man or woman that is dressed with anger and impatience, wears pride under their robes, and immodesty above.

8. Hither, also, is to be reduced singular and affected walking, proud, nice, and ridiculous gestures of body, painting and lascivious dressings: all which together God reproves by the prophet: "The Lord saith, Because the daughters of Sion are haughty, and walk with stretched-forth necks and wanton eyes, walking and mincing as they go, and make a tinkling with their feet; therefore the Lord will smite her with a scab of the crown of the head, and will take away the bravery of their tinkling ornaments." And this duty of modesty, in this instance, is expressly enjoined to all Christian women by St. Paul: "That women adorn themselves in modest apparel, with shamefacedness and sobriety, not with broidered hair, or gold, or pearl, or costly array, but (which becometh women professing godliness) with good works.

9. As those meats are to be avoided which tempt our stomachs beyond our hunger, so, also, should prudent persons

decline all such spectacles, relations, theatres, loud noises, and outcries, which concern us not, and are besides our natural or moral interest. Our sense should not, like petulant and wanton girls, wander into markets and theatres without just employment; but when they are sent abroad by reason, return quickly with their errand, and remain modestly at home under their guide till they be sent again.

10. Let all persons be curious in observing modesty towards themselves, in the handsome treating their own body, and such as are in their power, whether living or dead. Against this rule they offend who expose to others their own, or pry into others' nakedness beyond the limits of necessity, or where a leave is not made holy by a permission from God. It is also said, that God was pleased to work a miracle about the body of Epiphanius to reprove the immodest curiosity of an unconcerned person who pried too near, when charitable people were composing it to the grave. In all these cases and particulars, although they seem little, yet our duty and concernment is not little. Concerning which I use the words of the son of Sirach, "He that despiseth little things, shall perish by little and little."

HENRY DAVID THOREAU
1817–1862

When Henry David Thoreau was dying, his Aunt Louisa asked if he had made his peace with God. "I have never quarreled with Him," he replied, and no reply could have been more typical of the man. He was always a nonconformist, but his nonconformity did not proceed from any rebellion against God or His universe. It was what "the mass of men" insisted on doing with the universe that he took exception to, and his calm assurance in pursuing this quarrel, whether on minor or on major issues, seemed to indicate that he believed God agreed with him. To us, looking back over a hundred years, the pure logic of his position in most cases indicates that he was probably right. At the completion of his Harvard studies, for example, he refused to pay the five-dollar diploma fee. What act could be more rational? He had needed the education; he did not need the sheepskin. Because he disapproved of military purposes to which the public tax was being devoted, he went to jail rather than pay his share. Again, his logic was irrefutable, so much so that it set a pattern for the conscience of succeeding generations. The same clarity of judgment, the same refusal to compromise with error or irrationality, inform every sentence of the accompanying essay, "Life Without Principle," which was first published in the *Atlantic Monthly* for October, 1863. Yet nowhere in Thoreau does logic become self-righteousness or intolerance. His eye for the absurd in human affairs resulted in wit, not scorn, the wit that could put his Aunt Louisa in her place, even from his deathbed.

Life Without Principle

At a lyceum, not long since, I felt that the lecturer had chosen a theme too foreign to himself, and so failed to interest me as much as he might have done. He described things not in or near to his heart, but toward his extremities and superficies. There was, in this sense, no truly central or centralizing thought in the lecture. I would have had him deal with his privatest experience, as the poet does. The greatest compliment that was ever paid me was when one asked me what *I thought,* and attended to my answer. I am surprised, as well as delighted, when this happens, it is such a rare use he would make of me, as if he were acquainted with the tool. Commonly, if men want anything of me, it is only to know how many acres I make of their land,—since I am a surveyor,—or, at most, what trivial news I have burdened myself with. They never will go to law for my meat; they prefer the shell. A man once came a considerable distance to ask me to lecture on Slavery; but on conversing with him, I found that he and his clique expected seven eighths of the lecture to be theirs, and only one eighth mine; so I declined. I take it for granted, when I am invited to lecture anywhere,—for I have had a little experience in that business,—that there is a desire to hear what *I think* on some subject, though I may be the greatest fool in the country,—and not that I should say pleasant things merely, or such as the audience will assent to; and I resolve, accordingly, that I will give them a strong dose of myself. They have sent for me, and engaged to pay for me, and I am determined that they shall have me, though I bore them beyond all precedent.

So now I would say something similar to you, my readers. Since *you* are my readers, and I have not been much of a traveller, I will not talk about people a thousand miles off but come as near home as I can. As the time is short, I will leave out all the flattery, and retain all the criticism.

Let us consider the way in which we spend our lives.

This world is a place of business. What an infinite bustle! I am awaked almost every night by the panting of the locomotive. It interrupts my dreams. There is no sabbath. It would be glorious to see mankind at leisure for once. It is nothing but work, work, work. I cannot easily buy a blank-book to write thoughts in; they are commonly ruled for dollars and cents. An Irishman, seeing me making a minute in the fields, took it for granted that I was calculating my wages. If a man was tossed out of a window when an infant, and so made a cripple for life, or scared out of his wits by the Indians, it is regretted chiefly because he was thus incapacitated for—business! I think that there is nothing, not even crime, more opposed to poetry, to philosophy, ay, to life itself, than this incessant business.

There is a coarse and boisterous money-making fellow in the outskirts of our town, who is going to build a bank-wall under the hill along the edge of his meadow. The powers have put this into his head to keep him out of mischief, and he wishes me to spend three weeks digging there with him. The result will be that he will perhaps get some more money to hoard, and leave for his heirs to spend foolishly. If I do this, most will commend me as an industrious and hard-working man; but if I choose to devote myself to certain labors which yield more real profit, though but little money, they may be inclined to look on me as an idler. Nevertheless, as I do not need the police of meaningless labor to regulate me, and do not see anything absolutely praiseworthy in this fellow's undertaking any more than in many an enterprise of our own or foreign governments, however amusing it may be to him or them, I prefer to finish my education at a different school.

If a man walk in the woods for love of them half of each day, he is in danger of being regarded as a loafer; but if he spends his whole day as a speculator, shearing off those woods and making earth bald before her time, he is esteemed an industrious and enterprising citizen. As if a town had no interest in its forests but to cut them down!

Most men would feel insulted if it were proposed to employ them in throwing stones over a wall, and then in throwing them back, merely that they might earn their wages. But many are no more worthily employed now. For instance: just after sunrise one summer morning I noticed one of my neighbors walking beside his team, which was slowly drawing a heavy hewn stone swung under the axle, surrounded by an atmosphere of industry—his day's work begun, his brow commenced to sweat, a reproach to all sluggards and idlers—pausing abreast the shoulders of his oxen, and half turning round with a flourish of his merciful whip, while they gained their length on him. And I thought, Such is the labor which the American Congress exists to protect,—honest, manly toil,—honest as the day is long,—that makes his bread taste sweet, and keeps society sweet,—which all men respect and have consecrated; one of the sacred band, doing the needful, but irksome drudgery. Indeed, I felt a slight reproach, because I observed this from the window, and was not abroad and stirring about a similar business. The day went by, and at evening I passed the yard of another neighbor, who keeps many servants, and spends much money foolishly, while he adds nothing to the common stock, and there I saw the stone of the morning lying beside a whimsical structure intended to adorn this Lord Timothy Dexter's premises, and the dignity forthwith departed from the teamster's labor, in my eyes. In my opinion, the sun was made to light worthier toil than this. I may add that his employer has since run off, in debt to a good part of the town, and, after passing through Chancery, has settled somewhere else, there to become once more a patron of the arts.

The ways by which you may get money almost without exception lead downward. To have done anything by which you earned money *merely* is to have been truly idle or worse. If the laborer gets no more than the wages which his employer pays him, he is cheated, he cheats himself. If you would get money as a writer or a lecturer, you must be popular, which is to go down perpendicularly. Those services which the community will most readily pay for it is most disagreeable to render. You are paid for being something less than a man. The State does not commonly reward a genius any more wisely. Even the poet-laureate would rather not have to celebrate the accidents of royalty. He must be bribed with a pipe of wine; and perhaps another poet is called away from his muse to gauge that very pipe. As for my own business, even that kind of surveying which I could do with most satisfaction my employers do not want. They would prefer that I should do my work coarsely and not too well, ay, not well enough. When I observe that there are different ways of surveying, my employer commonly asks which will give him the most land, not which is most correct. I once invented a rule for measuring cordwood, and tried to introduce it in Boston; but the measurer there told me that the sellers did not wish to have their wood measured correctly,—that he was already too accurate for them, and therefore they commonly got their wood measured in Charlestown before crossing the bridge.

The aim of the laborer should be, not to get his living, to get "a good job," but to perform well a certain work; and, even in a pecuniary sense, it would be economy for a town to pay its laborers so well that they would not feel that they were working for low ends, as for a livelihood merely, but for scientific, or even moral ends. Do not hire a man who does your work for money, but him who does it for love of it.

It is remarkable that there are few men so well employed, so much to their minds, but that a little money or fame would commonly buy them off from their present pursuit. I see advertisements for *active* young men, as if activity were the whole of a young man's capital. Yet I have been surprised when one has with confidence proposed to me, a grown man, to embark in some enterprise of his, as if I had absolutely nothing to do, my life having been a complete failure hitherto. What a doubtful compliment this to pay me! As if he had met me halfway across the ocean beating up against the wind, but bound nowhere, and proposed to me to go along with him! If I did, what do you think the underwriters would say? No, no! I am not without employment at this stage of the voyage. To tell the truth, I saw an advertisement for able-bodied seamen, when I was a boy, sauntering in my native port, and as soon as I became of age I embarked.

The community has no bribe that will tempt a wise man. You may raise money enough to tunnel a mountain, but you cannot raise money enough to hire a man who is minding *his own* business. An efficient and valuable man does what he can, whether the community pay him for it or not. The inefficient offer their inefficiency to the highest bidder, and are forever expecting to be put into office. One would suppose that they were rarely disappointed.

Perhaps I am more than usually jealous with respect to my freedom. I feel that my connection with and obligation to society are still very slight and transient. Those slight labors which afford me a livelihood, and by which it is allowed that I am to some extent serviceable to my contemporaries, are as yet commonly a pleasure to me, and I am not often reminded that they are a necessity. So far I am successful. But I foresee, that, if my wants should be much increased, the labor required to supply them would become a drudgery. If I should sell both my forenoons and afternoons to society, as most appear to do, I am sure that, for me, there would be nothing left worth living for. I trust that I shall never thus sell my birthright for a mess of pottage. I wish to suggest that a man may be very industrious, and yet not spend his time well. There is no more fatal blunderer than he who consumes the greater part of his life getting his living. All great enterprises are self-supporting. The poet, for instance, must sustain his body by his poetry, as a steam planing-mill feeds its boilers with the shavings it makes. You must get your living by loving. But as it is said of the merchants that ninety-seven in a hundred fail, so the life of men generally, tried by this standard, is a failure, and bankruptcy may be surely prophesied.

Merely to come into the world the heir of a fortune is not to be born, but to be stillborn, rather. To be supported by the charity of friends, or a government-pension,—provided you continue to breathe,—by whatever fine synonyms you describe these relations, is to go into the almshouse. On Sundays the poor debtor goes to church to take an account of stock, and finds, of course, that his outgoes have been greater than his income. In the Catholic Church, especially, they go into chancery, make a clean confession, give up all, and think to start again. Thus men will lie on their backs, talking about the fall of man, and never make an effort to get up.

As for the comparative demand which men make on life, it is an important difference between the two, that the one is satisfied with a level success, that his marks can all be hit by point-blank shots, but the other, however low and unsuccessful his life may be, constantly elevates his aim, though at a very slight angle to the horizon. I should much rather be the last man,—though, as the Orientals say, "Greatness doth not approach him who is forever looking down; and all those who are looking high are growing poor."

It is remarkable that there is little or nothing to be remembered written on the subject of getting a living; how to make getting a living not merely honest and honorable, but altogether inviting and glorious; for if *getting* a living is not so, then living is not. One would think, from looking at literature, that this question had never disturbed a solitary individual's musings. Is it that men are too much disgusted with their experience to speak of it? The lesson of value which money teaches, which the Author of the Universe has taken so much pains to teach us, we are inclined to skip altogether. As for the means of living, it is wonderful how indifferent men of all classes are about it, even reformers, so called,—whether they inherit, or earn, or steal it. I think that Society has done nothing for us in this respect, or at least has undone what she has done. Cold and hunger seem more friendly to my nature than those methods which men have adopted and advise to ward them off.

The title *wise* is, for the most part, falsely applied. How can one be a wise man, if he does not know any better how to live than other men?—if he is only more cunning and intellectually subtle? Does Wisdom work in a treadmill? or does she teach how to succeed *by her example?* Is there any such thing as wisdom not applied to life? Is she merely the miller who grinds the finest logic? It is pertinent to ask if Plato got his *living* in a better way or more successfully than his contemporaries,—or did he succumb to the difficulties of

life like other men? Did he seem to prevail over some of
them merely by indifference, or by assuming grand airs? or
find it easier to live, because his aunt remembered him in
her will? The ways in which most men get their living, that
is, live, are mere make-shifts, and a shirking of the real business of life,—chiefly because they do not know, but partly
because they do not mean, any better.

The rush to California, for instance, and the attitude, not
merely of merchants, but of philosophers and prophets, so
called, in relation to it, reflect the greatest disgrace on mankind. That so many are ready to live by luck, and so get the
means of commanding the labor of others less lucky, without
contributing any value to society! And that is called enterprise!
I know of no more startling development of the immorality of
trade, and all the common modes of getting a living. The
philosophy and poetry and religion of such a mankind are
not worth the dust of a puffball. The hog that gets his living
by rooting, stirring up the soil so, would be ashamed of such
company. If I could command the wealth of all the words by
lifting my finger, I would not pay *such* a price for it. Even
Mahomet knew that God did not make this world in jest. It
makes God to be a moneyed gentleman who scatters a handful of pennies in order to see mankind scramble for them.
The world's raffle! A subsistence in the domains of Nature a
thing to be raffled for! What a comment, what a satire, on
our institutions! The conclusion will be, that mankind will
hang itself upon a tree. And have all the precepts in all the
Bibles taught men only this? and is the last and most admirable
invention of the human race only an improved muck-rate? Is
this the ground on which Orientals and Occidentals meet?
Did God direct us so to get our living, digging where we never
planted—and He would, perchance, reward us with lumps of
gold?

God gave the righteous man a certificate entitling him to
food and raiment, but the unrighteous man found a facsimile
of the same in God's coffers, and appropriated it, and obtained food and raiment like the former. It is one of the most
extensive systems of counterfeiting that the world has seen.
I did not know that mankind was suffering for want of gold.
I have seen a little of it. I know that it is very malleable, but
not so malleable as wit. A grain of gold will gild a great surface, but not so much as a grain of wisdom.

The gold digger in the ravines of the mountains is as much
a gambler as his fellow in the saloons of San Francisco. What

difference does it make whether you shake dirt or shake dice? If you win, society is the loser. The gold digger is the enemy of the honest laborer, whatever checks and compensations there may be. It is not enough to tell me that you worked hard to get your gold. So does the Devil work hard. The way of transgressors may be hard in many respects. The humblest observer who goes to the mines sees and says that gold digging is of the character of a lottery; the gold thus obtained is not the same thing with the wages of honest toil. But, practically, he forgets what he has seen, for he has seen only the fact, not the principle, and goes into trade there, that is, buys a ticket in what commonly proves another lottery, where the fact is not so obvious.

After reading Howitt's account of the Australian gold diggings one evening, I had in my mind's eye, all night, the numerous valleys, with their streams, all cut up with foul pits, from ten to one hundred feet deep, and half a dozen feet across, as close as they can be dug, and partly filled with water—the locality to which men furiously rush to probe for their fortunes—uncertain where they shall break ground—not knowing but the gold is under their camp itself—sometimes digging one hundred and sixty feet before they strike the vein, or then missing it by a foot—turned into demons, and regardless of each others' rights, in their thirst for riches—whole valleys, for thirty miles, suddenly honeycombed by the pits of the miners, so that even hundreds are drowned in them—standing in water, and covered with mud and clay, they work night and day, dying of exposure and disease. Having read this, and partly forgotten it, I was thinking, accidentally, of my own unsatisfactory life, doing as others do; and with that vision of the diggings still before me, I asked myself why *I* might not be washing some gold daily, though it were only the finest particles—why *I* might not sink a shaft down to the gold within me, and work that mine. *There* is a Ballarat, a Bendigo for you—what though it were a sulky-gully? At any rate, I might pursue some path, however solitary and narrow and crooked, in which I could walk with love and reverence. Wherever a man separates from the multitude, and goes his own way in this mood, there indeed is a fork in the road, though ordinary travelers may see only a gap in the paling. His solitary path across lots will turn out the *higher way* of the two.

Men rush to California and Australia as if the true gold were to be found in that direction; but that is to go to the very opposite extreme to where it lies. They go prospecting farther and farther away from the true lead, and are most unfortunate when they think themselves most successful. Is not our *native* soil auriferous? Does not a stream from the golden mountains flow through our native valley? and has not this for more than geologic ages been bringing down the shining particles and forming the nuggets for us? Yet, strange to tell, if a digger steal away, prospecting for this true gold, into the unexplored solitudes around us, there is no danger that any will dog his steps, and endeavor to supplant him. He may claim and undermine the whole valley even, both the cultivated and the uncultivated portions, his whole life long in peace, for no one will ever dispute his claim. They will not mind his cradles or his toms. He is not confined to a claim twelve feet square, as at Ballarat, but may mine anywhere, and wash the whole wide world in his tom.

Howitt says of the man who found the great nugget which weighed twenty-eight pounds, at the Bendigo diggings in Australia: "He soon began to drink; got a horse, and rode all about, generally at full gallop, and, when he met people, called out to inquire if they knew who he was, and then kindly informed them that he was 'the bloody wretch that had found the nugget.' At last he rode full speed against a tree, and nearly knocked his brains out." I think, however, there was no danger of that, for he had already knocked his brains out against the nugget. Howitt adds, "He is a hopelessly ruined man." But he is a type of the class. They are all fast men. Hear some of the names of the places where they dig: "Jackass Flat"—"Sheep's-Head Gully"—"Murderer's Bar," etc. Is there no satire in these names? Let them carry their illgotten wealth where they will, I am thinking it will still be "Jackass Flat," if not "Murderer's Bar," where they live.

The last resource of our energy has been the robbing of graveyards on the Isthmus of Darien, an enterprise which appears to be but in its infancy; for, according to late accounts, an act has passed its second reading in the legislature of New Granada, regulating this kind of mining; and a correspondent of the *Tribune* writes: "In the dry season, when the weather will permit of the country being properly prospected, no doubt other rich *guacas* [that is, graveyards] will be found." To emigrants he says: "Do not come before December; take the Isthmus route in preference to the Boca del Toro one; bring no useless baggage, and do not cumber yourself with a tent; but a good pair of blankets will be necessary; a pick, shovel, and axe of good material will be almost all that is required"; advice which might have been taken from the "Burker's Guide." And he concludes with this line in italics and small capitals: *"If you are doing well at home,* STAY THERE," which may fairly be interpreted to mean, "If you are getting a good living by robbing graveyards at home, stay there."

But why go to California for a text? She is the child of New England, bred at her own school and church.

It is remarkable that among all the preachers there are so few moral teachers. The prophets are employed in excusing the ways of men. Most reverend seniors, the *illuminati* of the age, tell me, with a gracious, reminiscent smile, betwixt an aspiration and a shudder, not to be too tender about these things—to lump all that, that is, make a lump of gold of it. The highest advice I have heard on these subjects was groveling. The burden of it was—It is not worth your while to undertake to reform the world in this particular. Do not ask how your bread is buttered; it will make you sick, if you do— and the like. A man had better starve at once than lose his innocence in the process of getting his bread. If within the sophisticated man there is not an unsophisticated one, then he is but one of the devil's angels. As we grow old, we live more coarsely, we relax a little in our disciplines, and, to some extent, cease to obey our finest instincts. But we should be fastidious to the extreme of sanity, disregarding the gibes of those who are more unfortunate than ourselves.

In our science and philosophy, even, there is commonly no true and absolute account of things. The spirit of sect and bigotry has planted its hoof amid the stars. You have only to discuss the problem, whether the stars are inhabited or not, in order to discover it. Why must we daub the heavens as well as the earth? It was an unfortunate discovery that Dr. Kane was a Mason, and that Sir John Franklin was another. But it was a more cruel suggestion that possibly that was the reason why the former went in search of the latter. There is not a popular magazine in this country that would dare to print a child's thought on important subjects without comment. It must be submitted to the D.D.'s. I would it were the chickadee-dees.

You come from attending the funeral of mankind to attend to a natural phenomenon. A little thought is sexton to all the world.

I hardly know an *intellectual* man, even, who is so broad and truly liberal that you can think aloud in his society. Most

with whom you endeavor to talk soon come to a stand against
some institution in which they appear to hold stock, that is,
some particular, not universal, way of viewing things. They
will continually thrust their own low roof, with its narrow sky-
light, between you and the sky, when it is the unobstructed
heavens you would view. Get out of the way with your cobwebs; wash your windows, I say! In some lyceums they tell
me that they have voted to exclude the subject of religion.
But how do I know what their religion is, and when I am
near to or far from it? I have walked into such an arena and
done my best to make a clean breast of what religion I have
experienced, and the audience never suspected what I was
about. The lecture was as harmless as moonshine to them.
Whereas, if I had read to them the biography of the greatest
scamps in history, they might have thought that I had written
the lives of the deacons of their church. Ordinarily, the inquiry is, Where did you come from? or, Where are you going?
That was a more pertinent question which I overheard one
of my auditors put to another once—"What does he lecture
for?" It made me quake in my shoes.

To speak impartially, the best men that I know are not
serene, a world in themselves. For the most part, they dwell in
forms, and flatter and study effect only more finely than the
rest. We select granite for the underpinning of our houses
and barns; we build fences of stone; but we do not ourselves
rest on an underpinning of granitic truth, the lowest primitive
rock. Our sills are rotten. What stuff is the man made of who
is not coexistent in our thought with the purest and subtilest
truth? I often accuse my finest acquaintances of an immense
frivolity; for, while there are manners and compliments we
do not meet, we do not teach one another the lessons of
honesty and sincerity that the brutes do, or of steadiness and
solidity that the rocks do. The fault is commonly mutual,
however; for we do not habitually demand any more of each
other.

That excitement about Kossuth, consider how characteristic,
but superficial, it was!—only another kind of politics or dancing. Men were making speeches to him all over the country,
but each expressed only the thought, or the want of thought,
of the multitude. No man stood on truth. They were merely
banded together, as usual one leaning on another, and all
together on nothing; as the Hindus made the world rest on an
elephant, the elephant on a tortoise, and the tortoise on a

serpent, and had nothing to put under the serpent. For all fruit of that stir we have the Kossuth hat.

Just so hollow and ineffectual, for the most part, is our ordinary conversation. Surface meets surface. When our life ceases to be inward and private, conversation degenerates into mere gossip. We rarely meet a man who can tell us any news which he has not read in a newspaper, or been told by his neighbor; and, for the most part, the only difference between us and our fellow is that he has seen the newspaper, or been out to tea, and we have not. In proportion as our inward life fails, we go more constantly and desperately to the post office. You may depend on it, that the poor fellow who walks away with the greatest number of letters, proud of his extensive correspondence, has not heard from himself this long while.

I do not know but it is too much to read one newspaper a week. I have tried it recently, and for so long it seems to me that I have not dwelt in my native region. The sun, the clouds, the snow, the trees say not so much to me. You cannot serve two masters. It requires more than a day's devotion to know and to possess the wealth of a day.

We may well be ashamed to tell what things we have read or heard in our day. I do not know why my news should be so trivial—considering what one's dreams and expectations are, why the developments should be so paltry. The news we hear, for the most part, is not news to our genius. It is the stalest repetition. You are often tempted to ask why such stress is laid on a particular experience which you have had— that, after twenty-five years, you should meet Hobbins, Registrar of Deeds, again on the sidewalks. Have you not budged an inch, then? Such is the daily news. Its facts appear to float in the atmosphere, insignificant as the sporules of fungi, and impinge on some neglected *thallus*, or surface of our minds, which affords a basis for them, and hence a parasitic growth. We should wash ourselves clean of such news. Of what consequence, though our planet explode, if there is no character involved in the explosion? In health we have not the least curiosity about such events. We do not live for idle amusement. I would not run round a corner to see the world blow up.

All summer, and far into the autumn, perchance, you unconsciously went by the newspapers and the news, and now you find it was because the morning and the evening were full of news to you. Your walks were full of incidents. You

attended, not to the affairs of Europe, but to your own affairs
in Massachusetts fields. If you chance to live and move and
have your being in that thin stratum in which the events that
make the news transpire—thinner than the paper on which
it is printed—then these things will fill the world for you; but
if you soar above or dive below that plane, you cannot remember nor be reminded of them. Really to see the sun rise
or go down every day, so to relate ourselves to a universal
fact, would preserve us sane forever. Nations! What are nations? Tartars, and Huns, and Chinamen! Like insects, they
swarm. The historian strives in vain to make them memorable.
It is for want of a man that there are so many men. It is
individuals that populate the world. Any man thinking may
say with the Spirit of Lodin,

> "I look down from my height on nations,
>   And they become ashes before me;—
> Calm is my dwelling in the clouds;
>   Pleasant are the great fields of my rest."

Pray, let us live without being drawn by dogs, Esquimaux-
fashion, tearing over hill and dale, and biting each other's
ears.

Not without a slight shudder at the danger, I often perceive how near I had come to admitting into my mind the
details of some trivial affair—the news of the street; and I
am astonished to observe how willing men are to lumber their
minds with such rubbish—to permit idle rumors and incidents
of the most insignificant kind to intrude on ground which
should be sacred to thought. Shall the mind be a public arena,
where the affairs of the street and the gossip of the tea-table
chiefly are discussed? Or shall it be a quarter of heaven itself—
an hypethral temple, consecrated to the service of the gods? I
find it so difficult to dispose of the few facts which to me are
significant, that I hesitate to burden my attention with those
which are insignificant, which only a divine mind could illustrate. Such is, for the most part, the news in newspapers
and conversation. It is important to preserve the mind's
chastity in this respect. Think of admitting the details of a
single case of the criminal court into our thoughts, to stalk
profanely through their very *sanctum sanctorum* for an hour,
ay, for many hours! to make a very barroom of the mind's
inmost apartment, as if for so long the dust of the street had
occupied us—the very street itself, with all its travel, its bustle,
and filth, had passed through our thoughts' shrine! Would it

not be an intellectual and moral suicide? When I have been compelled to sit spectator and auditor in a courtroom for some hours, and have seen my neighbors, who were not compelled, stealing in from time to time, and tiptoeing about with washed hands and faces, it has appeared to my mind's eye, that, when they took off their hats, their ears suddenly expanded into vast hoppers for sound, between which even their narrow heads were crowded. Like the vanes of windmills, they caught the broad but shallow stream of sound, which, after a few titillating gyrations in their coggy brains, passed out the other side. I wondered if, when they got home, they were as careful to wash their ears as before their hands and faces. It has seemed to me, at such a time, that the auditors and the witnesses, the jury and the counsel, the judge and the criminal at the bar—if I may presume him guilty before he is convicted—were all equally criminal, and a thunderbolt might be expected to descend and consume them all together.

By all kinds of traps and signboards, threatening the extreme penalty of the divine law, exclude such trespassers from the only ground which can be sacred to you. It is so hard to forget what it is worse than useless to remember! If I am to be a thoroughfare, I prefer that it be of the mountain brooks, the Parnassian streams, and not the town sewers. There is inspiration, that gossip which comes to the ear of the attentive mind from the courts of heaven. There is the profane and stale revelation of the barroom and the police court. The same ear is fitted to receive both communications. Only the character of the hearer determines to which it shall be open, and to which closed. I believe that the mind can be permanently profaned by the habit of attending to trivial things, so that all our thoughts shall be tinged with triviality. Our very intellect shall be macadamized, as it were, its foundation broken into fragments for the wheels of travel to roll over; and if you would know what will make the most durable pavement, surpassing rolled stones, spruce blocks, and asphaltum, you have only to look into some of our minds which have been subjected to this treatment so long.

If we have thus desecrated ourselves—as who has not?—the remedy will be by wariness and devotion to reconsecrate ourselves, and make once more a fane of the mind. We should treat our minds, that is, ourselves, as innocent and ingenuous children, whose guardians we are, and be careful what objects and what subjects we thrust on their attention. Read not the Times. Read the Eternities. Conventionalities are at length as bad as impurities. Even the facts of science may dust the mind by their dryness, unless they are in a sense effaced each morning, or rather rendered fertile by the dews of fresh and living truth. Knowledge does not come to us by details, but in flashes of light from heaven. Yes, every thought that passes through the mind helps to wear and tear it, and to deepen the ruts, which, as in the streets of Pompeii, evince how much it has been used. How many things there are concerning which we might well deliberate whether we had better know them—had better let their peddling-carts be driven, even at the slowest trot or walk, over that bridge of glorious span by which we trust to pass at last from the farthest brink of time to the nearest shore of eternity! Have we no culture, no refinement—but skill only to live coarsely and serve the Devil?—to acquire a little worldly wealth, or fame, or liberty, and make a false show with it, as if we were all husk and shell, with no tender and living kernel to us? Shall our institutions be like those chestnut burs which contain abortive nuts, perfect only to prick the fingers?

America is said to be the arena on which the battle of freedom is to be fought; but surely it cannot be freedom in a merely political sense that is meant. Even if we grant that the American has freed himself from a political tyrant, he is still the slave of an economical and moral tyrant. Now that the republic—the *res-publica*—has been settled, it is time to look after the *res-privata*—the private state—to see, as the Roman senate charged its consuls, *"ne quid res-*PRIVATA *detrimenti caperet,"* that the *private* state receive no detriment.

Do we call this the land of the free? What is it to be free from King George and continue the slaves of King Prejudice? What is it to be born free and not to live free? What is the value of any political freedom, but as a means to moral freedom? Is it a freedom to be slaves, or a freedom to be free, of which we boast? We are a nation of politicians, concerned about the outmost defenses only of freedom. It is our children's children who may perchance be really free. We tax ourselves unjustly. There is a part of us which is not represented. It is taxation without representation. We quarter troops, we quarter fools and cattle of all sorts upon ourselves. We quarter our gross bodies on our poor souls, till the farmer eat up all the latter's substance.

With respect to a true culture and manhood, we are essentially provincial still, not metropolitan—mere Jonathans.

We are provincial, because we do not find at home our standards; because we do not worship truth, but the reflection of truth; because we are warped and narrowed by an exclusive devotion to trade and commerce and manufactures and agriculture and the like, which are but means, and not the end.

So is the English Parliament provincial. Mere country bumpkins, they betray themselves, when any more important question arises for them to settle, the Irish question, for instance—the English question why did I not say? Their natures are subdued to what they work in. Their "good breeding" respects only secondary objects. The finest manners in the world are awkwardness and fatuity when contrasted with a finer intelligence. They appear but as the fashions of past days—mere courtliness, knee-buckles and smallclothes, out of date. It is the vice, but not the excellence of manners, that they are continually being deserted by the character; they are cast-off clothes or shells, claiming the respect which belonged to the living creature. You are presented with the shells instead of the meat, and it is no excuse generally, that, in the case of some fishes, the shells are of more worth than the meat. The man who thrusts his manners upon me does as if he were to insist on introducing me to his cabinet of curiosities, when I wished to see himself. It was not in this sense that the poet Decker called Christ "the first true gentleman that ever breathed." I repeat that in this sense the most splendid court in Christendom is provincial, having authority to consult about Transalpine interests only, and not the affairs of Rome. A praetor or proconsul would suffice to settle the questions which absorb the attention of the English Parliament and the American Congress.

Government and legislation! these I thought were respectable professions. We have heard of heaven-born Numas, Lycurguses, and Solons, in the history of the world, whose *names* at least may stand for ideal legislators; but think of legislating to *regulate* the breeding of slaves, or the exportation of tobacco! What have divine legislators to do with the exportation or the importation of tobacco? what humane ones with the breeding of slaves? Suppose you were to submit the question to any son of God—and has He no children in the Nineteenth Century? is it a family which is extinct?—in what condition would you get it again? What shall a State like Virginia say for itself at the last day, in which these have been the principal, the staple productions? What ground is there for patriotism in such a State? I derive my facts from statistical tables which the States themselves have published.

A commerce that whitens every sea in quest of nuts and raisins, and makes slaves of its sailors for the purpose! I saw, the other day, a vessel which had been wrecked, and many lives lost, and her cargo of rags, juniper berries, and bitter almonds were strewn along the shore. It seemed hardly worth the while to tempt the dangers of the sea between Leghorn and New York for the sake of a cargo of juniper berries and bitter almonds. America sending to the Old World for her bitters! Is not the sea-brine, is not shipwreck, bitter enough to make the cup of life go down here? Yet such, to a great extent, is our boasted commerce; and there are those who style themselves statesmen and philosophers who are so blind as to think that progress and civilization depend on precisely this kind of interchange and activity—the activity of flies about a molasses-hogshead. Very well, observes one, if men were oysters. And very well, answer I, if men were mosquitoes.

Lieutenant Herndon, whom our government sent to explore the Amazon, and, it is said, to extend the area of slavery, observed that there was wanting there "an industrious and active population, who know what the comforts of life are, and who have artificial wants to draw out the great resources of the country." But what are the "artificial wants" to be encouraged? Not the love of luxuries, like the tobacco and slaves of, I believe, his native Virginia, nor the ice and granite and other material wealth of our native New England; nor are "the great resources of a country" that fertility or barrenness of soil which produces these. The chief want, in every State that I have been into, was a high and earnest purpose in its inhabitants. This alone draws out "the great resources" of Nature, and at last taxes her beyond her resources; for man naturally dies out of her. When we want culture more than potatoes, and illumination more than sugar-plums, then the great resources of a world are taxed and drawn out, and the result, or staple production, is, not slaves, nor operatives, but men—those rare fruits called heroes, saints, poets, philosophers, and redeemers.

In short, as a snowdrift is formed where there is a lull in the wind, so, one would say, where there is a lull of truth, an institution springs up. But the truth blows right on over it, nevertheless, and at length blows it down.

What is called politics is comparatively something so superficial and inhuman, that practically I have never fairly recognized that it concerns me at all. The newspapers, I perceive, devote some of their columns specially to politics or government without charge; and this, one would say, is all that saves it; but as I love literature and to some extent the truth also, I never read those columns at any rate. I do not wish to blunt my sense of right so much. I have not got to answer for having read a single President's Message. A strange age of the world this, when empires, kingdoms, and republics come a-begging to a private man's door, and utter their complaints at his elbow! I cannot take up a newspaper but I find that some wretched government or other, hard pushed and on its last legs, is interceding with me, the reader, to vote for it—more importunate than an Italian beggar; and if I have a mind to look at its certificate, made, perchance, by some benevolent merchant's clerk, or the skipper that brought it over, for it cannot speak a word of English itself, I shall probably read of the eruption of some Vesuvius, or the overflowing of some Po, true or forged, which brought it into this condition. I do not hesitate, in such a case, to suggest work, or the almshouse; or why not keep its castle in silence, as I do commonly? The poor President, what with preserving his popularity and doing his duty, is completely bewildered. The newspapers are the ruling power. Any other government is reduced to a few marines at Fort Independence. If a man neglects to read the Daily Times, government will go down on its knees to him, for this is the only treason in these days.

Those things which now most engage the attention of men, as politics and the daily routine, are, it is true, vital functions of human society, but should be unconsciously performed, like the corresponding functions of the physical body. They are *infra*-human, a kind of vegetation. I sometimes awake to a half-consciousness of them going on about me, as a man may become conscious of some of the processes of digestion in a morbid state, and so have the dyspepsia, as it is called. It is as if a thinker submitted himself to be rasped by the great gizzard of creation. Politics is, as it were, the gizzard of society, full of grit and gravel, and the two political parties are its two opposite halves—sometimes split into quarters, it may be, which grind on each other. Not only individuals, but states, have thus a confirmed dyspepsia, which expresses itself, you can imagine by what sort of eloquence. Thus our life is not altogether a forgetting, but also, alas! to a great extent, a remembering, of that which we should never have been conscious of, certainly not in our waking hours. Why should we not meet, not always as dyspeptics, to tell our bad dreams, but sometimes as *eu*peptics, to congratulate each other on the ever-glorious morning? I do not make an exorbitant demand, surely.

JAMES THURBER
1894–1961

James Thurber once drew a cartoon of a man sitting at his typewriter and staring at a pile of crumpled papers on the floor. His wife, one of those predatory Thurber females, inquires: "What's the matter? Has your pen gleaned your teeming brain?" That was a fate Thurber never had to worry about. A jet-propelled pen could not have gleaned his brain of all its fantasy and humor, and Thurber's pen was slowed for many years by failing eyesight. He was always writing, however, with his mind if not with his hand. At parties or at dinner he often lapsed into absent-mindedness until his wife, who knew the symptoms, ordered: "Dammit, Thurber, stop writing." For what he wrote, of course, there was an inexhaustible market; but it is an ironic note that Thurber himself might have invented, that the first thirty articles he sent to the *New Yorker* were returned, and the next batch too. His first drawing of a seal was likewise haughtily dismissed, until he and E. B. White published *Is Sex Necessary?* with illustrations by Thurber, which immediately became popular. Then *New Yorker* editor Harold Ross, who by this time had Thurber on his staff, inquired, "Say, why can't you give us some of your drawings?" Thurber did, and rapidly populated books and periodicals across the country with his droopy men and women and his sad, intelligent hounds. No wonder that, as he relates in this essay, "How to Name a Dog," he eventually met up with a number of canines christened "Thurber."

How to Name a Dog

Every few months somebody writes me and asks if I will give him a name for his dog. Several of these correspondents in the past year have wanted to know if I would mind the use of my own name for their spaniels. Spaniel-owners seem to have the notion that a person could sue for invasion of privacy or defamation of character if his name were applied to a cocker without written permission, and one gentlemen even insisted that we conduct our correspondence in the matter through a notary public. I have a way of letting communications of this sort fall behind my roll-top desk, but it has recently occurred to me that this is an act of evasion, if not, indeed, of plain cowardice. I have therefore decided to come straight out with the simple truth that it is as hard for me to think up a name for a dog as it is for anybody else. The idea that I am an expert in the business is probably the outcome of a piece I wrote several years ago, incautiously revealing the fact that I have owned forty or more dogs in my life. This is true, but it is also deceptive. All but five or six of my dogs were disposed of when they were puppies, and I had not gone to the trouble of giving to these impermanent residents of my house any names at all except Shut Up! and Cut That Out! and Let Go!

Names of dogs end up in 176th place in the list of things that amaze and fascinate me. Canine cognomens should be designed to impinge on the ears of dogs and not to amuse neighbors, tradespeople, and casual visitors. I remember a few dogs from the past with a faint but lingering pleasure; a farm hound named Rain, a roving Airedale named Marco Polo, a female bull terrier known as Brody because she liked to jump from moving motor cars and second-story windows, and a Peke called Darien; but that's all.

Well, there is Poker, alias *Fantôme Noir,* a miniature black poodle I have come to know since I wrote the preceding paragraphs. Poker, familiarly known as Pokey, belongs to Mr. and Mrs. J. G. Gude, of White Plains, and when they registered him with the American Kennel Club they decided he needed a more dignified name. It wasn't easy to explain this to their youngest child David, and his parents never did quite clear it up for him. When he was only eight, David thought the problem over for a long while and then asked his father solemnly, "If he belongs to that club, why doesn't he ever go there?" Since I wrote this piece orginally, I have also heard about a sheep dog named Jupiter, which used to belong to Jimmy Cannon, journalist, critic, and man about dog shows. He reported in a recent column of his that Jupiter used to eat geraniums. I have heard of other dogs that ate flowers, but I refuse to be astonished by this until I learn of one that's downed a nasturtium.

The only animals whose naming demands concentration,

hard work, and ingenuity are the seeing-eye dogs. They have to be given unusual names because passers-by like to call to seeing-eyers—"Here, Sport" or "Yuh, Rags" or "Don't take any wooden nickels, Rin Tin Tin." A blind man's dog with an ordinary name would continually be distracted from its work. A tyro at naming these dogs might make the mistake of picking Durocher or Teeftallow. The former is too much like Rover and the latter could easily sound like "Here, fellow" to a dog. Ten years ago I met a young man in his twenties who had been mysteriously blind for nearly five years and had been led about by a seeing-eye German shepherd during all of that time, which included several years of study at Yale. Then suddenly one night the dog's owner began to get his vision back, and within a few weeks was able to read the fine print of a telephone book. The effect on his dog was almost disastrous, and it went into a kind of nervous crack-up, since these animals are trained to the knowledge, or belief, that their owners are permanently blind. After the owner regained his vision he kept his dog, of course, not only because they had become attached to each other but because the average seeing-eye dog cannot be transferred from one person to another.

Speaking of puppies, as I was a while back, I feel that I should warn inexperienced dog-owners who have discovered to their surprise and dismay a dozen puppies in a hall closet or under the floor of the barn, not to give them away. Sell them or keep them, but don't give them away. Sixty per cent of persons who are given a dog for nothing bring him back sooner or later and plump him into the reluctant and unprepared lap of his former owner. The people say that they are going to Florida and can't take the dog, or that he doesn't want to go; or they point out that he eats first editions or lace curtains or spinets, or that he doesn't see eye to eye with them in the matter of housebreaking, or that he makes disparaging remarks under his breath about their friends. Anyway, they bring him back and you are stuck with him—and maybe six others. But if you charge ten or even five dollars for pups, the new owners don't dare return them. They are afraid to ask for their money back because they believe you might think they are hard up and need the five or ten dollars. Furthermore, when a mischievous puppy is returned to its former owner it invariably behaves beautifully, and the person who brought it back is likely to be regarded as an imbecile or a dog-hater or both.

Names of dogs, to get back to our subject, have a range almost as wide as that of the violin. They run from such plain and simple names as Spot, Sport, Rex, Brownie to fancy appellations such as Prince Rudolph Hertenberg Gratzheim of Darndorf-Putzelhorst, and Darling Mist o' Love III of Heather-Light-Holyrood—names originated by adults, all of whom in every other way, I am told, have made a normal adjustment to life. In addition to the plain and fancy categories, there are the Cynical and the Coy. Cynical names are given by people who do not like dogs too much. The most popular cynical names during the war were Mussolini, Tojo, and Adolf. I never have been able to get very far in my exploration of the minds of people who call their dogs Mussolini, Tojo, and Adolf, and I suspect the reason is that I am unable to associate with them long enough to examine what goes on in their heads. I nod, and I tell them the time of day, if they ask, and that is all. I never vote for them or ask them to have a drink. The great Coy category is perhaps the largest. The Coy people call their pets Bubbles and Boggles and Sparkles and Twinkles and Doodles and Puffy and Lovums and Sweetums and Itsy-Bitsy and Betsy-Bye-Bye and Sugarkins. I pass these dog-owners at a dog-trot, wearing a horrible fixed grin.

There is a special subdivision of the Coys that is not quite so awful, but awful enough. These people, whom we will call the Wits, own two dogs, which they name Pitter and Patter, Willy and Nilly, Helter and Skelter, Namby and Pamby, Hugger and Mugger, and even Wishy and Washy, Ups and Daisy, Fitz and Startz, Fetch and Carrie, and Pro and Connie. Then there is the Cryptic category. These people select names for some private reason or for no reason at all—except perhaps to arouse a visitor's curiosity, so that he will exclaim, "Why in the world do you call your dog *that*?" The Cryptic name their dogs October, Bennett's Aunt, Three Fifteen, Doc Knows, Tuesday, Home Fried, Opus 38, Ask Leslie, and Thanks for the Home Run, Emil. I make it a point simply to pat these unfortunate dogs on the head, ask no question of their owners, and go about my business.

This article has degenerated into a piece that properly should be entitled "How Not to Name a Dog." I was afraid it would. It seems only fair to make up for this by confessing a few of the names I have given my own dogs, with the considerable help, if not, indeed, the insistence, of their mistress. Most of my dogs have been females, and they have answered, with apparent gladness, to such names as Jennie, Tessa, Julie, and Sophie. I have never owned a dog named Pamela, Jennifer, Clarissa, Jacqueline, Guinevere, or Shelmerdene.

About fifteen years ago, when I was looking for a house to buy in Connecticut, I knocked on the front door of an attractive home whose owner, my real-estate agent had told me, wanted to sell it and go back to Iowa to live. The lady agent who escorted me around had informed me that the owner of this place was a man named Strong, but a few minutes after arriving at the house, I was having a drink in the living room with Phil Stong, for it was he. We went out into the yard after a while and I saw Mr. Stong's spaniel. I called to the dog and snapped my fingers, but he seemed curiously embarrassed, like his master. "What's his name?" I asked the latter. He was cornered and there was no way out of it. "Thurber," he said, in a small frightened voice. Thurber and I shook hands, and he didn't seem to me any more depressed than any other spaniel I have met. He had, however, the expression of a bachelor on his way to a party he has tried in vain to get out of, and I think it must have been this cast of countenance that had reminded Mr. Stong of the dog I draw. The dog I draw is, to be sure, much larger than a spaniel and not so shaggy, but I confess, though I am not a spaniel man, that there are certain basic resemblances between my dog and all other dogs with long ears and troubled eyes.

Perhaps I should suggest at least one name for a dog, if only to justify the title of this piece. All right, then, what's the matter with Stong? It's a good name for a dog, short, firm, and effective. I recommend it to all those who have written to me for suggestions and to all those who may be at this very moment turning over in their minds the idea of asking my advice in this difficult and perplexing field of nomenclature.

Since I first set down these not too invaluable rules for naming dogs, I have heard of at least a dozen basset hounds named Thurber, a Newfoundland called Little Bears Thurber and a bloodhound named Tiffany's Thurber. This is all right with me, so long as the owners of Thurbers do not bring them to call on me at my house in Connecticut without making arrangements in advance. Christabel, my old and imperious poodle, does not like unannounced dog visitors, and tries to get them out of the house as fast as she can. Two years ago a Hartford dog got lost in my neighborhood and finally showed up at my house. He hadn't had much, if anything, to eat for several days, and we fed him twice within three hours, to the high dismay and indignation of Christabel, who only gets one big meal a day. The wanderer was returned to its owner, through a story in the Hartford *Courant,* and quiet descended on my home until a handsome young male collie showed up one night. We had quite a time getting him out of the house. Christabel kept telling him how wonderful it was outdoors and trotting to the door, but the collie wasn't interested. I tried to pick him up, but I am too old to pick up a full-grown collie. In the end Christabel solved the problem herself by leading him outside on the promise of letting him chew one of the bones she had buried. He still keeps coming back to visit us from time to time, but Christabel has hidden her bones in new places. She will romp with the young visitor for about twenty seconds, then show her teeth and send him home. I don't do anything about the situation. After all, my home has been in charge of Christabel for a great many years now, and I never interfere with a woman's ruling a household.

LEO TOLSTOY
1828–1910

Among world writers, the critic Marc Slonim suggests in *The Epic of Russian Literature,* only Shakespeare and Tolstoy have possessed an "unlimited range of characterization." Every one of the 559 characters in Tolstoy's *War and Peace,* for example, from Napoleon to the humblest peasant, is a distinct, memorable individual. In the same way, each act performed by each of these characters is distinct, memorable, and significant. For Tolstoy's vision encompasses not only an infinite variety of human beings, but an infinite number of their actions; and these actions, trivial and weighty alike, link together in Tolstoy's eyes into the vast, inevitable pattern of history. It is this view of history, breathtaking in its scale, completely unromantic in its reduction of conventionally "great" events to the common level, that is the basic premise of *War and Peace;* and the following essay, which is the introduction to Section Nine of *War and Peace,* presents this premise in microscopic form.

When the Apple Is Ripe

Towards the end of the year 1811, there began to be greater activity in levying troops and in concentrating the forces of Western Europe, and in 1812 these forces—millions of men, reckoning those engaged in the transport and feeding of the army—moved from the west eastward, towards the frontiers of Russia, where, since 1811, the Russian forces were being in like manner concentrated.

On the 12th of June the forces of Western Europe crossed the frontier, and the war began, that is, an event took place opposed to human reason and all human nature. Millions of men perpetrated against one another so great a mass of crime—fraud, swindling, robbery, forgery, issue of counterfeit money, plunder, incendiarism, and murder—that the annals of all the criminal courts of the world could not muster such a sum of wickedness in whole centuries, though the men who committed those deeds did not at that time look on them as crimes.

What led to this extraordinary event? What were its causes? Historians, with simple-hearted conviction, tell us that the causes of this event were the insult offered to the Duke of Oldenburg, the failure to maintain the continental system, the ambition of Napoleon, the firmness of Alexander, the mistakes of the diplomatists, and so on.

According to them, if only Metternich, Rumyantsev, or Talleyrand had, in the interval between a levee and a court ball, really taken pains and written a more judicious diplomatic note, or if only Napoleon had written to Alexander, "I consent to restore the duchy to the Duke of Oldenburg," there would have been no war.

We can readily understand that being the conception of the war that presented itself to contemporaries. We can understand Napoleon's supposing the cause of the war to be the intrigues of England (as he said, indeed, in St. Helena); we can understand how to the members of the English House of Commons the cause of the war seemed to be Napoleon's ambition; how to the Duke of Oldenburg the war seemed due to the outrage done him; how to the trading class the war seemed due to the continental system that was ruining Europe; to the old soldiers and generals the chief reason for it seemed their need of active service; to the regiments of the period, the necessity of re-establishing *les bons principes;* while the diplomatists of the time set it down to the alliance of Russia with Austria in 1809 not having been with sufficient care concealed from Napoleon, and the memorandum, No. 178, having been awkwardly worded. We may well understand contemporaries believing in those causes, and in a countless, endless number more, the multiplicity of which is due to the infinite variety of men's points of view. But to us of a later generation, contemplating in all its vastness the immensity of the accomplished fact, and seeking to penetrate its simple and fearful significance, those explanations must appear insufficient. To us it is inconceivable that millions of Christian men should have killed and tortured each other, because Napoleon was ambitious, Alexander firm, English policy crafty, and the Duke of Oldenburg hardly treated. We cannot grasp the connection between these circumstances and the bare fact of murder and violence, nor why the duke's wrongs should induce thousands of men from the other side of Europe to pillage and murder the inhabitants of the Smolensk and Moscow provinces and to be slaughtered by them.

For us of a later generation, who are not historians led

away by the process of research, and so can look at the facts with common sense unobscured, the causes of this war appear innumerable in their multiplicity. The more deeply we search out the causes the more of them we discover; and every cause, and even a whole class of causes taken separately, strikes us as being equally true in itself, and equally deceptive through its insignificance in comparison with the immensity of the result, and its inability to produce (without all the other causes that concurred with it) the effect that followed. Such a cause, for instance, occurs to us as Napoleon's refusal to withdraw his troops beyond the Vistula, and to restore the duchy of Oldenburg; and then again we remember the readiness or the reluctance of the first chance French corporal to serve on a second campaign; for had he been unwilling to serve, and a second and a third, and thousands of corporals and soldiers had shared that reluctance, Napoleon's army would have been short of so many men, and the war could not have taken place.

If Napoleon had not taken offence at the request to withdraw beyond the Vistula, and had not commanded his troops to advance, there would have been no war. But if all the sergeants had been unwilling to serve on another campaign, there could have been no war either.

And the war would not have been had there been no intrigues on the part of England, no Duke of Oldenburg, no resentment on the part of Alexander; nor had there been no autocracy in Russia, no French Revolution and consequent dictatorship and empire, nor all that led to the French Revolution, and so on further back: without any one of those causes, nothing could have happened. And so all those causes— myriads of causes—coincided to bring about what happened. And consequently nothing was exclusively the cause of the war, and the war was bound to happen, simply because it was bound to happen. Millions of men, repudiating their common sense and their human feelings, were bound to move from west to east, and to slaughter their fellows, just as some centuries before hordes of men had moved from east to west to slaughter their fellows.

The acts of Napoleon and Alexander, on whose words it seemed to depend whether this should be done or not, were as little voluntary as the act of each soldier, forced to march out by the drawing of a lot or by conscription. This could not be otherwise, for in order that the will of Napoleon and Alexander (on whom the whole decision appeared to rest)

should be effective, a combination of innumerable circumstances was essential, without any one of which the effect
could not have followed. It was essential that the millions of
men in whose hands the real power lay—the soldiers who
fired guns and transported provisions and cannons—should
consent to carry out the will of those feeble and isolated
persons, and that they should have been brought to this acquiescence by an infinite number of varied and complicated
causes.

We are forced to fall back upon fatalism in history to
explain irrational events (that is those of which we cannot
comprehend the reason). The more we try to explain those
events in history rationally, the more irrational and incom-
prehensible they seem to us. Every man lives for himself,
making use of his free will for attainment of his own objects,
and feels in his whole being that he can do or not do any
action. But as soon as he does anything, that act, committed
at a certain moment in time, becomes irrevocable and is the
property of history, in which it has a significance, predestined
and not subject to free choice.

There are two aspects to the life of every man: the personal
life, which is free in proportion as its interests are abstract,
and the elemental life of the swarm, in which a man must
inevitably follow the laws laid down for him.

Consciously a man lives on his own account in freedom of
will, but he serves as an unconscious instrument in bringing
about the historical ends of humanity. An act he has once
committed is irrevocable, and that act of his, coinciding in
time with millions of acts of others, has an historical value.
The higher a man's place in the social scale, the more con-
nections he has with others, and the more power he has over
them, the more conspicuous is the inevitability and pre-
destination of every act he commits. "The hearts of kings are
in the hand of God." The king is the slave of history.

History—that is the unconscious life of humanity in the
swarm, in the community—makes every minute of the life
of kings its own, as an instrument for attaining its ends.

Although in that year, 1812, Napoleon believed more than
ever that to shed or not to shed the blood of his peoples
depended entirely on his will (as Alexander said in his last
letter to him), yet then, and more than at any time, he was
in bondage to those laws which forced him, while to himself
he seemed to be acting freely, to do what was bound to be
his share in the common edifice of humanity, in history.

The people of the west moved to the east for men to kill one another. And by the law of the coincidence of causes, thousands of petty causes backed one another up and coincided with that event to bring about that movement and that war: resentment at the nonobservance of the continental system, and the Duke of Oldenburg, and the massing of troops in Prussia—a measure undertaken, as Napoleon supposed, with the object of securing armed peace—and the French Emperor's love of war, to which he had grown accustomed, in conjunction with the inclinations of his people, who were carried away by the grandiose scale of the preparations, and the expenditure on those preparations, and the necessity of recouping that expenditure. Then there was the intoxicating effect of the honours paid to the French Emperor in Dresden, and the negotiations too of the diplomatists, who were supposed by contemporaries to be guided by a genuine desire to secure peace, though they only inflamed the *amour-propre* of both sides; and millions upon millions of other causes, chiming in with the fated event and coincident with it.

When the apple is ripe and falls—why does it fall? Is it because it is drawn by gravitation to the earth, because its stalk is withered, because it is dried by the sun, because it grows heavier, because the wind shakes it, or because the boy standing under the tree wants to eat it?

Not one of those is the cause. All that simply makes up the conjunction of conditions under which every living, organic, elemental event takes place. And the botanist who says that the apple has fallen because the cells are decomposing, and so on, will be just as right as the boy standing under the tree who says the apple has fallen because he wanted to eat it and prayed for it to fall. The historian, who says that Napoleon went to Moscow because he wanted to, and was ruined because Alexander desired his ruin, will be just as right and as wrong as the man who says that the mountain of millions of tons, tottering and undermined, has been felled by the last stroke of the last working-man's pickaxe. In historical events great men—so called—are but the labels that serve to give a name to an event, and like labels, they have the least possible connection with the event itself.

Every action of theirs, that seems to them an act of their own freewill, is in an historical sense not free at all, but in bondage to the whole course of previous history, and predestined from all eternity.

E. B. WHITE
1899——

Irwin Edman declared on the first page of the *New York Times Book Review:* "E. B. White is the finest essayist in the United States." Other authorities might nominate a handful of other candidates, but the field is distinctly limited. If White is not the finest by unanimous acclaim, he is one of the few finest, and in his particular vein he has no rival. No one else could have done exactly what White did for so many years with the first page of *The New Yorker,* where his Notes and Comments "represent," said Morris Bishop, "the apotheosis of the paragraph. . . . His paragraphs have an opening quality; they seek to break a hole in the texture of time which confines us; they hint of eternity." That hint of eternity is present almost everywhere in White, whether he is dealing with Maine, New York City, or the world; whether with people, dogs, or sheep; or, as in the essay below, with the mere hope of a cow. Yet eternity does not subdue Mr. White, as it has often subdued lesser men. His wit remains irrepressible, his humor delicious, his way with the English language a marvel. And he keeps his sense of enchantment. "As a writing man, or secretary," he admits, "I have always felt charged with the safekeeping of all unexpected items of worldly or unworldly enchantment, as though I might be held personally responsible if even a small one were to be lost."

Getting Ready for a Cow

This month an event is scheduled to take place here which is the culmination of four years of preparation. I am going to get a cow. Perhaps I should put it the other way round—a cow is going to get me. (I suspect I am regarded hereabouts as something of a catch.)

To establish a herd, even to establish a herd of one, is a responsibility which I do not lightly assume. For me this is a solemn moment, tinged with pure eagerness. I have waited a long time for this cow, this fateful female whom I have yet to meet. Mine has been a novitiate in which I have groomed myself faithfully and well for the duties of a husbandryman; I feel that now, at the end of these years, I have something to offer a cow.

Of course I could have got a cow immediately on arriving here in the country. There is no law against a man getting a cow before he, or she, is ready. I see by *Life* magazine that Chic Johnson, the Hellzapoppin farmer of Putnam County, N. Y., established his herd by "buying the World's Fair Borden Exhibit." This struck me as a rather clearcut case of a man who was perhaps not ready for his cows. He probably had not even had himself tested for Bangs. "At the dairy," said the article, describing a party the actor was throwing, "cows were milked and ridden bareback." Mr. Johnson was photographed in the act of trying to strike up an acquaintance with one of his own cows, but I noticed she had averted her gaze. He was wearing shorts and a jockey cap. From the photograph I judged that the cows were in clean, modern quarters, and there seemed to be a great many of them (I counted forty cows and ten milkmaids—enough to keep an actor in cream); but I think probably it will suit me better to have one cow with whom I am well acquainted than a barnful of comparative strangers in all stages of lactation.

I knew from the very first that some day there would be a cow here. One of the first things that turned up when we bought the place was a milking stool, an old one, handmade, smooth with the wax finish which only the seat of an honest man's breeches can give to wood. A piece of equipment like that kicking around the barn is impossible to put out of one's mind completely. I never mentioned the name "cow" in those early days, but I knew that the ownership of a milking stool was like any other infection—there would be the period of incubation and then the trouble itself. The stool made me feel almost wholly equipped—all I needed was the new plank floor under the cow, the new stanchion, the platform, the curb, the gutter, the toprail, the litter alley, the sawdust, the manger, the barn broom, the halter, the watering pail, the milk pail, the milk cans, the brushes, the separator, the churn, the cow, and the ability to milk the cow.

And there was the barn itself, egging me on. There it stood, with the old tie-ups intact. Every morning the sun rose, climbed, and shone through the south windows into the de-

serted stalls, scarred and pitted from bygone hooves. I tried
not to look. But everytime I walked past I admired the ingenious construction of the homemade stanchions, set in a solid
wooden curb and locked with pegs and tumblers, everything
handhewn by a man who had fashioned, with ax and chisel,
whatever he had needed for himself and his creatures. Men
familiar with the habits and desires of cows have advised me
to take those old stanchions out because of their rigidity,
which is too confining for a cow, and I have already begun the
work, but not without many misgivings and a feeling of guilt.
The urge to remodel, the spirit of demolition, are in the blood
of all city people who move to the country, and must be
constantly guarded against. I have seen too many cases of
farmhouses being torn limb from limb by a newly arrived
owner, as though in fright or in anger.

There is something bumptious in the common assumption
that an old house or an old barn must be hacked to pieces
before it is a fit place in which to settle. The city man coming
suddenly to the country customarily begins his new life by
insulting someone else's old one; he knocks blazes out of his
dwelling house, despite its having served former owners well
for a hundred years or more. My own house is about a hundred and forty years old—three times my age—yet I, a mere
upstart, approached it as though it didn't know its business
and weren't quite fit for me the way it was, when the truth, as
I now see it, was that I was not quite fit for *it*. Quite aside
from the expense and inconvenience of razing one's newly
acquired home, there is a subtle insult in the maneuver, the
unmistakable implication that the former inhabitants lived
either in squalor or in innocence, and that one's neighbors,
in houses of similar design and appointments, are also living
in squalor or innocence. Neither is true. But the demolition
goes right ahead. The place of a newly arriving city man always looks more like a battleground than a home; earthworks
are thrown up around the foundation wall, chimneys are
reduced to rubble, and on the front lawn a cement mixer
appears, with its little wheels and big round abdomen. It
would be a comical sight if it were not so dispiriting.

I don't know why people act in this panicky way. I do
know for a fact that a man can't know the quality of his home
until he has lived in it a year or two; and until he knows its
good and bad qualities how can he presume to go about re-
modeling it? In the frenzy of resettlement one often does
queer things and lives to regret his mistakes. When I go into

my neighbors' "unimproved" houses in the dead of winter and feel how comfortable they are and cheerful, the sills banked with spruce boughs, the little heating stoves standing in candid warmth in the middle of the room, the geraniums and flowering maples blazing away in tin cans on the sunny shelf above the sink, with no pipes to freeze under the floors and no furnace around which huddle full ash cans like gloomy children, I always chuckle over the commotion city people make in their determination that their farmhouse shall be "livable." They have no idea how livable a farmhouse can be if you let it alone. We have too many preconceptions, anyway, about life and living. There is nothing so expensive, really, as a big, well-developed, full-bodied preconception.

But as far as my cow was concerned, it was not so much any hesitancy at ripping things up and changing things around, not so much a matter of equipment and housing; it was simply that I felt the need of a personal probationary period. If a man expects his cow to have freshened before he gets her she has a right to expect that some important change will have been worked in him too. I didn't want a cow until I could meet her on her own ground, until I was ready, until I knew almost as much about the country as she did—otherwise it would embarrass me to be in her presence. I began this probation in 1938. For more than a year I kept my cow in the hindmost region of my thoughts. It was almost two years before I even allowed myself to dwell on her form and face. Then I began to lay the groundwork of my herd.

My first move was to purchase fifteen sheep and a case of dynamite. The sheep, I figured, would improve my pasture, and the dynamite would keep me out of mischief in the meantime. Before they were done, the sheep managed to serve another useful purpose: I had no desire to have a cow on the place until I had learned how an udder worked, and my first lambing time taught me a lot about that. The way to learn to sail a big boat is first to sail a little one, because the little one is so much harder to manage. The same is true of udders. I can milk a sheep now, with her small cleverly concealed udder, and so I have no hesitancy about going on to a larger and more forthright bag. The dynamite also turned out to have a second purpose—it had the advantage of letting people know something was going on around here.

That fall when we dynamited for my cow was a great time. I set out to revive a run-out hayfield, and while I was at it I thought I would remove the rocks. I hadn't the slightest notion of what I was getting into, except that I knew I was establishing a cow, and, true to form, thought first of demolition. The rocks didn't look like much when I made my preliminary survey, but I discovered as time went on that a rock is much like an iceberg—most of it is down-under. A very great deal of spadework had to be done around the horse-size rocks before you could hook on to them with the team, and of course the others had to be drilled before they could be exploded. Hand drilling is tedious business, but I didn't have sense enough to charter an air-drill, which I learned later I could have done. The cow receded. There were days when I almost forgot her, so engrossed did I become in the amazing turn which my probation had taken. It was the end of summer; the days were hot and bright. Across the broad field, newly plowed, would come the exultant warning cry of "Fie-ah!" Then the breathless pause, then the blast, and the dunnage and rock fragments flying into the sun, then another pause and the sound of falling wreckage.

Although the field had been turned over by the plow, the fragmentation from the blasting left it looking more like a gravel pit than a seedbed. There was a tremendous lot of work to be done just hauling away the debris after the bombing was over. The plowman hooked his team to the drag and I borrowed a tractor and another drag from a neighbor, and together we went at it. Day after day we loaded the drags, hauled them to the edge of the woods, and tossed the rocks off, creating a kind of hit and miss stone wall. I learned to throw the chain over a big rock with a "rolling holt," back the tractor up to it, and ease the rock on to the drag by giving it a nudge of power. The cow seemed a long way off, but I held her firmly in my thoughts, as a soldier holds the vision of home and peace through a long campaign in a foreign land. Rivers of sweat flowed into the dry, chewed-up soil, mountains of granite slogged along the dragways, all to achieve, in some remote time, the blade of new grass, the tiny jet of yellow milk. The whole thing seemed like a strangely tangential episode, as if I had wandered off on an idiot's holiday.

And after the rocks had been torn from the earth and removed, then there was the matter of dressing the field. Having no cow, I had no dressing, except a small amount of sheep manure and hen manure which would be needed for the gardens. The field would need thirty or forty spreader loads. After much exploring, some dressing was located in a barn cellar within reasonable trucking distance, and for some days I lived close to a dung fork. This phase of the work had a cow smell and seemed somehow closer to the main issue.

All winter the land and I lay waiting. In spring the frost opened cracks and seams in the field to receive the seed. I marked out courses with guide stakes and sowed the long lanes, working on a windless morning. The rains of spring never descended that year, and summer ushered in one of the most blistering droughts on record. The new grass drooped, the weeds jumped up and sang. The result of a year's labor seemed meager, doubtful. But it turned out that there was established in spite of the dry season what a farmer calls a good bottom. As soon as it got half a chance the field picked up miraculously. This summer, under benign rains, it has become a sweetly rolling green, like something Grant Wood might have sent me.

Meantime the sheep had been at work in the pasture, quietly, with no dynamite. Their golden hooves had channeled among the rocks and ferns, and they had fertilized easily as they went. The time was approaching when I might take unto myself a cow. I began to see her as a living being who was growing closer to me, whose path and mine were soon to cross. I began having the sort of daydreams I used to have at fifteen: somewhere in the world (I would think) is the girl who is some day to be my wife. What is she doing? Where is she? What is she like?

Of course there was still the matter of the barn—a fit place for this dream creature to spend her winter nights. The thought of a concrete floor flashed through my mind, and was quickly gone. I had invested in one concrete floor when I built my henhouse, and one concrete floor is enough for any man's lifetime. The sensible thing would be to lay a good smooth plank floor, with a six-inch platform, and perhaps a gutter. I turned, as one always does turn in any critical time, to the mail order catalogue and began a study of floor plans—stalls and gutters and curbs and stanchions and rails and partitions. I learned about stanchions, stanchion anchors, alignment devices; I began to pit the high curb against the low curb, the single post stall against the double. One evening after dark I went to the barn with a two-foot rule and a flashlight and measured up the job, working carefully and late, in pitch black except for the concentrated beam of the flash—an odd tryst, as I think back on it, but part of my beautiful romance. When I returned to the house I made a plan, drawn to scale, showing a maternity pen, three stalls, a raised platform, an eleven-inch curb hollowed out to six inches at the anchor point, and a gate, everything worked out to the inch. The platform is to be cut on the bias—a long stall (4 foot 10) at one end, in case my lovely girl turns out to be an Amazon, a medium-size stall (4 foot 4) for a medium-size bride, and a short stall (3 foot 8) for the heifer which will inevitably bless this marriage.

There have been setbacks and reverses. Priorities worked against me and I soon found out that barn furnishings were almost unobtainable. I sent to Sears for their Russet Cow Halter, 32D449, the one with the adjustable crown and the brown hardware to match her eyes and hair, but they returned the money, with a grim note, Form Number 7, rubber stamped. Where they got the rubber for the stamp I have no idea.

Tomorrow the carpenter arrives to start tearing out the old floor. When the last stanchion is anchored and the last brushful of whitewash has been applied to wall and rafter, I shall anoint myself and go forth to seek my love. This much I know, when the great day comes and she and I come marching home and pause for a moment in the barnyard before the freshly whitened door, *she's* got to carry *me* across the threshold. I'm tired.

VIRGINIA WOOLF
1882–1941

At the conclusion of her essay on "How to Read a Book," Virginia Woolf imagines that on the Day of Judgment, when all the meritorious of the earth come to receive their rewards, St. Peter will say of a certain group to the Lord: "Look, these need no reward. We have nothing to give them here. They have loved reading." And surely the lovers of reading who have enjoyed the perfection of Virginia Woolf's novels and essays have already experienced a large measure of their eternal reward.

Daughter of Sir Leslie Stephen, who was editor of the *Dictionary of National Biography,* and wife of journalist, editor, and publisher Leonard Woolf, Mrs. Woolf wrote as naturally as the rest of us breathe. But while we generally breathe without thought or effort, she took infinite pains with her writing. On it, said her friend, E. M. Forster, she "concentrated her entire vision"; and this concentration intensified and refined her natural gift, gave it that peculiar combination of transparency and toughness that was Virginia Woolf's own mark, whether in a complete novel, such as *To the Lighthouse,* or in the miniature compass of the accompanying essay, "The Death of the Moth."

The Death of the Moth

Moths that fly by day are not properly to be called moths; they do not excite that pleasant sense of dark autumn nights and ivy-blossom which the commonest yellow-underwing asleep in the shadow of the curtain never fails to rouse in us. They are hybrid creatures, neither gay like butterflies nor sombre like their own species. Nevertheless the present specimen, with his narrow hay-coloured wings, fringed with a tassel of the same colour, seemed to be content with life. It was a pleasant morning, mid-September, mild, benignant, yet with a keener breath than that of the summer months. The plough was already scoring the field opposite the window, and where the share had been, the earth was pressed flat and gleamed with moisture. Such vigour came rolling in from the fields and the down beyond that it was difficult to keep the eyes strictly turned upon the book. The rooks too were keeping one of their annual festivities; soaring round the tree tops until it looked as if a vast net with thousands of black knots in it had been cast up into the air; which, after a few moments sank slowly down upon the trees until every twig seemed to have a knot at the end of it. Then, suddenly, the net would be thrown into the air again in a wider circle this time, with the utmost clamour and vociferation, as though to be thrown into the air and settle slowly down upon the tree tops were a tremendously exciting experience.

The same energy which inspired the rooks, the ploughmen, the horses, and even, it seemed, the lean bare-backed downs, sent the moth fluttering from side to side of his square of the window-pane. One could not help watching him. One was, indeed, conscious of a queer feeling of pity for him. The possibilities of pleasure seemed that morning so enormous and so various that to have only a moth's part in life, and a day moth's at that, appeared a hard fate, and his zest in enjoying his meagre opportunities to the full, pathetic. He flew vigorously to one corner of his compartment, and, after waiting there a second, flew across to the other. What remained for him but to fly to a third corner and then to a fourth? That was all he could do, in spite of the size of the downs, the width of the sky, the far-off smoke of houses, and the romantic voice, now and then, of a steamer out at sea. What he could do he did. Watching him, it seemed as if a fibre, very thin but pure, of the enormous energy of the world had been thrust into his frail and diminutive body. As often as he crossed the pane, I could fancy that a thread of vital light became visible. He was little or nothing but life.

Yet, because he was so small, and so simple a form of the energy that was rolling in at the open window and driving its way through so many narrow and intricate corridors in my own brain and in those of other human beings, there was something marvellous as well as pathetic about him. It was as if someone had taken a tiny bead of pure life and decking it as lightly as possible with down and feathers, had set it dancing and zigzagging to show us the true nature of life. Thus displayed one could not get over the strangeness of it. One is apt to forget all about life, seeing it humped and bossed and garnished and cumbered so that it has to move with the greatest circumspection and dignity. Again, the thought of all that life might have been had he been born in any other shape caused one to view his simple activities with a kind of pity.

After a time, tired by his dancing apparently, he settled on the window ledge in the sun, and, the queer spectacle being at an end, I forgot about him. Then, looking up, my eye was caught by him. He was trying to resume his dancing, but seemed either so stiff or so awkward that he could only flutter to the bottom of the window-pane; and when he tried to fly across it he failed. Being intent on other matters I watched these futile attempts for a time without thinking, unconsciously waiting for him to resume his flight, as one waits for a machine, that has stopped momentarily, to start again without considering the reason of its failure. After perhaps a seventh attempt he slipped from the wooden ledge and fell, fluttering his wings, on to his back on the window sill. The helplessness of his attitude roused me. It flashed upon me that he was in difficulties; he could no longer raise himself; his legs struggled vainly. But, as I stretched out a pencil, meaning to help him to right himself, it came over me that the failure and awkwardness were the approach of death. I laid the pencil down again.

The legs agitated themselves once more. I looked as if for the enemy against which he struggled. I looked out of doors. What had happened there? Presumably it was midday, and work in the fields had stopped. Stillness and quiet had replaced the previous animation. The birds had taken themselves off to feed in the brooks. The horses stood still. Yet the power was there all the same, massed outside indifferent, impersonal, not attending to anything in particular. Somehow it was opposed to the little hay-coloured moth. It was useless to try to do anything. One could only watch the extraordinary efforts made by those tiny legs against an oncoming doom which could, had it chosen, have submerged an entire city, not merely a city, but masses of human beings; nothing, I knew, had any chance against death. Nevertheless after a pause of exhaustion the legs fluttered again. It was superb this last protest, and so frantic that he succeeded at last in righting himself. One's sympathies, of course, were all on the side of life. Also, when there was nobody to care or to know, this gigantic effort on the part of an insignificant little moth, against a power of such magnitude, to retain what no one else valued or desired to keep, moved one strangely. Again, somehow, one saw life, a pure bead. I lifted the pencil again, useless though I knew it to be. But even as I did so, the unmistakable tokens of death showed themselves. The body relaxed, and instantly grew stiff. The struggle was over. The insignificant little creature now knew death. As I looked at the dead moth, this minute wayside triumph of so great a force over so mean an antagonist filled me with wonder. Just as life had been strange a few minutes before, so death was now as strange. The moth having righted himself now lay most decently and uncomplainingly composed. O yes, he seemed to say, death is stronger than I am.